W9-CRT-182

Constantinople (Istanbul)

Cyzicus

Prusa (Bursa)

Ancyra
(Ankara)

Sigeum
Troy (Hisarlik)
Alexandria
Troas

Assos

Mytilene
Pergamum (Bergama)

Dikeli

Aizanoi (Ayazin)

Thyatira

Smyrna
(Izmir)

Sardis

Teos

Apollonia
In Pisidia

Colophon

SAMOS

Ephesus
Scala Nova (Kuşadası)

Magnesia
Aphrodisias

Miletus
Priene
Lagina

TMOS
Didyma
Mylasa

KALYMNOS
Iasos

Halicarnassus (Bodrum)

LYCIA

Antalya

KOS

Oenoanda

Cnidus

Tlos

Trysa
(Gölbaşı)

Xanthus

Antiphellus

RHODES

GREECE AND WESTERN TURKEY:
Showing places mentioned in the text

0 ————————————— 100 mls
0 ————————————— 100 km

LAND OF
LOST GODS

LAND OF LOST GODS

The Search for Classical Greece

RICHARD STONEMAN

HUTCHINSON
LONDON MELBOURNE AUCKLAND JOHANNESBURG

© Richard Stoneman 1987

First published in 1987 by Hutchinson, an imprint of
Century Hutchinson Ltd, Brookmount House, 62–65 Chandos Place,
London WC2N 4NW

Century Hutchinson Australia Pty Ltd
PO Box 496, 16–22 Church Street, Hawthorn, Victoria 3122, Australia

Century Hutchinson New Zealand Ltd
PO Box 40–086, Glenfield, Auckland 10, New Zealand

Century Hutchinson South Africa (Pty) Ltd
PO Box 337, Berglvei, 2012 South Africa

Stoneman, Richard
Land of lost gods: The search for Classical Greece
1. Excavations (Archaeology) – Greece
2. Greece – Antiquities
I. Title
938'.0072   DF77

ISBN 0-09-167140-X

Photoset by Rowland Phototypesetting Ltd
Bury St Edmunds, Suffolk
Printed in Great Britain by
Redwood Burn Ltd, Trowbridge, Wiltshire
and bound by WBC Bookbinders Ltd
Maesteg, Mid-Glamorgan

Contents

FOR OLGA

Ancient shipwrecked cities
tell us of the omnipotence of Silence,
of her sudden overwhelming floods within their walls;
the snows of time are heaped on her breast;
in a slow movement voyaging,
the icebergs of millenniums proceed . . .
All set out from the primordial space of Silence
and return to her once more;
all are weighed on her bronze shield,
our words, our footsteps,
and our most deeply hidden thoughts.
Nothing can be lost,
Not a secret tear, not the leaf of a tree,
not a single raindrop on the grass.

Melissanthi

Chronology

1580–1120 BC	Mycenaean Civilization
1300 c–1250	Destruction of Troy VII (earthquake)
1200 c	Destruction of Troy VIIa (fire)
776	First Olympiad (first, legendary, celebration of first Olympic Games)
670	First Temple of Hera on Samos
570	Later Temple of Hera on Samos
560	First Temple of Artemis at Ephesus
550 c	Temple of Apollo, Corinth
500–400	Heroön of Gölbaşı-Trysa
480s	Temple of Aphaia, Aigina
470	Curse inscriptions from Teos
450 onwards	Temple of Apollo Epicurius, Bassae
450 c	Cephisodotus fl.
440	Great Temple of Artemis at Ephesus dedicated
447–38	Construction of Parthenon, Athens Phidias fl. (b. 490 c)
400 c	Nereid Monument, Xanthus
364	Praxiteles fl.
356	Temple of Artemis at Ephesus burnt down; birth of Alexander the Great
353	Mausoleum of Halicarnassus built
350 c	Myron fl.
334	Monument of Lysicrates, Athens
334	Alexander the Great invades the Persian Empire

328	Lysippus fl.
300 c	Construction of Temple of Apollo at Didyma
263	Attalid Dynasty established in Pergamum, Marmer Parium erected
175–150	Temple of Dionysus at Teos
146	Sack of Corinth by Rome
100–0	Tower of Winds, Athens
64 BC–AD 21	Strabo
25–20	Temple of Augustus and Rome, Ancyra
AD 37–68	Nero (Emperor from 54)
76–138	Hadrian (Emperor from 117)
127–48	Ptolemy the Geographer fl.
117	Dedication of Temple of Poseidon, Cyzicus
121–80	Marcus Aurelius (Emperor from 161)
150	Pausanias fl.
285–337	Constantine the Great (Emperor of the whole Empire from 324)
324	Foundation of Constantinople
346–93	Theodosius I (Augustus from August 379)
393	Last Celebration of the Olympic Games
482–565	Justinian (Emperor from 522)
Eighth Century	*Parastaseis Syntomoi Chronikai*
Tenth Century	*Patria Constantinopoleos*
1204	Sack of Constantinople by the Fourth Crusade
1414	Cristoforo Buondelmonti in Greece
1415	Castle of St John at Bodrum begun (with fragments of Mausoleum)
1435–53	Cyriac of Ancona in Greece
1439	Council of Florence
1452	Death of Gemistus Plethon
1453	Capture of Constantinople by Ottoman Turks
1527	Sack of Rome
1547	Pierre Gilles in Constantinople
1583	Pierre Belon in Greece
1584	Martin Crusius, *Turcograecia*
1612–14	Earl of Arundel in Rome
1622 onwards	Sir Thomas Roe and William Petty in Constantinople and Greece

1874	Foundation of German Archaeological Institute in Athens
	Excavation of Olympia begun
1876	Schliemann excavates Mycenae
1880	Otto Benndorf and Georg Niemann's expedition to Gölbaşı-Trysa
1882	Museum in Constantinople founded by Osman Hamdi Bey, director of the archaeological service
	American School of Classical Studies in Athens founded
1883	Kunsthistorisches Museum, Vienna, completed
1886	British School of Archaeology in Athens founded
1896	Olympic Games re-established by Baron Coubertin

Acknowledgements

Acknowledgement is due to the Efstathiadis Group for permission to reproduce part of 'Ancient Shipwrecked Cities' by Melissanthi, from *Modern Greek Poetry* edited by Kimon Friar; to Jonathan Cape Ltd for permission to reproduce 'We who set out' from *Mithistorima* by George Seferis; and to Chatto and Windus Ltd for permission to reproduce part of *Ithaca* by C. P. Cavafy.

Preface

Greece has never been more visited than it is now. Every day thousands of feet tramp up and down the steep ascents of the Athenian Acropolis, the hill of Mycenae, and the sanctuary of Delphi; wander over the level column-strewn pleasances of Epidaurus and Olympia; gaze at the gold of Agamemnon and the great bronze Zeus of the National Archaeological Museum in Athens. What is it that draws them here?

These hordes of enthusiastic tourists, assuredly here not only for the sun and sea – scarcely to be enjoyed in the air-conditioned coaches or in the sultry heat of Athens – are perhaps the best argument for the continuing force of the classical tradition – of the admiration of antiquity, be it ever so little understood – as the source of our culture.

Yet the classical tradition is not the inert dictator its detractors sometimes suppose. Every piece of antiquity, every relic of its literature or fragment of its art, has been recovered through love and dedication. It is my contention that at least as much has been done by the travellers, especially the great mavericks who set out to make Greece their own. Purveyors of a live tradition, too, were the architects who took classical models and transformed them into bricks and mortar, marble and plaster in their own countries. Academic concerns are incidental to their achievements.

Institutions ossify, and career connoisseurs make dull company. Archaeology, a latecomer to academe, has never been a pure pursuit. For centuries it was the pursuit of any who had the time, the passion and the resources to dig, discover, interpret and use. And its devotees were many.

It is the story of these men (there is scarcely a woman among them) which I aim to tell in this book. The story has its intrinsic interest besides the light it throws on the changing history of taste, of scholarship and of art. It took men of determination, endurance, imagination and courage to travel in the Levant, even until quite recently. There were few roads, transport was slow, plague and malaria endemic, food poor, Turkish rulers obstructive and brigands a menace. War added its hazards, not only to the travellers but to the survival of the monuments they went to study. There are men here whose acquaintance I count myself the richer for making, quite apart from the achievements that preserve their names.

Yet the true heroes of the tale are really the monuments of ancient Greece: her buildings, her statues and reliefs, her inscriptions and vases. Like the heroes of the *Iliad*, they are destroyed constantly as the story advances – many of them in the first few pages – but those that survive dominate the passing centuries.

I have set myself continually to ask of the men who populate these pages, 'Why did you go to Greece?' The answers are many, and include ambition, for self or nation or for art, connoisseurship, acquisitiveness, even scenery – and not least the genuine desire to know and understand the ancient Greeks.

This history is the history of ourselves. It is our relationship with the classical past that has made us what we are. This book is an exercise in remembrance, an effort to understand how we and our forebears have striven to rescue the ancients, Giants immersed in time as they are, from the depredations of time.

My debts are numerous. Above all I am grateful for the facilities of several libraries whose generous provision of books alone made my work possible: the British Library, the Bodleian Library, the Ashmolean Library in Oxford and the Institute of Classical Studies Library in London, the Gennadeion in Athens and above all the London Library. The whole text has been read by Professor John Boardman and Dr Olga Palagia, who should not be held responsible for its shortcomings. Parts were also read by Professor Averil Cameron, Dr Arthur MacGregor and Dr J. M. Wagstaff, to whom the same applies. I am grateful to Richard Smail and his colleagues and pupils at Radley College for helping me to clarify my ideas about the Picturesque. Part of Chapter 5 appeared in a different form in *Boreas 8* (1985).

My wife has borne the tedium of a husband whose talk is all of obscure foreigners and little green index cards, with her usual patience and good humour.

RICHARD STONEMAN

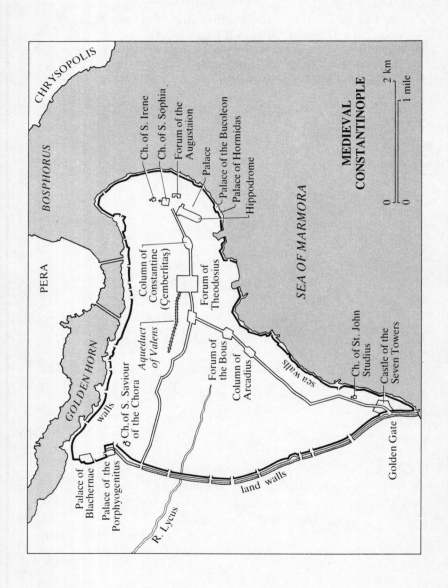

CHRYSOPOLIS

BOSPHORUS

PERA

GOLDEN HORN

Ch. of S. Irene
Ch. of S. Sophia
Forum of the Augustaion
Palace
Palace of the Bucoleon
Palace of Hormidas
Hippodrome

Column of Constantine (Çemberlitaş)
Forum of Theodosius

Aqueduct of Valens

Ch. of S. Saviour of the Chora

walls

SEA OF MARMORA

Forum of the Bous
Column of Arcadius

sea walls

Ch. of St. John Studius
Castle of the Seven Towers

Palace of Blachernae
Palace of the Porphyogenitus

R. Lycus

land walls

Golden Gate

MEDIEVAL CONSTANTINOPLE

0   1 mile
0   2 km

CHAPTER ONE

Prologue: The Treasures of Constantinople

Even the borrowed splendour, in which Constantine decked his city, bore in it something which seemed to mark premature decay. The imperial founder, in seizing upon the ancient statues, pictures, obelisks, and works of art, acknowledged his own incapacity to supply their place with the productions of later genius; and when the world, and particularly Rome, was plundered to adorn Constantinople, the Emperor, under whom the work was carried on, might be compared to a prodigal youth, who strips an aged parent of her youthful ornaments, in order to decorate a flaunting paramour, on whose brow all must consider them as misplaced. (Sir Walter Scott, *Count Robert of Paris*)

April in Constantinople is the cruellest month. In April the Bosphorus begins to lay aside its winter anger; the European and the Asian shores begin to acquire their spring carpet of flowers. Poppy, chrysanthemum and cranesbill, delphinium and asphodel colour the hills and the crevices of the two castles, Rumeli Hisar and Anadolu Hisar. Fresh breezes bring new life to the sodden damps of the unhealthy city.

But April held a special meaning for the Greeks who lived here in the last two and a half centuries of the Byzantine Empire. For it was in April 1204, sixteen centuries after the creation of the earliest and greatest of the innumerable works of art that adorned the City of Gold, that more than half of those treasures were destroyed – destroyed at the hands of Christians who but a few weeks previously had been regarded in Byzantium as allies.

The Fourth Crusade, a host of warriors from all the nations

of Europe, known collectively to the Byzantine Greeks as
'Franks', had set out from Venice in 1203 with the blessing of
the Pope on its project to recover the holy places of Asia. Their
instructions were to enlist the aid of the Byzantine Empire in
the war against the Turk. But with them was Alexius, son of
the deposed Emperor of Constantinople, who had ends in
view beyond the conquest of Islam. As the fleet sailed up the
Bosphorus towards the Golden Horn, and the mighty clus-
tered domes of St Sophia (then unrelieved by the vertical
thrust of any minarets) hove into view, surrounded by the
glint of marble, gold and bronze from the statued population
that lined every public place, disaster began to impend.

The monument that had long been a landmark to guide
ships into harbour, the mighty Athena of Phidias that had been
made to grace the Acropolis of Athens, stood with its hand
outstretched to the west, and the people said that it was
beckoning the army to destroy the city. The Emperor Alexius
III, who had deposed the old Emperor Isaac eight years before,
sat insecure in his palace. At the news that Isaac's son was at the
port with a crusade, he fled the city. In a quandary, the
government reinstated Isaac, and agreed to make his son joint
Emperor, as Alexius IV.

In January 1204 a riot, accompanied by a disastrous fire, was
organised by dissatisfied nationalists led by Murzuphlus, one
of the sons-in-law of Alexius III, the main purpose of which
seems to have been to destroy the offending statue of Athena,
which was blamed for the presence of the hostile army. A
month later Murzuphlus invaded the palace; Alexius was
chained, imprisoned and eventually strangled in his dungeon.
Murzuphlus began to call himself Alexius V, and was not slow
to repudiate the agreement with the Crusaders entered into by
his predecessor.

The challenge did not long go unanswered. On 6 April
the Crusaders attacked, but were repulsed; on 13 April
they breached the walls against the Golden Horn. The
Emperor's bodyguard fled, fire again swept through the city,
Murzuphlus slipped out through the Golden Gate, and in the
morning a suppliant procession announced the submission of
the Greeks.

The cruelty and lust of the invaders, wrote Gibbon, 'were
moderated by the authority of the chiefs and feelings of the

soldiers', though Pope Innocent III complained of nuns and children and married women defiled; 'but a free scope was allowed to their avarice, which was glutted, even in the holy week, by the pillage of Constantinople.'

Once given the run of the city, the Franks forgot all thoughts of their former enemy, and set about looting and destroying the gold and silver and jewels, the precious stuffs and coinage, the marbles and alabasters, even the books and manuscripts of the glorious city. Constantinople, which for nearly a thousand years had been the destination of the choicest works of art of the known world, was stripped of its glory in a riot of greed and wanton destruction.

From the very commencement [wrote the Greek historian Nicetas Choniates] the Latins exhibited their national covetousness; and struck out a new system of rapine, which had escaped all the former despoilers of the Imperial City; for they opened and plundered all the tombs of the Emperors in the Heroum, at the great Church of the Apostles. They sacrilegiously laid their hands upon every golden ornament, and every chalice which had been studded with pearls and precious stones. They gazed with admiration at the body of Justinian, which after so many centuries exhibited no mark of decay; but they refrained not from appropriating to themselves the sepulchral ornaments. These western barbarians spared neither the living nor the dead; but beginning with God and his servants, they shewed themselves, upon all occasions, indiscriminately impious . . . They cast their eyes on the brazen statues, and consigned them to the flames.

Among the victims that fell a sacrifice to Christian barbarity were a colossal Juno, so large that four oxen could scarcely move it, which was melted down to make coins; a figure of Paris presenting the apple to Venus; the bronze weather-vane that was one of the peaks of Byzantine artistry; a statue called Bellerophon (or Joshua); the Heracles; the ass with his driver; the lion-wrestler; the sphinxes, elephant and stallion; the magical bronze eagle of Apollonius of Tyana; the statue of Helen which 'though cast in brass, seemed fresh as the descending dew, while her swimming eyes provoked love'; the victorious charioteer; a pair of mysterious creatures variously interpreted as a basilisk and an asp or a Nilotic hippopotamus and crocodile, locked in combat as savage as that of the 'nations who have waged war against us Romans; they have massacred and destroyed each other [he ends with a pious wish] by the favour of Christ towards us, who . . . causes the just man "to tread upon the Basilisk and the Asp", and "to trample the lion and the dragon under his feet".'

Meanwhile the pretender Murzuphlus had been recaptured, and the Crusaders, having elected Count Baldwin of Flanders as their own Emperor in Constantinople, had him put to death in a way which the Frankish chronicler Villehardouin describes:

Towards the centre of Constantinople there stood a marble column (the column of Arcadius), one of the highest and most finely carved that ever man's eye has seen. Murzuphlus was to be taken to the top of that column, and made to leap down in the sight of all the people, because it was fitting that such a signal act of justice should be seen by everyone. Murzuphlus was led to the column, and taken to the top, while all the people in the city flocked to the place to see that amazing sight. Then he was cast down, and he fell from such a height that every bone in his body was broken as soon as he reached the ground.

Now let me tell you of a marvellous coincidence. On that column from which Murzuphlus fell were figures of various kinds, and among them was one representing an emperor falling headlong. Now a very long time before it had been prophesied tht an emperor would be cast down from that very column. Thus the prophecy, as portrayed in the marble figure, came true.[1]

There were many such prophecies contained, as we shall see, in the stones of Constantinople.

As Sir Steven Runciman has written:

There never was a greater crime against humanity than the Fourth Crusade. Not only did it cause the destruction or dispersal of all the treasures of the past that Byzantium had devotedly stored, and the mortal wounding of a civilization that was still active and great; but it was also an act of gigantic political folly. . . . It upset the whole defence of Christendom.[2]

The first encounter of the Christians of West and East was thus hardly auspicious, in view of the importance that that same Greek art, and Greece itself, with its antiquities, would assume in the eyes of the Crusaders' descendants in Western Europe for generations to come. Greece, the fountainhead of Western art and thought, where, until Athens' glorious heyday, 'Art's deathless dream lay veiled by many a vein/Of Parian stone', had, in perhaps two hundred years, produced works of art, in marble, bronze and paint, that were to be envy of every conqueror and the admiration of every artist for centuries to come. If most of the artists had come from Athens, a city which as Pericles boasted was an education to Greece, artists like Phidias and Ictinus in the fifth century, Praxiteles and Lysippus in the fourth, had filled Greece with works of art wherever patrons could commission them. A population of statues more numerous than the human seemed to rub shoulders with onlookers whose main pleasure in them went no further than wonderment at their naturalism.

The story of their long journey from their homes to Constantinople begins in the heyday of the Roman Republic, when Rome's victorious generals were adding Greece and Asia Minor to the growing Empire. The first impact was made by M. Acilius Glabrio in 191/0 BC, when he captured various works of art in bronze and marble from the camp of King Antiochus III after defeating him at Thermopylae and in Actolin and took them to the Capitol in Rome as spoils of war. But a far greater devastation was caused by the sack of Corinth by L. Mummius in 146 BC, one of the crucial encounters in Rome's conquest of the Greek peninsula.

Some writers tell us that Mummius wept to see the destruction of what had been one of the most charming and hospitable cities in Greece (and not only because of the fame of its prostitutes). He could not, however, more than any other commander, restrain his soldiers from using paintings as gaming boards and wreaking other destruction.[3] Many statues were brought to Rome and exhibited in Mummius' triumph. Others were sold to the King of Pergamum, where since 210 BC a remarkable collection had been built up, and critical standards developed which were to influence the judgements on art later expressed by Cicero and Quintilian. Of those brought to Rome, a statue of Philip II from Thespiae was taken for an image of Zeus (and, one supposes, labelled accordingly), and two marble youths from Arcadia were exhibited as figures of the aged heroes of the Trojan War, Nestor and King Priam. Though the public may have enjoyed the spectacle, they can scarcely have been very enlightened.

The next Roman general to ravage the glories of Greece was L. Cornelius Sulla, later dictator. From 88–4 BC he was engaged in campaigns against Mithridates VI of Pontus.

Mithridates' army had occupied the Piraeus, and in 87 Sulla launched an attack on Athens and Piraeus. He hacked down the groves of the Academy and the Lyceum, where Plato and Aristotle had taught, to build siege towers. Athens fell in 86, and Sulla took control of its government. At the same time he removed choice pieces of its antiquities, including some columns and capitals from the Temple of Olympian Zeus, only erected in 175–64 BC by Antiochus IV Epiphanes. These fragments were probably later used for the Temple of Jupiter Optimus Maximus in Rome.[4] He also acquired a number of manuscripts, paintings and other *objets d'art*.

Sulla's siege of Athens had been expensive; to pay for it he had levied contributions on the wealthiest cities of Greece, among which were the major shrines of Epidaurus, Olympia and Delphi. At the latter place his agent Caphis, who was sent to make an inventory of the treasure, reported hearing the supernatural sound of a lyre within the temple. Frightened by this, he referred to Sulla, who replied that music was a sign of Apollo's favour to the conqueror – and removed the treasure.

It took many ships to carry all this plunder to Rome; and we know of one which sank off the treacherous Cape Malea, depriving the world of several masterpieces. In 1907 a sunken ship was found, not off Cape Malea but off Mahdia in Tunisia, which proved to contain a quantity of marble columns, several bronze sculptures including an Eros four feet high, a bust of Dionysus and several smaller figures, as well as numerous marbles – 'a bust of Aphrodite, a small Pan, a Niobe, two Niobids, two satyrs, one youth, two torsoes of young boys and several statuettes' – and other items such as lamps, candelabra, furniture, ornaments and marble columns. The bust of Dionysus, which was signed by Boethus of Chalcedon, dated the collection not earlier than the second century BC. The anchors of the ship were of first-century type, and various other pieces of circumstantial evidence led the excited director of antiquities in Mahdia to identify the ship with one of Sulla's convoy.[5] This may well have been a Sullan ship, but it may equally have contained the loot of another campaign, or legitimate merchandise. There was a flourishing trade in reproduction classical marbles by the first century BC, and one shipment of such materials is represented by the finds from another ship recovered from the Piraeus harbour in 1959.

Another ship, found off Cerigotto in 1900 – again by a sponge-diving fleet – contained a cargo of the Augustan period. Perhaps many more such treasure troves await discovery: we shall be fortunate if we can discover the exact historical fortunes of any of these hoards, which all reflect the eagerness of new Rome to emulate its older neighbour.

Other generals followed Sulla's example, among them L. Licinius Lucullus, whose triumph over Mithridates VI in 63 included an extensive exhibition in the Gardens of Lucullus, mainly of works looted from Sinope by L. Aemilius Paullus, who apparently really admired Greek culture, and took time off after his conquests in Greece in 167 BC to make a short tour of the ancient sites. He seized an Athena by Phidias, the fifth-century master, and dedicated it at Rome; but he was content to leave in place the gigantic statue of Zeus by the same hand, which was the pride of Olympia. It was of ivory and gold, and stood over thirty-five feet high. Four centuries were to pass before this was finally removed.

Julius Caesar had an extensive private collection of Greek art, acquired by plunder as well as purchase. But perhaps the most notorious of the despoilers was the governor of Sicily, L. Verres, whom Cicero prosecuted to such devastating effect in 70 BC, accusing him of laying all Greece under requisition to satisfy his greed; seizing statues, reliefs, dedications, paintings and jewellery from the unfortunate Sicilians, and indeed from other parts of the Greek world, to enrich his own collection.

Cicero himself, for all his love of Greece, was no less willing than Verres to adorn his villa with Greek *objets d'art*. Though his lust, like his purse, was more modest, his discrimination was scarcely great:

I am already quite enchanted with your Pentelic herms with the bronze heads, about which you write to me, so please send them and the statues and any other things you think would do credit to the place in question and to my enthusiasm and to your good taste, as many and as soon as possible, especially any you think suitable to a lecture hall and colonnade.   (To Atticus, February 67 BC, *ad Att* I, 8)

The historian Polybius censured the Roman practice of looting works of art, not solely because he was a Greek and therefore the loser, but because, being habituated to 'a life destitute of all superfluous wealth, and manners far removed from elegance and splendour', the Romans had indeed corrupted their own morals by their acquisitions. It would have been more prudent '. . . to have established the glory of their own country, not by the vain ornaments of pictures and statues, but by a gravity of manners, and a magnanimity of conduct.'

Words on deaf ears; but they chime with the obsessive desire of historians to seek for some corrupting cause that ensured the eventual decline and fall of the Republic.

Certainly the Romans learnt how to make the best of their vices – though vices to many observers they remained. With the progress of empire and the increase of wealth, Rome transmuted the base instinct for looting into a sometimes over-refined connoisseurship. Corinthian bronzes were particularly prized (Corinthian bronze was said to be made in a special way, copied from the unintentional results of fire on the local metalwork during the sack of the city), so it is not surprising to find the younger Pliny congratulating himself with ill-feigned modesty on having acquired one:

. . . only a small one, but an attractive and finished piece of work as far as I can judge. . . It appears to have the true colour of a genuine antique. . . However, my intention was not to keep it in my house (I have not any Corinthian bronzes there yet) but to place it in some public position in my native town, preferably in the Temple of Jupiter.   (*Letters*, III, 6)

It was a rare public spirit that put such works on public display rather than keeping them for private gratification, or as conversation pieces to impress guests.

In that generation the most refined of connoisseurs was Novius Vindex, less generous than Pliny: a bronze statuette of Heracles, said to be an original by Lysippus, had gone through many vicissitudes before reaching his gallery:

> This one the Macedonian youth possess'd,
> Who soone the whole world conquered, soon deceased;
> Then Hannibal to Libya coasts translated;
> Who Sylla's stern commanding power abated.
> Brooking no longer swelling tyrants' courts,
> T' a private dwelling he at length resorts;
> And, as he once was kind Molorchus' guest,
> So with learn'd Vindex now this god will rest.
>
> (Martial IX, 43)

The piece seems to have been celebrated, since Statius devoted a poem of 109 lines to this same piece of elegant tableware (*Silvae* IV, 6).[6] Vindex, he said, could also display 'bronzes that kept the intellectual Myron up late, marbles which live through the chisel of laborious Praxiteles; ivory chased by the thumb of Pisatan Phidias, metal cast in the kilns of Polycleitus, and lines which confess the touch of old Apelles.' In other words, possession of Greek art, original or copy, is a matter for praise and self-praise.

Collectors like these enlarged their holdings through purchase and exchange. But the Emperor Nero, who counted among the Greeks for a Philhellene because 'to the nation which among his subjects was noblest and most beloved of Heaven he had granted Freedom' (Plutarch), was responsible for the largest influx ever of Greek art to Rome, and had no need to respect such niceties. From Delphi alone he took 500 bronze statues. (But one must remember that even after this there remained as many as 3,000 more in that single town.)[7] He also took a good deal from Olympia, and an Eros by Lysippus from Thespiae: this was later destroyed in Rome by fire. Athens he scarcely touched. But it was the Greek cities of Asia that bore the brunt of Nero's acquisitive mania: from them all he acquired masterpieces by the most famous sculptors: Phidias, Praxiteles, Cephisodotus, and even Styppax, famous only for his 'Man Cooking Tripe'. Among the statues found in the remains of the villa he built at his birthplace, Antium, were three of what were to become the most famous statues of antiquity: the Apollo Belvedere, the Borghese Gladiator, and the Venus with the Beautiful Backside. Nero thus had a direct influence on the taste of future centuries.

After Nero's acquisitive ardour was for ever extinguished, Greece did not again come under the hammer until the foundation by Constantine the Great in 324 of his new Christian Rome in the East. Now all Rome's Greek treasures retraced their steps eastward, to the Greek city of Constantinople. (From now on its Greek inhabitants would refer to themselves as 'Romans'.)

With the Empire's brief return to paganism, under Julian 'the Apostate' or 'Philosopher', many pagan religious sites were restored, among them the oracle of Apollo at Didyma and the sanctuary of Demeter at Eleusis. The latter was however finally destroyed not long afterwards, most likely at the hands of Alaric the Goth, who penetrated deep into Greece before General Stilicho drove him back. But he could not save Athens, where, according to Zosimus, the figures of the goddess Athena and the hero Achilles were seen striding upon the ramparts of the Acropolis , defending the citadel against the Goths. (Achilles indeed seems to have acquired quite a magical reputation in Athens: in 372 the Eleusinian hierophant had protected Athens from an earthquake by placing a magical figure of the hero under the shield of the statue of Athena Parthenos.)

Goths and the advance of Christianity vie for the honour of the most destructive onslaught on the ancient sites. Gibbon had no doubt which was worse:

In almost every province of the Roman world, an army of fanatics, without authority and without discipline, invaded the peaceful inhabitants; and the ruin of the fairest structures of antiquity still displays the ravages of *those* Barbarians, who alone had time and inclination to execute such laborious destruction.

Certainly Alaric's sack of Rome in 395 was no greater a blow to Greek civilisation than the closure of the Olympic Games by Theodosius I in the previous year. The oracles were now truly dumb, the sanctuaries silent, the Games a ghostly echo. It was at this time that the chryselephantine Zeus of Phidias was at last removed and taken to Constantinople. It became part of the large collection in the palace of Lausus, 'praepositus sacri cubiculi' of Theodosius II (406–50), which also included such major works of the fourth century BC as the Lindian Athena, the Cnidian Aphrodite of Praxiteles, the Samian Hera of Lysippus and Bupalus, the Kairos (Opportunity) of Lysippus, and others. The Zeus was subsequently destroyed, in the reign of Zeno the Isaurian (474–91), by one of the fires that plagued the medieval city.

Constantinople now rapidly became the greatest repository of ancient art in the world, a position it was to retain until 1204. Constantine brought many of the choicest items of Greek and Roman art from Rome. He also brought several monuments from Delphi, including the 'serpent column' which remains in the Hippodrome to this day (though one head was removed by Mehmed the Conqueror, and the other two apparently by the Polish ambassadors in the seventeenth century).[8] The Christian tradition reported that he brought these pagan 'idols' to be figures of fun for the pious citizens of Constantinople, but it is clear that he was continuing that tradition of ostentatious culture and learned display which had characterised many of his imperial predecessors.

Procopius (c 500 – after 562) in his work *On the buildings of Justinian*, describes the collection which was later housed in the bath of Zeuxippus. This house stood near the Forum of Augustus, the principal square of ancient Constantinople, in the area at present contained by the Blue Mosque at one end and Hagia Sophia at the other. In this square was also the Chalke or Brazen House, the vestibule of the Imperial Palace, where further treasures were housed. West of the Forum of Augustus was a second square, the Basilica, around which stood the law-courts, the university, the library and a book-market. This early public museum thus shared the company of buildings of similar purpose, in the manner of many a modern city.

Here our Emperor constructed a court standing outside the city, intended as a promenade for the inhabitants, and a mooring-place for those who sail past it. Its basement, its columns, and its entablature are all covered with marble of great beauty, whose colour is of a most brilliant white, which glitters magnificently in the rays of the sun; moreover, many statues adorn it, some of brass and some of marble, composing a sight well worth mention; one would conjecture that they were the work of Phidias the Athenian, of Lysippus of Sicyon, or of Praxiteles.

A Coptic poet called Christodorus (*fl* 491–518) compiled a long description of the collection, with specific descriptions of over eighty statues: portraits of the poets, especially Homer; of the Homeric heroes and the gods of Greece; of classical writers; and even three of Roman notables. Again one has a picture of a city peopled with statues, as Christodorus praises these works (whose date it is impossible to determine) for their naturalism:

Simonides, you have not laid aside your love of the dance, but lust after the strings . . . ; your sculptor should have mingled sweet music with the bronze; the dumb bronze would have been shamed, and sung to the rhythm of the lyre.

Unhappy Hecabe, mother of Hector, who of the immortals taught you to weep in your silent beauty? Not even bronze restrained you from lamentation, nor did the lifelessness of art take pity on you and release you from your bitter madness.

That naturalism not only enhanced the distinction of the statues in the connoisseur's eye: it could make them, on occasion, uncanny.

Other works erected by Constantine are listed in the tenth-century account of the treasures of Constantinople, the *Patria Constantinopoleos*, which goes under the name of Codinus, though it cannot be by this author. In the Brazen House were four Gorgoneia from the Temple of Artemis at Ephesus (another four were in the Forum of the Bull), and two horses which stood in the apse above them. These were said by the twelfth-century Al-Harawy to have been placed here by the magician Apollonius of Tyana 'to prevent horses from quarreling'.[9] The very gate of the Temple was here, carved with reliefs showing the Battle of the Gods and Giants: it had been presented to the city of Ephesus by the Emperor Trajan. It was of this work that the poet Constantine the Rhodian wrote (in his 'Lines on the Wonders of Constantinople') 'by such errors was the foolish race of Greece deceived, paying evil homage to the filthiness of these impieties', claiming as an excuse for its presence that Constantine had brought it 'as a laughing-stock for the city, and a plaything for children'.

Here too stood the Athena of Lindos, and an Amphitrite surrounded by Sirens. Only seven out of twelve remained in the tenth century when the author of the *Patria Constantino-poleos* described the group. The porphyry column which Constantine brought from Delphi stood in the Forum of Constantine (modern Çemberlitaş); the statue of Apollo-Helios was transformed into a statue of the Emperor himself, and it was inscribed with a dedication to Christ. The statue fell down in 1091 and killed ten people. The statue of Helen destroyed by the Crusaders also arrived at this time. In the Senate stood the statue of Zeus of Dodona, and two of Pallas Athena. One of them faced a statue of Thetis surrounded by crabs, and the ignorant called the pair 'Earth and Sea'.

Bronze and wooden works, as well as columns, were brought from all the cities of the Empire: from Great Antioch (or perhaps from Corinth) came the statue of Bellerophon slaying the Chimera, which stood in the Forum of the Bull (and which pious opinion later re-interpreted as a figure of Joshua). On its pedestal, according to the *Patria*, as well as its source, the eighth-century *Parastaseis*, a remarkable collection of lore about medieval Constantinople, were inscriptions telling of the last days of Constantinople, and of how the city would fall in due time to the Russians.

From Rome came the Fortune of the City which stood in the Forum, along with a statue of the Sun God from Phrygia. Pierre Gilles (1490–1555), who arrived in the city in 1547 to acquire manuscripts and codices for Francis I of France, and spent several years studying its antiquities, tells us that it had formerly stood elsewhere and acted as a guide to ships entering the city. At the Iron Gate stood another porphyry column from Rome, which according to the *Patria* took three years to make the journey because of its immense weight.

In the Hippodrome stood sixty statues brought from Rome, including one of Augustus. Many came also from all the cities of East and West: from Nicomedia and Nikopolis, from Athens, Chios, Crete and Rhodes, from Cyzicus, Caesarea and Sardis, Tralles, Tyana, Antioch and Iconium, Smyrna and Nicaea.

Also in the Hippodrome stood the group of four gilded bronze horses (then pulling a chariot) which now adorn St Mark's Cathedral in Venice. They were supposed to have been brought by Theodosius II from Chios, though another story said that they had been a present from King Tiridates of Armenia to the Emperor Nero. Whichever it was, the group closely resembled that made by Lysippus and dedicated at Delphi by the Rhodians in the fourth century BC: most probably it was a Hellenistic copy, but perhaps the stations of these marvellous beasts' pilgrimage had included both Delphi and Chios before ending in Constantinople.[10] Certain it is that other works besides this did indeed find their way to Venice, but more were wantonly destroyed at once.

The rate of influx of ancient treasures decreased after the reign of Constantine. Theodosius I, as we have seen, brought several pieces from Greece. He also erected the Golden Gate in about 390. The outlines of its triple archway are still visible, embedded in the walls of Istanbul. The gates were plated with

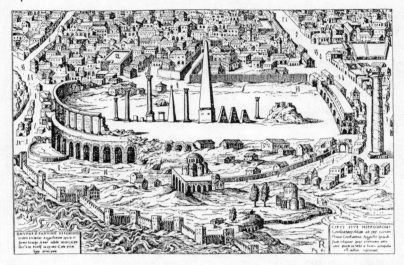

The ruins of the Hippodrome, as they appeared in AD 1450, after Onophrius
Panvinius of Verona.

gold, and adorned with various sculptures, including a famous
group of four elephants. According to Pierre Gilles the other
sculptures, on the smaller outer gate of marble, were brought
by Theodosius II from the temple of Ares at Athens. They
included a bronze gilt victory, and scenes of the Labours of
Heracles and the punishment of Prometheus – appropriate
scenes for a proud and vengeful victor. No one seems to know
where the elephants came from, though they were supposed to
recall those on which Theodosius made his triumphal entry
into the city. The gate was still intact in 1550 when the Dutch
artist Pieter Coeck van Aalst drew it, and at the visit of
Bernard de Montconys in 1648; Spon and Wheler saw five or
six of the reliefs in 1674; thereafter it decayed gradually,
and pieces were removed by the Turks for other buildings,
until in 1795 James Dallaway, who made a study of the
Walls of Constantinople (published in *Archaeologia*, 1803),
could observe nothing left but two porphyry columns with
sculptured capitals.

The next major building programme in Constantinople was
that of Justinian (527–565), whose greatest achievement was
the church of Hagia Sophia, and who changed Constantinople
to a much more ostentatiously Christian city. But even in

the changed atmosphere of his reign, over 100 works of art were acquired, according to the *Parastaseis* and *Patria*. What Titus took from Jerusalem, and Genseric the Vandal from Rome, came, when Belisarius defeated the Vandals, to Constantinople. The very columns of Hagia Sophia came from several sites of Asia Minor. Very often it is impossible to pinpoint the date of arrival, the provenance or the subject of the innumerable statues which we are told adorned the City.

The growth of the Christian ideology of the Empire put these abundant relics of the pagan past in an anomalous position. The popular attitude to images which occasioned the iconoclast controversy, and the series of 'Iconoclast' emperors who attempted to stamp out the use of icons because they were venerated in themselves rather than for the access they gave to the saints and to the divine nature, manifested itself also in popular superstitions which became attached to the ancient statues. The statues were inhabited, largely, by maleficent demons. We have seen the roots of this belief as early as the fourth century in the use of a figure of Achilles as a talisman at Athens. It is a hard question, why this new conception of the power of works of art should have arisen, unless it derives in part from the sometimes uncanny realism of classical art compared to that typical of the Byzantium of Justinian and his successors. A partial explanation can no doubt be found in accidents like that of Himerius, the friend of one of the contributors to the *Parastaseis*, who was killed by the collapse of a statue at the Kynegion; whereupon one John, a philosopher, appeared and announced that the writings of Demosthenes contained a prophecy that a man of worth would be killed by this statue. In this context it is striking that the very word for statue in Byzantine Greek, *stoicheion* (in ancient Greek, 'element'), has come in modern Greek to mean 'ghost'.

By the tenth century a number of very curious legends had come to be attached to the ancient works of art preserved in the city. There was, for example, the magic statue of Aphrodite in the hostel of Theophilus at Zeugma. If there was a dispute about the virginity of a bride, she was presented to the statue. If she was 'guilty' her skirts would fly up around her and expose her genitals. This statue, 'Codinus' tells us, was destroyed by the wife/sister of Justinian, who was exposed by it unawares. She must have been a very depraved woman, for storms sprang up whenever she sailed on the water at Blachernae.

Another useful relic was a sculptured prow at Neoris, on which stood a statue with four horns. If a man who suspected his wife of infidelity approached this, he could be sure of his cuckoldry if the massive marble revolved a third of a circle; if it remained still, his honour was assured.

In the Hippodrome was a bronze eagle which, according to Nicetas, had been constructed by the wonder-working sage of the first century AD, Apollonius of Tyana. It was designed to reduce the dangerous effects of the bites of Byzantine serpents. Unfortunately, Apollonius had made the bird of such a sleepy appearance that its effectiveness was annulled. The hours of the day were incised on its wings as on a sundial.

Other sages were credited with the construction of other wonders of the city. Perhaps the most absurd is that mentioned – though only, it must be admitted, by Evliya Celebi, the seventeenth-century traveller who was at one time the Sultan's ambassador to Vienna – which was a statue of a gnat, constructed by the great Plato (whom the Turks called Iflatun) to ward off all gnats from Constantinople. Goodness knows what real object this description travestied; we can at least be fairly sure it did not work either. Evliya also attributed to a mysterious sage called Surendeh the construction of the serpent column, which was meant to keep all serpents out of Constantinople. It had worked well until the removal of the head which looked to the west. Snakes immediately appeared in the western parts of the City, and by Evliya's time were common in all its parts.

Another treasure was the Bronze Bull at the harbour Neorion, which roared once a year (according to Pierre Gilles) or whenever a disaster was imminent (according to 'Codinus'). Pierre Gilles learnedly assumed that this legendary property had been borrowed from the accounts given by Pindar and Callimachus of the bronze bulls which inhabited Mt Atabyrius in Rhodes, and roared whenever calamity impended.

Another Bronze Bull, in the Forum of the Bull, was said to be that in which the infamous Sicilian tyrant Phalaris had roasted his victims. Typically, the *Parastaseis* tell us instead that it was Julian 'the Apostate' who had roasted *Christians* in it – including, as Pierre Gilles had been told, the martyr Antipas. Thus was legend overlaid with legend.

There were also various wonders to which no legend was attached, but which it must be regarded as a sore loss not to have seen, so intricate and exquisite must their workmanship have been – 'such forms as Grecian goldsmiths make Of hammered gold or gold enamelling To keep a drowsy Emperor awake.' One such was the Wind-vane of Anemodoulion, also called Boukinon (*Parastaseis*) or Tetrasceles (Pierre Gilles). This masterpiece of Byzantine workmanship was made in the time of Theodosius the Great. It was a machine with four bronze walls, sculpted with figures of birds, farmers, flocks, the sea with its fish, fruits, naked cupids. Atop was a pyramid on which stood a female figure, which revolved in the wind. On the four corners stood bronze youths with trumpets, which sounded in turn according to the direction of the wind.

But most persuasive among the legends which the last centuries of Byzantium attached to the antique works was that which made them prophets of the fall of the city. The 'dumb column' of the Xerolophus had reliefs which were supposed to depict the downfall of the city.[11] So, as we have seen, did the legends inscribed on the Bellerophon. The obelisk in the Hippodrome was inscribed with hieroglyphs which, as the key to the Egyptian script had long been lost, seem to have received a similar interpretation. Evliya is, however, our only source in this instance:

Sixteenth talisman. This is also an obelisk of red coloured stone, covered with various sculptures, and situated in the At-meidan [Hippodrome]. The figures on its sides foretell the different fortunes of the city. It was erected in the time of Yanko–ibn–Madiyan [Justinian], who is represented on it sitting on his throne, and holding a ring in his hand, implying symbolically 'I have conquered the whole world, and hold it in my hands like this ring.' . . . On another [side] are the figures of three hundred men engaged in erecting the obelisk, with the various machines used for that purpose.

Jacques Spon (see Chapter 4) drew these reliefs, and as the obelisk still stands we can identify the scenes as typical Egyptian hieratic representations.

Many oracles were current which foretold the end of the city. Pierre Gilles found a collection in the works of the scholar John Tzetzes. In 1204, as we saw, the statue of Athena by Phidias, which stood in the Forum, was destroyed by rioters because it pointed to the west, from which the Crusaders already encamped by the walls had come. Constantinople was indeed a city which contained within itself the seeds of its own destruction. Top-heavy with wealth, burdened with treasure which scarcely any could understand or appreciate, the city was a mausoleum of the past. The popular mind was only too right to interpret those relics of a glorious past as harbingers of doom – doom from the West which would, in due time, understand those works better than their bigoted and ceremonious guardians had ever done. But the West must first destroy the thing it was to love. Byzantium, which kept intact so much else that had been destroyed – the works of the ancient poets most notably – was also the scene of the largest single destruction of antique art the world had ever seen.

It was only when Constantinople had been sacked, when fragmentary Greek empires had re-surfaced at Nicaea, in Epirus and at Trebizond, that scholars of Byzantium began to mourn what had been lost. There had, it is true, been some savants in medieval Constantinople, who paid attention to what might be called archaeological matters as well as to letters. Even as early as the fourth century BC, the Athenian historian Philochorus, and later, in the second century BC, one Polemon, had collected inscriptions from the numerous dedicatory statues of the Greek world. Polemon even acquired the sobriquet of *stelokopas*, or 'statue-breaker', for his pains. The inscriptions of Thebes were collected by one Aristodemus. All these collections were treasured in Byzantium, and made the foundation of the collection, put together in the tenth century by the priest and scholar Constantine Cephalas, which became the Palatine Anthology.

In the ninth and tenth centuries several scholars had interested themselves in such matters:[12] Cephalas' master, Gregory Magister, had transcribed epigrams from monuments in Greece and Asia Minor, and one collection of epigrams from the town of Cyzicus now forms Book III of the *Anthology*. But, such is the perversity of mankind, it was the site of a ruin that inspired the most moving reaction of the medieval Greek mind to the classical past.

Early in the thirteenth century, the future Emperor of Nicaea, Theodore II Lascaris, undertook an educational tour of Asia Minor, visiting the great cities of history. Much of his voluminous correspondence is concerned with doctrinal matters, but in a few of his letters to his tutor George Acropolites, he sounds a different note. Troy impresses him, as 'the work of men of heroic fame', but it is at Pergamum that his eloquence is truly stirred.

We arrived at Pergamum, a city as it were celestial, a dwelling not for spirits, but for men as a protection against demons (who these may be, must be surmised). It is hard to view thoroughly, and no less hard to ascend. It is full of theatres, these being so aged and wasted by time that the brilliance is to be seen as it were in a glass. . . . It is full everywhere of the majesty of the Hellenic spirit, and the vestiges of their wisdom: the city itself demonstrates this in its disdain for us, mere latecomers to the greatness of its ancestral glory. For these buildings are overwhelming compared with the structures of today – although Aristotle writes that, in general, everything is less than wonder leads us to suppose. Walls rise up no less high than the brazen heaven, great in artistry. Through the middle runs a river, bridged by spreading arches. By the governor of the poles!, one would hardly think them made by hand, but as it were of a piece with the earth and of solid stone. If Phidias or any sculptor should see them, he would be amazed at their regularity and purity of line. Among the buildings are low cells, which appear to be the refuse of perished dwellings, and fill the beholder's sight with pain. . . . On either side of the walls of the great theatre stand cylindrical towers, vying with each other in the smoothness of their stonework, and girdled with zones. These could never be the work of hands, or the conception that of a modern mind: they astonish the onlooker. . . . Looking at the citadel, how did we despond, how did we leap and dance, transported in joy mixed with pain and weeping through our delight.

It might almost be Petrarch speaking, imagining the renascent glory of ancient Rome in medieval Italy. But there was no Renaissance in Greece. As Theodore had not perhaps the power, or the resources, or even the imagination, to build anew on the ruins of the old. Fixated in literature on the reproduction, in ever more contorted form, of the style of the ancients, the Byzantines were unable to absorb that spirit for creative purposes. Yet to investigate the past scientifically might be to dethrone it from its pedestal. So Pergamum remained a ruin.

By the fifteenth century things had changed somewhat. The Western Renaissance had given a stimulus to the study of antiquity also in the Greek East, and scholars began to flourish in Constantinople. In the reign of the learned and cultivated Emperor Manuel II Palaeologus (1391–1425) we encounter Manuel Chrysoloras (whom we shall meet again later: p 26) making a catalogue of the statues in Constantinople, 'without fables or exaggeration'.[13] This aim does not, apparently, preclude enthusiasm for the 'gates, pavements, vestibules, columns, tessellations, marble veneers, glass, bronze, lead, iron, sapphires and gold' which Chrysoloras says he could never adequately describe. Nevertheless, the task he set himself must have been considerably easier than it would have been three centuries earlier. The quantity of material had been disastrously and permanently reduced.

After the Turkish conquest of 1453 interest in the remains of antiquity was again dissipated. The Turks smashed many images for doctrinal reasons. Columns from Troy were used to build the Mosque of the Sultan's Mother, and columns from elsewhere in the city were incorporated in the Suleimaniye Mosque. The same happened elsewhere in the Empire. The temple of Poseidon in Cyzicus was demolished to build a mosque (see pp 32–4); and in some cases what the Turks left undone the Franks completed, as when the Knights of St John demolished the Mausoleum of Halicarnassus to build the castle of St Peter at Bodrum.

All Greek learning fled, notably to Mistra. Those Greeks who remained in Constantinople were uninterested or demoralised – a sore disappointment to the stream of educated westerners who began to flock to the city. The first of these was Pierre Gilles. His comments are vigorous:

Add to this the passive ignorance of the Greeks, who seem to have drunk dry the River of Forgetfulness. Not one of them can be found who knows where the remnants of the ancient monuments are situated, or cares to know; not even the priests recognise the places where, only a few years before, sacred temples were destroyed. Furthermore, they are quite amazed if anyone inquires. I myself, for fear of becoming a victim of too great leisure, when I was waiting for the moneys allotted by the King for the acquisition of ancient codices, tried, by whatever clues I could, to track down the monuments of antiquity, which any one may learn who makes a similar attempt.

Posterity has remained for ever in his debt.

Soon afterwards came Jan Dousa, a Dutchman, who collected and published many inscriptions. His comments – in a letter to his father – are equally biting:

Who would not be enraged by the supine idleness of the Greeks who can be convicted of such incuriousness as to their own relics, that none of them today even wishes to know where any ancient monument formerly stood? Not only are they innocent of all science of antiquity, but they even place obstacles in the way of foreigners, to prevent them daring to speak freely about the matter.

But we have anticipated our story. There, on the verge of the seventeenth century and a new beginning, we may leave the sad and silent city of Constantinople, once capital of the world. According to Greek legend, when the Turks stormed into the city, the priests and deacons who were solemnly celebrating the last mass in Haglia Sophia disappeared into the walls. They will re-emerge when the city becomes Greek again. But will they ever recognise it, shorn of all the treasures of Greece?

CHAPTER TWO

Cyriac of Ancona and his Contemporaries

Throughout the world you hunt out ruined temples, and the names of every ancient gymnasium. Then you hunt out the writings of the divine Homer, and all that the old man of Ascra wrote. You even clean up tombs covered with brambles, and return to the sight of men the verses of the ancients.   (Carolo Arretino: see p 27)

Any day in 1421 a young man of thirty could have been seen bent over a drawing-board by the harbour at Ancona. The harbour of this little town on the Adriatic coast of Italy was being dredged and reconstructed to improve the roadstead for the ships of commerce from the Levant, with their cargoes of silks, drugs and spices from Turkey, Persia and the further East. The town of Ancona had been an important port since antiquity, and Trajan had honoured it with one of the arches with which he was so prodigal. But the harbour works had been erected long before his time and now, dilapidated but with still solid foundations, were being reconstructed.

The young man's name was Ciriaco Pizzicolli. He was already well known for his antiquarian interests, and had made an intensive study of the arch of Trajan, as well as teaching himself Latin – insisting on doing so the hard way by plunging directly into the *Aeneid*. His learning, his knowledge of Latin and his understanding of antiquities had made him a suitable candidate, in the eyes of Cardinal Gabriel Condulmieri (the future Pope Eugene IV), for the task of supervising the harbour reconstruction, a task which engaged him for much of that year. From this contact the two men became firm friends, and Condulmieri's patronage was to be valuable to Cyriac (as he is usually called) for years to come. By the end of his life he had made himself the greatest living expert on the antiquities of Greece. How had this come about?

Cyriac (c1391–c1453) came from a family of merchants, and had already been on trading voyages as far as Egypt, Cyprus and Constantinople, as well as the Dalmatian coast. No doubt the house of the Pizzicolli was often full of the tales of seafarers from distant parts and the strange things they had seen, as well as of the information Cyriac himself had picked up and loved to retail. There were the tales of the endless deserts of the East and the 'sole Arabian tree'; of the men with faces in their chests, or with a single foot which they used as an umbrella to ward off the intense heat; of the gold-mining ants of India. Current too were tales of lands that seem less exotic now, notably of Greece. Pilgrims to the Holy Land had travelled via Greece and Constantinople and recorded their strange legends in their books; for example Niccolo Martoni's account of the Gorgon's head on the south face of the Acropolis of Athens, which had the power to sink approaching ships.[1]

Legend and fact blended in the work of the Florentine priest Cristoforo Buondelmonti (b c1385), of whose books Cyriac certainly owned copies in later life. Buondelmonti made a tour of the Greek islands in 1414, apparently under commission from the humanist Niccolò Niccoli to collect Greek books. He wrote two books himself: the *Description of Crete* (1417) and the *Book of the Islands of the Archipelago* (1422) in which he gives details of seventy-nine islands (Constantinople is made to count as one). Both books became best sellers, being translated into several languages, including Greek. The dedication of the first indicates clearly his aims and his limitations.

I expound the form of the isles, their greatness and the events of which they have been the theatre at various epochs up to our own day. . . . You will see, briefly told, numerous pleasant tales of the men of antiquity and of the exploits of heroes; you will see mountains green and white with snow, springs, pastures, plains where nymphs descend; goats wandering on arid rocks; ports with capes and neighbouring rocks, strong cities, stretches of sea.

A geographical account above all, then, with classical overtones. Anyone who visits Greece today, with its scrubbed and weeded ruins, trampled daily by a thousand feet and surrounded by sellers of flokati rugs, leatherwork and trinkets, will find it hard to picture the country as a depopulated wilderness, unexplained marbles poking through the herbage, partially legible inscriptions buried in the sand and brambles, crumpled columns a haunt for storks and hares. The effort is easier in some of the remoter parts of Turkey. But this is how the country must have seemed when the first visitors came from the west; a daunting labyrinth of riddling stones and ill-discerned ground plans, reluctant to give up their secrets even to those to whom the recovery of the classical past was an almost religious quest. One must admire a man who wrests any information from the wreckage in such unfavourable circumstances.

The information Buondelmonti gives about the islands is mainly derived from his classical reading, interspersed where appropriate with quotations from Virgil and anecdotes from Livy. He sometimes describes a relief or a statue, like that he saw on Melos, of Cybele in a chariot with a mural crown, accompanied by Galli and lions; more often he simply refers to 'numerous and magnificent marbles' and the like.

The ruins of Gortyn in Crete inspire him to a longer outburst:

Here Minos reigned, justest of kings. Alas, what shall I say, what shall I tell of first when I see such things? Let all the Cretans mourn over such destruction, let the women tear their thinning hair. There was a mountain standing separate from the others, further north and close to the water, and round it were walls, where an undamaged gate was still to be seen. The Palace of Minos can be seen, its decaying windows wide open, and from there a water conduit descended from the mountain and then sprinkled the whole city, which is about as big as our Florence, though Gortyn is fuller, and has no walls. . . . I counted the marble columns and stones, upright or lying on the ground, and there were fourteen hundred of them; and there were also endless numbers of marble sheets and tombs.

He is one of our earliest witnesses to the 'labyrinth of Cnossus' (actually an old quarry on a hill above Kastelli near Gortyn, which has been sealed up since about 1980), and the first to mention the 'tomb of Zeus' on Mt Juktas. Occasionally he recounts a fascinating legend such as that current in Cos, that every six or eight years the spectre of the physician Hippo- crates' daughter would appear in the town, recounting her woes and praying for release. This is obviously a version of the widespread medieval legend, told in Mandeville's *Travels* and elsewhere, that Hippocrates' daughter, in the form of a dragon, besought men to kiss her to restore her human form – but to no avail.[2] On Tinos, he tells of a sorceress who, when an approaching fleet was sighted, would go to a mountain top, strip naked and pronounce incantations, which invariably brought on a storm. The fleet would be wrecked, and the Tiniots would despoil the ships and enslave the survivors. Clearly this is a garbled story relating to the prevalence of pirates; it also recalls the similar powers of Martoni's Gorgon at Athens.

But such travellers' tales could not be enough to drive one man, almost alone, to make Greece and its antiquities the object of his quest and passion, the theme of his diaries and the anvil of his inexhaustible energies. If Greece extended its lure through such tales as these, the passion to understand had other roots, and to appreciate these we have to envisage the passion for antiquity that lay at the roots of the Italian Renaissance, in which Cyriac's talents and energies were nurtured.

That passion at its height is the subject of Chapter 3. But it was Petrarch (1304–74), who, though his interests were mainly literary, began the quest to rediscover classical antiquity and to apply its lessons to the contemporary world. He was, for example, the first to assemble an extensive coin collection, the aim being to acquire a chronological series of the Roman emperors.

In Cyriac's time it was the collecting of manuscripts and codices that most engaged the interest of the humanists. Though Cyriac's interests were in buildings and monuments, the task of providing the humanists in Italy with fresh materials helped to fund his frequent journeys, after he had lost sight of his original avocation as a merchant.

Among his closest acquaintances were the Florentine humanists, above all Francesco Filelfo (1398–1481). Filelfo had himself visited Greece, and 'fired with ardent enthusiasm for Greek letters, went to Parnassus to drink of Hippocrene and among the ruins of Athens trod in the footsteps of the immortal philosophers' (Paolo Giovio). He translated Homer at the behest of Pope Nicholas V, and established a considerable literary reputation by his voluminous output of translations and treatises. He also acted informally as ambassador for the Emperor Constantine Palaeologus to the Pope and Francesco Sforza.

Other acquaintances included Niccolò Niccoli and Cosimo de' Medici himself. Important too was Manuel Chrysoloras (*c*1350–1415), whose daughter Filelfo had married, and who was the teacher of Greek, it sometimes seems, to half the humanists of the Renaissance, from Rome to Germany; and Francesco Scalamonti, who was to become Cyriac's biographer. Filelfo wrote an interesting reference for Cyriac to Lorenzo Giustinian in Venice on 30 December 1442:

I do so the more willingly, as I am aware that you will find the man pleasant company, particularly because he will bring with him several monuments of great antiquity, eulogies [?] and epigrams, and other numerous writings collected from most ancient stones in Asia and Greece. Cyriac never rests, and regards it as his most valuable merchandise if he can find, and bring to Italy, something worthy of record from among those first men of Arcady (who, as they say, existed before the sun and moon) . . .

That was nearly twenty years after Cyriac's first journey with an archaeological purpose. The reconstruction of Cyriac's chronology is not altogether easy, since many of his own manuscript journals are lost, but it may be worthwhile to indicate the scope of his major journeys.

His first journey in 1412 took him beyond Constantinople to Egypt, a journey which no doubt sowed the seeds of the archaeological interests he began to develop in 1425. Then, he had been in Constantinople on business for the Contarini. Here he set about learning Greek, starting, like Heinrich Schliemann after him, with Homer. He must also at this time have acquired some knowledge of Ptolemy's *Geography*, a work of the early second century AD which was a major source for ancient topography, for he cites it regularly in his later travels.

He began to build his reputation rapidly. Already in 1427 Filelfo speaks of Cyriac's task of 'restoring antiquity, or rather redeeming it from extinction'. A poem addressed to Cyriac by one Carolo Arretino begins by hailing him as a poet, a rhetor, an historian; alluding to his visit to the Pyramids in 1412, and his copying of some hieroglyphic inscriptions (which he could not, of course, interpret), Arretino credits him with a knowledge of most of the other Seven Wonders of the World, including one that no longer existed:

Now an expert surveys the miracle of the Pyramids; and you read inscriptions in an unknown tongue. Now you seek the remains of Babylon, its hanging gardens, and the extent of its broad walls. Now shall Caria be despoiled of its ancient sepulchre, and the noble work of Mausolos be revealed.[3] Throughout the world you hunt out ruined temples, and the names of every ancient gymnasium. Then you hunt out the writings of the divine Homer, and all that the old man of Ascra [Hesiod] wrote. You even clean up tombs covered with brambles, and return to the sight of men the verses of the ancients. . . . Whatever inscribed panels show, or bronze or marble statues, all this is copied down in your notebooks.

In 1435 he toured the Ionian Islands, Epirus, Northern Greece and the Peloponnese, returning to Egypt the following year (or perhaps 1437). Between 1443 and 1449 he was again in Greek lands, after a period of holding municipal office in Ancona. In 1444 he was in the Northern Aegean; met the Sultan in Adrianople (Edirne) and the Emperor in Constantinople. The next year he was in Crete, and in 1446 he visited the islands. 1447–8 were spent in the Peloponnese. If he came home at all during these periods we know nothing of it. The next years are particularly ill-recorded, and the last glimpse we see of Cyriac, in 1453, is a particularly tantalising one (see below, p 36).

Everywhere he went, he drew temples and reliefs, copied inscriptions (some, like the Royal Inscriptions of Didyma or those on the Monument of Philopappus in Athens, subsequently lost or destroyed), and recorded them in his notebooks or *Commentaria*, almost all of which perished, probably in the fire of the Sforza Library in Pesaro in 1514. The only surviving one in Cyriac's hand records his journey of 1447–8: laconic entries on day-to-day movements, careful and largely accurate copies of inscriptions in Greek and Latin, interspersed with sketches, untutored in style, but conscientious.

For all his importance as a collector of inscriptions, many of which are now lost or defaced, and for which he is the only witness, it is important to realise what Cyriac was not. He had little interest in ancient topography or in the identification of

buildings. He had read his Homer, and expected to find
Homer's world awaiting him. One is startled to read in his
notebook that he took ship from Gytheion, a fishing boat,
before dawn on 15 October 1447, and arrived 'before the sixth
hour from sunrise' at Homer's sandy Pylos, until we realise
that where he is actually visiting is near Vitylo, similarly
situated on a deep bay, but on the wrong promontory of the
Peloponnese. Likewise he sanguinely identifies nearby Las
with Homer's Asine. At Delphi he sneers at the villagers of
Castri who 'have no idea where the ancient Delphi was',[4] and
then refers to 'the round temple of Apollo' (obviously the
fourth-century tholos, or rotunda):

I came to Delphi, where I saw at first magnificent, and for the most
part ancient, walls in dilapidation, distinguished by a variety of
architectural riches. Then the circular temple of Apollo, collapsed on
all sides, and close by a wonderful amphitheatre with thirty-three
steps of great stones, and on the topmost citadel, below extremely
high rocks, a hippodrome adorned with marble steps, 600 paces
long. And I saw broken statues here and there. And epigrams, in
both Greek and Latin letters, and within as well as out in the fields
huge marbles, and elaborate tombs, and rocks marvellously carved.

The first journey of which we have a detailed record is that
of 1436–7, of which a copy was fortunately made by another
hand before the destruction of Cyriac's own manuscript. In
January 1437 he was staying with Carlo II, the Venetian ruler
of Cephalonia and Zakynthos, at Arta. From here he visited a
site which he took to be Dodona. It was actually Nikopolis,
the city founded by Augustus to celebrate his victory at
Actium; but the mistake is understandable since Strabo,
whom Cyriac was using, himself remarks that most of the area
is desolate, habitations vanished, and the difficulty of identification great. But at least as amusing as the site (with its, to us,
evidently Roman ruins) was the enterprise of getting there. In
a letter of 20 May 1437 he describes his visit: 'to omit the rest,
we swam briskly across the three courses of the Acheron'; he
later recrossed, in a 'hollow log', by night.

It was in the spring of this year that he first visited Athens.
The case of Athens exemplifies most of Cyriac's preoccupations and limitations. He first visited it only after he had been
travelling for twenty-four years: such was its lack of allure,
prestige and civilisation at this time. Such travellers as visited

Athens before Cyriac are unanimous in their laments over its fallen state. The cry began even in the fourth century with Bishop Synesius, and became regular with the pilgrims of the late Middle Ages. Athens was a shadow of its former self, though liberally sprinkled, then as now, with ancient ruins. Scarcely one of these was correctly identified in Cyriac's time. The Parthenon, it is true, was always known as the 'Temple of Minerva', despite the church in its midst. The Propylaea had been converted into a palace for Nerio Acciaiuoli, the Duke of Athens, and Cyriac stayed in the house of one Antonio Balduino, on the Acropolis itself. (Cyriac is, incidentally, the first modern writer to call it 'Acropolis'.)

Cyriac systematically explored the city, recording inscriptions, for example all five of those on the Monument of Philopappus, two of which are now lost; but he made few attempts to criticise the identifications of buildings current at the time. The writings of Niccolò Martoni, who had been in Greece in 1394, and a brief anonymous list, in Greek, of the monuments of the city, preserved in a manuscript in Vienna and hence known as the 'Vienna Anonymous', provide an interesting farrago of identifications.

The Temple of Olympian Zeus, perhaps because of its position beyond the arch announcing the border of the City of Hadrian, was universally held to be Hadrian's Palace. The Library of Hadrian was known as the Palace of Themistocles, and other buildings were identified as the houses of Solon and Thucydides. The Tower of the Winds was known as the School of Socrates (or sometimes as the Tomb of Socrates). The School of Plato was identified with a lone tower of Frankish date in the suburb of Ambelokipi. The Theatre of Dionysus was called the School of Aristotle, and so, on occasion, was Hadrian's aqueduct. The School of Epicurus was put in the Propylaea, and that of Pythagoras, more outrageous than the rest, in the Temple of Nike. The so-called Lantern of Demosthenes (the choragic monument of Lysicrates) had acquired its sobriquet even in the time of Bishop Michael Acominatus (before 1204), and it is a puzzle to know when and how these names might have arisen. They seem to predate the renascent Hellenism of the thirteenth century, after the fall of Constantinople to the Crusaders. Perhaps they go back even to the Dark Ages. Even today the

prison of Socrates is solemnly pointed out at the foot of
Philopappus Hill.

One point on which Cyriac challenges the accepted lore
is the identification of the Tower of the Winds, which he
describes as a Temple of Aeolus. This was a good guess but
betrays an ignorance of the architectural form appropriate to a
temple. His account of it is careful and factual:

> We revisited the octagonal Temple of Aeolus, which has at the top of
> the walls eight winged fingers of the winds, sculpted with their
> attributes with wonderful art, and each image has above it its name in
> large letters of Attic style, as we saw from nearby.

On 22 April 1436 Cyriac left Athens; in the course of that
single day he visited Piraeus, where he observed the marble
lion which was subsequently removed by Francesco Morosini
to stand before the arsenal in Venice, where it remains; went
on to Eleusis, sketched and noted the ruins; thence continued
to Megara, the Isthmus, and finally Corinth. Five days later he
was at Kalavryta, being entertained by George Cantacuzenus
and making the most of his host's copious library of Greek
books. Two days seem to have been enough for him to digest
the essence of these treasures – or at least to acquire itchy feet –
and on 29 April he was on his way again.

He was heading straight for Mistra, then supposed to be the
site of ancient Sparta, and for him it is Sparta, not Athens, that
is the true destination of the lover of antiquity. The democratic
fervour of a Rienzo was exceptional, and the idealisation of
Athenian democracy is a creation of nineteenth-century liber-
alism. For the Renaissance, it was Sparta that embodied the
true central virtues of classical civilisation. Before 1402 P. P.
Vergerio had praised Sparta in his treatise on manners for
young princes, and the neo-Latin poet (a Greek by birth)
Michael Marullus[5] waxed enthusiastic on Spartan cold baths.
In this the Italian writers were no doubt reflecting the ideal that
had been constructed by Byzantine emperors and their
advisers on the basis of their reading of Plutarch. And this
admiration for the pride, valour and restraint of the Spartans of
old was shared by the greatest luminary of the Greek intellectual world, Gemistus Plethon, who was at this time living at
Mistra. It was above all to see him that Cyriac had come.

Plethon's admiration for classical antiquity and the theories of Plato had not endeared him to the Christian government of the Byzantine Empire. He had retired in semi-exile to Mistra to elaborate his theories of Platonic communism and his grandiose plans for a re-Hellenisation of the Empire and the conquest of the encroaching Turk. Cyriac may be supposed to have sympathised with this latter aspiration, which had been the motivation of many who voted for the union of the Greek and Roman churches at the Council of Florence, which both Plethon and Cyriac had attended in 1439. The two men lamented together the passing of classical Sparta.

I decided to make a detour to visit the ruins of the once noble city of Sparta. For I felt that a duty of mourning was owed to those great and noble cities now collapsed or destroyed. I felt that more bitterness was in that calamity of the human race than in the distinguished cities of the world. We saw wonderful temples and beautiful statues, and other noble ornaments of human power and art crumbled from their former splendour. What a decline did that pristine human virtue and famous probity of soul seem to have suffered! . . .

When Cyriac was inspired to an epigram in Italian on Sparta, Plethon translated it into Greek.[6]

> Sparta, kind queen of broad Laconia,
> Glory of Greece, example to the world,
> Temple and training ground of war and honour,
> Mirror of every virtue, and its spring,
>
> When I survey your policy and laws,
> Your customs and your every excellence,
> I stand by the Eurotas and exclaim
> In wonder to Diana, your kind queen:
>
> Where is your good Lycurgus, where are Castor
> And Pollux, the divine twin sons of Zeus?
> Where Anaxandridas, Orthriadas and Gylippus?
> Eurystheus, and Leonidas and Agis?
> Where are Pausanias, and the great Lysander?
> Agesilaus, Aristus and Xanthippus?
>
> Not Rome, not Philip,
> But now, in Mistra here, a lowlier age
> Has brought you to Byzantine vassalage.

The anti-Byzantine classicism is explicit, and would have warmed Plethon's heart. The lines also convey something of the world Cyriac was seeking to recover, and what its values were. The romance of legend, civic probity, the ringing names of gods and heroes, coalesce to a thumbnail sketch of an ideal world which contemporaries could, perhaps, do well to imitate.

After this visit, and although he failed to unearth more than a few fragments of the real Sparta, his further travels could perhaps only be an anti-climax. Yet it is his last voyage, to Northern Greece and the Propontis in 1444–7, that produced the results which have had more permanent influence than anything else he did. For different reasons, his visits to Cyzicus and to Samothrace have earned themselves places in archaeology and art history respectively.

He visited Cyzicus in August 1444. Situated on the sea of Marmora, under Mt Dindymon, the throne of Rhea, Mother of the Gods, Cyzicus was one of the most important trading ports of the Greek world. Its glory had been the great temple of Zeus, which had been many centuries in the building; it was still unfinished when it was felled by an earthquake in 123 AD. The Emperor Hadrian, who showered honours on Greek cities, had it reconstructed, and it was dedicated probably in 167 AD. Its pillars were, at sixty-seven feet, taller than those of the temple of Olympian Zeus at Athens. Its life was prolonged by use as a church in Byzantine times.

Cyriac had visited the site before, in 1431. He took the temple for that of Persephone, the most honoured goddess of Cyzicus, because an altar dedicated to her stood close by the temple. He also copied an inscription recording its dedication to her, which is now lost and which has been suspected, unreasonably, of being his own invention. The error in identification is of small significance beside his service in recording not only the inscriptions but the appearance of the building.

In 1431 he had seen thirty-three columns and a large part of the pediment still *in situ*: the pediment, with its statues of Zeus and other gods, was 'undamaged and intact, almost in its original splendour'. In 1444 two more columns had gone, removed by the Turks who now controlled the area, for the building of mosques and other purposes. Quarrying was still going on as late as 1946;[7] nothing today remains beyond a mound of earth, unapproachable with holly bushes, which covers the well-preserved vaulted passages of the foundations. These were known throughout the centuries as the Labyrinth, or the Caves. Even in the twentieth century they were reputed to be the haunt of demons.

Cyriac made careful drawings of the column capitals, bases and other architectural remains, and made measurements of the whole. Pliny (*Nat Hist* 36, 98) mentions a temple at Cyzicus in whose walls a gold thread (or gold tubes? – the passage is a vexed one) was embedded: Cyriac claims that he observed this here. The passage is a crux of interpretation, for Pliny claims that the gold thread or tubes somehow shed a mystic illumination on the statues within the temple. It is almost certain that Cyriac here is using his imagination, finding what he thinks he ought to find on the basis of his reading. Pliny does not even say that this was the temple concerned.

This makes one the more suspicious of the measurements he made, and he has been accused of fantasy in these too. But if some allowance be made for the difficulty of interpretation of an uncleared site piled high with the rubble of ruins, Cyriac's

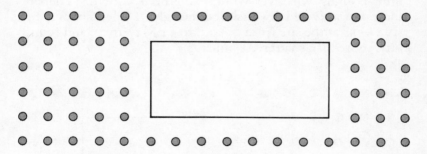

S. Reinach's reconstruction of the Temple at Cyzicus

figures can be made to work. Nothing is now visible on the
ground to aid reconstruction. S. Reinach produced a plan of a
temple which followed Cyriac's data for the numbers of
columns, but it cannot be made to fit the dimensions Cyriac
gives, of 240 by 110 cubits, if the intercolumniations were at all
regular. F. Hasluck, in 1910, preferred to reject Cyriac's
statement on the dispositions of the columns, and reconstructed an octastyle temple with a broad central doorway.
This would admittedly be a normal plan for a temple of this
size, and corresponds closely to that of a temple at Aizanoi; but
it seems cavalier to reject Cyriac's evidence on what would
have been the easiest detail to observe, namely the disposition
of columns at either end. If Cyriac is not to be assumed to have
observed the five rows of four columns, and four rows of
three, correctly, what virtue is there in keeping his totals of
twenty (assuming the inclusion of two in antis) and twelve
(assuming the exclusion of two in antis)?

The question seems scarcely amenable to speculation alone,
though one must admit Cyriac's temple would have looked
rather odd. At least Cyriac has given archaeologists the entertainment of trying to reconstruct a building of which, but for
him, nothing whatever would have been known. (The site
thereafter attracted few visitors, though Dr John Covel spent
six weeks at the site from 2 April to 14 May 1677, and found
little more than shattered remnants.)[8]

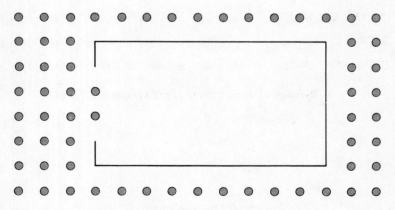

F. W. Hasluck's reconstruction of the Temple at Cyzicus

On Samothrace, his interests took a different direction. Here his mind was full of the meeting of Philip and Olympias, parents of Alexander the Great, on the island. So when he came upon a poorly preserved bearded torso, now identified as the prophet Tiresias, it was for him unquestionably a portrait of Aristotle, the tutor of Alexander. He made a sketch. It became known in the artistic circles of Italy, and derivatives of this sketch established the iconography of Aristotle for the Renaissance. The error of identification does not invalidate his recording of the bust, which has suffered the ravages of another half-millennium since Cyriac saw it. As Ashmole puts it, 'not only was he trying to make a true record of the objects, but was succeeding so well that he occasionally puts later investigators to shame.'[9]

Another piece of sculpture he copied on Samothrace had equally interesting repercussions. This was a marble relief of dancing figures, which he described as nymphs. A subsequent copyist of the drawing labelled six of the ten dancers with the names of Muses. Cyriac would not so have committed himself, but the error must be early, for these 'Muses' became the models for the Muses in Andrea Mantegna's painting *Parnassus*.[10]

The extent to which Cyriac had embedded himself in an ancient world of literary and Virgilian tone is evident from the description of his journey from Thasos, then in fee to the Gattilusi Dukes of Lesbos, to Ainos. He wrote in a letter to Johannes Pedemontanus:

The night after the New Year celebrations in Thasos, we made our farewells and returned to our boat to make for ancient Aenos [Enos on the Thracian coast]: the omens were good. The sailors slept 'spread over their oars' (Virg *Aen* 5,837), but 'sleep did not seize Cyriac' (Hom *Il* 2,2). But long before 'the crested bird' (Ov *Fast* 1,455–6) called forth the warm dawn, I woke my companions and the captain with a cry of 'Alleluia!'; when the towering waters had settled and the sky cleared . . . we launched the ship and resumed our pleasant journey. We left the noble and peaceful port of Ieramoulinte [?] on Thasos and bade farewell to the Empire of the Gattilusii. Night breezes blow, and the pale moon does not refuse her course, 'the sea trembles with her silver light' (Virg *Aen* 7,7–9). Then, cutting the furrow of liquid Neptune, we point out the summit of Thasos, reach the confines of Thrace, and graze the shores of savage Diomede, who, we are told, was accustomed to give his visitors as fodder to his huge horses. To prevent us pious souls from suffering such a fate, or entering on his shore, our very own Mercury filled our sails with wind, and a company of Nereids escorted us on either side. On one side Doris, her blonde companion Doto, and Galatea 'ploughed the watery way' (Virg *Aen* 9, 102–3), while on the right Panopea, Amphitrite and Parthenia Glauce gently assisted us with their white arms, and the finest of them all. Cymodocea, swam in the deep sea and gently bedewed me from time to time with her kisses, buoying up from below the iron craft.

This loss of touch with the real Greece perhaps accounts for the last glimpse, and the most astonishing of all, which the lacunose record of history affords us of Cyriac of Ancona.

It is strangely incongruous with the rest. It is May 1453. Outside the walls of Constantinople, Mehmed the Conqueror is encamped. As he prepares through the long vigil of the night the final assault that will shatter the Byzantine Empire, who is at his side to soothe his mind? None other than the Italian humanist, lover and preserver of Hellenic culture, intimate friend of Greece's last champion, Gemistus Plethon, reading to its destroyer from the works of Diogenes Laertius, Herodotus, Livy and Quintus Curtius, as well as Chronicles of the Popes, Emperors and Kings of the Franks and Lombards. Presumably the Sultan – a particular admirer of Alexander the Great – benefited from all these martial tales in his own assault, which he regarded as vengeance against the Greeks for the sack of Troy.[11] It is perhaps unworthily cynical to suggest that Cyriac got the codices he wanted when they entered the city. Much more was lost for ever. Whatever he did get, in 1514 it went the same way as the books burned by the conquering Turks to roast a celebratory ox.

But this bitter conclusion should not colour our estimation of Cyriac's real achievement. Ferdinand Gregorovius hailed him as a Pausanias reincarnate (on Pausanias, see p 145). Certainly his service to archaeologists is of the same kind, if not on the same scale, as the great Baedeker of thirteen centuries before. Unlike Buondelmonti, Cyriac is a true son of the Renaissance. Though sunk into obscurity in succeeding centuries, his example was of immense significance for the development of Italian antiquarianism, and hence archaeology; and his work forms the basis of much of the codification of knowledge that has occupied scholars in the last 150 years.

CHAPTER THREE

Collectors and Antiquaries:
The Arundel Marbles

The general reasons why God admits some such diversities in his book, prevail also for this place which is now under our consideration; which are, first, to make men sharp and industrious in the inquisition of truth, he withdraws it from present apprehension, and obviousness. For naturally great wits affect the reading of obscure books, wrastle and sweat in the explication of prophesies, dig and thresh out the words of unlegible hands, resuscitate and bring to life again the mangled and lame fragmentary images and characters in Marbles and Medals, because they have a joy and complacency in the victory and achievement thereof.   (John Donne, *Essays in Divinity*)

The Collectors

We invite you to take a turn through the galleries of the Palace of Fontainebleau. Francis I (1494–1547) has recently become King of France, and he intends to make his court a centre of Renaissance culture. From the Sack of Rome in 1527 he has been able to reap some benefit; illustrious Italian artists have come to his court, the first of whom is Il Rosso, who since 1530 has been engaged in turning the old medieval hunting lodge in the forest south-east of Paris into a residence fit for a king and a connoisseur. Two years later he is joined by Francesco Primaticcio.

Galleries, pavilion, court and ballroom, arcades and Golden Gate, all have been decorated by them with the elaborate symbolism of the ripe Renaissance and the attention to ornate detail that tips the style over into Mannerism. Strapwork and cartouches frame paintings of classical and mythological subjects (few religious themes here), and Primaticcio's latest task (since 1540) is to acquire antique statuary – either originals from Italy and its impoverished collectors, or casts – to recreate an entire classical world in the corridors of Fontainebleau.

Primaticcio came back from his first trip with 133 cases, containing 125 statues, busts and torsos, as well as numerous casts. It seems to have been the advent of these Italian painters which opened Francis' eyes to the wealth of antique art available in Italy, and to its merits. But these acquisitions of Primaticcio were certainly not the first. As early as 1515 Francis had been bargaining with Lorenzo de' Medici for the copy of the Laocoön (see p 112) in the Pope's collection (it had been discovered in the ruins of Nero's Golden House in 1506). The piece was not for sale, however, and Baccio Bandinelli was commissioned to produce a marble copy for the King. Unfortunately, when the Pope saw the copy he liked it so much that he decided to keep that as well, and to send Francis some other statues instead. In the end the King did acquire a Laocoön, but it was a bronze cast.

Other works that entered the King's collection in the form of casts (by Giovanni Bologna) were the Commodus Hercules, the Apollo Belvedere, the Zingara or Gipsy, and the Cleopatra – all of them statues which continued for centuries to be among the canonical great works of antique art. Not all of them would receive much respect today. Almost all the works admired by the Renaissance and later centuries were Roman copies of Greek originals, often of post-classical date. The late fourth century and the Pergamene baroque of the Laocoön were what was known and therefore admired: few had yet paid any attention to the surviving works of classical Athens, for few had been in Greece to see them. Of the works Francis received, the Zingara was a heavily doctored ancient marble torso, fitted out with modern bronze extremities. The Cleopatra kept its reputation longer, being copied for the grotto at Stourhead where it was accompanied by a couplet of Alexander Pope, and even featuring in *Middlemarch* as a background for the unfortunate Dorothea Casaubon when sighted by Ladislaw on her honeymoon in Rome.

Benvenuto Cellini, who was also by this time in the King's

service, describes the accommodation of the pieces of Fontainebleau in a room

> more than a hundred paces in length, [which] was richly furnished, and was hung with a number of paintings from the hand of our splendid Florentine, Rosso; under the paintings were grouped a great many pieces of sculpture, some in the round and others in low relief. The room was about twelve paces across. Bologna had brought here all his antiques, beautifully cast in bronze, and had arranged them magnificently with each one raised on its own pedestal.

The centrepiece of the display was Cellini's own Jupiter, which moved the king to admiration, though Mme d'Etampes considered that it looked tawdry beside the magnificent antique works.

Undoubtedly Francis cherished every one of his antiques. The atmosphere of his court can be gauged from the literary effort that went into celebrating a single statue, that of Venus. The statue, though it apparently was holding an apple, was almost certainly a version of the *Standing Venus* from the Vatican collection, one of the closest extant copies of the most famous of all statues of Aphrodite, that made by Praxiteles for her temple at Cnidus (see pp 113–4). But this association would have been unknown to Francis, who no doubt enjoyed it mainly for its supposed resemblance to favourite ladies of the court, whom he could tease with allusions to the likeness.

> Plus inconneue a moi et transformée
> Est cette chair, si long temps estimée,
> Qui n'est à vous qui desirez me veoir,
> Car ne trouvant vos coeurs chaux, par debvoir,
> Marbre m'ont fait par grand froid congelée.
>
> Et qu'il soit vray, l'amour est transfynée
> Par long desir en la pensée aymée,
> Dont ne suis plus, estant sans le sçavoir
> Plus inconneue.

Besides this poem by the King himself, the statue, which had been sent to him by Renzo da Ceri in 1530, provoked a series of nine Latin epigrams from another poet, Germain de Brice, which play on the conceit that the work is virtually alive, as well as shorter tributes from six other poets.[1]

In all this Francis was only following the tradition of the

Italian princes. The Renaissance had recreated the idea of 'fine art', and of its appreciation as a pursuit fit for gentlemen. The great Medici in Florence, Cosimo and Lorenzo, had acquired large collections of ancient gems and bronzes (now in the Archaeological Museum in Florence). In 1489 Lorenzo had made his villa near San Marco at once a museum of marbles and an academy for young artists. Here it was that Michelangelo served his apprenticeship. The fashion spread throughout northern Italy.

It was not only themes that the artists took from antiquity. Already the classical past was acquiring the status of a lost paradise, an ideal for art rather than a model for life. The artists increasingly reproduced ancient pieces directly in their own works: sculptures, reliefs and architectural details recur constantly. Raphael's Apollo in his *Parnassus* was the Orpheus of an early Christian sarcophagus, and his Olympus in the *Council of the Gods* was the Belvedere Torso. Sphinxes, sarcophagi, Muses, Demeters and the Dioscuri of Monte Cavallo all appear in his paintings. Giulio Romano borrowed pyramids and columns from the city of Rome, as well as sarcophagi, statues and draperies to make his classical subjects authentic. Bronzino could even borrow an angel from a Roman coin. Titian's *Bacchus and Ariadne* is a cento of ancient motifs, including the Laocoön in reverse. Myron's Cow appears in both Tintoretto's *Golden Calf* of 1560 and in Nicolas Poussin's painting of the same subject in London. And so on.[2]

Andrea Mantegna, as we saw in Chapter 2, liked to use recondite sources of imagery such as the drawings of Cyriac of Ancona, and may even preserve a memory of Constantinople in his *Christ in the Garden* in London.[3] He was a notably scholarly artist who had a special house in Mantua for his own antiquities. Close by was Vespasiano Gonzaga's gallery of statues and reliefs at Sabbioneta. Isabella d'Este was perhaps the most rapacious collector of all; she suborned the nephew of Baldassare Castiglione, a knight of Malta called Fra Sabba Castiglione, (d.1533), to obtain marbles from Halicarnassus and the Greek islands;[4] she was not above pressing Mantegna, even at the point of death, to sell her his most treasured pieces; and when Urbino was sacked by Cesare Borgia, she wrote immediately to obtain the collection that had belonged to her conquered cousin, Federigo da Montefeltro.

One of the most popular forms of collection was a cabinet of coins, such as had first been assembled by Petrarch. Many who followed him in this also thought to read all the moral lessons of antiquity in a silver tetradrachm. For a man with a passion for antiquity but limited means, a collection of coins was both cheap and portable. The habit became an obsession in Europe. By 1550 there were over 380 cabinets of medals in Italy, as well as more than 200 in the Low Countries, 175 in Germany, and 200 in France. After another century of collecting John Evelyn could anatomise and approve the passion:

Marbles with their deepest inscriptions crumble away, and become no more legible: pictures and colours fade . . . 'Tis deplorable even to consider, what irreparable loss the learned world has suffered by so many conflagrations and funest accidents, as have not only dissipated, but quite consumed infinite numbers of volumes; so as of all that noble and venerable store, so very few in comparison are left us, that there is hardly to be found a manuscript in the whole world which can honestly pretend to above eight hundred, or a thousand years antiquity, and to have so long escaped the rage of fire, wars, or (what is worse) barbarous ignorance, and fanatick zeal: whilst Medals (though even these likewise, as all other sublunary things, be not wholly exempt from diminution, through the avarice of some, who have melted down all they could get of them of gold or silver) have survived, and outlasted the most ancient records and transmitted to us the knowledge of a thousand useful things of twice a thousand years past.[5]

Almost as popular as collections of coins were collections of drawings. Many famous painters were to be schooled in the antiquities of Roman Italy. Jacopo Bellini (d1470) not only drew sculptural works but copied inscriptions. Not much later, Andrea Mantegna would do the same; and, as we shall see, he made good use of Cyriac's drawings from Greece, too. Like coin collecting, drawing became an obsession whose impetus continued for two centuries; P. P. Rubens (1577–1640) when he visited Rome made his own personal collection of every antiquity he could find; Nicolas Poussin was employed to record the buildings of ancient Rome, a task already essayed a generation earlier by the Fleming, Marten van Heemskerck (1498–1574). Poussin's patron in this was Cassiano dal Pozzo (1589–1657), antiquarian and connoisseur, whose aim and achievement was to compile the completest collection possible of such drawings, which he called his Museum Chartaceum or Paper Museum. He was only just in time, for by 1650 the antiquities of Italy were rapidly leaving the country for the collections of wealthy connoisseurs abroad.

The collecting of art, ancient and otherwise, had gone beyond connoisseurship to become an instrument of international power politics. Princes vied with princes to have the most spectacular and comprehensive collections. In the circumstances it would be a wonder if respect for the arts themselves survived, despite the generous patronage offered to living artists. The latter could appreciate and learn from the antiquities thus amassed; but it was rare for their owner to take such a disinterested attitude.

In the wake of the Continental Renaissance came England. Charles I (1600–49) was the first monarch to form a collection of fine art. This had been built up by the spoliations of loyal privateers as well as by purchase, for example, of the Gonzaga collection at Mantua. At the time of his execution the King's collection at Whitehall comprised 36 statues, 400 coins, and 42 reliefs, as well as 73 paintings, 75 miniatures, and 54 finely bound books; he had a further 175 pictures and sculptures in two galleries, and still more at Greenwich. In all there were 1,387 paintings and 399 sculptures. When the collection was sold by Parliament, much of it was acquired by Cardinal Mazarin, and became the nucleus of what was to become the Louvre (see Chapter 5).[6] The rest was destroyed in a fire at Whitehall in 1697.

It is against this background of what one might call conspicuous acquisition, that we should see the collections amassed by peers of less than princely rank like the Earl of Arundel and the Duke of Buckingham. The story of the two men is inevitably intertwined.

The Arundel Marbles

To his liberal charges and magnificence, this angle of the world oweth its first sight of Greek and Roman statues, with whose admired presence he began to honour the gardens and galleries of Arundel House about twenty years ago, and hath ever since continued to transplant old Greece into England. (Henry Peacham, *The Compleat Gentleman* 1634)

Thomas Howard, Earl of Arundel (1586–1646) was a thoroughly exceptional Englishman. His dress – all his portraits show him in sober dark habit or in sombre armour; his demeanour – 'he knew and kept greater distance towards his Sovereign than any person I ever observed', wrote his secretary, and that distance was evident also in the hauteur of the first peer of England to lesser men; his simplicity of life in all but his collecting; his valuation of true friendship; his wealth – he would spend £10,000 on 'medals' (coins) from the 'cabinet' (collection) of Daniel Nys, and if he had a fault it was prodigality in collecting; but above all his taste, marked him out from the common run of noble connoisseurs, collectors and antiquarians. For the scholar, poet and translator of Montaigne, Robert Cotton, he was the perfect nobleman. Though in his youth he took part in the Court Masques, it is clear that he found more enjoyment in the refined and cultured atmosphere of learning that surrounded the young Prince Henry, already a discriminating collector of paintings and medals.

His was a genuine, serious, knowledgeable love of art. Rubens called him 'one of the four evangelists, and a great upholder of our art.' He would have shared the high valuation put on the arts by his librarian Franciscus Junius (1589–1677), whose *De Pictura Veterum* ('On the painting of the ancients') made them important moral influences on ancient life and, by implication, gave ancient art the opportunity to play a similar serious role in modern life.[7]

As well as collecting, at a time when, as Defoe said, 'all Europe had been rummaged for fine paintings', he patronised living artists; his collections included drawings as well as paintings of great masters, surely a sign of a discriminating eye rather than one to be deflected by flamboyance and colour. As we shall see, his interest in his antiquities, too, went beyond the conventional and was of unique importance for the growth of archaeological studies in England. The novelty of the collection the Earl of Arundel had assembled can be gauged from Sir Francis Bacon's reaction on visiting Arundel House in the Strand in 1626:

Coming into the Earl of Arundel's garden, where there were a great number of ancient statues of naked men and women, [he] made a stand, and as astonished cried out: The Resurrection!

He had developed his archaeological interests early, on his first visit to Rome in 1612–14 – in itself a suspect destination for an Englishman, especially a Catholic, in those days. He travelled with Inigo Jones, and paid due attention to the architecture and other glories of Italy; Jones sketched and made notes on the buildings of Rome. Arundel went so far as to obtain a licence to dig, and began to excavate on his own account, finding a number of statues of Roman consuls and others, which he sent back to England. (One was the so-called Caius Marius that is now, like the majority of the surviving marbles, in the Ashmolean Museum.)

It was surely with his patron the Earl in mind that Peacham wrote:

The pleasure of them [*sc* antiquities] is best known to such as have seen them abroad in France, Spain and Italy, where the gardens and galleries of the great men are beautified and set forth to admiration with these kinds of ornaments. . . . But the profitable necessity of some knowledge of them will plainly appear in the handling of each particular.

Arundel was plainly well able to 'handle the particulars'. There can be little ground for hesitation in dismissing the Earl of Clarendon's assessment of his connoisseurship as a calumny:

He was willing to be thought a scholar, and to understand the most mysterious parts of antiquity, because he made a wonderful and costly purchase of statues whilst he was in Italy and Rome (some whereof he could never obtain permission to remove from Rome, though he had paid for them), and had a rare collection of the most curious medals; whereas in truth he was only able to buy them, never to understand them, and as to all parts of learning he was almost illiterate, and thought no other part of history considerable, but what related to his own family, in which no doubt there had been some very memorable persons.

The sketch would fit almost any contemporary connoisseur better than Arundel. Though an affected or actual superiority might antagonise those who misunderstood his passions, it is clear that his interest in Italian and classical culture stemmed above all from a veneration of the grandeur and seriousness of Rome, so different from the superficial elegance, the malice and jockeying for position, the corruption and perversity of the court of James I during the ascendancy of Buckingham. The two could not but become arch rivals, especially after Arundel's elevation to the office of Earl Marshal in 1621.

In the few years that intervened between this distinction and his fall from grace and imprisonment in the Tower in 1626, soon after the accession of Charles I, Arundel devoted great energy to the extension of his collection with items from ancient Greece. As with earlier collectors like Isabella d'Este, it must have been opportunity above all that prompted the development of the taste. Sir Thomas Roe (c1580–1644) had been newly appointed ambassador to the Porte Sublime at Constantinople, and in 1621 the Earl approached him with the commission to acquire marbles for his collection. Though his specifications were no doubt reasonably precise, they were scarcely enough to outweigh Roe's indifference to ancient art, and his nervousness about making unsatisfactory purchases as a result of his ignorance. Nevertheless, he reported promptly on his arrival at Constantinople on 27 January 1622:

Concerning antiquities in marbles there are many in diverse parts, and especially at Delphos [by which he meant Delos], unesteemed here; and, I doubt not, easy to be procured for the charge of digging and fetching, which must be purposely undertaken.

In May 1623 Roe wrote again:

On Asia side, about Troy, Zizium [ie Cyzicus] and all the way to Aleppo, are innumerable pillars, statues and tombstones of marbles, with inscriptions in Greek; these may be fetched at charge and secretly; but if we ask leave, it cannot be obtained; therefore Mr Markham [his assistant] will use discretion, rather than power, and so the Turks will bring them for their profit.

Such things as he did obtain caused him much anxiety by their battered condition:

Now I am offered a lion to the waist, of pure white, holding a bull's head in his claws; but the very nose and mouth is defaced, the rest very fair, and, they say, a l'antiqua: I have not yet seen it, but expect it hourly.

Later, in Angora, he apologised for the acquisition of a 'half-woman', lacking hand, nose and lip, 'so defaced that she makes me think of an hospital'.

By 1625, unknown at first to Arundel, Roe had accepted a second commission from the Duke of Buckingham (1592 –1628) to perform the same services for him. Meanwhile, Arundel had sent to assist Roe his chaplain, William Petty (b c1585). The two naturally fell into dispute, Petty believing that all he found with Roe should go to Arundel, Roe wishing rather to displease neither, hedging his bets on the ascendancy of the two rivals, and proposing to share the spoils. He wrote honestly to Buckingham (1/11 May 1625):

By conference with Mr Petty, sent hither by my Lord of Arundel, I have somewhat bettered my skill, in such figures as your grace hath commanded me to seek: at least, he hath made me more assured to venture upon some things, which I should myself have little esteemed, for the defacings, either by age or accident.

Arundel can have little relished the advantage his dangerous rival obtained from his own agent's efforts.

It is clear too that Buckingham was much less fit to appreciate such marbles as Roe might acquire than his rival was. He wrote to Roe in 1626:

Neither am I so fond of antiquity (as you rightly conjecture) as to court it in a deformed or misshapen stone; but where you shall meet beauty with antiquity together in a statue, I shall not stand upon any cost your judgment shall value it at.

This was of course a much harder brief to fulfil than Arundel's. However, Roe and Petty began their cooperative venture enthusiastically enough, with an audacious attempt to obtain the reliefs from the Golden Gate at Constantinople:

We have searched all this city, and found nothing but upon one gate, called anciently Porta Aurea, built by Constantine, beautified with two mighty pillars, and upon the sides and all over it, twelve tables of fine marbles, cut into histories, some of a very great rilievo, set into the wall, with small pillars, as supporters. . . . They are, in my eye, extremely decayed; but Mr Petty doth so praise them, as that he hath not seen much better in the great and costly collections of Italy. . . . There are but six of them that are worth the taking down. . . . The four to which I have the most affection, are fuller of work: the one is (as we comment) an Endimion carelessly sleeping by his sheep; Luna

COLLECTORS AND ANTIQUARIES 47

descending from the sky with a torch in her hand, representing
night: and a cupid hovering in the air, to signify her love . . . The
next is an history I understand not, either of some race, or game; in
the midst is a horse, a young man naked running by it, and reaching
to pull another off. . . . The third is a Pegasus, with the Nymphs, or
Muses. . . . The last is a Satyr, skipping between the Hercules, or a
wild man, and a woman, which he seems to avoid: the one hath a
whip in his hand, the other a pot of water held behind her, and may
signify a rescue from ravishment: these are above the life, and rather
great and stately, than delightful. . . . I will endeavour to get them.
Promise to obtain them I cannot, because they stand upon the ancient
gate, the most conspicuous of the city, though now mured up, being
the entrance by the castle called the Seven Towers, and never opened
since the Greek Emperors lost it: to offer to steal them, no man dares
to deface the chief seat of the Grand Signor: to procure them by
favour, is more impossible, such envy they bear unto us. There is
only then one way left; by corruption of some churchman, to dislike
them, as against their law; and under that pretence, to take them
down to be brought into some private place; from whence, after this
matter is cold and unsuspected, they may be conveyed. I have
practised this for the four, and am offered to have it done for 600
crowns. To send them home chested, and freight, with some other
bribes at the water side, may cost 100 more. This is a great price, and
yet I rather despair of obtaining them.

Roe was right to be pessimistic, for it proved impossible to put
the plan into effect. The final defeat came, after three months
and the expense of 500 dollars, when the Great Treasurer
announced that the statues were enchanted, and that to remove
them would cause 'some great alteration' in the City.

It would have been as well if the reliefs could have been
obtained, since they are now altogether lost (see p 14).

After the failure of this project, William Petty began to
pursue an independent course, travelling indefatigably around
Pergamum, Samos and Ephesus. 'There was never man,'
wrote Roe to Arundel in March 1626, 'so fitted to an employment, that encounters all accident with so unwearied patience;
eats with Greeks on their worst days; lies with fishermen on
planks, at the best; is all things to all men, that he may obtain
his ends, which are your lordship's service.' Off Ephesus he
was wrecked with all the marbles he had obtained so far, and
imprisoned as a spy until his bona fides was vouched for and
secured his release. From there he went to Smyrna, where he

obtained the large collection already assembled by the agent of the Provençal savant Nicolas Claude Fabri de Peiresc, who had been imprisoned and his marbles confiscated. Among these was the greatest treasure of the Arundel Marbles, the Marmor Parium, a chronological table compiled in antiquity which forms the basis of much of our dating of Greek history.

By November 1626 Petty was in Athens, and the collection he had amassed, of 200 items, reached Arundel House in January 1627. The house with its newly constructed sculpture gallery (the first of its kind in England) was ready to receive them.

The Roman statues that so astonished Sir Francis Bacon had been a great wonder; these Greek pieces were the first such ever to reach England. The inscriptions, in particular, were a unique acquisition for a nobleman's collection at this date, and it says a good deal for Arundel's scholarly integrity – against the sneers of Clarendon – that the learned Sir Robert Cotton was with him at their unpacking, and that the two immediately summoned John Selden, (1584–1654) the antiquary and politician, who agreed to begin the work of decipherment the following day.

Selden's *Marmora Arundeliana* (1628) is the first major work of classical archaeological scholarship in England, and a worthy landmark in the development of the profession. It is naturally no detriment to Selden's work that he made good use of the assistance of the Dutch scholar Daniel Heinsius in composing the commentary. Even the worsted Peiresc could only praise the scholarly quality of the edition.

The handsome folio volume published twenty-nine inscriptions from the 'cimelia' of William Petty, accompanied by learned and often voluminous notes. Conjectural restorations of missing letters were printed in red: this became standard practice thereafter. An elaborate chronological table and 'arguments' were appended to elucidate the Marmor Parium.

This great inscription is a stone about six feet seven inches high and two feet three inches broad, which had been set up at Paros; when Arundel's piece was found it was already broken, and the remaining part was found in 1897 and is now in the Paros Museum. Its authorship is unknown, but it contains a chronology of major events of Greek history from the time of Cecrops, the first (legendary) king of Athens, down to the date it was set up, 264–3 BC. It includes information on a miscellany of political, military, religious and literary history, and is sufficiently detailed to provide the basis of much of the chronology of Greek history as it is now established. Selden's edition, as we shall see, came none too soon.

Meanwhile, Roe's labours for Buckingham had been far from vain. Having learnt from Petty something of ancient art, he had sent a variety of agents to Greece, while Petty was in the islands. He had bought two statues at Zia (Ceos), and a variety of statues and fragments from the Morea, especially from Corinth, including one head supposed, with singular improbability, to be that of Corinth's destroyer, Lucius Mummius. Urns from Corinth, items from Sparta, reliefs from Andros and marbles expected from Proussa and Sinope – some of the pieces weighing twenty hundredweight; no one could have accused Roe of idleness.

If you please to continue this search [he wrote to Buckingham], there will be found daily many rare matters, the poor people being set on work, in hope of gain, and all these parts full of the enquiry made by me and Mr Petty: all above ground being gone to Venice, we must trust, like miners, to chance; but I find, that the old Christians, to prevent the envy of the Turks, did in all Greece and the islands, bury their antiquities, which time and diligence will discover.

On 27 June 1628 he wrote to Buckingham that the marbles were being shipped from Patras. On 23 August, Buckingham was assassinated.

The assassination enabled Arundel's star to rise again to something like its former glory, and his acquisition of antiquities continued apace. In 1636 he was still writing to Petty about new acquisitions, but his health was already failing. The outbreak of the Civil War found him abroad, and he determined to remain in exile, where he died in 1646, at Padua.

At his death Arundel possessed 37 statues, 128 busts and 250 inscriptions, as well as sarcophagi, altars, fragments, coins and medals, books and manuscripts. His collection rivalled even the King's. It is an indication of the unusualness of Arundel's taste in England, as well as an object lesson in the dangers of archaeological expropriation, that his son, who inherited these treasures on the death of his father, should have neglected them so shamefully. The Parian Marble, for example, was converted into a hearthstone. Lines 1–45 of the inscription were lost at this time, and Selden's edition is the only record of this part of the inscription. Many more had been built by Arundel himself into the garden walls as picturesque decorations – for they could scarcely be studied there – and others were piled in disorder around the grounds. It was John Evelyn, the diarist, who first exerted himself to bestow them in a safer place:

These precious monuments, when I saw miserably neglected and scattered up and down about the Gardens and other places of Arundel House, and how exceedingly the corrosive air of London impaired them, I procured him to bestow upon the University of Oxford; this he was pleased to grant me, and now gave me the key of the gallery, with leave to mark all those stones, urnes, altars etc, and whatever I found had Inscriptions on them that were not statues. This I did, and getting them removed and piled together, with those which were incrusted in the garden walls, I sent immediately letters to the Vice-Chancellor what I procured, and that if they esteemed a service to the University (of which I had been a member) they should take orders for their transportation. (*Diary* 19 September 1667).

Even in Oxford the stones had to suffer the indignity of being immured in the circuit wall of the Sheldonian Theatre, though Evelyn did ensure that a holly hedge was planted before them to prevent curious passers-by from damaging them further. By the time the marbles reached their present home in the Ashmolean Museum, in the nineteenth century, weather and time had taken their toll.

Worse still, many marbles remained at Arundel House. D. E. L. Haynes[8] describes how these were disposed of when Henry Howard decided to pull down the house in 1677. Some were sold to Thomas Herbert, later Earl of Pembroke, who removed them to Wilton House near Salisbury. The remainder were left behind a wall, in a spot which became used as a workmen's rubbish dump, and many were buried in the rubble of Arundel House only to be rediscovered when Norfolk and Howard Streets were excavated for redevelopment. Other sculptures were disposed of by Henry's widow, many of them going to the seat of Sir William Fermor, Easton Neston in Northamptonshire, and the residue was simply dumped on some waste ground in Kennington. The whole story is little short of tragic.

But despite the insouciance with which they were originally

kept and displayed, and despite their seclusion in Arundel House, the marbles made an impact not only on scholars but on at least one distinguished artist. In about 1620 the Earl of Arundel commissioned from Anthony Van Dyck a painting, *The Continence of Scipio*, as a gift for the Duke of Buckingham. (The portrait of Scipio is an idealised version of Buckingham's features.) As local colour, the artist included in the scene a section of a Roman frieze which is certainly from the Arundel collection. Its original was in fact discovered on a building site in London in 1972, where Arundel House had formerly stood.[9] Antiquities have their exits and their entrances.

The introduction of John Selden into the story calls for comment. His background had very little in common with the aristocratic milieu of the Earl of Arundel. It is a tribute to the Earl that he knew where to find not only artists, but men of learning, when he had need of them.

Learning at that time was by no means exclusively housed in the Universities. Many men developed and indulged antiquarian tastes. Selden was one, and others, like Robert Cotton or Edward Lhwyd, devoted their energies to British antiquities. Outstanding was William Camden, author of the *Britannia*, 'the nourrice of antiquity/And lantern unto late succeeding age/To see the light of simple verity/Buried in ruins.'

They were all of them men who would willingly go forty miles out of their way to see a ruined monastery or a Druid stone circle. Books, shards, manuscripts, coins and localities were all material for their omnivorous curiosity. Men like these devoted most of their time to what was near at hand. If Selden spent more time on British antiquities than on the classical past, John Evelyn found equal fascination in his Italian journey; but even he delighted as much in the new cabinets of curiosities he visited as in the antiquities of Rome.

Curiosities indeed they were, in many cases. Men with less disciplined minds than either the connoisseurs or the numismatists, but who sincerely believed that the world was open to their full understanding if they could amass sufficient evidence, these collectors put their energies into the acquisition of natural and man-made objects of every kind. It is the passion of the stamp collector in the guise of learning. The virtuoso, as he called himself, was indeed given to 'the study of all things' –

of natural history, alchemy, mechanics, as well as the stocking of galleries and cabinets of coins, gems and rarities. These cabinets, as German Bazin has put it, by their 'profusion signified the inexhaustible richness of nature's creatures and the ingeniousness of means used by man to penetrate their mysteries.'[10] The cabinet John Evelyn visited in Rome is fairly typical:

Being arrived at Rome on the 13th Feb we were again invited to Signor Angeloni's study, where with greater leisure we surveyed the rarities, as his cabinets and medals especially, esteemed one of the best collections of them in Europe. He also showed us two antique lamps, one of them dedicated to Pallas, the other Laribus Sacru', as appeared by their inscriptions; some old Roman rings and keys; the Egyptian Isis cast in iron; sundry rare bass-rilievos; good pieces of painting, principally the Christ of Correggio, with this painter's own face admirably done by himself; divers of both the Bassanos; a great number of pieces by Titian, particularly the Triumphs; an infinity of natural rarities, dried animals, Indian habits and weapons, shells, etc; divers very antique statues of brass; some lamps of so fine an earth that they resembled cornelians for transparency and colour; hinges of Corinthian brass, and one great nail of the same metal found in the ruins of Nero's Golden House.

Evelyn was enraptured, as his contemporaries Tradescant and Ashmole were to be, by this kind of hotchpotch (or, in Samuel Johnson's definition, 'repository of learned curiosities') – he also enjoyed the trick chairs that spouted water that were on exhibit in another cabinet – and went so far in antiquarian enthusiasm as once to state he would rather have a portrait from antiquity than one of the great paintings of Titian. Aesthetic sense was no part of an antiquary's apparatus, and it laid him open to mockery.

Some would collect literally anything. The best examples are the Copenhagen cabinet of Ole Worm (1588–1694), an early print of which shows a shark slung from the ceiling, boxes along the walls with specimens of indeterminate nature, and tables spread with further objects and antiquities; or above all 'Tradescant's Ark', the extraordinary collection formed by the gardener John Tradescant senior, which in 1683 became the nucleus of the Ashmolean Museum. Some of his rarities included, besides fragments of birds, beasts and fishes, 'mechanick artificiall works in carvings, turnings, sowings

and paintings . . . the Roman measure called Ligula; the
martyrdome of the bishop of Amphipolis done in alabaster;
. . . a piece of the stone of Sarigo-Castle where Helen of
Greece was born; . . . warlike instruments, garments, . . .
utensils' and, of course, a rich hoard of coins.

The antiquary's cabinet became a microcosm of nature.
Some classical scholars in the true sense shared this magpie
frenzy, like Isaac Casaubon who thought to know the ancient
world whole, devoted his life to the acquisition of knowledge
from books, and died of a stoppage because he would not take
the time off to visit the lavatory. (His editions of Strabo were,
however, of great use to those who visited Greece.) But other
antiquarians would specialise, at least to a degree. Many
concentrated on the lumber which we would today regard as
the province of the archaeologist, men like the antiquary of the
Microcosmography (1628) of the sardonic John Earle:

. . . a man strangely thrifty of time past, and an enemy indeed to his
maw, whence he fetches out many things that are now all rotten and
stinking. . . . He is of our religion, because we say it is most ancient;
and yet a broken statue would almost make him an idolater. A great
admirer he is of the rust of old monuments, and reads only those
characters, where time hath eaten out the letters. . . . Printed books
he contemns, as a novelty of this latter age, but a manuscript he pores
on everlastingly, especially if the cover be all moth-eaten, and the
dust make a parenthesis between every syllable. . . . His chamber is
hung commonly with strange beasts' skins, and is a kind of charnel-
house of bones extraordinary; and his discourse upon them, if you
will hear him, shall last longer.

It was perhaps scarcely surprising that men with interests like
these should often be seen as useless, self-indulgent, perverse
and perhaps slightly insane. One thing the majority of them
could not be accused of was malice. Mostly they derived from
their humane pursuits a humane sodality with like-minded
virtuosi. Their connections were international, and one of the
epicentres was the most typical virtuoso of all, Nicolas Claude
Fabri, Lord of Peiresc near Aix-en-Provence (1580–1637). A
correspondent of most of the learned spirits of his day – among
them Johan Meurs, Robert Cotton, J. J. Scaliger, Cassiano dal
Pozzo, the patron of Poussin, and Peter Paul Rubens – he was
honoured, fortunately for us, by an elaborate biography or
encomium by Pietro Gassendi. This was completed in 1639,

published in 1641, and translated into English (with a dedication to John Evelyn) in 1657. Gassendi includes everything
that could interest us, and much that cannot: he enthuses over
the charm of Peiresc's appearance, which lowers savagely and
shaggily at us from the frontispiece of his book, apologising
for the failure of any painter to do him justice.

Like the English antiquaries, and like Spon (see Chapter 4)
after him, Peiresc began his antiquarianism at home, with
studies of the antiquities of his native Provence. At eighteen he
travelled to Rome where he spent some years studying its
topography and monuments, capitalising on his time by
studying in the hours which others devoted to 'games and
plays, in compotations, or dalliance with women'.

In 1604 he was back at Aix, his head already well-stocked,
and ready also to stock his library and his cabinet. Here he
became a senator and a judge. But nothing was beyond his
ken. He also qualified as a doctor, and interested himself in
genealogy, heraldry, numismatics, optics and anatomy; his
collections included books, coins, Roman measures, shrubs
and Angora cats. In 1610 he was anxious to obtain a telescope,
and in 1613 he gave equal attention to the two discoveries in
Dauphine of some coins of Marius and of a 'Giant' (or
elephant).

Much ingenuity went into his stratagems for the acquisition
of new antiquities. As we saw, he maintained an agent in the
Levant. He also had an agent in Cairo, a Venetian named
Seghezzi, and was not above promoting his cause as the next
French consul there, with an eye to the advantages learning
might secure from political power.

In 1620 he acquired an engraved sardonyx and an agate, and
three years later the first of these formed the subject of his first
letter to the painter Peter Paul Rubens, himself an eager
collector of gems and an enthusiast for the art of antiquity. (He
was indeed a true antiquary in his own right: he thought the
treaty between Smyrna and Magnesia the most fascinating
item in the whole of the Earl of Arundel's collection – a
surprising judgement for an artist.)

Peiresc was always generous with his collection, often
lending books with no hope of their ever reappearing, swap-
ping coins and inscriptions. He published nothing, and all his
delight was in contemplation of his learning, and in sharing it

with his learned friends. So it is no surprise that he regretted not at all the loss of the marbles for which his agent Samson had paid fifty crowns. When these were acquired by Petty for the Earl of Arundel, envy could not have been further from his mind: no, he rejoiced 'when he heard that these rare monuments of antiquity, were fallen into the hands of so eminent an hero; and the rather, because he knew his old friend Selden had happily illustrated the same.' His only complaint was that Petty's role in saving the marbles 'from barbarism' was insufficiently acknowledged by Selden.[11]

Gassendi does not spare us the infirmities of the sedentary scholar – piles, strangury, backache – while he treats us in full to Peiresc's delight at acquiring his first tulips, his curing a sick puppy with treacle, his preparation of a map of Provence, his researches on winds and tides, mermen, eclipses, coral and the antiquities of Fréjus; his search for a copy of the *Thracian Bosphorus* of Dionysius of Byzantium; his letters to Selden on the orientation of English churches; or his attempts to breed chameleons. Coins and statues he valued because from them 'we may know what was the countenance and habit of renowned men and illustrious women, whose actions we delight to hear related' – a view that his contemporaries, and perhaps Montaigne, would have shared.

Men like Peiresc are passed over in the progress of archaeology: the scholars like Scaliger and the artists like Rubens maintain their fame; but the burning coal nursed by Peiresc and his peers in their bosoms is that of a true love of learning and of the past. Peiresc's conversation and his correspondence were tirelessly fascinating, though now, like Cyriac, he seems continually to elude our grasp. But when such virtuosos ceased to hold their place in the counsels of the learned, the world became a duller place.

CHAPTER FOUR

Antiquaries and Explorers:
The Visit of Jacques Spon and
George Wheler

When Europe was roused from barbarism, her first thoughts were
directed to Athens. 'What is become of Athens?' was the universal
cry: and when it was known that her ruins still existed, the learned
and the ingenious flocked thither as if they had discovered the lost
ashes of a parent.   (Chateaubriand)

Greece in the 1670s

In the National Gallery in Cardiff there is a painting by Nicolas
Poussin, *The Body of Phocion Carried Out of Athens*. Painted in
1648, it shows in the foreground the small figures of Phocion's
pallbearers, while in the background tower the buildings of
Athens. The representation of the city is completely imaginary. Two hundred years after Cyriac made the first drawings
of the Parthenon, Poussin had to rely solely on his imagination
and on some written descriptions for his picture. A circular
tower topped by a victory weathervane faintly recalls the
Tower of the Winds, which Poussin probably knew from
the description in Vitruvius; other buildings have more
resemblance to the monuments of Rome, notably a domed
one like the Pantheon. Others are conventional classicising
inventions with a Roman cast.

   It is true that Poussin had no thought of making a representation of Athens which anyone might use as a *guide
illustré*, and in this he is in the tradition of artists like the one
who illustrated the *Liber Chronicarum* of Hartman Schedel
(1493), where several cuts of standard cities do duty for more
than one location.

The ignorance and indifference of even the learned world is nicely exemplified in the comments of Robert Burton in the *Anatomy of Melancholy*:

The lanthorn in Athens was built by Xenocles, the theatre by Pericles, the famous port Piraeus by Musicles, the Palladium by Phidias, the Pantheon [sic] by Callicrates; but these brave monuments are decayed all, and ruined long since, their builders' names alone flourish by mediation of writers. (III, i, 3)[1]

Despite all the fascination of antiquity for the antiquaries, and their endurance of travel and hardship, they did not on the whole set foot on Greek soil. In England the antiquaries were digging, and their successes made the practice commendable. But the vogue was not extended to the Greek world. It was not until 1686 that French antiquarian Baudelot de Dairval could see travel and the study of antiquities as the beginning of wisdom, and wrote his book *De l'Utilité des Voyages et de l'Avantage que la Recherche des Antiquitez procure aux sçavans*.

It was a lucky chance that united in one man the character of the antiquarian and of the traveller. That man was Jacques Spon, who spent the months from July 1675 to March 1676 in Greece and Asia Minor, and wrote the most authoritative account of its antiquities, which was to hold the stage for a century. The book of his travelling companion George Wheler achieved an equal celebrity, at least in England, though much of its information was derived from Spon's account, and it was more diffuse, interlarded with botany, observation of Turkish mores, and acid comments (which Wheler called 'Divine Reflections') on Islam and the Orthodox Church. (On his return, Wheler became a priest of the Church of England.)

Those who visited Greece in the first three-quarters of the seventeenth century were mainly classically educated adventurers or Grand Tourists *avant la lettre*. When Spon and Wheler set out there were a handful of accounts in print, though nothing which engaged closely with the antiquities of Greece. On the English side there were the travel journals of men like the irrepressible Tom Coryate, 'traveller to the wits'; the dogged Fynes Moryson and solemn Henry Blount, who did their duty and assembled their observations. More lasting is the appeal of the pugnacious and disenchanted, baroque and splenetic William Lithgow, a Scot who had left his native

Lanark under a cloud in 1610. His *Rare Adventures and Painefull Peregrinations* was a popular book and has been reprinted many times, though it is scarce now. By turns dour, self-pitying and abrasive, Lithgow seems to have had a talent for attracting trouble. Captured by pirates at one time, at another deliberately embroiling himself to assist the escape of a Huguenot in Candia accused of murder; tortured by the Spanish Inquisition; given the gloomy task of night watch in Euboea by the sailors who endured his company as a passenger; sleeping rough in Argos 'with earth for pillow . . .'; one nevertheless forgives him his foolishness and discontent for the marvellous ebullience of his writing. He liked to flaunt his classical learning, mentioning the labyrinth of Crete, and blithely confusing Olympia with Mt Olympus. He made much of his visit to 'Troy', where like Alexander the Great he ran round the tomb of Achilles – though unfortunately what he actually visited was Alexandria Troas. But entertaining though he was he could not offer much to the learned traveller or the autodidact.

The most recent traveller to publish an account, Sir George Sandys, was a different matter, and his book was the most learned production seen to date from an English pen. He was a man of many talents. Born in 1578, he had been one of the founding fathers of the Virginia expedition of 1611, which settled the first colony in the rich lands of the American South. (While there, he had employed his time in the composition of a complete translation of Ovid's *Metamorphoses*, which became the standard translation at least until the time of Dryden.) His first foreign journey, undertaken in 1610, had followed the established pilgrimage route to the Holy Land: his account of his journey deploys a far wider range of classical learning than that of any pilgrim or tourist before him. There is no sign that Wheler or Spon made much use of Sandys' book, and their sketches and maps, though indifferent, are an improvement on his topographical indications.

The French travellers had even less to offer. In 1583 the King's chief botanist, Pierre Belon, had passed through the Aegean; but his eye had been mainly on natural history, though he spared some attention for the antiquities of Crete, Lemnos and the Troad. In the seventeenth century, most travellers passed through Greece only *en route* to more distant destinations: Tavernier (1631) and Chardin (1664–70) for Persia and its commercial opportunities; Thévenot (1655) as the perfect tourist, bound after Constantinople for Alexandria and Jerusalem. There had been the riotous Sieur La Boullaye le Gouz, ambassador to Isfahan from 1665; Bernard de Monconys in 1645; and Antoine des Barres, 'the Don Juan of the Archipelago' in 1673. Antiquarian interests were strictly incidental to their aims.

More scholarly progress came from an unexpected quarter. The Catholic kings, especially the French, were busy sending out missions to convert the Greeks: among them were the Capuchins in Athens (since 1658), and the Jesuits in Negropont and Santorini (of which Père Richard wrote a full history, including one of our earliest Greek vampire stories). Venetian rule in the islands had given Catholicism a foothold, though a feeble one; and the presence of the missions inevitably increased the awareness of Greece in their parent countries.

It was the Capuchins of Athens, housed in a monastery whose kitchen garden wall incorporated the Monument of Lysicrates, who prepared the first map of ancient Athens. And it was a Jesuit, Père Babin, who compiled the first written account of Athenian topography from autopsy.

But there is little to prepare us for the dedication with which Spon and Wheler set about their study of Greece and its remains, about the recovery of a past civilisation worthy of all respect for its own sake, and with values to offer the modern world.

The Levant at this period was by no means an easy or welcoming destination. War smouldered perennially between Venice, which until recently had ruled much of the archipelago, and Turkey, now ruler of the islands and mainland Greece. Locally the tension was expressed in the constant friction of the Catholic and Orthodox communities on the islands. At the level of international politics the unease focused on the siege of Candia, which the Turks had invested in 1645 and which they did not finally drive into submission until 1669. The long siege had already inspired more than one scheme in Italy or France for a new Crusade; France had even sent ships to the Venetian side in 1661, a move which naturally had not pleased the Turks. They had retaliated by curtailing the French trading privileges, or capitulations, in their

Empire. In 1673 the Marquis de Nointel had been sent as ambassador to renew the capitulations on terms more favourable to France – a task only partially achieved when he was recalled six years later.

If Turkey was willing to show force against Crete and Venice, it was unable to combat the more general menace of the Barbary corsairs who made navigation in the Mediterranean so hazardous that a sailor in his hammock at night might find himself a galley-slave at dawn, with release a matter of chance, bold escape, or decades of waiting.

Turkish rule was cruel, bloody and extortionate. It was also inefficient. Much of the time the populations were left to their own devices, provided they paid the poll tax. The child levy, which in former times had been imposed on every Christian family to swell the ranks of the janissaries at Constantinople, had recently been abolished. But many abuses remained. Fynes Moryson noted many in his diary but forbore to include them in the published version. Sandys seems to have deluded himself so far as to see in the life of the citizens of Lesbos a veritable idyll:

Their ordinary drink being water; yet once a day they will warm their bloods with a draught of wine, contented as well with this, as those that with the varieties of the earth do pamper their voracities. . . When they will they work, and sleep when they are weary; . . . so cheerful in their poverty, that they will dance while their legs will bear them, and sing till they grow hoarse: secured from the cares and fears that accompany riches.

But Greece was poor, and most of the people lived in quite brutish conditions. Travellers of quality, however, could be sure of reception at the houses of the great men of the cities, and in particular of the foreign consuls.

In Athens, the consul was Jean Giraud (1658– after 1688), who seems to have been host to a constant stream of visiting Franks. Like his countryman Fauvel a century and a half later, he was cicerone and host, adviser and entertainer to every foreign visitor to the dilapidated city. Entertainment they will certainly have found, if a contemporary description is indeed to the life:

This Giraud is a nimble man, and understands well enough, but he loves his pleasure, and particularly play; for there are gamesters at

Athens as well as at other places: when he was turned out of the consulship for the French, he struck in with some people, and got himself made consul there for the English and Dutch. He is a person that loves to make a noise and a parade, and with his bustling got a young lady of the house of the Palaeologi; and married her much to his advantage; for there is still a branch of that illustrious family in Athens.

This description by Guillet de St Georges (of whom more later) is scarcely kind, though his facts are correct. Spon was later indignantly to rebut this caustic portrait of the consul who lost his consulship through an imagined insult to a passing French citizen. As we shall see, Giraud was also very knowledgeable on Athens and Attica and their antiquities; occupations cannot have been so very plentiful for a Frank in Athens that one should forbid him a hand of cards or a jape like the one he and his equally high-spirited wife played on the local priest.

A gardener had unearthed in the Ceramicus – which was then known as the 'Academy' or 'School of Plato' – a statue of Athena made of marble, and sold it to Giraud for two crowns. As the lifesize figure stood around the house, no doubt getting in the way, the consul's wife took it into her head to dress the statue in a nightshirt and put it to bed. Then she called for the priest to attend her 'sick maid'. The priest was apparently easily fooled; getting little response to his questions from the statue, he turned in puzzlement to Mme Giraud. 'Speak a little louder,' she advised, 'she is not only very sick, but deaf as well.' It is not recorded how long the priest persisted in his attempt, or what he said when the trick was explained. The whole story might be out of Boccaccio, and casts a ray of cheerful and domestic light into the colourless gloom of Turkish Athens.

It was to Giraud, inevitably, that Spon and Wheler eventually came. But we must begin at the beginning.

Jacques Spon and his voyage

Jacques Spon (1647–85) was a doctor from Lyon, the son of a doctor, who had early become addicted to the study of antiquities, especially the fine Roman remains of his native Provence. As with Cyriac and the English antiquaries, scholarship began at home. Spon had learnt something of numismatics from Charles Patin while studying in Strasbourg in 1662, and from acquaintance with Pierre Carcavy, also of Lyon, who since 1664 had been director of the Cabinet Royal des Médailles. In 1674 the antiquarian J. F. F. Vaillant was embarking on a journey to Greece for Colbert, Louis XIV's minister, to collect manuscripts and antiquities. He was one of the earliest of a long line of such learned emissaries (see Chapter 5). Spon was offered the opportunity to travel with Vaillant and eagerly accepted it.

The party left in October 1674, and their first adventure took place before they had even left France. At Marseille they were alarmed by the near approach of a 'Turkish' corsair. Fearing slavery, and mindful of the possible need to buy his freedom, Vaillant immediately swallowed the collection of twenty ancient gold coins which he was carrying. The corsair departed, however, without molesting anyone, and an urgent consultation of doctors followed, as to the best way to retrieve the coins. Opinion being divided between an emetic and a purgative, poor Vaillant was left to recover his coins at the rate nature herself permitted – which he duly accomplished, afterwards selling them to his friend Dufour from Lyon. Such were the incidental privations of the learned travellers. Spon was to suffer more before his travels were over.

After a leisurely journey through Provence and northern Italy, they reached Venice. Spon early showed his antiquarian mettle by proving an inscription in the Aldorovandi Cabinet at Bologna to be a fake, by the simple method of pointing out that the Roman name on it was incorrect in form, containing two nomina and no praenomen.

At Venice Spon fell in with George Wheler (1650–1723). Wheler was the son of Royalist parents who had been forced into exile by the Civil War. Though England was by this time safe again for such men, he seems to have acquired a taste for travel, which in any case was at this time an approved pursuit for a young gentleman of quality. There is no knowing what course his plans might have taken but for his meeting Spon; but it was this meeting which gave him an aim and a cause, which was to culminate in his writing the book which made his reputation and gained him a knighthood.

The two swiftly determined to join forces and leave

Vaillant, for an independent expedition to Greece and Turkey. (It is significant that both Spon and Wheler entitled their books as accounts of journeys to *Greece*; the classical name was scarcely current as Greece was swallowed up in the Turkish Empire, and earlier travellers had seen its lands as simply part of the tourist or pilgrim route through the Ottoman dominions.) They increased the party further with two more Englishmen, Francis Vernon (?1637–77), a Fellow of the Royal Society, and Giles Eastcourt. No doubt not the least attraction for Spon was the comparative wealth of the young men, an advantageous support for a penniless and often sickly young medic with an obsession to gratify. They departed from Venice on 20 June 1675.

After coasting Dalmatia, the four reached Corfu, which in common with many before and since they identified with the legendary Phaeacia of the Odyssey – though Sir William Temple already admitted the role of the imagination in Homer's picture: 'the garden of Alcinous, described by Homer, seems wholly poetical, and made at the pleasure of the painter; like the rest of the romantic palace in that little barren[!] island of Phaeacia or Corfu.' Here for the first, but by no means the last, time, they were taken for spies; but this problem was surmounted, and they enjoyed the society of the brother of the priest, Nicolas Bulgari, who was a member of the Corfiot 'Academy' and had a cabinet of medals and engravings. They visited the plain beyond Palaiopolis, which they took for the garden of Alcinous, and the river Chrysida, where – to quote Waller Rodwell Wright, a poet admired by no less than Byron – 'sequester'd midst embowering shades, / The bright Nausicaa sported with her maids.'

They went on to Cephalonia, and thence to Thiaki (Ithaca) and Zante. On arrival here, Vernon and Eastcourt left them, to travel overland. Eastcourt died of a fever at Delphi; and though they met Vernon again later, and spent some time with him at Athens, he too was doomed: he was murdered in Isfahan in a quarrel over a penknife.

We can pass over the rest of their route around the Peloponnese, except for a frustrating excursion on the charmless Cerigo (Cythera) to see the 'Palace of Helen' (two Doric columns) and the 'Baths of Helen' (a hole in the ground, which had been more thoroughly explored by Nicolas de Nicolay in

1551 and William Lithgow in 1609). They came next to
Seriphos, and Tinos, where Spon remarked on the food. 'One
would suppose that to eat quantities of raw cucumber, even
with sour milk, would be enough to kill a horse. However, all
those who have been in the Levant know that it is one of the
greatest delicacies of the Turks, and that no one has ever been
incommoded by it in those countries.' Some of the attractions
of Greece do not change!

Their next call was at Delos, which was a treasure-trove and
a cynosure for other visitors too. Spon's account laid the
foundations for most later work on the site, while he was also
the earliest witness to give an account of what was visible then
but may since have disappeared. The island was an obvious
attraction since so many of the marble remnants, including the
colossal cult statue of Apollo of the early sixth century BC,
whose shoulders were as broad as a man is high, lay still above
the surface of the ground for the taking. It had been pillaged
but little in the days of Frankish rule, which was based in its
mainland strongholds, and as little under the Venetians, since
from antiquity onwards it had been uninhabited. A rich crop
awaited the inspection of the curious traveller.

The tiny island, uninhabited through sanctity as birthplace
of Apollo and Artemis his twin, to which there yearly flocked

> so many an Ionian,
> With ample gowns that flow down to their feet
> With all their children, and the reverend sweet
> Of all their pious wives
> (Homeric Hymn to Apollo)

to participate in the festival of Apollo which, with its athletic
contests, its dancing competitions and rivalry of song, had
been one of the religious focal points of Greece. Legend said
that it had been a floating island until it was selected by Leto for
her place of labour: 'then four mighty pillars, shod in adamant,
sprang upright from the bottom of earth, and held the rock on
their brows; and there she gave birth to her blessed son.'
(Pindar, *Hymn to Delos*)

Such was the island's prestige, and its position in the centre
of the Cyclades, that it rapidly acquired a political importance.
It was the titular centre of the fifth-century Delian League of
Athens and her allies, which developed into the Athenian

Empire. Before all allied tribute began to be siphoned into the building of the Parthenon, the sanctuary of Delos benefited from this various wealth to sprout a variety of temples, statues, dedications and ornaments, including the famous Lion terrace, as well as water cisterns and a sacred lake large enough to stage mock sea-battles.

Declining like all Greece under Roman rule, it found a new champion in the Emperor Hadrian, who restored many of the monuments and built a new complex which he called New Athens, to the south of the fifth-century site.

The remains of these splendours began to suffer in the seventeenth century. By 1687 it was common knowledge that 'the ruins are carried away by all ships who come to anchor there, so as part are in England, France, Holland, but most at Venice.'[2] Among the most notorious of these predators was Sir Kenelm Digby. He mounted an expedition to harry the Turkish coast in 1627, hoping thereby to gain the favourable attention of Charles I. Thomas Roe had clearly left many stones unturned, for Digby's account is enough to make one's blood run cold:

With half my ship went to Delphos [sic], which is a very good port, and there I spent my time taking in some marble stones and statues. . . Because idleness should not fix their minds upon any untamed fancies (as is usual among seamen), and together to avail myself of the conveniency of carrying away some antiquities there, I busied them in rolling of stones down to the seaside, which they did with such eagerness as though it had been the earnestest business that they came out for, and they mastered prodigious massy weights: but one stone, the greatest and fairest of all, containing four statues, they gave over after they had bin, three hundred men, a whole day about it.

There was nevertheless still plenty to see on Delos. George Sandys, writing up his visit of 1610, had had but little to say of the antiquities, being more concerned to reproduce the ancient legends; so Spon and Wheler were able to make the first serious survey of its ruins.

Wheler wrote in his account, 'the ruins of Apollo's temple are here yet to be seen, affording fair pillars of marble to such as will fetch them.' (An unusual light is cast on this comment by John Evelyn's remark, in his *Elysium*, that the best garden rollers were made of pillars from Greece.)

The companions landed at the port and, a mere fifty paces off, they came to eleven standing columns (the Portico of Philip, of which rather fewer columns stand today). These, Spon acutely took to be part of a school or gymnasium, for he found an inscription referring to a gymnasiarch; in addition, the traditional name given to this island by the Christian corsairs was, he remarks, 'Les Ecoles'.

With his copy of Strabo's *Geography* (the most voluminous work of Greek geography, written in the first century AD) in hand, he explored the ruins, and was surprised to find dedications of Mithridates Euergetes and Mithridates Eupator who, according to that author, had sacked and destroyed the isle. Moving south to the Sacred Lake, which he interpreted as a lake for staging sea-battles, they returned via the Temple of Apollo and the colossal statue of the god, now a prostrate torso. It was six feet across the shoulders, and Spon knew it was Apollo from its long hair (for had not Horace called the god *intosum Cynthium?*). The Venetian proveditore of Tinos, he notes, had recently sawn off the face as a souvenir. According to Wheler, 'as Signior Georgio, our landlord at Micone, informed me, an Englishman who was there, called, as he said, Signior Simon, Captain of the St Barbara, endeavoured to carry it away, but finding it impossible, he brake off its head, arms and feet, and carried them with him.' (I have not identified this Simon, and the story sounds garbled.)

Beyond this Spon noted the celebrated Lion terrace, and they made their way to a portico 'facing Rheneia' (the Sacred Way), where there were marbles inscribed with the names of the 'Kings of Greece' (Philip of Macedon and Dionysius Eutyches). In the centre of the complex they saw the dedication of the Naxians, and beyond it the theatre.

By this time evening was drawing on. A storm had arisen and, as often happens, the strait between Delos and Myconos had become unnavigable. They had no food or water with them, and faced the prospect of a night on the island. They dined frugally off the scant vegetation, including something Spon calls 'polion montanum', probably hulwort – which Dioscorides calls 'polion ye mountainous, which also is called Teuthris, and of which there is use': it is apparently an antidote to poison, and a purgative as well as a healing agent, but it hardly sounds appetising.

The next day was still stormy. Very thirsty by now, they searched, as Spon sagely remarks, in vain for the River Inopus mentioned by Strabo, which, according to Pliny, rises and falls with the Nile. Wheler found more foundations, which he attributed to the 'New Athens' of Hadrian, but no water. They even tried straining sea water through sand, an experiment which had recently been tried in England by no less than Robert Boyle as an expedient for producing drinkable water – small beer compared with the usual ludicrous and ghastly experiments of the Royal Society. Eventually their companion, Dr Crescentio, found a cistern.[3] Thirst allayed, they were able to hunt some hares, and provide themselves with a game stew for their second evening as castaways.

At the next dawn they were able to get off and return to Myconos; but, having missed their ship, they were unable to proceed thence until 24 August.

Their next extended call was at the Troad, where they arrived on 26 August, and they seem to have stayed until 3 September. The ruins they visited were those of Alexandria Troas, though they took them for Troy. Many columns, Spon tells us, had been removed from the extensive ruins for the new Mosque of the Sultan's Mother at Constantinople.

Further on, at Heraclea, they found plenty of antiquities, including inscriptions to copy, but they had lost their pens – an item hard to procure where the natives used only sharpened reeds. At last they found a goose quill lying in the road, and another of the scholars' difficulties was solved.

They arrived in Constantinople on 23 September, and stayed there until 16 October. Most of Spon's observations repeat what we have learnt from earlier travellers, though it is interesting to learn that they met, besides a Scottish bibliophile called 'Vatz' (ie Watts), the English chaplain John Covel, himself a man of considerable archaeological interests, who had explored the ruins of Cyzicus and other cities as well as studying the walls of Constantinople. Wheler used Covel's drawings when he wrote his own book. Covel also showed the visitors his collection of Turkish songs, and noted their visit in his diary:

Last year were here one Mr Wheeler, a pretty ingenious youth, our countryman, and one Mr Le Spon, a Frenchman, who certainly

have made the best collection in the world, and intends to print them
when he comes home. He hath gathered up and down at least 10,000
that never yet saw light in Greek or any other author. I have a very
great intimacy with him, and maintain a strict correspondency with
him, and I shall certainly give him all I have which he wants.[4]

They embarked now on a tour of Asia Minor: Prousa (Bursa),
Thyatira (Ak-hisar, 'White Castle'), and Smyrna, where Spon
identified a temple of Janus in the town centre as Strabo's
temple of Homer. (A bust of Janus had been found there, and
bought by the Venetian consul Lupazzolo.) Here they met Sir
Paul Rycaut, the author of a learned work on the Greek
church, and bought a number of medals from Mr Falkner, an
English merchant. They stayed there a month.

    Next stop was Ephesus, *en route* to which they were briefly
held up by bandits, but frightened them off. Of Ephesus, Spon
writes: 'I do not believe there is a city in the world which has
such great and such melancholy ruins of ancient splendour.'
They visited the 'Temple of Diana' (actually some of the ruins
at the foot of the Bülbüldağ) and the Cave of the Seven
Sleepers, where they did not stay long for fear, as Spon says, of
nodding off for a century or two. Then to Pergamum,
Laodicea, Sardis, Philadelphia, Hierapolis, Miletus (which he
correctly located at Palatschia – modern Balat – and not, like
the geographers, at Melasso), Askem Kalesse which they took
for Iasus (though others made it Halicarnassus), Melasso/
Mylasa and Bodrum/Halicarnassus. Besides these new and
correct identifications, Spon identified eight other sites: a
substantial contribution to the topography of ancient Ionia.

    On 28 November they embarked at Smyrna and returned to
Zante, where they arrived on 3 January 1676. Their second
tour went overland from Zante to Athens. This time their first
important call (after Patras, Lepanto and Salona) was at Delphi, the most important sacred centre of ancient Greece, which
they reached at the end of January. Many identified Salona
with Delphi, but Spon found an inscription which proved it to
be Amphissa. Their host at Salona told them of ruins at Castri,
which they rightly assumed would represent the site of Delphi. Elated at arriving at so famous a city, than which only
Athens would offer a greater excitement, Spon indulged his
fancy by composing a little Greek song – but after two verses
'my poetic vein abruptly left me'.

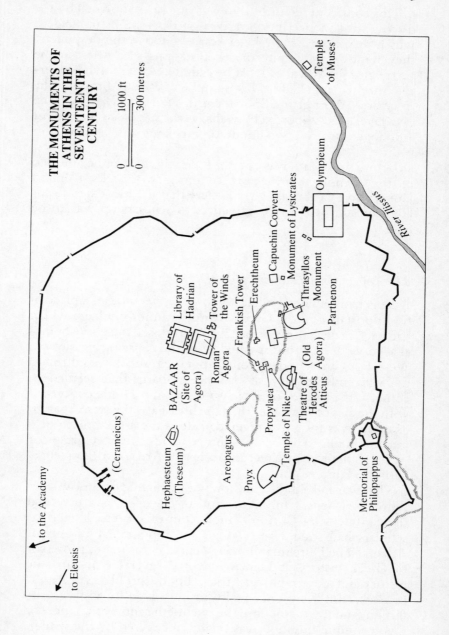

THE MONUMENTS OF
ATHENS IN THE
SEVENTEENTH
CENTURY

1000 ft
0

300 metres
0

River Ilissus

Temple
'of Muses'

Olympieum

Capuchin Convent
Monument of Lysicrates

Thrasyllos
Monument

Parthenon

Erechtheum

Library of
Hadrian

Tower of
the Winds

Frankish Tower

Roman
Agora

BAZAAR
(Site of
Agora)

(Old
Agora)

Theatre of
Herodes
Atticus

Propylaea

Temple of Nike

Areopagus

Hephaesteum
(Theseum)

(Cerameicus)

Pnyx

to the Academy

to Eleusis

Memorial of
Philopappus

This confident identification was quickly confirmed by the discovery of an inscription referring to Delphi. In an incident which puts Spon and Wheler scarcely above the despoilers, they removed it despite the protestations of a priest at the sacrilegious removal of what he claimed was Church property; but 'we mocked at his scruples'. Wheler brought the inscription to England. Spon identified the Church of St Elias, on a level area supported by walls, as the site of the Temple of Apollo; excavation two hundred years later was to prove him right.

Before the month was out, the indefatigable pair had pushed on to Athens where they stayed about two weeks, from 27 January to 15 February. It was here that the most significant contribution of the two travellers to scholarship was to be made.

The Topography of Athens

Athens had remained what it was in Cyriac's time, a place of no importance in the Greek world, an untidy village which had been in decline ever since Justinian closed the philosophical schools. It had almost faded from the consciousness of the West. For Cyriac and his contemporaries, and indeed through the sixteenth century, it had been Sparta that seemed to embody the virtues of ancient Greece. To minds concerned with the arts of life rather than the life of art, the stern Spartan example was the most revered. But as the arts came to be a pursuit indulged in as an adjunct to life, respect grew for 'Athens, the Eye of Greece, Mother of Arts/And Eloquence, native to famous Wits.'

That was indeed the emotion with which Spon and Wheler came to Athens. Only a handful of travellers had preceded them. It was by Burton's 'mediation of writers' alone that scholars had sought to establish the topography of ancient Athens. The Dutchman Johan Meurs (1579–1639), professor of Greek history at Leiden, devoted several works to the history and topography of Attica,[5] but the problems of Pausanias' account were only really to be solved by visits to the terrain (and it was not until the twentieth century that most of the ground in question was finally uncovered by the spade).

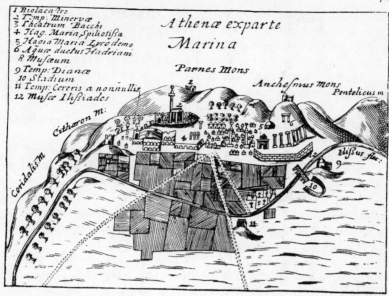

1 Biolaca?ro
2 Temp: Minervæ
3 Theatrum Bacchi
4 Hag. Maria Spiliotissa
5 Hagia Maria Lycodemo
6 Aquæ ductus Hadriani
8 Musæum
9 Temp: Dianæ
10 Stadium
11 Temp: Cereris a nonnullis
12 Musæ Ilissiades

Athenæ exparte Marina

Parnes Mons

Anchesmus mons

Pentelicus m

Cithæron m:

Coridalis m

Hissus fluc:

George Wheler's map of Athens

Meurs' assemblage of evidence had its uses, but a map could do the job much more simply.

One of the few men who had studied the topography of Athens on the spot was the Consul Jean Giraud. He had profited from his conversations with the Capuchin monks, and had made it his business to develop an expertise in Latin and Greek history, geography and antiquities. No doubt this helped to sustain him against the inevitable longueurs of a consul's life. He had prepared descriptions of Athens and of Attica; compiled a chronology of the Morea; given to the French traveller Robert de Dreux in 1665–9 a memorandum of the best antiquities of Athens; and acted as a cicerone to many foreign visitors. Spon and Wheler were his ideal audience. He provided them with plenty of information, not all of which Spon accepted at face value, particularly in his identifications of buildings; and he collected inscriptions.

But perhaps the most significant of Spon's predecessors was the Prussian soldier J. G. Transfeldt (1648–85).[6] This man had led a colourful life which was fairly typical of that of many soldiers of fortune. Enlisting in the Polish army, he was caught up in the war against the Turks when it was resumed in August 1672; enslaved at the battle of Batow, he became at the end of 1674 a galley-slave of a Turkish merchant at Nauplia. After only a few weeks he contrived to slip his chains during a shipwreck off the east coast of Attica. Albanian shepherds rescued him from the sea; he came to Athens where he lodged for a year in the Capuchin cloister, came to know Giraud and also met Spon.

When he moved in later years to Aleppo he remained in contact with Spon as his numismatic agent, until Spon's death in 1685. He also acted as agent for other scholars. His autobiography survives, as does part of his account of Athens, which no doubt incorporated the result of discussions with both Giraud and the Capuchins. He apologises (significantly) for treating the monuments of Athens in a different order from Pausanias'; beginning, like the ancient bards, from Zeus, he starts with the splendid flourish of correctly identifying the Temple of Olympian Zeus, hitherto known as the Palace of Hadrian. All that was needful, apparently, was to consult the detailed description of the edifice in the Roman architectural writer, Vitruvius. It is surprising that this evidently correct identification did not gain instant acceptance.

Transfeldt gives careful descriptions of the Arch of Hadrian, of the Lantern of Demosthenes, of the 'Temple of Socrates' (Tower of the Winds), with its human figures, 'winged like angels', whose accoutrements he illustrates with quotations from Virgil and Ovid. This passage makes it clear that he wrote after Spon's work had been published, for it includes a long and tedious polemic on the ancient nomenclature of the Winds.

It is hard to know what in this is Transfeldt's own, and what came from discussion with others. What sticks is the vivid picture of the Capuchin monks, the sprightly and fey Lyonnais consul, the pinched and sickly Spon, the travel-stained German, and the solemn Englishman, all sitting, perhaps, in the Capuchins' vegetable garden under the Lantern of Demosthenes, poring over plans, exchanging notes, arguing windily about winds and capping quotations to illustrate their theses. Oh, the freshness of the first pilgrims in an antique land, and the joy of every tiny fact established!

The Capuchins must have stood amazed on the occasion of the most celebrated visit to Athens, that of the Marquis de Nointel in December 1674, and at the ease with which he obtained what most Westerners were denied, access to the Acropolis which was the home of the military garrison. Nointel had been some years as ambassador at Constantinople, endeavouring to re-establish the trading privileges of the French nation which the Porte had curtailed. He lived in a grand style at Constantinople, despite his little success in so much as obtaining interviews with the Sultan; and devoted his leisure, like his predecessor Busbecq (1554–62), to collecting antiquities and to a long tour of the Archipelago. His own description of his arrival at Athens is full of relish at the pomp of an ambassador of his Most Christian Majesty:

Melos did not detain me, and it was at Piraeus that I cast anchor, hoping that the Athenians, those master depositories of science, art and law, would vouchsafe me some secret. Their dealing with the rest of the world hinted it to me, their civility in my reception persuaded me of it. The commandant of the famous castle promised it to me when he introduced me to the town, drums beating, ensigns flying, and with the sound of cannon, through a numberless crowd which gazed at me, well and richly mounted as I was, surrounded by a great number of footmen, followed by forty horsemen and preceded by my trumpeters, by a company of infantry and by several Turkish officers.

Nointel was allowed to enter the Acropolis:

There are many accounts of it [he wrote], but I can assure you that no one has enjoyed all the means which were at my disposal to examine all its artistic treasures; one may say of those which are to be seen in the castle, around the temple of Minerva, that they surpass even what is most beautiful in the reliefs and statues of Rome. I entered for the first time, in procession and to the sound of cannon, into the treasury where these marvels are kept, and I returned incognito five or six times to admire them better and to study the beautiful drawings which my painter made of the most beautiful of them, which contain up to two hundred figures, beyond and above the natural, in high and low relief, some entire and some mutilated. There are men, women and centaurs, battles and victories of the latter, triumphs, sacrifices, and if it were possible for me to express the rich confusion which such beautiful order, such fine composition, and the expression of such varied passions have left in my soul, I should undertake it with pleasure.

The drawings have generally been attributed to Jacques Carrey of Troyes; but they may have been made by an otherwise unknown artist, since Cornelio Magni, who accompanied Nointel, says specifically that the artist was a Fleming. They have proved the most valuable of all drawings of the Parthenon sculptures, in view of the subsequent destruction of pediments and some of the frieze. These had to be sufficient to content the Marquis, who was anxious to acquire the marbles themselves – or at least some of them – for the King's cabinet. He insisted that they needed protection from their Turkish masters. But this honour was to be reserved for a later ambassador, and of another country. Nointel did however acquire various ancient statues, including the inscription of the Erechtheid warriors who died in 456 BC, which became the first item of the French Epigraphic Collection.

Nointel's career ended in dishonour and poverty. On his death his collection was dispersed, and the drawings all lost except those of the Parthenon. Even these were missing from 1764 to 1797, when they were found in the Bibliothèque Nationale. (One series was burnt in the Louvre fire of 1871.) One marble inscription went to the collection of Baudelot de Dairval, thence to the Académie, and ultimately to the Louvre. Various paintings were also dispersed, to the Chateau de Berry and elsewhere. One, of Nointel entering Athens, has now reached the National Gallery in Athens.

Nointel could rejoice in the privilege of being perhaps the first traveller since Cyriac to look carefully at the most beautiful surviving building of antiquity, the Parthenon or Temple of Athena Parthenos. This edifice, now the symbol of the Greek nation, and symbol also, in its brilliant whiteness, of the dazzling light in which Aegean Greece is bathed, was in its time a monument rather to Athenian aggrandisement than to any nationalist ideal.

It stood, like most Greek temples, on the site of several earlier temples, the latest of which was that destroyed during the Persian siege of the Acropolis in 480–79 BC. As the funds of the Delian League insensibly turned to the tribute of an Athenian Empire, the Athenian democracy under Pericles turned its income to the beautification of the chief city of the League. The architects Ictinus and Callicrates were employed to produce a fitting house for the ivory and gold statue of

Athena by the master-sculptor Phidias, and they produced the subtlest and most harmonious yet of their temples – utterly different from the later, imitative Temple of Hephaestus that peers up at it from the Agora.

It was executed between 447 and 438 BC, though the sculptures were still being worked on at the outbreak of war in 432. It is grander and more spectacular than any other temple on the Greek mainland. It contained an ambulatory of columns in which the visitor could walk right around the great statue, by Phidias, who was also the master sculptor of the frieze and pediments, perhaps the greatest surviving glories of Greek art. The east pediment showed the birth of Athena, the west the contest of Athena and Poseidon for possession of Attica, while the frieze portrayed the procession of the Panathenaic festival.

A Panhellenic gesture then, if one which emphasised Athenian leadership, while the pediments were devoted to Attic interests. Plutarch tells us that Pericles' opponents said that 'Greece cannot but regard it as an insufferable affront, and consider herself to be tyrannised over openly, when she sees the treasure, which was contributed by her upon a necessity for the war, wantonly lavished out by us upon our city, to gild her all over, and to adorn and set her forth, as it were some vain woman, hung round with precious stones and figures and temples, which cost a world of money.'

Little of this was known to visitors in the seventeenth century, who on the whole were content to stand and admire the newly recognised beauties of the temple. Spon made, here as in other Athenian matters, tangible contributions to the scientific description of the monument. Less favoured than the Marquis de Nointel, it cost the companions five okes (about twelve and a half kilograms) of coffee in bribes to obtain admittance to the Acropolis. Spon made a detailed description of the pedimental sculptures, and his description of one of the pediments is worth quoting in full, for it is the last record of the sculptures before their destruction by Venetian artillery in 1687. Unfortunately the interpretation is of less value than the observation, since Spon, by an egregious error, has tried to fit the figures of the west pediment to the scene known from Pausanias to be featured on the east!

Jupiter, who is below the peak of the pediment, has his right arm broken; in it, he apparently held the thunderbolt. His legs are slightly apart, no doubt to make room for the eagle. Although these two features are missing, one cannot fail to recognise him by his beard and by the majesty which the sculptor has given him. He is naked, as he is often represented, and particularly by the Greeks, who made most of their figures nude. On his right is a statue with mutilated head and arms, which one may judge to be a Victory, preceding the chariot of Minerva, the two horses of which she leads. They are the work of a hand both strong and delicate, which would perhaps not have yielded to the famous Phidias or Praxiteles. One seems to see in their air a certain fire, a certain pride which Minerva inspires in them as they draw her chariot. She is seated upright rather in the guise of Goddess of Wisdom than of War, for she is not dressed as a warrior, having no helmet, no buckler, no head of Medusa on her breast. She has a youthful air, and her hairstyle is different from that of Venus. Another female figure, without a head, is seated behind her, with a child whom she holds on her knees. I will not tell you what it is, but I had no difficulty in recognising the two following figures, which are the last on that side. They are the Emperor Hadrian, seated and semi-nude, and close to him his wife Sabina. They seem both to be looking with pleasure at the triumph of the goddess. I do not think anyone before has observed this remarkable detail.

To the left of Jupiter are five or six figures, of which some have lost their heads, and these are apparently the circle of the gods, to whom Jupiter is introducing Minerva, to have her recognised as his daughter. So here is a little commentary on Pausanias.

The judgement that two of these figures represented Hadrian and Sabina was to have far-reaching consequences, in diluting the enthusiasm of the reception of the marbles when Lord Elgin brought what was left of them to England.

Besides the monuments of the Acropolis, Spon, Vernon and Wheler visited and identified many of the sites: the temple of 'Theseus', where Vernon's signature is still visible though Spon's and Wheler's are now obliterated;[7] the Theatre of Dionysus, where Vernon narrowly escaped being shot down by an over-zealous guard while taking its dimensions; the Temple of Olympian Zeus, which Spon established could not be the Palace of Hadrian, though he was unable to offer a positive identification; the Lantern of Demosthenes, which Spon recognised for a monument not a dwelling, though he surmised (like Vernon) that it was a dedication to Heracles; the Tower of the Winds (of which he had seen the drawing by

F. Giambetti after Cyriac in the Barberini Library in Rome); the entrance to the Roman agora, which they were unable to identify though they rejected accounts which identified it with the Dipylon Gate or the Gymnasium of Ptolemy; the Monument on the Hill of the Muses which Spon, like Cyriac but unlike his other predecessors, associated with the name of its dedicator Philopappus; the Library of Hadrian, which Spon took for the Temple of Olympian Zeus (following a false reading in Thucydides (II, 15) which placed the latter north of the Acropolis), rather than the traditional name, the Palace of Themistocles; and the bazaar which they surmised might correspond to the Ceramicus – a surmise not altogether incorrect, though they were not to know that the entire fifth-century agora – the agora 'in Ceramicus' lay underneath to await disclosure only in the twentieth century.

Apart from the Capuchin plan, Spon had for reference the account of the monuments of Athens by the Jesuit Father J. P. Babin, which Spon himself had published a few months earlier in 1674.[8] This also contained a pictorial 'map' of Athens. It is remarkable that Spon could achieve such good results. But in publishing his account, the most reliable so far, and criticising the accounts of previous travellers and geographers, he stirred up something of a hornet's nest in the form of Guillet de St Georges, author of the *Athènes Ancienne et Nouvelle* (1675), which purported to be a transcript of the adventures of Guillet's brother, Guillet de la Guilletière. Guillet de St Georges (c1625–1705) was an Auvergnat who became the first historian of the Académie Royale de Peinture et Sculpture. His other works included a treatise on swordsmanship, a history of the Grand Viziers Mehmed and Ali Köprülü, and a life of Mehmed II: but his *Athens* became a bestseller, being translated into English in 1676, in which year he also followed it with a similar work on Sparta. Guillet's credit in his account of Athens has scarcely stood the test of time or the arguments of Spon, who repeatedly in his account draws attention to Guillet's fabrications, misinterpretations, incorrect locations of ancient monuments, and omissions. Guillet's map is a straight copy of the Capuchin map, into which he has imported over 100 identifications of buildings, some roughly right, many barely plausible or clearly wrong.

Some of Guillet's more obvious mistakes include the information that the Monument of Philopappus was an 'Arch of Trajan' (when it is not even an arch!), the placing of a marble lion before the Parthenon, the claim to have admired the inscription 'To the Unknown God' on the very entablature of the 'Temple of Minerva',[9] and the reporting of the stadium twice, once as the stadium, once as the Theatre of Bacchus – the latter being placed in an obscure but impossible site due to the misreading of his topographical information. He also claims to have seen the Stoa Poikile, of which in fact no remains were extant, and a building called the Lantern of Diogenes, quite different from the Lantern of Demosthenes.

Whatever was not in the ancient sources seems to have come from the Capuchins. It is to their work that we must attribute several correct identifications: the Tower of the Winds, the Temple of the Muses (or perhaps of Demeter in Agra)[10] on the Ilissus (now destroyed) and the Cimonian Wall. The same source may have provided Guillet with the curious legend attached to the marble lion *couchant* not far from the Temple of Theseus. The wife of a janissary was said to have become obsessed with this stone beast to such a degree that she dreamt of it every night. Eventually she became pregnant, and in due course gave birth to a monstrous child with a lion's head. This creature was immediately smothered in a pit of stones by the disdar, or military commander. (Spon is not above repeating this colourful story.)

If Guillet had access to some source of information on Athens, it was at any rate not enough to enable him to produce a recognisable picture of the topography. Spon at first accepted Guillet's claim to have been seven days at Athens, but afterwards declared that Guillet de la Guilletière was a figment, and that Guillet de St Georges had never been there. He made as much clear in his own account of Athens.

Guillet responded angrily to the publication of Spon's *Voyage*, and issued a series of *Letters* (1689) in which he accuses Spon of 'making an anatomy [ie dissection] of many of our authors, and in his guise of antiquary, he has censured Strabo, Ptolemy, Pliny, Stephanus, Meursius, Ferrarius, Ortelius, Monsieur de Monconys, M. Baudran, la Guilletière, and two or three of our most celebrated geographers.' Clearly the written word was still paramount in antiquarian studies; to study the terrain at first hand was a maverick task. The attitude remained long entrenched, and is the reason for the relatively late dates at which schools of archaeology were established in our universities. Antiquities could be admired, copied, even stolen; but to study them was sacrilege against the written word.

Guillet accused Spon, legitimately, of some minor errors. Spon fought back in 1679 with a Response, addressed to the Dauphin, in which he fancifully envisages himself and Guillet as 'rivals for an ancient but still beautiful mistress – the city of Athens.' He goes on to give a list of 122 errors in Guillet's work – a list which is less devastating than it seems, since only a dozen or so refer to matters of fact rather than interpretation or opinion. Ultimately the controversy was a rather fruitless exercise, and an illustration more of Gallic waspishness and scholarly pique than of anything momentous.

Spon's great achievement was this account of Athens, but the work of the travellers was by no means over. The culminating point had, however, been achieved. In his portfolio Spon already had 100 inscriptions, which he printed in his *Voyage* and in his subsequent works. Wheler had a quantity of marbles which, after he entered holy orders in 1683, he presented to the University of Oxford. They had still several sites left to visit, however, including Corinth, where they had their last major adventure, while drawing the twelve Doric columns of the Temple of Apollo (Spon took this incorrectly for the temple of Diana of Ephesus mentioned by Pausanias.) Their archaeological activity attracted the attention of the authorities:

The curiosity we showed in going to study and measure these columns was bound to result in a tiresome affair, although we supposed ourselves unseen by anyone except a servant of the voyvode, who had himself offered us a pole to measure their height. For when we returned to our lodgings, the Cadi [judge] sent two or three Albanians to fetch us to speak with him. We went thither, accompanied by our dragoman, to whom he said that he had learnt that we were going about studying the buildings of Corinth, and that we had been seen taking some measurements; were we not perhaps spies of the Franks, who had come to discover the weakness of the place? Mourati replied that we were Englishmen, and that on coming to Corinth we had espied some antiquity which had attracted our attention, so that we could tell, on our return to our own country, of the remarkable things we had seen in each place.

The Cadi wished to know who he was himself: Sultanum, he said, I am the dragoman of the English consul at Athens, and there before you is Panagioti Cavallari, who has known me a long time. But, said the Cadi, have you letters from the Sultan, allowing you to go with these strangers to all these towns? I never travel without them, replied Mourati; here is what you require. And he at once presented to him a patent which the consul had obtained from the Grand Seigneur, to secure him and his companions from all inconveniences in his journeys. The Cadi took and read it, and seeing that it was from the English consul, and that we were under his protection, Ah, well, he said, the English are good friends of our Emperor, you are welcome, go where you please.

The work of Wheler and Spon has been largely forgotten, or overlaid by the researches of later writers who could scarcely have travelled without the book of the one or the other. Yet, as we have seen, Spon was the first correctly to identify many ancient sites; even his mistakes, such as his dating of the Parthenon pediments, were of central importance for the development of archaeology.

As for Wheler, the traveller E. D. Clarke (see Chapter 7) makes a generous assessment:

Respecting the merits of Wheler, as a traveller, there can be but one opinion among those who have had an opportunity of judging. That he was diligent in his researches, intelligent, faithful, a good naturalist, and a zealous antiquary, cannot be disputed. That he was profoundly learned, will perhaps not be so readily admitted. It may be said, that for the erudition displayed in his book of travels, he was mainly indebted to his companion Spon; a charge easily urged, and after all not so easy to be proved. Wheler confesses, that he copied into his work some passages as he found them already published by his fellow-traveller: but the facts, to which those passages relate, may have existed previously in his own journal; and, with regard to the erudition by which they are accompanied, the later writings of Wheler sufficiently prove that his literary attainments enabled him to supply every illustration of this nature.

It was natural that English travellers should make more use of Wheler's handsome folio volume than of Spon's cramped duodecimo, and make his book the vade-mecum of a century; but it was only the publication of Spon's own account that impelled Wheler to publish his version, lest he be thought to be co-author of the book in which Spon described 'their' travels.

Again, it is to Francis Vernon (see above, p 63) that the honour properly belongs of the first attempt to survey Greece scientifically. E. D. Clarke gave too much praise to Wheler in saying of him what was true of Vernon, that:

. . . he was the first traveller in Greece, who adopted the practice of taking a mariner's needle to the tops of mountains for the purpose of making observations of the relative positions of places, and thereby reducing those positions into triangles.

Still, Wheler's achievement was momentous in its way. He dedicated his book to Charles II, and made political capital out of its appearance by some remarks in the Preface:

A country once mistress of the civil world, and a most famous nursery both of arms and sciences; but now a lamentable example of the instability of human things, wherein your majesty's discontented and factious subjects, if their own late calamities will not sufficiently instruct them, may see the miseries that other nations are reduced to, and behold, as in a picture, the natural fruits of schism, rebellion, and civil discord.

The stage was thus being set for the representation of Greece as the ideal of liberty crushed, which was eventually to result in the stream of Philhellenes who went to fight for Greece in the War of Independence.

Though others would devote more attention, like Stuart and Revett, to Athens, or would, like the Abbé Fourmont, copy more inscriptions, or, like Elgin, collect more marbles, the achievement of these two men in studying with attention the whole extent of the Greek world was not to be bettered until the work of W. M. Leake (Chapter 7).

Spon and Wheler were also the last Europeans to see the Parthenon in its comparatively undamaged state. Though it had undergone various modifications, through conversion to a Christian church, and the subsequent building of a mosque in its midst, its outer structure had remained intact, as is clear from Spon's description and his pictorial map.

In 1663 the Ottoman Empire had renewed its attacks on mainland Europe. Now came the opportunity for those who had advocated a new crusade against the Turk to see some at least of their programme put into action. In 1669 the new Pope Clement IX gave his blessing to the fleet which sailed for

Crete. The French consistently held aloof from the war, through their traditional friendship with the Turk and in the hope of reaping the benefits of unopposed trading rights. It was to secure this latter form of favour that the Marquis de Nointel had been despatched to Constantinople in 1673.

The siege of Crete lasted until 1669 when, after twenty-four years' resistance, it fell to the Turks. The Venetians made no attempt on Constantinople, but in 1687 the Doge Morosini led his forces against Athens. Encamped on the Hill of the Nymphs, his army began the bombardment of the Acropolis. The mosque within the Parthenon was at that time being used as a powder magazine, and the result was inevitable. One of Morosini's bombardiers, the Russian Cristoforo Ivanovich, has left an account of the bombardment.[11]

On the twenty third of September Morosini sent to the field four light cannons, two newly invented heavy cannons, and four mortars, all of which were drawn by the galley crews. The army pushed on to the Borgo without any obstruction from the enemy, who was closed up in the fortress. The general drew up the attack the same day, and at the timely arrival of the above-mentioned cannons and mortars, they began to fire on the fortress with the assistance of the captain general himself, who had decided to move to the field to be better able to oversee the undertaking. From the continuous shelling, the besieged suffered considerable damage to the narrow enclosing wall of the fortress. His Excellency, informed that the Turks' ammunition, together with the principal women and children, were in the temple of Minerva, the latter believing themselves safe there on account of the thickness of the walls and vaults of this temple, His Excellency ordered Count Mutoni to direct his fire at that part. Even from the beginning, a certain disorder appeared in the tossing of the bombs, which were falling outside, and this was because of the inequality of the weight which varied 130 pounds from one to the next; but through practice and adjustment not a single one fell outside, so that one of them, striking the side of the temple, finally succeeded in breaking it.

There followed a terrible explosion in the fire of powder and grenades that were inside, and the firing and reverberations of the above munitions made tremble all the houses of the Borgo, which seemed a great city, and put a tremendous fear in the besieged. In this way that famous temple of Minerva, which so many centuries and so many wars had not been able to destroy, was ruined.

The north and south walls of the cella, and the rows of columns on those sides, were blown out by the explosion.

The Venetians who had taken so much of the wealth of Greece when they looted Constantinople over four centuries before had now contributed to the destruction of the most famous and beautiful building of antiquity. Unabashed, Morosini decided to remove a few souvenirs from the intact portions of the Parthenon. He selected the statue of Jupiter in his chariot from the west pediment. He succeeded, however, merely in smashing the sculpture:

In the plans for abandoning Athens, I conceived the project of taking some of the beautiful ornaments, especially those which could add to the splendour of the Republic. With this intention, I instigated the first steps for detaching from the facade of the Temple of Minerva – where there are the most beautiful sculptures – a statue of Jupiter and the reliefs of two magnificent horses. But hardly had the workers started to remove the large cornice than it all fell from this extraordinary height, and it is a miracle that no harm came to the workers.

The blame for this accident lies in the construction of the temple, built with stones placed on top of one another, without mortar and with a marvellous art, but which were all dislocated by the shock resulting from the explosion.

The impossibility of erecting scaffoldings and of taking yard arms from the galleys and other machines to lift heavy weights up to the top of the Acropolis, makes any other attempt difficult and danger-ous. I have forbidden it, so much the more that having deprived it of that which was the most remarkable, all that remains seems to me inferior in some limb by the corrosive action of time.

Instead, he decided to take a pride of marble lions; his officers removed the lion *couchant* which was near the Temple of Theseus, and the lion of Piraeus: the latter still stands before the Arsenal in Venice as a memorial of acquisitive connoisseurship, and a reminder of what had been lost.

CHAPTER FIVE

Marbles for the French King, 1667–1789

It is not a matter of indifference to a painter, nor to a poet, nor to a writer, after a profound study of nature, the first mistress of all, source of all beauties and of every sublime imitation, to be ignorant or familiar with the most beautiful things that Antiquity has transmitted to us.   (Diderot, to Naigeon (?), 1765 or 1774, *Oeuvres* 1971, 1003)

Curiosity is not a taste for what is good or beautiful, but for what is rare, unique, because one possesses it and others do not. It is not an attachment to what is perfect but to what is sought after, what is fashionable. It is not an amusement but a passion, often so violent that it yields to love and ambition only by the pettiness of its object.
   (La Bruyère, *Caractères* xiii)

Spon's *Voyage*, for all its learning, and its epoch-making contribution to the knowledge of ancient topography and inscriptions, made little impact on the world at large. He had not even the glory which Wheler could claim, of a royal dedicatee for his book. Peiresc, who could have appreciated it, was dead; Nointel was disgraced. The book was, of course, used by subsequent travellers to Greece, but the significant point is that most of those travellers were engaged in an enterprise which resembled that of Spon's predecessors more than his own, and were largely unaffected by the standards he admired.

The court of Louis XIV (1638–1715), the most powerful monarch in Europe, could not shirk the emulation of other courts in the assembling of works of antique art. His father's minister of state, Cardinal Richelieu (1585–1642), had been interested on his own account in antiquities and a letter to Richelieu of 1638 from the ambassador in Venice, Du Houssay, shows clearly what the Cardinal expected from him:

Since the most beautiful monuments of antiquity seem to have survived the injuries of so many centuries only to be judged worthy of a lodging in your library and your cabinets, I can assure your Eminence that, in order to obtain for them so glorious a home, I have already written through the Levant, and issued the necessary orders, in every place where there are consuls of France, to search diligently for everything which may be found worthy of Your Eminence.

Another minister, Cardinal Mazarin (1602–61) continued this interest and enhanced his own collection by the acquisition of a number of the antiquities that had belonged to Charles I, on the latter's execution. Many of these were taken back to England by the Earl of Pembroke at the Cardinal's death; but others were less fortunate. They passed to his nephew, the Duc de Mazarin, a man of extreme and eccentric piety and narrowness of vision, who one day tried to redeem his collection from its sinful suggestiveness by smashing off the private parts of all the statues with a large hammer.

Where Cardinals led, a King must follow. Jean Baptiste Colbert (1619–83), who became Louis' chief minister in 1661, made it one of the many duties of his almost vice-monarchical role to ensure that a substantial royal library and gallery should be developed. To this end he employed a series of agents in the Levant to collect books, manuscripts, medals and inscriptions. As soon as one failed or ran out of steam he set another to the task. It was as if he could not afford to allow the stream of antiquities to dry up for a moment.

It must be said that books were always of more interest than objects of art.

The achievement of Guillaume Budé in building up Francois I's library at Fontainebleau provided a pattern for emulation, and in the learned world rumours abounded of priceless works of classical literature, lost to knowledge, which might yet lie in their entirety in the Seraglio Library at Constantinople. The favourite hope for recovery rested on the lost books of Livy, which Pierre de Carcavy, (d 1684) the royal librarian and keeper of the Royal Cabinet in the Palace, had been assured by 'a famous traveller' were to be seen somewhere in the Levant, though possibly in Arabic translation.

At the same time there was no doubt that anything found by French agents belonged to the King, and it was the King's bidding which was in all cases to be followed. Perhaps this was not the least of the reasons for Nointel's disgrace – that he had acquired a collection of antiquities of his own in which he took pride, over which he exulted and which he displayed to all his visitors, in his palace over the Golden Horn.

The first of Colbert's emissaries were MM de Monceaux and Laisné. The latter, a scientist, was charged also with the collection of natural curiosities and plants. Among manuscripts, the chief quarry – apart from Livy – was to be religious works, though the botanical work of Dioscorides was also of interest to the naturalist Laisné. Detailed instructions were also given on the types of medals they should look for: they were to be large, struck, not moulded or sand-cast (to insure against fakes); with reverses of historical interest or including several figures, in fine condition, and lettered in Greek or Latin 'around the Emperor's head'. It was clearly assumed that most coins found would be Roman imperial ones.

The two men departed in 1667 and stayed in the Levant until 1675. By 1670 Monceaux, residing at Constantinople, was suggesting to the itinerant Laisné that they should remove the eight bas-reliefs from the Golden Gate. Like Petty's, their attempt was unsuccessful, and the works remained *in situ* for Spon and Wheler to describe, and thereafter to fall into decay. They also had a try at three bas-reliefs from a triumphal arch at Nicaea but the kaimakam refused to sell them.

The next of Colbert's emissaries set out four years later, in 1671: this was the German Dominican Father Wansleben. He was instructed to make drawings of all figures and 'implements', and adjured to copy inscriptions 'in the same language in which they are written' – surely a minimal requirement, and one which shows how carefully an agent's terms of reference might need defining. His mission was on the whole unsuccessful, and an outbreak of plague in Smyrna in 1674 would hardly be enough to account for his failure to obtain anything worthwhile. About June 1675 Pierre de Carcavy took him to task for sending only 'five small parcels' in four years: if Wansleben's productivity did not improve, his annual allowance of 2,000 livres would be cut off. A letter from Colbert followed, to which Wansleben did not reply until November.

You speak in your journal of nothing but the visits you have made, the entertainment you receive from your friends, and the good or bad humour of the Consuls. Look, if you please, to your instructions, which mention nothing of all that. And as the time and our expense are already considerable, you will please to manage both items rather better.

In January 1676 the Father was summoned to return, and to face charges of embezzlement. These he escaped, but his work was done. It is hard not to have some sympathy with the poor man, the demands on whom were obviously more than his learning or entrepreneurship enabled him to fulfil. How poor Spon would have been delighted with even a half of those 2,000 livres, and what solid results he would have procured!

A year before Wansleben's return, late in 1674, Colbert obviously despaired of the feckless Father, and despatched J. F. F. Vaillant (1655–1708), the numismatist, who as we have seen gave Spon his passage as far as Italy. He too, in three separate voyages, acquired at Constantinople and Smyrna only a few books and coins.

By this time the Marquis de Nointel had become ambassador at Constantinople, and with him went the orientalist Antoine Galland, later famous as the translator of the *Arabian Nights*. This man was given the task that Wansleben had failed to carry out; and he was a good deal more effective. Even before Spon's visit he had been to Patmos, had become excited at finding a life of Alexander with a hundred illustrations, and had given twenty écus for it on the spot. Back in Paris in 1675, he was off again in 1679 with even more detailed instructions from Colbert: that he should 'make such observations as we can make in voyages to the Levant'; should seek out manuscripts, parchments, medals and gems; should have his Pausanias always in his hand to illuminate the topography and lead him into spots of antiquarian interest; should take views of the Vale of Tempe, Mt Parnassus, Delphi and Athens, making copies of every drawing as a precaution against loss or accident; and should bring back inscriptions. Colbert also detailed the titles of a number of books he was specifically to search for (most of them highly obscure) known to be available in particular locations.

But as soon as Galland received these instructions, his luck ran out. He began his tour in Melos in October 1679; by

January 1680 he was in Candia, but still almost empty-handed; he saw some statues for sale, drew a statue of Apollo Pythius, and collected a few heads and inscriptions which he sent to Spon for his own collections. On Chios in May, he got a copy of Homer and some religious works, but on Mytilene a month later he got nothing at all. The last letter from him was dated October 1680, from Constantinople. We know that he was in Smyrna during the earthquake of 1688, and must assume that he had been pensioned off or lost interest. He seems to have spent his time translating works of Arab history into French, an enjoyable task which prepared him for his *magnum opus*. The list of his acquisitions amounts to a number of coins, several vases of agate, and some 'other curiosities'. Scarcely a scholar's haul.

Some other agents were employed for a time, to even less effect. But the last of Louis XIV's collectors was a different matter altogether. The indefatigable Paul Lucas (1664–1737), a merchant who was by the way a naturalist and antiquarian, was employed for a series of missions between 1699 and 1725. He had made a collection of medals which he had presented to the Cabinet du Roi in 1696, which no doubt gained him the post. He wrote up his first voyage, in which he had traversed almost the entire Levant, in 1704. In the same year he departed with a detailed commission from the First Secretary, the Comte de Pontchartrain, to hunt for 'plants, medals and other curiosities'; to visit Constantinople, Smyrna, Thessalonica and the Archipelago, as well as Pergamum, Ephesus, Sardis, Caesarea and Ancyra. He was to collect only such coins as were not already known to Vaillant, and only such large fine marbles as were fit for the cabinet of a king. When he rendered his accounts in 1708, he had acquired nearly 2,000 medals at a cost of 2,122 livres, 24 manuscripts, many precious stones and bronze figures, and a copy of the Monumentum Ancyranum (see pp 117–8) which cost him 40 livres. Total cost: 7,650 livres. The king was well pleased with his bargain.

In 1714 he was off again, and at Smyrna the following year he was pleased to find a marble relief, one and a half feet square, weighing sixty pounds and portraying six figures accompanied by an inscription 'which no one is able to interpret'. Unfortunately his accounts, detailed as they are, omit any specifications of the works he acquired, so that it is not possible to identify with any precision what he discovered, or whether it is still in the Louvre or Bibliothèque Nationale.

Lucas clearly made a good impression on his masters: the Abbé Bignon (1662–1743), Royal Librarian since Carcavy's death, referred to him as 'the marvellous Paul Lucas', and his energy was certainly equal to that of Cyriac, if his scholarly acumen was less. Chateaubriand, indeed, gave him very short shrift as a traveller:

Paul Lucas enjoys a high reputation among the class of travellers, and I am astonished at it: not but that he amuses us with his fables; the battles which he fights single-handed against fifty robbers – the prodigious bones which he meets with at every step – the cities of giants which he discovers – the three or four thousand pyramids which he finds on a public road, and which nobody besides himself ever saw, are diverting stories enough: but then he mangles all the inscriptions that he copies, his plagiarisms are incessant, and his description of Jerusalem is copied verbatim from that of Deshayes. Lastly, he speaks of Athens as if he had never been there, and what he says of that city is one of the most glaring falsehoods that ever traveller had the impudence to publish.[1]

Luckily for him, Bignon was not in a position to check his facts.

In 1723 he was given a further mission, with an allowance of credit up to 5,000 livres for acquisitions of special merit. He was, again, to draw inscriptions and reliefs, collect marbles, medals and vases, to note geographical names and plant names, and bring back seeds and roots. The returns on this last trip were inevitably less: of five hundred new medals, only fourteen were of types not already represented in the King's collection. Lucas now opened a museum of his own at Paris for the surplus: the centrepiece of this institution was a 'Ceres' from Athens, described in a kind of advertisement in the *Mercure de France* of December 1732:

I know of no cabinet in Paris more worthy of attention. . . . The most remarkable piece is the figure of the goddess Ceres which he brought from Athens more than forty [?] years ago. She is two feet and a few inches high. She is seated on a very singular seat, of beautiful florid oriental jasper. All the extremities of the figure are of bronze, including the head, hands, feet and the attributes she carries, to wit a torch of straw in the right hand and an ox's horn in the left. The base is of flawless stone, touchstone. Her clothing is of white

alabaster. . . . The cabinet is full of a great quantity of bronzes from
Egypt and all the other countries of the Levant, Greece and Mace-
donia. They include two bronzes unique in Europe: they portray
two gymnosophists, and he brought them from Persia.

This florid Demeter would scarcely merit an archaeologist's
serious attention today, but its ornateness appealed to the taste
of that century as the marbles of the Parthenon, say, could
never have done. The collection was further enriched by six
cabinets of medals and three thousand plants. All this, of
which an Ashmole could have been proud, was dispersed on
Lucas' death in 1737.

But a far more important contribution to knowledge than that
made by all the vain acquisitions of these variously random
collectors, was that of Joseph Pitton de Tournefort (1656–
1708), a botanist, who in 1683 had become Professor of
Botany at the Jardin Royal des Plantes in Paris. His brief was
rather different.

After the Treaty of Karlowitz of 1699, which severely
limited the Turks' powers in Europe, the King was anxious to
learn more about the state of the Ottoman dominions. The
Secretary, the Comte de Pontchartrain, selected Tournefort as
the man who could best carry out a fact-finding mission. He

proposed to his Majesty at the end of 1699 to send abroad persons
capable of making observations, not only on natural history and on
ancient and modern geography, but also on matters of the commerce, religion and customs of the different peoples who inhabit
them.

I was overjoyed [writes Tournefort] at this farther opportunity of
gratifying the strong passion I always had to travel into remote
places, where, by personally studying nature and men, a much surer
foundation is laid, than by reading in one's closet.

Tournefort departed from Paris in March 1700, accompanied
by the German doctor Gundelsheimer and the painter Aubriet
(whose name is forever linked with his discovery of that
favourite flower of front driveways, the aubrietia). By early
May they had reached Crete, where Tournefort set about his
task energetically. But the island did not make a good impression. He begins his first letter to Pontchartrain by dutifully
describing the plants of Candia: juliane, prickly acanthus,

gnaphalium maritimum, chicory, thyme, stachys and orchid – but comments that Crete, contrary to what the ancient botanists had led him to believe, contained scarcely a dozen plants peculiar to itself.

We went to Candia purely for the sake of sampling, upon the veracity of Pliny and Galen, who give the plants of this island precedence of all others throughout the world. We ever and anon looked at one another without opening our mouths, shrugging up our shoulders, and sighing as if our very hearts would break, especially as we followed those pretty rivulets which water the beauteous plain of Canea, beset with rushes and plants so very common, that we would not have vouchsafed them a look at Paris; we whose imagination was then full of plants with silver leaves, or covered with a rich down soft as velvet, and who fancied that Candia could produce nothing that was not extraordinary!

The natives pleased him no better. When they celebrate the feast of Bairam:

in every house there's merry-making; some dancing, others eating and drinking: here they repeat verses, there they range the streets with musical instruments; while others take their pleasure on the water. In short, this nation, so grave, and which always seems to be on one pin, is of a sudden quite off the hinges, and runs about like so many mad things: happy that these festivals return no oftener!

Abandoning for a time the search for plants, the party turned their attention to antiquities. They visited the city of Gortyn, scarcely examined since the visit of Buondelmonti three centuries before, though Prince Nicholas Radziwill had spent some months on Crete in 1583–4, in the course of a pilgrimage to Jerusalem, and had informed his public that the city of Gortyn had been founded by one King Taurus (or Bull), had failed to read the inscriptions on the 'Tomb of Zeus' and had of course visited the 'Labyrinth'. Tournefort was moved to melancholy by the ruins of Gortyn, and indignation at its present inhabitants:

In the room of those great men who had caused such stately edifices to be erected, you see nothing but poor shepherds, who are so stupid as to let the hares run between their legs, without meddling with them; and partridges bask under their noses, without offering to catch them.

Of the remains, such of them as had not been carried off by
the Turks to build villages, he was ready to identify gaily the
temples of Diana and Jupiter; he copied a few inscriptions
which had not previously been noted. On 1 July the party
made the obligatory expedition to the Labyrinth (the Cave at
Kastelli: see p 24), which was generally identified by classically
minded travellers with that built by Daedalus for King Minos
to house the Minotaur, the hideous offspring of his wife
Pasiphae and her favourite bull. He was suitably awed by the
cave:

If a man strikes into any other path, after he has gone a good way, he
is bewildered among a thousand twistings, turnings, twinings,
sinuosities, crinkle-crankles, and turn-again lanes, that he could
scarce ever get out again.

They accordingly posted guards at the entrance, fastened
papers at every turning, and scattered twigs and straw in their
wake. It is a wonder they did not borrow a local girl with
classical features and stand her at the entrance with a ball of
string, as Ariadne had done for Theseus millenia before . . .[2]
They added their names to the series carved by previous
visitors to the caves, the earliest dating from 1444. Tournefort
decided against Belon's view that the caves were a quarry,
regarding them as natural formations. The matter continued
to be disputed, many travellers remaining anxious to see the
Daedalic hand at work; the final decision seems to be that of
J. B. S. Morritt in 1795, who plumped for the quarry solution
and closed the question.

The party left Crete in July, and visited the other islands of
the archipelago, and also penetrated deep into Armenia and
Georgia. Reports on plants became increasingly intermittent,
though comments on the depravity of the inhabitants remain
plentiful; political and diplomatic affairs also recede into the
background, but a good deal of attention is devoted to antiquities. Among the many sites Tournefort visited and dis-
cusses with notable acuity are the ruins of Delos; but the most
interesting account is perhaps that of Samos, where he has
scored a first in his account of the Heraion. No previous writer
had much to say on this site. One reason for the detailed
account of this island is no doubt that they found it nearly
impossible to get off. They reached it in January 1702, *en route*

homewards from Constantinople, after a long tour deep into Turkey, Armenia and Georgia which offered little classical fodder beyond the Monument of Augustus at Ancyra or Angora (a city which Tournefort pronounced 'one of the most illustrious of the Levant': see pp 117–8). In February they tried to set sail for Icaria, but were blown back to the Samian shore nine miles from Carlovassi; biscuits and water ran short, the incessant rain made hunting and fishing impossible, and they were marooned for a week. Then they got as far as Patmos, only to be blown back to Carlovassi. On 21 February it was still raining, but by now they had reached the comparative comfort of a convent, Our Lady of the Thunder, and Tournefort was cheered up by finding a clump of blue ranunculus. On 24 February they were able to depart for Vathy; but they did not leave the island until mid-March.

Despite these privations, Tournefort wrote approvingly of the island, describing it as 'populous and well-manured', though its women were both ugly and lazy. Noting its richness in such commodities as pitch, silks, scammony, wildfowl, iron, ochre, emery stone and white marble, he was not above mentioning the wolves and tigers alleged to swim over from the mainland.

In more serious vein, he turned his attention to the ruins at Tigani (now Pithagorio):

Going down from the theatre to the sea, you behold a world of broken pillars, most of 'em either channel'd or in pannels . . . There are also several other columns with different profiles on some adjacent risings; their disposition still is round or in squares, which makes one guess they serv'd for temples or porticoes.

Here, in fact, was the site of the ancient temple of Hera, which 'the more ingenious sort of Papas still call . . . by the name of Juno's temple'. The spot had long been held sacred as the birthplace of the goddess Hera under an agnus castus tree (still plentiful in the neighbourhood). The first temple was said to have been erected by the Argonauts, on their return from the quest for the Golden Fleece; they established a sanctuary with a wooden image of the goddess, revealed to them in Argos by a miracle.

In historical times the site inspired continual rebuilding. The

temple itself was rebuilt four times, first in the early eighth
century, being enlarged by a peristyle about fifty years later.
Destroyed by flooding about 670 BC, it was rebuilt larger than
before, and in about 640 a walled peribolos was added. By 570
the tremendous leaps in architectural style made this, too,
seem inadequate. The architect Rhoecus was engaged to erect
a much larger structure, this time in full-blown Ionic, elegant
and airy, a miracle of art from the intricate bases to the curling
capitals of its 104 columns. Such was its effect that the
inhabitants called it a labyrinth, implying thereby an almost
magical status.

This temple too was destroyed – how short-lived were these
glories! – perhaps in the unrest that accompanied the rise to
power of the tyrant Polycrates, who could however, as a
patron of art whose tame poets included the graceful Anac-
reon, scarcely afford not to outdo his predecessor. His reach
exceeded his grasp: the temple was never finished; Polycrates
was betrayed to the Persians, crucified and left to rot, 'washed
by the rain and anointed by the sun', as the prophecy foretold.
Some desultory attempts to complete the building continued
to the late fourth century, but thereafter the Roman Empire
and the Christians left it to moulder into its present state.
There stands but one column, rickety and headless, where
once soared over a hundred.

Not surprisingly, Tournefort's attempts to work out the
ground plan underlying this complicated mass of ruins were
unsuccessful. He did however note the unusual capitals of the
proto-Ionic temple – a worthwhile observation. He also saw
two columns and bases:

of the beautifullest marble I ever saw. Some years ago the Turks,
imagining that one of these columns was full of gold and silver,
attempted to demolish it by firing some cannon at it from on board
their gallies; and accordingly damaged it very much.

Besides exploring the Heraion, they visited the church of
Metelinous, where an ancient bas-relief had been found by a
priest in a field. Tournefort's description is so accurate that it is
possible to identify the type despite his complete misinter-
pretation of the scene. Mindful of the healing sanctuary of the
god Asclepius (the Roman Aesculapius) on the island, he
describes:

a marble 2′4″ long, by 15″ or 16″ high, and 3″ thick; but as it is not far above the ground, the heads have been damaged. The relief contains seven figures, and represents a ceremony to implore the assistance of Aesculapius in the sickness of a person of importance.

The 'sick man' is described as in a bed; a table beside him with three goat's feet, and on it stand a pineapple, two flagons and three pyramids. A slave pounds drugs in a mortar. The border shows a horse's head, flames, a helmet and a cuirass. In fact the stone is clearly a characteristic form of funerary relief, where the dead man is shown at his last meal in the tomb; the horse, symbol of the underworld, peers through a window while the family offer delicacies to the dead. One can only admire Tournefort's accuracy of description, and scarcely condemn his over-eagerness to understand what he could not.

Diligent as he was, Tournefort clearly preferred France to the barbarous realm of the Turks, and was pleased to return soon after this to Paris and the Jardin des Plantes. In 1708 he was crushed against a wall by a cart and killed; the Abbé Bignon made himself responsible for the publication of his work, which appeared in 1717, to be followed in 1718 by English and German editions, which clearly appealed to the taste for accounts of Oriental adventure that was infecting the west.

The great era of royal collecting under Louis XIV seemed to have come to an end with Paul Lucas. But a project which has been gathering momentum for over thirty years is unlikely to cease through an incidental event like the death of a monarch. The Abbé Bignon ensured that the new reign should aim to be equally fruitful. It was under his patronage that one of the first great frauds of classical Greek archaeology was perpetrated, by the highly eccentric Abbé Michel Fourmont.

Fourmont was to claim the discovery of many important historical inscriptions at Sparta, whose authenticity was accepted for several decades, until proofs were adduced in 1791 that they must be forgeries. The acceptance of these proofs led to scholars dismissing all of Fourmont's other finds as fraudulent also, and it is only in recent years that a more discriminating assessment of his discoveries has been made. The chronology of his voyage through Greece, and the accompanying changes in his mental state, are important to the understanding of his purposes.

Fourmont's expedition was to be positively the last foray of the King of France. It had its preliminaries in a renewed interest in the possible contents of the Seraglio Library. In 1727 the Académie was informed that a Turkish press was to be set up by one Zaid Aga, son of Mehmet Effendi whom Bignon had himself visited in 1721. This was one of the most noticeable effects of the short period of foreign (French) influence known in Turkish history as the Tulip period. Bignon wrote quickly to both Zaid and Mehmet, inquiring whether there was any chance of the press printing any of the Greek or Latin classical manuscripts believed to reside there. Zaid Aga's reply was simple: his press was only equipped with Turkish types, and as there were no scholars of Greek and Latin at Constantinople, he was unable to produce editions of works in those languages.

The second difficulty at least could easily be remedied, and undaunted, the Abbé Bignon proposed in December 1727 that two scholars should be sent to ascertain whether there were any manuscripts worth copying. Though the mission was approved by the First Minister, Cardinal Fleury, in March 1728, the instructions were not drawn up until 18 August. Finally on 1 September, two Abbés, Sevin and Fourmont, departed for Constantinople. Such were the elephantine ways of the Royal pleasure.

They were able to take with them not only Bignon's instructions but, no doubt, a copy of the memoir drawn up by the learned Benedictine, Bernard de Montfaucon (1655–1741), who had visited Italy but not Greece, and in 1719 had published *L'antiquité explorée et representée en figures*, perhaps the most authoritative treatment of Greek art before Winckelmann. The memoir was composed in 1720 and included instructions relative to inscriptions, manuscripts of poets, historians, geographers and others as well as holy writ and ecclesiastical works.

Busts, statues and bas-reliefs are not for everybody. It is generally princes and great lords who have them brought, to adorn their cabinets and gardens. Although many of these kinds of monument may serve to illustrate antiquity, nothing approaches the utility one can derive from inscriptions, of which Greece and the cities of Asia are all full; and of these we shall speak in detail.

One can find there, without doubt, incomparable things which will illustrate history and chronology, and fill admirably the lacunae which historians have left us in the accounts of time. The countryside is full of these kinds of monument – in Athens, around Athens, at Thebes, at Eleusis, that celebrated place, at Megara and in the Peloponnese, at Corinth, at Argos, of which I know not even if the location is well-known today, at Sparta, at Patras and above all on the West coast, opposite the isle of Zante, that is Elis, that part of the Peloponnese where were celebrated the Olympic Games, so famous in antiquity.

Montfaucon goes on to mention Crete, Cyprus, the isles, Smyrna, Ephesus, Ancyra, where:

there remain enough [inscriptions] to make a decent volume. Mr [William] Sherard, the Englishman, has copied a good number in different places, which are being printed, at this very moment according to report, in England. But what are these in comparison with the great finds which one could make if some powerful prince should send there persons capable of transcribing accurately, and should pay their expenses. Those who copy, however clever, should take care, in cases of doubt, to write nothing by conjecture, but to represent all the marks as they are on the marble, and to put their conjectures in the margin.

We shall see how faithfully Fourmont followed this just requirement.[3]

When Fourmont and Sevin arrived in Constantinople in the late autumn of 1728, it was to find that most of the collection in the Seraglio had just been sold to the Prince of Wallachia. Sevin remained in Constantinople to pursue the search for manuscripts and books, while Fourmont left the city on 8 February 1729 to make enquiries in other parts of Turkey and Greece. Sevin's search for the Imperial Library was fruitless, though twenty years later Lord Charlemont was still hoping to find the lost books of Livy and Tacitus there. In fact, J. D. Carlyle in 1801 was the next Westerner to gain access to the Seraglio Library; and he was able only to repeat Pierre Giraudin's discovery of 1685 that it contained hardly a single classical work.

Fourmont went first to Chios, where he began a stream of illnesses by catching a bad cold, and then sailed on to Athens, arriving about 12 April. He gives a startling picture of the pomp in which he proceeded around the city:

Our procession at Athens was quite extraordinary. A janissary
preceded us; the sieur Cortrica, dragoman of France, and the son of
the consul followed to indicate the quarter, the name of the street, of
the church, of the house, and to warn people that the women should
retire. They were followed by people, one of them carrying a bill
hook, a mattock and a pair of tongs to unearth and remove the
marbles; another had a ladder and ropes to climb the walls, to
descend into abandoned enclosures and to hoist themselves into the
air and scramble over the church roofs and bell towers. This second
had also in his hand a bucket full of water, sponges, a broom to clean
away the earth and make the characters visible. Myself and my
nephew followed, armed with notebooks, as if we had been commissioned to take the census, or rather to extract the *carasch* [*harac*: the
poll-tax].

Wherever he went, he tells us, people would run up to him and
cry 'Afendis Fourmont, einai grammata, einai grammata'. He
tells us that he would even explore wells in search of inscriptions. He has already lost all interest in any search for books,
and is devoting himself entirely to material antiquities, especially inscriptions and reliefs. His nephew, Claude-Louis
Fourmont, who accompanied him, tells us that his purpose
was not to admire the beauty of the cities he visited but 'to
extract information to clarify certain matters of Greek history'. In this he expressed, indeed, a respectable aim, and one
in keeping with the aims of predecessors like Jacques Spon.
But it was far from being the King's objective, for his interest
was in enhancing his prestige by the beauty of his collection of
books and marbles. By the end of his travels, Fourmont was
claiming – somewhat hysterically – that his collection was
superior even to the Arundel Marbles. It should be noted,
however, that his idea of 'collecting' was not to transport
antiquities home, but to copy inscriptions and leave them *in
situ* – again, in the tradition of Spon and Wheler, rather than of
the unscrupulous bounty hunters of earlier generations; but it
was not a procedure to earn great rewards from the royal
Collector.

   He claims discovery of 130 inscriptions, 20 marbles, and
other items at Athens. His 'Relation Abrégée' notes that he
collected, among other things, victor lists of young men, lists
of magistrates and lists of priests and Amphictyons. This is
one of the rare cases where Fourmont is at all precise about his

findings, before his reports from Sparta, and it is possible to identify these lists with those attributed to him by Boeckh in his *Corpus* of Greek inscriptions.[4]

Between April and July he visited Eleusis, Megara, Salamis and Aegina, Sunium, Porto Rafti and Marathon. At Aegina he had an attack of sunstroke which laid him up for ten days. At the end of this period he laid claim to a total of 900 inscriptions, many of them not noted by Spon and Wheler. On 15 September Fourmont left Attica, and on 20 September he was in Nauplia. At nearby Hermione he spent a period variously given by him in his letters as ten or nineteen days, in which time fifteen workmen unearthed forty inscriptions, and he believed himself to have identified the temples of Apis, Venus Limnia, Neptune, Minerva on the Hill, Vesta and Apollo near the theatre by the sea. Here he was struck down by a fever, which was still afflicting him when after a forty-day journey from Argos he reached Patras on 22 December. Whatever his faults, there can be no doubt that the Abbé Fourmont drove himself exceedingly hard.

By February 1730 he was in Modon, and on 17 February he wrote to Cardinal Fleury from Ithome, with an account of the Mani. 20 April is the date of his first letter from Sparta. It is here that the mental life of the researcher begins to part company with reality.

Sparta represented an almost *tabula rasa* for an archaeologist, because it had had so few public buildings in classical times. However, a few remains are visible even now, though many of them are of Roman date. Against the Acropolis nestles the classical theatre. To the east of the Acropolis, near the river, is the sanctuary of Artemis Orthia, probable scene of the performance of the lovely maiden songs of Alcman, and north of this on the river bank, the altar of Lycurgus, the semi-legendary law-giver of Sparta.

How disappointing are these relics of the second city of classical Greece, particularly when we read the long description by Pausanias of the rich dispositions of buildings, colonnades, tombs, altars and statues that could be seen there in his day. According to his usual method, Pausanias begins from the agora, and describes the sights of the city in a series of excursions radiating from this central point and returning to the centre before making the next radius. But alas we cannot even be sure where his streets ran, named though they are, so little remains on the ground. He seems to have begun by setting out southwards along the road Aphetais; then south-west via the Canopy to the tombs of Castor, Idas and Lynceus (plausibly identified by modern archaeologists); then to the west, 'towards the setting sun' to the tomb of Brasidas and the theatre (easy enough). Then he describes the racecourse, the *platanistas* or plane-tree park where the young men's gymnas-tic contests were held, with its colonnade. These appear to have lain to the west though their site is unknown. His next site is 'east of the racecourse' – presumably retracing his steps on this spoke of his trip. His final excursion is clearly east-wards, to the lake sanctuary of Artemis, which has been found by the river. Finally he climbs briefly northward to the Acropolis itself, to the temple we mentioned and a temple of Aphrodite, before leaving the city altogether for Amyclae.

In view of the paucity of information recoverable even now, it is somewhat surprising to find that Guillet de St Georges was able to identify a number of Spartan sites with confidence in

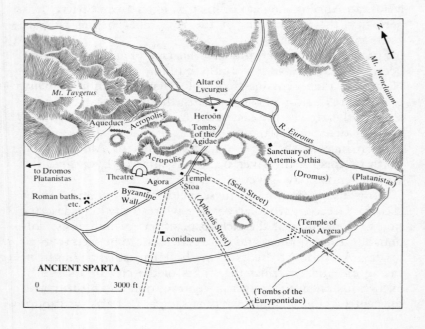

ANCIENT SPARTA

0 _____ 3000 ft

his book of 1679. He had followed up the success of his *Athens* of 1676 with a similar work on *Sparta*, of whose almost 300 pages some 40 are dedicated to its topography. We have seen good reason to believe that he never visited Athens. The case can be substantiated in the case of Sparta as well.

Clearly some fantasy is at work. For example, he tells us that in the agora, amid five or six ancient buildings the most remarkable are the Stoa Persike or 'houses of Menelaus', the temples of Helen, of Hercules, of Aphrodite in arms; and the racecourse and *platanistas*. Again, in apparent contradiction of Pausanias' testimony, he places the Dromos and *platanistas* and Temple of Olympian Zeus on the road to the bridge, with the south on the right. Now, it is possible that he read Pausanias' ambiguous words as implying that the first two lay to the east of the town; but Pausanias has no reference to a Temple of Olympian Zeus here or elsewhere. It is perhaps equally possible that a local antiquarian should bear-lead a visitor to one of the few visible relics of the city (the amphitheatre of Artemis was still visible in 1900) and tell him that these were the racecourse, and the temple, and that the *platanistas* was nearby. Particularly since the Turks were accustomed to ride, shoot and practise archery in this very spot (Guillet 256), it would seem a natural location. But was it Guillet himself who visited Sparta? or did he, as from the Capuchins in Athens, get his information from some now unidentifiable source?

A certain proof of the latter is to be found in his site for the city as a whole. He states clearly that Mistra was built on the ruins of Sparta. Now this was clearly impossible since the River Eurotas never ran through Mistra; and a century later Chateaubriand bemoaned the error when he climbed up to the Byzantine citadel in a search for the classical city. Chateaubriand's guide was able to tell him clearly enough that Sparta lay in the plain, at Palaeochori. As at Athens, Guillet had taken information acquired at second hand, misunderstood it and garbled it, and produced an impossible topography which, as much as Fourmont's deceits, was to baffle succeeding visitors.

In any case his *Sparta* did not achieve the success of his *Athens*, perhaps because a larger proportion of it was devoted to miscellaneous and unoriginal reflection on the history of the city, and there is no way of knowing whether any subsequent traveller beside Chateaubriand made use of it. Fourmont makes

no reference to it (or to any other book!). Apart from what
Cyriac had been able to observe three centuries before, the
ancient city of Sparta lay as a clean slate before Fourmont, to
reveal and design the archaeological record as he could or
would.

The record Fourmont offers is truly remarkable. In his own
words:

For a month now, despite illness, I have been engaged with thirty
workmen in the entire destruction of Sparta; not a day passes but I
find something, and on some I have found up to twenty inscriptions.
You understand, Monsieur, with what joy, and with what fatigue, I
have recovered such a great quantity of marbles: I am blind to the
fatigue, for this inconvenience has given me the time to write to you.
I have been in Amyclae, I returned loaded; digging is continuing
there under my orders, and finds are being made continually.

For what I have already, I can tell you that we have an almost
complete series of priests and priestesses, of ephors, of elders, of
gymnasiarchs, of agoranomoi and several things of the bidiaei [a
kind of educational officer]. Good fortune has willed that I should
discover the tombs of Lysander and Agesilaus (that of Lysander is
no doubt purely an honour, as he was buried near Thebes), bases
which supported statues of various philosophers, rhetors, captains
and other personages of this country, unknown until now, many
inscribed columns and a quantity of other things of that nature.

As I am not the only seeker here, I believed that I ought to be the
first to strike great blows and (as far as the plague permitted me) in
the places of greatest consequence. Hermione deserved some attention, Troezen and Argos as well, but I wanted Sparta above all; it is a
quarry of inscribed marbles which I must excavate without scruple.
If by overturning its walls and temples, if by not leaving one stone on
another in the smallest of its sacellums, its place will be unknown in
the future, I at least have something by which to recognise it, and
that is something. I have only this means to render my voyage in
the Morea illustrious, which otherwise would have been entirely
useless, which would have suited neither France, nor me.

I am becoming a barbarian in the midst of Greece; this place is not
the abode of the Muses, ignorance has driven them out, and it is that
which makes me regret France, whither they have retreated. I should
have liked to have more time to bring them at least more than bare
nourishment, but the orders I have just received obliged me to finish.

Few archaeologists can have rejoiced so blatantly in the
destruction of the record they came to recover.

At the same time, he continues to complain of illness, and of the exhaustion his researches are bringing on. Alas, his masters in France were not impressed. Sevin conveyed to him the order from Court that he was to give up his pursuit in Greece. He left Sparta reluctantly, and sailed from Nauplia on 23 June 1730, and in October presented his accounts, which revealed a total expenditure of 9,410 livres. Requests for funds to publish his discoveries were refused. Fourmont died on 5 February 1746, and his papers remained in the Bibliothèque Nationale for nearly a century before being properly collated. His nephew Claude (1713–80) who had accompanied him, planned to publish their *Voyage de l'Argolide*, but it was never printed.

But it is to those inscriptions of Sparta that particular attention needs to be paid. In November 1740 Fourmont lectured on them to the Académie des Inscriptions et Belles Lettres, and at the end of his account he writes 'the things which I have said here, are only views which I formed at the time I unearthed these marbles; I express them, without wishing that anyone should follow them or feel constrained by them.' This apparently admirable disclaimer conceals in fact a wholesale forgery. To have found inscriptions contemporary with the legendary past of Sparta would be inconceivable; it is fascinating to observe that none of the academicians at this time had the scholarly equipment to perceive this. It was left to Richard Payne Knight, in his *Essay on the Greek Alphabet* of 1791, to show that the letter forms in Fourmont's careful drawings were incompatible with this or indeed any period of Greek orthography. In doing so he singled out many of the features which had been noted by the Abbé Barthélémy in an article of 1756 as particularly characteristic of the seventh or eighth century BC (from the latter of which we have in fact not a single inscription).

But even more entertaining than Fourmont's spurious lists of magistrates are the circular bas-reliefs from the 'Temple of Onga' at Amyclae. A moment's glance at the drawings re-printed in Caylus' edition, side by side with the versions in the Earl of Aberdeen's publication of 1817, will persuade one that Fourmont's claims can be attributed only to preconception, near-blindness or total paranoia. These inscriptions show illustrations of slippers, toilet trays, mirrors and cosmetic

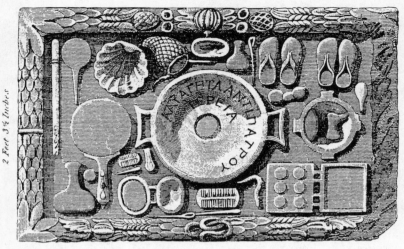

3 Feet 6 Inches

2 Feet 3½ Inches

. 2 Feet 10 Inches .

2 Feet 11 Inches

Engraved by P. W. Tomkins.

Fourmont's marbles from Amyclae, from Lord Aberdeen's 'Remarks on the Amyclaean Marbles', plate facing p 46.

Pl. LI.

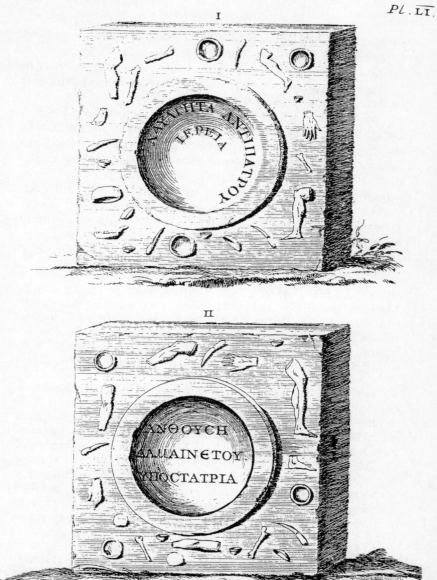

Fourmont's marbles from Amyclae, from Comte de Caylus, Recueil d'Antiquités.

cases, clearly votives offered to a deity of females; Fourmont had interpreted them as pictures of razors, cleavers and severed limbs, testifying to a 'pre-Trojan' custom of human sacrifice in Laconia. The fantasy is worthy of the archaeological delusions of Bouvard and Pécuchet.

The French academicians, sorely wounded by the English 'attacks', fought back in vain to establish Fourmont's credit. In the march of history even his real achievements have been largely forgotten, though the excavations in Sparta in the early twentieth century rehabilitated a number of his finds, which had been dismissed as part of the forgery, and even specific readings which epigraphists had emended away. Fourmont's reputation remained largely as it was bound to be after the final *coup de grâce* of Edward Dodwell (see Chapter 7), who had been in Sparta in 1801, and wrote in 1819:

After I had taken copies of some of these inscriptions, I observed Manusaki [his guide] turning them over and concealing them under stones and bushes. When I inquired his motive for such unusual caution, he informed me that he did it in order to preserve them, because many years ago a French *milord* who visited Sparta, after having copied a great number of inscriptions, had the letters chiselled out and defaced. He actually pointed out to me some fine slabs of marble from which the inscriptions had evidently been thus barbarously erased.

The fact is generally known at Misithra, and it was mentioned to me by several persons as a received tradition. This must doubtless have been one of the mean, selfish and unjustifiable operations of the Abbé Fourmont. . . It is conjectured by many, and perhaps not without reason, that his principal object in obliterating the inscriptions was, that he might acquire the power of blending forgery and truth without detection, and that his fear of competition was subordinate to that of being convicted of palaeographical imposture.

On his return to France he produced a vast mass of inscriptions, many of which are authentic, and have since been copied in Greece, and published by various travellers. But the most curious part of his collection, and that in which his authenticity is particularly questionable, are his inscriptions of Sparta and Amyklai, in which perfect confidence ought not to be reposed without great caution.

Since the time of Alaric, Greece never had so formidable an enemy. . . .

Not surprisingly, the débâcle of Fourmont's expedition – not so much his forgeries as his failure to deliver anything the King actually wanted – put an end to any further royal interest in sending agents to the East to collect antiquities. But by this time an extensive network of private wealthy connoisseurs had developed in France and elsewhere; the torch of antiquarianism was handed by default to these men, who were responsible for the scientific development of the subject and could travel both to collect and survey the land – when even D'Anville, the greatest of the eighteenth-century geographers of ancient Greece, scarcely ever stirred from Paris and never visited the Levant.

They abounded, these independent collectors of choice marbles, who profited from diplomatic or government postings to indulge their antiquarian taste, and to hold a voluminous correspondence on their treasures. The set-up is little different from that of a century before, when Scaliger the philologist, Meurs the historian, Peiresc the antiquary and Rubens the artist could all share their erudition in conversation and correspondence.

Such tastes were no longer the prerogative of Northern Europe. The rule of Italian states in the archipelago gave plenty of scope to a man like the Venetian proveditore of Melos since 1702, Antonio Nani, who assembled marbles from Melos and from the Peloponnese; content, however, merely to admire, he bequeathed his collection to his son Bernardo (b 1712), who entrusted publication of the whole to the savant P. M. Paciaudi, who can fairly be called (with Scipione Maffei, whose 'Lapidarium' – Verona, begun in 1744, can still be visited) the founder of the scientific study of inscriptions.[5]

Paciaudi is the link too, through his correspondence, with the last and greatest of the French connoisseurs, a species perhaps aptly castigated by La Bruyere (epigraph), and abruptly obliterated in the French Revolution. Anne Claude Philippe de Tubières, Comte de Caylus (1692–1765), spent three years travelling in the Levant (1714–1717), and on his return to Paris rapidly became one of the leading lights of the antiquarian world. Most extensive in his collections, most voluminous in his correspondence, most noble in his published *Recueil d'Antiquités* in seven volumes (1752–67) and most erudite in commentary, he was from 1742 an active member of the Académie des Inscriptions et Belles Lettres, the prestigious body founded in 1701 by Louis' Minister, the Comte de Pontchartrain, and his librarian, the Abbé Bignon. Its purpose was not only to encourage the serious study of antiquities, but to ensure the composition of appropriate mottoes for medals struck to commemorate the exploits of Louis XIV. The scholarly purpose of this august body was far in advance of the public ambition of any other country. The Académie des Inscriptions was above all the home of history, though its members ranged in their interests over such fields as Greek architecture, ancient religions, the alphabet, Greek law, Assyrian chronology, the Greek calendar and (in the second half of the century) classical geography. As Fourmont (and Richard Payne Knight) dabbled in all these, so too did Caylus: but it was art not history that gave the focus to his interests.

Besides owning one of the most distinguished private collections in France – or rather three of them, since he filled his house three times with his acquisitions, and presented each in turn to the King – Caylus was deeply interested in the art of the ancient world. He spent four-fifths of his income on antiquities from Egypt and Etruria, as well as Greece and Rome; he corresponded not only with Paciaudi but with the Abbé Sevin on his book-hunting expedition to Constantinople; he even invented a style of painting on wax which he believed to correspond to the encaustic technique of the ancients (and which was loudly ridiculed by Diderot).[6] Such practical application of scholarship was typical of the time and his inclinations. All the ancient world was his oyster.

Unlike Peiresc and his friends, he was interested in the arts for their own sake and not simply in the relics of ancient time; but though he came to antiquity through the arts, his artistic sense was slender. His eye was better than his taste[7] – a desiccated connoisseurship that would repel those who, like Denis Diderot, sought to seize a living and life-giving flame from the writings of the ancients. For Diderot, antiquarianism was a kind of sickness: it arose from a distrust of, even a contempt for, the contemporary world, which was quite at odds with the ideals of the Enlightenment.[8]

'His eye was better than his taste': that phrase could be used to damn alike the wild imaginings of Fourmont or the misplaced enthusiasms of Lucas. The Comte de Caylus was the apogee of his age, and Diderot summed him up once for all in his epitaph: 'Ci gît un antiquaire acariâtre et brusque. Ah! qu'il est bien logé dans cette cruche étrusque.'

There is a perceptible piety in Chateaubriand's benign statement that his compatriots had done more than any other nation to advance the understanding of ancient Greece. To say the least, he shows inadequate discrimination in including Guillet and Fourmont in his litany. But a tradition that began with Peiresc and Spon, included the endeavours of Lucas and the contributions of Tournefort, as well as the publications of Bernard de Montfaucon and the Comte de Caylus, and saw also the foundation of the first institution devoted solely to the study of ancient remains, deserves, despite its limitations, our respect and serious commemoration. Chateaubriand could look back too on a literary tradition which had abandoned the frigid classicism of Racine to attempt a real modernisation of classic form in the *Télémaque* of Fénélon (1699: see also Chapter 6) – though who can endure it now? – and had followed that up with the almost equally unreadable *Voyage d'Anacharsis* of the Abbé Barthélémy (1788). The Battle of the Books, the quarrel of Ancients and Moderns, was reflected also in the increasing disparagement of the sinewy intellectualism of Poussin for the fleshy transformations of antique art in the works of Rubens, one of whose heirs is the painter closest in spirit to the Arcadian Never-Never-Land of Fénélon: Antoine Watteau (1684–1721).

Greece seemed really to have got under the skin of French culture. If the momentum in the eighteenth century reverted to the English students of Greece, it is just to affirm that they could not have achieved what they did without the work of their French predecessors.

CHAPTER SIX

The Society of Dilettanti and the Greek Revival

Then lead, ye Powers
That o'er the garden and the rural seat
Preside, which, shining through the cheerful land
In countless numbers, blest Britannia sees –
Oh! lead me to the wide extended walks,
The fair majestic paradise of Stowe!
. . .
While there with thee the enchanted round I walk,
The regulated wild, gay fancy then
Will tread in thought the groves of Attic land;
Will from thy standard taste refine her own,
Correct her pencil to the purest truth
Of nature, or, the unimpassioned shades
Forsaking, raise it to the human mind.

(James Thomson, *Autumn* 1744)

The Greek Taste

Surely the most striking, if not the most distinguished, monument of the Greek Revival in English architecture is W. H. Inwood's Church of St Pancras in London, with its porches modelled quite blatantly on the Erechtheion (Temple of Erechtheus) on the Athenian Acropolis. The building was erected in 1822, hard on the heels of the arrival of the Elgin Marbles in London, and Inwood published a monograph on the Erechtheion itself in 1831. But this building was the culmination of a process of classicising architecture which had been begun by James Stuart in 1750. What had happened to bring these architectural and sculptural forms, scarcely modified, from sunny Greece and its marble mountains to the chill north and grey foggy damps of London?

The story begins at least a century earlier, and its prologue contains many elements. First among these is the new enthusiasm for Homer that began to infect Europe at the beginning of the eighteenth century. The fashion had begun in the France of Louis XIV, with the publication in 1699 of Fénélon's *Télémaque*, a continuation of the Odyssey which placed Homer's heroes in a setting which contemporaries no doubt thought authentic, but which was about as Greek as Marie Antoinette's Petit Trianon was truly pastoral.

But the Homeric taste was born. There followed soon Mme Dacier's translation of Homer, translated into English in 1714 by Broome, Ozell and Oldisworth, and then the illustrious *Iliad* and *Odyssey* of Alexander Pope, the standard translation and classic reading of at least three succeeding generations. The virtues Pope found in Homer's art are interesting for the correspondence they show to the virtues discovered a little later by critics in Greek sculpture.

Our Author's work is a wild paradise, where if we cannot see all the beauties so distinctly as in an order'd garden, it is only because the number of them is infinitely greater. . . It is to the strength of this amazing invention we are to attribute that unequal'd fire and rapture, which is so forcible in Homer, that no man of a true poetical spirit is master of himself while he reads him.

Homer encapsulated and prefigured the main trends of the Greek Revival: consummate artistry, truth to nature, and a genius which rapt the beholder with ecstasy. To be Greek meant to exhibit a matchless simplicity and naturalness.

J. J. Winckelmann's writings on Greek art pointed to the same focus as the critical understanding of Homer. The study of antique art was transformed by the publication in 1755 of Winckelmann's *Gedanken* (*Reflections on the Imitation of Nature in Greek Art*; translated into English by Henry Fuseli in 1765). Almost no systematic study of ancient art had appeared in England before this, though in France, Bernard de Montfaucon had compiled a massive dossier of more than 30,000 pieces of antique art in *L'Antiquité Explorée* – a work later dismissed by Thomas Carlyle as 'mere classical ore and slag'.

Eighteenth century taste had, despite Montfaucon's labours, been based on a relatively small number of statues, mostly in Rome, though some were in Florence and elsewhere. But no attempt had been made by collectors or scholars to attribute works – other than portraits – to particular periods on stylistic grounds. Scarcely indeed was a distinction made between Greek and Roman art. In England, in fact, taste generally favoured the Roman over the Greek, partly because of the presence of Roman antiquities in the British Isles, but also for more intangible reasons. A collector like Dr Richard Mead, or Sir John Clark of Penicuik, forming collections in the 1720s, concentrated on Roman items. The collection of Sir Charles Townley (1737–1805) consisted overwhelmingly of Roman works (though some were copies or imitations of Greek works or styles) acquired from Rome. Richard Payne Knight (1750–1824), the arbiter of taste for half a century, collected above all Roman coins and bronzes. (Sir William Hamilton in Naples would soon begin to collect Greek vases: but he thought they were Etruscan).

Of seventeen major collections in England described by James Dallaway in his book on contemporary collections,[1] which included those of the Earl of Leicester at Holkham, of Robert Walpole at Houghton, of the Earl of Egremont at Petworth, of Horace Walpole at Strawberry Hill, every one contained pieces that were almost without exception of Roman origin. Whatever was to be seen in Rome was good, was a standard of taste and excellence, and among its vast store were a dozen or two statues that had become benchmarks of taste. There was the Laocoön, a work of the Pergamene school which represented the scene described by Virgil in the *Aeneid*, where the priest and his two sons are engulfed by an enormous serpent: 'Twice round his waist their winding volumes rolled;/And twice about his gasping throat they fold/ . . . With both his hands he labours at the knots/ . . . His roaring fills the flitting air around.' (II, 286–92: tr John Dryden).

But, as G. E. Lessing says in his famous essay on the work, Laocoön does not scream; what he utters is, rather, a fearful and anguished sigh. Restraint, decorum, 'physical pain and nobility of soul' are evenly distributed in this work which for the eighteenth century (strangely, it may seem to us who know the Parthenon metopes) typified the classical ability to express violence through slight gestures.

There was the Medici Venus, another work fairly repugnant to modern taste in its frosty stiffness, but which sent the contemporaries of Byron into raptures:

> We gaze and turn away, and know not where,
> Dazzled and drunk with beauty, till the heart
> Reels with its fulness; there – for ever there –
> Chain'd to the chariot of triumphal art,
> We stand as captives, and would not depart.
> (*Childe Harold's Pilgrimage IV* 50)

There was the Belvedere Torso, which sent Winckelmann into ecstasies:

Ask those who know the best in mortal perfection whether they have ever seen a flank that can compare with the left side of this statue . . . You can learn here how a master's creative hand is able to endow matter with mind. The back, which appears as if flexed in noble thought, gives me the mental picture of a head filled with the joyful remembrance of his astonishing deeds, and, as this head full of wisdom and majesty arises before my inner eye, the other missing limbs also begin to take shape in my imagination . . .

There was the Farnese Hercules; and there was the Apollo Belvedere, which Winckelmann called 'the highest artistic ideal of all the surviving work of antiquity' and 'as much superior to all other images as the Apollo of Homer is superior to those of later poets . . . eternal spring decks his alluring manhood with delightful youth and plays with tenderness over the proud architecture of his limbs'. Winckelmann's biographer rightly dismisses this 'irredeemably antiquated prose hymn' to another statue which today draws few admiring eyes; but for the eighteenth century it was these works that embodied the Greek genius, and made the study of things Greek worthwhile.

In fact few Greek statues had survived the Roman period, and most of what was to be seen in Rome were copies, reasonably close, of Greek originals. Most interesting to us are the various more or less degenerate copies of the Aphrodite made by Praxiteles for her temple at Cnidus – perhaps the first authentic female nude of Western art – which elicited an appropriate response in those who saw it. Lucian (second century AD) describes the journey of two friends – only one of whom was a lover of women – to Cnidus expressly to see it. The first leapt forward to kiss it, while even his homosexual friend was lost in admiration of its beauty. This was blemished only by a mark on the thigh, which according to legend was the result of an ejaculation by an admirer who contrived to have himself shut up with the statue overnight.

The statue had been taken to Constantinople by Theodosius, and burnt in the fire in the Palace of Lausus in the eleventh century. The identification of the Venus Belvedere (of which Francis I had a copy) with the type of the Cnidian Venus was the achievement of the numismatists, who noted the similarity of her pose to that of a figure on the coins of Cnidus. The aesthetician, Ennio Quirino Visconti (1751–1818), later took up the identification, but it was almost too late, for the nineteenth century took against the goddess' immodesty and the Venus Belvedere, as well as other versions such as the Venus Colonna, were all consigned to the storerooms of their museums lest they shock the modest eyes of museum-goers.

Such might be the sad fate of the gods of Greece. But in the eighteenth century they still basked in a blaze of glory and set themselves up as standards of excellence in the arts of man, if they did not, like Rilke's Archaic Torso of Apollo, issue that peremptory command, 'you must change your life.'

Winckelmann adhered to this valuation of what was to be found in Rome, to the extent that he never travelled to Greece to survey its works of art in their own setting. He regarded the antique as a better model than nature. But already he was working towards the larger historical conception of his *History of Greek Art* (1764) which for the first time erected a periodic framework into which the classic works could be fitted. Considering the stylistic softening that resulted from these works being copies of lost originals, and the fact that no representatives of the classical fifth century were available for his study in Rome, he did this with remarkable accuracy. The result was that the use of 'antique' as a universal accolade was replaced by that of 'Greek' to describe works that reached the highest ideal of perfection; and this was just, for most of these works were Greek in their original conception, however it had been overlaid by the treatment of the Roman sculptor. For Winckelmann and his followers like Flaxman and Goethe, Roman art was synonymous with degeneracy. Nor was this revaluation affected by the discoveries – in which Winckelmann took a great interest – of the buried cities of Pompeii (1738) and Herculaneum with their hitherto unimagined riches of Roman painting and sculpture.

'The aim of a right criticism', said Walter Pater, 'is to place Winckelmann in an intellectual perspective, of which Goethe is the foreground.' Winckelmann is as much symptom as exponent of the change in taste that Goethe was to forge and embody in supreme complexity. Goethe's pursuit of the Greek ideal was a lifelong quest. From the time he saw the Elector of Mannheim's collection of ancient art in 1769, Greece was the focus of his aspiration. Profoundly influenced by Winckelmann's emphasis on the naturalism of the Greek genius, he was in tune with his century in regarding Homer as the unapproachable pinnacle of the Greek literary genius. Goethe himself collected antique art when he could; constant meditation on the Greeks and the struggle to absorb a model he regarded (like Diderot: see Chapter 5, p 108) as superior even to Nature's own, led him away from his youthful attempts to fuse Greek form and eighteenth-century bourgeois sensibility, to a recognition of the otherness of the Greeks and the impossibility of creating art in the same mould. All his effort was to outgrow his master Winckelmann.

Yet Winckelmann deserves appreciation for his new way of writing about Greek sculpture. 'Penetrating into the antique world by his passion, his temperament, he enunciated no formal principles, always hard and one-sided' (W. Leppmann). His *History of Greek Art* succeeded triumphantly in establishing a periodisation of Greek art history that has not in its essentials been contested.

He made as much impact on visitors to Rome by his presence as by his books. Always there, and always accessible, through the 1760s, his learning, passion and discrimination were at the service of all who wished to learn; among whom not the least was himself, constantly striving for greater clarity of understanding.

His death in 1768, in an inn in Trieste, murdered by a fellow guest for a few gold coins, is a story well known but still startling in its destructive absurdity. But his work was done. Having attained for himself a satisfactory perception of the Ideal, he succumbed to the temptation to tabulate its embodiments in the several features of the body: the eyes should be deeper set than in nature; foreheads should be low in youth, high in maturity; chins should not be dimpled; fingers should taper; breasts should 'resemble little hills running to a point'; of the testicles, the left is always larger; and so on. For lesser spirits he had provided a dangerously easy chart by which beauty could be recognised, dangerous in an age that sought to fit art to rules. But for those who wished to be told what to think, the answer was now there: for Beauty, seek Greek.

By 1779 Gavin Hamilton could say firmly to Charles Townley (p 112 above), 'Never forget that the most valuable acquisition a man of refined taste can make is a piece of fine Greek sculpture.' (Hamilton, a dealer in Rome, naturally had an interest in the matter.) But Townley's was one of the few English collections in which Greek materials made any significant showing at all. (He rather diminished the scholarly cachet of his collection by an arrangement of pieces according to 'symbolical values' and 'the mystic system of emanations'.)[2]

But among all this new valuation of things Greek it remained the tradition for any student of the arts, including architecture, to do his apprenticeship in Rome. For the sculptor and painter this made sense, and the habit of Rome had infected the artistic confraternity to such a degree that a Robert Adam could find all he required in Roman forms.

Even in 1781, a Goethe long in love with the idea of Greece would experience deep shock at the sight of the Greek temples of Paestum in South Italy and Segesta in Sicily, at the 'heavy' appearance of their 'crowded masses of stumpy conical pillars', which had none of the charm of Herculanean art. But 'in less than an hour,' says Goethe, 'I found myself reconciled to it.' Such is the mighty plunge of a change in taste.

Nothing like a Greek temple was to be seen in Rome: no Parthenon, no Temple of Concord like Agrigento's, no Bassae: taste knew only the graceful and miniature temples of Vesta and at Tivoli, the huge arches of the Baths of Diocletian and the colonnades of the Theatre of Pompey. So it might be seen as an act of considerable daring in an aspiring architect, or an indication of the strength of the idea that Greece must of necessity be a fertile source of excellence in inspiration, that the young architects James Stuart and Nicholas Revett should embark on a journey to Greece to study the antiquities and to form a portfolio of details, forms and ornaments.

To be sure, intrepid spirits had travelled from England to the Levant often in the past hundred years or more, but scarcely one Englishman had turned a knowledgeable eye on the antiquities in Greece since the visit of George Wheler with Jacques Spon in 1676. A rare exception was Edmund Chishull, who had arrived in the Levant in 1698 as British chaplain at Smyrna. With seven other Englishmen he had visited the ruins of Ephesus and other sites of Ionia; had sat and contemplated classical antiquity in a cave at Smyrna, where, according to the verse epistle he wrote on his travels, he was vouchsafed a vision of Homer – on the master's home ground; had thought of Hero and Leander as he passed Sestos and Abydos; admired the scenery of the Troad; and in general behaved like any young man with a good classical education. He also collected a significant number of new inscriptions, which he published, together with some gathered by the poetaster Samuel Lisle, in *Antiquitates Asiaticae* of 1728.

They included the lengthy decree of Antiochus Soter from Sigeum of 278 BC, which several travellers had described, and which was used by the Turks as a charm against illness. (The procedure was to roll the patient up and down on the stone, which did little for the clarity of the lettering.) Another was the famous dedication of Phanodikos from the same site which is one of the earliest examples of Greek writing, and may be as early as 600 BC. He also copied the long inscription from Teos which pronounces curses on those who infringe the laws of the city: 'if any make an insurrection, . . . or import new drugs, . . . or rob . . . or break or deface columns, let him be destroyed both himself and all his family.' This stone of about 470 BC has since disappeared, so Chishull's copy is of unusual value for the understanding of early Greek legislation. But the high point of Chishull's collection was undoubtedly the Monumentum Ancyranum from Angora (Ankara), the main source of the Emperor Augustus' record of his own achievements.

The temple had first been observed by Laisné in late 1670.[3] Tournefort in 1701, despite the effaced letters and the holes resulting from artillery bombardment, was able to make a copy of the inscription; and it was this copy which Chishull had obtained from him, in Smryna later that year.

Apart from the books of Tournefort and Chishull, there were few up-to-date works on which the traveller could rely. The lively books of Bernard Randolph, whose *Archipelago* and *Morea* were published in 1687 and 1689 respectively, were informative on political affairs, but had no classical learning.

In the early years of the eighteenth century appeared two ponderous tomes: Aaron Hill's *Full and Just Account of the Present State of the Turkish Empire* (1710), and Richard Pococke's *Description of the East* (1743–5). Hill has been described as 'an intolerable writer' and Pococke as 'the dullest man who ever travelled'.[4] Both were more interested in exotic contemporary detail than in antiquarian matters. Alexander Drummond, who was in the Levant from 1744 to 1756, and published his *Travels* in 1754, rejoiced more at his success in establishing a lodge of Freemasons at Smyrna than in ninety-nine inscriptions of antiquity – though he did mourn over Delos as over 'the ruins of some friend's habitation'. Charles Perry's *View of the Levant* of 1743 is, at least on Athens, 'a medley of ignorance and carelessness'.[5] The *Travels* of the Earl of Sandwich (whose fine collection of Egyptian mummies earned him the sobriquet of Mummius in Pope's *Dunciad*) in 1738–9 were not published until 1799; and Antony Askew who was in the East in 1747 apparently was a second Fourmont, who destroyed the inscriptions he copied.[6] Lord Charlemont was there in 1749 with Richard Dalton, but his diary too was not published in his lifetime.

A more interesting – and interested – traveller was Lady Mary Wortley Montagu, wife of the Ambassador to the Porte. She had visited the Troad, Homer in hand, and rejoiced to see the accuracy of Homer's epithets for the terrain – a thought that still rises up in the visitor to such places as rocky Chios, wooded Zakynthos, and windy Troy. She (tactfully?) refrains from observing how Pope has obliterated every local epithet in Homer in favour of a conventional Greek-rococo decor, or what Wood called 'a florid profusion of unmeaning ornament'. She realised that 'Troy' was of later date than Homer's Troy, though this did not lessen her enthusiasm at being close to its site.[7]

But these travellers offered little ground for a serious student of antiquity to build on. They reflected taste rather than making it.

As for the travellers with a professional interest in architecture, all their work before Stuart and Revett had been based on what could be seen in Rome and further north in Europe. No architect had bothered with Paestum or Sicily. Even Robert Adam's monumental work on the Palace of Diocletian at Split was an extension of the prevailing Roman taste. Furthermore, all attention that was paid to things Greek among the scholars and antiquarians had hitherto been given to coins, portable antiquities and inscriptions, of which at least the first and third could be seen as of value as illustrative of ancient literature, history and institutions. With Stuart and Revett's work began the study in England of a Greek art for its own sake.

There had, indeed, been one or two forerunners in the study of Greek architecture. Most notable among these was the lavish *Entwurf einer historischen Architektur* (1721) of Johann Bernhard Fischer von Erlach. This project to describe and illustrate the major stages of architectural history had begun with the Temple of Solomon at Jerusalem, the city of Babylon and the Pyramids; had covered the Greek world in seven plates and the Roman in thirteen, before going on to some masterpieces of Islamic architecture and a considerably more detailed survey of contemporary works. But Fischer's selection of Greek buildings is significant. The only ones, of those illustrated, standing in his day were the Temple of Olympian Zeus at Athens, the Parthenon, and the Acrocorinth (hardly, indeed, a building). He included five of the traditional seven Wonders of the World – the chryselephantine statue of Zeus at Olympia, the Mausoleum at Halicarnassus, the Temple of Diana at Ephesus, the Colossus of Rhodes and the Pharos of Alexandria – offering reconstructions on the basis of the ancient texts.

He also included one monument that was never built, the statue of Alexander the Great proposed to be carved out of Mt Athos, as well as the Labyrinth of Crete (the illustration for which was based on a coin design), and the Temple of Venus at Paphos.

Though scholarly in style, meticulous and exquisite in execution, these plates did not represent any new or useful additions to knowledge or understanding of Greek art, but a summa of the received tradition. For example, the Colossus of Rhodes is represented in the impossible posture, astride the harbour entrance, which had become canonical in illustrations; the Olympian Zeus is housed in a temple with an arched and coffered apse such as no Greek ever built; the Acrocorinth sprouts a non-existent temple on its precarious peak, while the eight fluted columns of the Parthenon are unequally spaced to allow a central door behind them. There could hardly be a clearer evidence of a preference for literary tradition over actual observation: for Vitruvius had stated that the central columns of eight should stand further apart to allow for a door, and Fischer followed this although no such allowance was made in the Parthenon. In terms of accuracy, Fischer's illustrations were no better than those of Cyriac, who was hampered only by lack of ability, and a regression from the crude sketches of Spon and Wheler. Stuart and Revett by contrast represented a real step forward.

It was in the tradition of the explorers as much as the scholars that the architects James Stuart and Nicholas Revett began their pilgrimage to Athens in 1749. There was however one circumstance which ensured that the results of their expedition were dramatically different from the minimal public repercussions of that of Spon or Wheler, or even from the acquisitive expeditions mounted by the nobility of England and the royalty of France. This was the existence of the Society of Dilettanti.

The Society of Dilettanti was founded in London, probably in 1734, as a dining club for aristocrats who had visited Italy: the first meeting of which minutes were kept was that of 6 March 1736. In May of that year it had forty-six members, of whom the leading spirit was a notorious rake, then aged twenty-eight, Sir Francis Dashwood. The acid tongue of Lady Mary Wortley Montagu had commented disparagingly on the characteristic pursuits of these self-styled lovers of the arts during their Grand Tour in Rome: they consisted, she alleged, almost entirely of gaming, drinking, gambling and keeping women; and even as late as 1783 Horace Walpole (who by this time had little love for antiquity or its admirers) could remark that 'the nominal qualification is having been in Italy, and the real one, being drunk; and the two chiefs are Middlesex and Dashwood, who were seldom sober the whole time they were in Italy.'[8]

Despite this perhaps unpromising start, the Society of Dilettanti did aspire to some measure of seriousness, recalling in its title the 'Society of Virtuosi' of 1689, a society of lovers or professors of the arts. The term virtuoso, by the 1730s largely outmoded, as were those it described, was used to denote the man of wide-ranging curiosity and intellect. It had been superseded by 'dilettante', which was in many ways its converse – a figure with a gentlemanly acquaintance with and appreciation of the forms of art as well as intercourse, but without the fanatic learning of a Peiresc or a Selden.

Their first few schemes to make some kind of cultural impact were all abortive. Starting with a plan to raise money by lottery to build a bridge at Westminster (1736), they turned seven years later to the more modest project of getting a permanent room for the Society in Cavendish Square. In 1742 they had a go at promoting Italian opera, and in 1748/9 tried their hand at founding an Academy of Arts. Luckily for their morale, this group of enthusiasts without a cause had by this time been presented by Fortune with a project worthy of their support, which would set the course of their activities for nearly a century.

James Stuart (1713–88), whose work was to earn him the sobriquet of Athenian Stuart, was born in London, the son of a Scottish sailor. A natural aptitude for drawing had helped to support his mother, brother and two sisters from an early age. He worked for some years as assistant to a fan painter named Louis Goupy, who had accompanied Lord Burlington on his first visit to Italy. It may have been he who inspired Stuart's eagerness to visit Rome. At all events, the young James set out on foot for the great city in 1742: he became a connoisseur of pictures, learnt the craft of engraving, and practised it on a newly discovered obelisk.

In Rome he met Nicholas Revett (1720–1804), who was studying painting. It was in April 1748, during a visit to Naples with Matthew Brettingham and Gavin Hamilton, both of whom dealt in antiquities, that the two men formed a plan to produce a scholarly record of the buildings of ancient Greece, similar to Antoine Desgodetz' *Edifices antiques de Rome* of 1682.

In their proposal of 1748 they explained their aims:

Athens, the mother of elegance and politeness, whose magnificence scarce yielded to that of Rome, and who for the beauties of a correct style must be allowed to surpass her, as much as an original excels a copy, has been almost completely neglected, and unless exact drawings from them be speedily made, all her beauteous fabricks, her temples, her theatres, her palaces will drop into oblivion, and Posterity will have to reproach us.

By January 1749 the plan was well advanced. Their work, in three volumes, was to comprise fifty-three views, a volume of plans, elevations and architectural details, and sixty-seven plates of sculpture. But now the financial question began to impose itself.

They were fortunate in obtaining the support of two members of the Society of Dilettanti living in Venice; Sir James Gray, the British Resident, and Joseph Smith, the British Consul. Their election to the Society in 1751 made them the first members drawn from the artistic professions. Besides the scholarly aim of recording buildings, and the artistic one of enhancing the architectural repertoire, part of the attraction was no doubt the very difficulty of the journey.[9]

In mid-1750 Stuart and Revett had reached Venice, where they were obliged to wait until January 1751 for a ship that would carry them to Greece. To fill in the time they made a shorter excursion to Pola in Dalmatia, where they drew the ancient Roman buildings which are included in Volume IV of the *Antiquities of Athens*. In March 1751 they reached Piraeus, where they immediately set about their task. They 'determined to avoid haste and system, those most dangerous enemies to accuracy and fidelity.' They accordingly spent almost two years in Athens, until March 1753 (contrasting this long stay proudly with Spon and Wheler's short seventeen or eighteen February days), returning briefly between June and September 1753. Of their day-to-day pursuits we know little. The travellers of the eighteenth century have not left any of those vivid and highly personal accounts that make their predecessors of a century earlier such a delight to study. A new sense of responsibility to their subject and its audience ensured that all their energy went into completing their appointed task with diligence and accuracy.

The four volumes of the *Antiquities of Athens*, with the supplement of 1830 (only the first volume was published in Stuart's lifetime) are beautiful books to look at, though somewhat of a trial if one has to lift them too frequently: perusal of all four really requires an empty table about fifteen feet long. They are not superior in beauty to the folios of illustrations of Greek architectural remains published shortly before by the Frenchman J. D. Le Roy and the Englishman Richard Dalton; but in accuracy they far excel them. [10]

The *Antiquities of Athens* in fact set new standards of accuracy in architectural drawing. Stuart and Revett could set themselves no humbler aim, in view of the stated purpose of the work:

The ruined edifices of Rome have for many years engaged the attention of those who apply themselves to the study of architecture; and have generally been considered as the models and standard of regular and ornamental building. Many representations of them drawn and engraved by skilful artists have been published, by which means the study of the art has been everywhere greatly facilitated, and the general practice of it improved and promoted . . . But although the world is enriched with collections of this sort already published, we thought it would be a work not unacceptable to lovers of architecture, if we added to those collections, some examples drawn from the antiquities of Greece.

The achievement of Stuart and Revett was more than this. They provided a scholarly account of all the main buildings of ancient Athens (as well as, in Volumes 3 and 5, some outside Athens: Volume 4 was devoted to Pola in Dalmatia). Revett did the measurements; Stuart drew and painted the monuments. Surprisingly, perhaps, they did not begin their publication with what we would regard as the major monuments of classical Athens: the Parthenon, the Theseion, the Temple of Olympian Zeus. Volume I was devoted to the Doric portico which they were the first rightly to identify as the entrance to the Roman agora; the Ionic Temple on the Ilissus, now altogether vanished; the 'Tower of the Winds'; the 'Lantern of Demosthenes' and the Library of Hadrian.

In the advertisement to the second volume, written in 1787, Stuart gave his reasons for this rather odd choice of edifices:

When Mr Revett and I returned from Athens, and received subscriptions for our first volume, uncertain whether we should be encouraged to proceed farther with this work, we selected such buildings for our proposed publication, as would exhibit specimens of the several kinds of columns in use among the ancient Greeks; that, if, contrary to our wishes, nothing more should be demanded of us concerning Athens, those who honoured us with their subscriptions to that volume, might find in it something interesting on the different Grecian modes of decorating buildings.

The words reflect Stuart's habitual diffidence; they indicate an excessive modesty in concentrating on ornament rather than any more fundamental architectural principles. In fact his own works by no means depend solely on ornament for their effect; but the prevailing taste in England persisted in seeing Grecian work as mainly decorative, more suitable for garden ornaments than for major buildings.[11]

Stuart and Revett faced considerable difficulties in their project of producing faithful drawings of the monuments. For example, the ground around the Tower of the Winds, more properly known as the Tower of Andronicus Cyrrhestes, an astronomer who had erected it in the first century BC as a sundial, water-clock and weathervane, had risen some fifteen or sixteen feet since antiquity, though on the north-east it had been lowered to permit continued use of the entrance, as the building was now used as a Turkish 'chapel' or Tekke (a Dervish convent), and regular performances of the famous dance of the whirling dervishes were given there, which have been described by several of the nineteenth-century travellers. One of the inhabitants obligingly pulled down his house to enable them to get a better view of the building, and they also obtained permission to break up the floor, from which they removed 2,700 cubic feet of earth before revealing the original marble pavement. It was on the illustration of this building, and of the choragic monument of Lysicrates (Lantern of Demosthenes) that they lavished their fullest care.

The latter building had been erected by Lysicrates in 334 BC as a memorial of his funding a chorus at one year's dramatic festival. The frieze accordingly illustrated a scene from the

legends of Dionysus, the god of tragedy – how he had been
once captured by pirates, but escaped, turned on them in the
form of a lion and frightened them overboard where they were
turned into dolphins:

> . . . all, for fear,
> Crowd to the stern, about the monster there,
> Whose mind he still kept dauntless and sincere,
> But on the captain rush'd and ramp'd, with force
> So rude and sudden, that his main recourse
> Was to the main-sea straight: and after him
> Leapt all his mates, as trusting to their swim
> To fly foul death; but so found what they fled,
> Being all to dolphins metamorphosed. [12]

A lovely cup by Exekias in Munich also shows the scene, a
vine sprouting from the wine-god's navel as he reclines at ease
in the now vacant boat.

The monument was now built into the walls of the
Capuchin monastery. In later years it was to be the home of the
French consul Fauvel, friend and cicerone to so many
archaeologically-minded travellers of the Napoleonic era.
Byron (and later the novelist John Galt) lived in it for a period.
Stuart's drawing shows the monument tucked in a corner of
the monks' kitchen garden. Hardly easy of access, Stuart and
Revett lavished on it all their care. It had long since been
broken into by hopeful treasure hunters, and the cupola, as
well as the tripod which had once topped the structure, had to
be restored from Vitruvius' description. As we shall see, it
became for a season one of the most famous, or notorious, of
Athenian buildings in England.

Stuart and Revett's greatest controversial energies were
reserved for their discussion of the Stoa now identified as the
Library of Hadrian. This had been taken by Spon and Wheler
for Hadrian's stoa of 120 columns of Phrygian marble mentioned by Pausanias. Stuart and Revett pointed out that the
marble was not Phrygian but Pentelic. Le Roy took it for the
Pantheon of Hadrian, and attached to it a description actually
suiting the Temple of Olympian Zeus (which was often called
the Palace of Hadrian). This large building, still relatively
intact, was now the residence of the voyvode of Athens. The
companions' own theory was that this was the Stoa Poikile or
Painted Portico of the fifth century BC. Though the style was

of the wrong period, the siting was not far off. In fact nothing remains of the Stoa Poikile above ground.

The publication of Volume I of the *Antiquities of Athens* in 1762 made an impact on the English scene in the most literal sense. It was dedicated to George III, whose accession in 1760 had aroused high hopes among lovers of the arts for new patronage for artists. Surely Stuart and Revett had an eye to possible commissions in making this dedication. But in the end Stuart had to content himself with more scattered commissions – yet they were not without impact. Although the volume covered only five buildings, within months of its appearance buildings began to spring up all over England, not only at the hands of Stuart, which either were close copies of Athenian buildings or made scrupulous use of motifs from those buildings. Among Stuart's own commissions were the Doric temples at Hagley Park (1758–9) and Shugborough (1764), both closely modelled on the Theseion; the 'Arch of Hadrian' (also 1764) and the 'Lysicrates Monument' (1770), both at Shugborough; and 15 St James' Square, London, whose columns were copies of those of the Erechtheion. In addition, details of his Hospital at Greenwich reproduced the capitals and entablature of the Erechtheion.

These works were soon followed by Revett's New St Lawrence Church at Ayot St Lawrence (1778–9), after the Temple of Apollo at Delos; James Wyatt's Radcliffe Observatory at Oxford (1773–94), a copy of the Tower of the Winds; and in 1804, by Wilkins, Grange Park in Hampshire, modelled on the Theseion with details borrowed from the Monument of Thrasyllus. Inwood's St Pancras has been mentioned, and his All Saints Camden (1822) is closely similar in inspiration.

Echoes of these few buildings became the leitmotif of much Grecising architecture of the next seventy years, spreading also to Ireland where St Stephen's, Mount Street, Dublin, sported copies of both the Lantern of Demosthenes and the Tower of the Winds.[13] The culmination was the virtuoso display of Cockerell's and Playfair's assemblage of monuments on Calton Hill in Edinburgh.

It is at least curious that neither Stuart nor Revett, unlike their successors, troubled (or dared?) to model himself on the outstanding grandeur of the Parthenon, preferring by and large the more gracious Ionic lines of later work.

Another tangible influence was on American architecture, where the same few buildings spawned a numerous progeny over the next sixty years. President Thomas Jefferson owned a copy of the *Antiquities*, though it made little impact on the style of his own architectural designs, which stuck to the Adam formulae. A very different matter was Benjamin H. Latrobe, a Yorkshireman with an American mother, who emigrated to America in 1796 after suffering bankruptcy in his English practice. Armed with good introductions, he soon got a commission for the Bank of Pennsylvania building in Philadelphia, which he executed in Erechtheion Ionic. His proficiency in the Grecian style has earned him the title of the American Soane: he wrote to Thomas Jefferson, 'My principles of good taste are rigid in Grecian architecture. I am a bigoted Greek in the condemnation of the Roman architecture of Baalbec, Palmyra and Spalatro.' His most elaborate commission, for the interior (1827) of the Capitol, exhibits Paestum Doric in the Supreme Court, fifth-century Ionic in the Senate Chamber and Lobby, the Corinthian of the Lysicrates Monument in the Hall of Representatives, and that of the Tower of the Winds at the Library entrance. But his American audience are perhaps fondest of his special invention, the tobacco and corn-cob capitals in the vestibule and stairs.

The Greek Revival took some bizarre forms in the works of Latrobe's followers, for example Thomas Cole's Ohio State Capitol (1838–61), a strange combination of Greek forms which recalls the architectural conglomerations of his series of paintings, *The Progress of Empire*. The culmination may be the Tennessee State Capitol (1845–59) of Latrobe's pupil William Strickland, where a double-ended octastyle temple is flanked on either side with hexastyle colonnades in the Ionic order of the Erechtheion, while the whole thing is topped off by a close copy of Stuart and Revett's reconstruction of the Lysicrates Monument – truly an all-or-nothing essay in Grecian Architecture! (The Merchant's Exchange in Philadelphia is also topped with the Lysicrates Monument.)

But both English and American taste had for the time being to content themselves with the fare offered in Volume I alone. This seems to have been quite enough to shock certain members of the architectural public. The original and unusually scholarly presentation of the *Antiquities of Athens* ensured that Stuart and Revett's account, and by implication their proposals, hit the architectural public as the project of two *enfants terribles*. One of the strongest opponents of the new style of architecture was the Architect of the Royal Works and first treasurer of the Royal Academy, Sir William Chambers. Though he is remembered as a Palladian architect, his Palladianism was far from pure, and was infected by the taste for chinoiserie which became evident in his designs for the various buildings of Kew Gardens. Horace Walpole's friend William Mason (in 1773) despaired of his controlling his extravagances:

> No! let Barbaric glories feast his eyes,
> August Pagodas round his Palace rise,
> And finish'd Richmond open to his view,
> A work to wonder at, perhaps a Kew.

He was hardly the man to take other architects to task for unconventionality, yet his notes for the second edition of his *Treatise of Civil Architecture* (1759) – published in modified form only in the third edition – are loud in sarcastic complaint:

It hath afforded occasion of laughter to every intelligent architect to see with what pomp the Grecian antiquities have lately been ushered into the world and what encomiums have been lavished upon things that in reality deserve little or no notice . . . A few remarks upon some of these celebrated trifles may here be permitted; they are not made with any invidious designs but merely to set them in a proper light, and with an intent to undeceive such as have been led astray by fine words and elegant publications . . . the celebrated Lantern of Demosthenes or Choragic Monument of Lysicrates or the Temple of Hercules with all its other names is in reality not quite so large as one of the sentry boxes in Portman Square: its form and proportions resemble those of a silver tankard excepting that the handle is wanting. Messrs Steward and Ryvet have given twenty six plates of this edifice . . . The celebrated Temple of the Winds or Tower of Andronicus Cyrrhestes to vulgar eyes resembles exactly one of the dove houses usually erected on Gentlemen's estates in the country of England, excepting that the roof is somewhat flatter and there is no turret for the pigeons to creep in and fly out at, but we are assured that a more nice observer will be greater pleased with its elegance and extraordinary beauty . . . What little magnificence the Grecians then displayed in their structures was confined to public buildings which were chiefly temples in which there appears to have been nothing very surprising either for dimensions or ingenuity of contrivance.[14]

Opposition from such a quarter could only retard the development of the Greek Revival. The Palladian tradition of architects like Chambers, and the Adam style, as well as the already incipient Gothic taste, all held their own alongside Grecianism for many decades. The new Grecian style also came in for some gentle mockery, for example from William Hogarth, who in 1761 produced a caricature of 'the five orders of PERRIWIGS . . . measured architectonically . . . taken from the statues, bustos and baso-relievos of Athens, Palmira, Balbec and Rome'. Stuart kept a copy of this engraving pasted on his firescreen, and always showed it to his visitors.

A further drawback to the general acceptance of the style was no doubt the price of the volume. John Flaxman could not afford to buy a copy until 1796, though, as David Watkin observes, his chill linear style reflected the emphasis on form praised in Greek art by Winckelmann, and so obviously emulated by Flaxman in his own designs.

It seems reasonable to mention at this point the remaining volumes of the *Antiquities of Athens*; Volume II was not published until 1788 (though dated 1787) after considerable wrangling only concluded by Stuart's death. Volume III only came out in 1794, some time after the further journeys sponsored by the Society to even more exotic locations.

Volume II illustrated the Parthenon, with thirty plates including the whole frieze; the pediments were still conceived to contain portraits of Hadrian and Sabina, but the heads were now thought to be replacements of Phidian originals. It also illustrated the Erechtheion (which they called the Temple of Minerva Polias and Pandrosus, and recalled the traditional origin of the distinctive Caryatids that supported the porch: according to Vitruvius, these were intended to recall female prisoners taken in war, just as the Persian Stoa at Sparta was decorated with Caryatids in the form of Persians). The other monuments included were the 'Theatre of Bacchus' (actually the Odeion of Herodes Atticus); the Choragic Monument of Thrasyllus; and the Propylaea.

Volume III was prepared for publication by Willey Reveley, at the request of Mrs Stuart, and many of the chapters are little more than an ordering of Stuart's loose notes. Reveley took the opportunity in his preface to castigate Sir William Chambers, whose views had now been made public in the third edition of his *Treatise* (1791), for his 'observations which have so little foundation in real facts, or in just taste, as must detract greatly from his weight and consequence as an author'. Hardly too stern a judgement in the light of posterity, if he could go so far as to think Gibbs' St Martin-in-the-Fields actually superior to the Parthenon!

The Antiquities of Ionia

> High towers, fair temples, goodly theatres,
> Strong walls, rich porches, princely palaces,
> Large streets, brave houses, sacred sepulchres,
> Sure gates, sweet gardens, stately galleries,
> Wrought with fair pillars and fine imageries;
> All those (O pity!) now are turned to dust
> And overgrown with black oblivion's rust.
> (Edmund Spenser, *The Ruins of Time*)

The Society of Dilettanti at least had the funds to continue to invest in further journeys. One of its members, Richard Dawkins, had died in 1759 leaving £500 to the Society, a sum which was used to finance an expedition to Asia Minor. The travellers this time were Richard Chandler (1738–1810), who had already distinguished himself by editing afresh the Arundel Marbles (*Marmora Oxoniensia* 1763), Nicholas Revett and William Pars (1742–82). Their brief included the instruction 'to keep a regular journal, and hold a constant correspondence with the Society'. For those who stayed at home, one of the chief purposes of these expeditions was to provide regular bulletins of exotic and sometimes hair-raising travellers' tales to enliven their meetings.

Chandler was provided with £200 for travel expenses, and credits of £800 per annum. They were to base themselves at Smyrna and make excursions from there. With hindsight, in the preface to the *Ionian Antiquities*, the Society was able to give the rationale behind the new expedition:

The Society directed them to give a specimen of their labours out of what they had found most worthy of observation in Ionia; a country in many respects curious, and perhaps, after Attica, the most deserv-

ing the attentions of a classical traveller . . . The knowledge of
Nature was first taught in the Ionic school: and as geometry,
astronomy, and other branches of the mathematics, were cultivated
here sooner than in other parts of Greece, it is not extraordinary that
the first Greek navigators, who passed the Pillars of Hercules, and
extended their commerce to the Ocean, should have been Ionians.
Here history had its birth; . . . the first writer who reduced the
knowledge of medicine or the means of preserving health, to an art,
was of this neighbourhood; and here the father of poetry produced a
standard for composition, which no age or country have dared to
depart from, or have been able to surpass. But Architecture belongs
more particularly to this country than to any other; and of the three
Greek Orders it seems justly entitled to the honour of having
invented the two first, though one of them only bears its name; for
though the temple of Juno at Argos suggested the general idea of
what was after called the Doric, its proportions were first established
here. As to the other arts which depend on design, they have
flourished nowhere more than in Ionia . . . Among the remains of
antiquity which have hitherto escaped the injuries of time, there are
none in which our curiosity is more interested than the ruins of those
buildings which were distinguished by Vitruvius and other ancient
writers, for their elegance and magnificence. . . . However mutilated and decayed these buildings now are, yet surely every fragment
is valuable, which preserves, in some degree, the ideas of symmetry
and proportion which prevailed at that happy period of taste.

Ionia was indeed a new venture for the Society, and for the
learned traveller presented an even more melancholy spectacle
than Greece proper. 'The provinces of the East', wrote Gibbon
at about this time, 'present the contrast of Roman magnificence with Turkish barbarism. The ruins of antiquity scattered
over uncultivated fields, and ascribed by ignorance to the
power of magic, scarcely afford a shelter to the oppressed
peasant or wandering Arab.'

The expedition departed for this Greek and Roman waste-
land on 9 June 1764. By 11 September they had taken up their
quarters with the consul at Smyrna. They had travelled by
way of Sigeum, where they had seen the inscription of Phanodikos observed by Lady Mary Wortley Montagu and copied
by Edmund Chishull. The Antiochus decree had already been
purchased by Edward Wortley Montagu in 1718 and removed
to Cambridge. They copied the former with its specimen of
Greek writing 'antiquated above two thousand years ago',
while regretting that it 'should be suffered to lie so neglected

and exposed. Above half a century has elapsed since it was first discovered, and it still remains in the open air, a seat for the Greeks, destitute of a patron to rescue it from barbarism, and obtain its removal into the safer custody of some private museum, or, which is rather to be desired, some public repository.'

From Smyrna their itinerary included sites on the whole much less frequented by Western travellers than Sigeum seems to have become. They visited all the major sites, though they avoided going as far south as Cnidus and Halicarnassus. The cities they studied are a litany which evokes a millennium of civilisation: Didyma, Miletus, Clazomenae, Erythrae, Teos, Priene, Tralles, Laodicea, Sardis, Philadelphia and Magnesia. No romance for them, as for George Wheler (see Chapter 4), in the 'Seven Churches of Asia': it is the classical aspect of the ruins that interests them.

At Magnesia the main relic was the temple of Artemis Leukophryene, 'the white-browed', which 'was larger than any in Asia, except the two at Ephesus and at Branchidae [Didyma]. It excelled the former in elegance and in the fitting up of the cell, but was inferior in the number of offerings. It was a pseudo-dipteros, and had eight columns in front and fifteen on the sides, counting the angular columns. The order was Ionic; and the architect the celebrated Hermogenes, who invented that species. He was a native of Alabanda; and a treatise on the fabric was once extant, written by him.'

This is perhaps sufficient of Chandler's prosing, which sets the tone for most of the book. At Didyma however, he lets enthusiasm briefly show, pronouncing it 'impossible perhaps to conceive a greater beauty and majesty of ruin. . . . A view of part of the heap, with plates of the architecture of this glorious edifice, has been engraved and published, with its history, at the expense of the Society of Dilettanti.'

How different is the tone from that of Theodore Lascaris' lament over the ruins of Pergamum three centuries before. Didyma, the oracular seat administered by the clan of the Branchidae, was Apollo's latest home. In the fifth century Xerxes had taken the bronze statue of the god to adorn his capital at Ecbatana; two centuries later King Seleucus returned it. He also rebuilt the whole site. Perhaps he too was touched by its majesty. The Emperor Trajan had built a road from

Miletus to Didyma, and the Emperor Julian had given a last lease of life to the banal but liquid flow of its oracles, until Theodosius' edict of 385 against extispicy and other forms of pagan prophecy doomed it for ever. It is hard to be very impressed by the pronouncements that survived, and are dutifully recorded by Chandler in *Ionian Antiquities* (43 ff).

They do however bring to life the day-to-day affairs of a great international sanctuary in a way the grand sagas of Herodotus never do. No Croesus here, but a diffident priest who wants to know whether he may erect a dedication to Kore the Saviour: 'pronounce then, Apollo, Sun of Didyma, if you order me to erect beside the altar of fruit-bearing Demeter an altar to her daughter.' Or here again is the god sonorously enacting the establishment of rites for Demeter, the great mother goddess of Asia Minor, and her daughter:

> All the mortal earthly race of men
> Must honour her who, sending the fruits of the barley on the
>   earth,
> Put an end to the savage, beast-eating ways of men,
> When, dwelling under the open roof of the mountains,
> They sated their hunger with raw meat,
> Even the dwellers on Nile where the long reeds grow:
> Do then holy and noble rites to them,
> The rituals of Deo and the daughter of Deo.

But most of the inscriptions are the lists and dedications of the priests and prophets of Apollo, or of the treasures of King Seleucus (which Cyriac had copied in 1446).[15] Didyma stands now, quiet yet magnificent, where the nervous visitors once tiptoed down the dark angled corridors to the central place of oracles. It is uncommonly well preserved, as can be seen now that it has been uncovered from the debris of earthquake and the centuries. A ruin but a speaking one, where less perhaps than elsewhere 'echoes list to silence now Where gods told lies of old.'

The account of the expedition to Asia Minor supersedes that of all previous travellers, though some of their site identifications were incorrect. They stayed a year at Smyrna, but on 20 August 1765 they were forced to leave by the rapidly approaching plague. The pictures and information they sent home so pleased the Society that they sent a further £500 to finance a roundabout return through the Morea and Magna Graecia.

In the course of nine months at Athens, they visited the sites of Attica, discussed the 'dark transactions of the once impenetrable' rite of Demeter at Eleusis, stayed in a roofless shed in Megara, lunched off samphire gathered from the Scironian rocks, spent a night trying unsuccessfully to land on Salamis, and were scared by a Barbary corsair off Aegina. At Epidaurus, after leaving Attica, they found some fragments, but seem to have lost heart for serious study; at Delphi they could only view inscriptions already copied by Wood. Resources were running low for topographising and study of the traditional kind. But they enlivened the last stretch of the route to Patras by detailed topographical observations:

It is matter of regret, that travellers too commonly hasten along in the beaten road, uninformed of the objects on the way; when, by consulting and following those invaluable guides [Strabo and Pausanias], they might increase their own pleasure, and at the same time greatly advance the general knowledge of ancient geography.

Chandler's words were to be put into effect, with a vengeance, within fifty years of his writing them.

On 1 September they departed from Zante for England, and on 2 December Chandler was able to hand over to his patrons his finds, drawings, copies and marbles, including 'a horse's head and bust of a man of exquisite workmanship' from the Parthenon at Athens. (This became the property of the Society, who in May 1738 gave Flaxman permission to model a bas-relief from it.)

Now began the agonies of publication. The Society decreed on 7 March 1767 that 'at least 150 copies of the first specimen of the intended work be engraved, and printed, for the use of the society.' Another two years passed before a selection of the material was published in the *Ionian Antiquities* of 1769. This first volume was devoted to illustrations of the temples at Teos, Priene and Didyma. The costs – £373 for the copper plates, among other items – were in the end met by Revett and Pars.

The volume represented another 'first' for the Society, for it was the first detailed publication of several major monuments from Ionia. The Temple of Athena Polias at Priene had in fact never been mentioned in print, except by Wheler. The inscriptions of Teos had all been published by Chishull, but the engraving of the Temple of Bacchus was a new contribution. They paid little attention to sites that had already been described, such as Ephesus and Miletus, but devoted several plates to Chandler's beloved Didyma.

Nonetheless, the publication had less effect on the English scene than its predecessor. Apparently the only building directly influenced by the new discoveries was Revett's portico (1771) at Despencer Park, West Wycombe, which imitated the order of the Temple of Bacchus at Teos. (The owner of the ground, Lord Despencer, was the erstwhile Sir Francis Dashwood of the Dilettanti – one of the sponsors of the original expedition.)

The reaction of Sir William Chambers could have been predicted, though he confined it to his private correspondence. He wrote to Charlemont:

The dilettanti book is published, and a cursed book it is, between friends, being composed of some of the worst architecture I ever saw; there is a degree of madness in sending people abroad to fetch home such stuff.[16]

Not all were so unsympathetic. It must be admitted however, that even the learned world betrayed little interest in these new publications. Although scholars in Germany were beginning to be aware of the value of archaeological evidence in interpreting literature, in England a rigorously philological tradition reigned supreme.

In 1774 Chandler published the inscriptions he had collected on the expedition, and in 1775 his *Travels in Asia Minor*, followed in 1776 by the *Travels in Greece*. The 1769 volume was dedicated to the Society, who awarded him a present of twenty-five guineas, and followed that with a similar gift for each of the following volumes. The second volume was not published until 1797, and one can find no other reason than dilettantish dilatoriness for the extraordinary delay.

The early years of the nineteenth century were not Grecian years; they were the years of the picturesque, and the years of Lord Elgin. In the face of these new forces the Dilettanti could only seem behind the times – and, as we shall see, one of them at least was rash enough to show it.

CHAPTER SEVEN

The Picturesque and the Topographers

Oh! where Dodona! is thine aged grove,
Prophetic fount, and oracle divine?
What valley echo'd the response of Jove?
What trace remaineth of the Thunderer's shrine?
All, all forgotten . . .

(Byron, *Childe Harold* II, 53)

At the end of the eighteenth century artists and aestheticians in Europe, and especially in England, started to look at landscape in a new way. Instead of the formality of the landscape garden, the explicit moral programme of the classical landscape, they began to admire something much more subtle – the picturesque. The picturesque is easier to recognise than to define, but that did not inhibit theorists from attempting a definition. The first in England was William Gilpin's *Observations on the River Wye . . . relative chiefly to picturesque beauty; made in 1770*. This was published in 1782, and Gilpin's aim was to describe and illustrate 'that kind of beauty which would look well in a picture'.

In the same year there appeared in Paris a magnificent folio volume, the *Voyage Pittoresque de la Grèce* by Comte Marie-Gabriel-Florent-Auguste de Choiseul-Gouffier (1752–1817). This last scion of a long line of savants to travel in Greece had learnt his enthusiasm not from the scholarly austerities of the Comte de Caylus or the Abbé Montfaucon, but from the picaresque romance of the Abbé Barthélémy, the *Voyage of the Young Anacharsis* (1788). This fanciful picture of life in classical

Greece became immensely popular in France and England. It combined the rococo inspiration of Fénélon's *Télémaque* with pretensions to inform on topography, political and social affairs, and history 'seen from the inside'. It was copiously illustrated with maps by Barbié du Bocage, which were compiled from a mixture of Ptolemy and other ancient sources with contemporary travellers' accounts and portolan charts.

Choiseul-Gouffier had made his voyage to the Levant in 1776. His wealth enabled him to employ numerous draughtsmen and collectors of antiquities, among them the young Louis-Sébastien Fauvel (see Chapter 8), the engineer Foucherot and the painter J. B. Hilair. It was the work of these men, interspersed with some scenes from Choiseul-Gouffier's own hand, that appeared in 1782 in the count's own name as the *Voyage Pittoresque de la Grèce*.

In producing such a publication, and in his methods, Choiseul-Gouffier had precedents. In 1749 the young painter Richard Dalton had travelled with Lord Charlemont to Greece and Turkey as his artistic amanuensis. It seems that they quarrelled: for Charlemont's diary was never published, though it might have been expected to appear, adorned by Dalton's hand. In fact Dalton published his views independently a few years later (see above, p 123). They are of importance especially for including the first views made of Cnidus and of the sculptures at Halicarnassus. Dalton's work, despite its errors, represented an advance over the fanciful landscape-engineering of Le Roy, who would never leave a monument on a mountain if he could move it to the beach, never represent a group of two buildings if a third could be imported with pictorial advantage. Le Roy's works were useless to the scholar (above, ibid); Dalton's were of some value. Choiseul-Gouffier's book was the acme of a tradition that was to influence artists and topographers for another half century.

The man's career is interesting in itself. His knowledge of the Levant procured him the post of ambassador at Constantinople, which he held from 1784 to 1792. He was far from popular, either with his foreign colleagues or with the Turkish court. Baron Dedem de Gelder, the son of the Dutch ambassador, has left a biting account of him:

M de Choiseul has all the qualities and the faults of a courtier. His taste for the arts limited itself to the desire for reputation; his works belonged to him because he had paid for them. He was surrounded by distinguished scholars and artists, who edited – and often provided – his Memoirs. His drawings were corrected by Fauvel [whom he had sent to Athens as his artistic representative], Heller and Kaufer [a cartographer], and he put his own name on them. Thoroughly lazy and negligent, travelling only to get the reputation of a famous traveller, but looking only superficially, he left to his companions the painstaking labours, and, when he had left them no time to study on the spot, his imagination supplied the lacunae. MM. Fauvel, Kauffer and Cassas [a painter and architect] have told me the most entertaining anecdotes on this subject. The story of the discovery of the tomb [sic] Ø Achilles and Patroclus, and of the sources of the Scamander, has by certain details authorised several European scholars to pour ridicule on the most interesting facts, which are owed, if not to the learning of M de Choiseul, at least to the direction he gave his artists, and still more to the money which he spent on excavations, on presents to the Turkish authorities, on freight and the many other expenses necessary to such an enterprise.[1]

This remarkably hostile account could perhaps be applied, if one wished, to many patrons of archaeological learning. It obscures the tangible achievement of Choiseul-Gouffier as a patron and connoisseur. His collection of marbles was large and valuable, and filled most of the ambassador's palace at Constantinople, which had housed so many such collections before on their way from Ottoman soil to the museums of France or oblivion.

When the Revolution came the Count was, of course, out of a job. He fled to Russia in 1792; his antiquities remained in Turkey, where twenty-five of fifty-one cases were destroyed in the fire of Smyrna in 1797. He was however able to return in 1802 to Napoleon's Paris, where he built a mansion, Idalie, (modelled on the buildings of Athens and Palmyra) on the Champs Elysées, to house the remains of his collection. He also completed the publication of his *Voyage*. Thus the last of the noble connoisseurs of France maintained his independence even into the years of Napoleon, who was to transform the style of artistic collecting in Europe in no uncertain manner. Choiseul-Gouffier died in 1817; and on 20 July 1818 the magnificent Hotel de Marboeuf, *dit* Idalie, echoed to the auctioneer's hammer as lot after lot (there were 469 in all) of the painfully acquired collection – busts, inscriptions, bronzes, copies, casts, paintings (including thirty watercolours by Fauvel) and drawings – were knocked down to private buyers or to the great Museum of the Louvre.

The fruits of the count's labours and expenditure were better presented in the two volumes of his *Voyage*. In the preface he speaks of his youthful passion to see Greece, and to pace its sites, Homer and Herodotus in hand; but wishes on reflection that he had visited the country in greater maturity, when reflection might temper sentiment. Reflection however has only hardened his indignation at Greece's slavish state, her subjection to the 'stupid Musulman', and he is sure that certain of the Greeks – at least the Albanians and the Maniotes – could still recall the virtues of their ancestors and throw off the Turkish yoke. (Furthermore, a new state of Greece would enfeeble Turkey and contribute to the stability of Europe.)

The *Voyage Pittoresque* has to be seen then, not merely as the gorgeous folio of a dilettante, but as an attempt – from the title vignette of Greece in chains among the tombs of the heroes, onwards – to arouse European sympathy, concern and admiration for the land of Greece as it then subsisted. He praises the charm and hospitality of the Greek people, which is known to all who have visited the country, and who will echo his call, 'Exoriare aliquis', 'let someone arise'.

A comparatively small number of plates is devoted to classical scenes, elevations and plans of buildings. The Picturesque tour is what it says. Not for him the tracing and deciphering of obscure and fragmentary inscriptions, the puzzling over topographical detail, the engagement with Strabo and Pausanias on the ground; not even the romance of the past that is to characterise the effusions of Chateaubriand. His is an aesthete's Greece. Not consciously, perhaps, he is the first representative of a new tone in the enthusiasm for Greece. The most striking characteristic of the generation that followed the publication of the third volume of the *Antiquities of Athens* was the interest in Greek topography. Once again the pendulum of scholarly interest swings far – away from the devoted adoption of Greek detail for purposes defined by English taste, and towards a disinterested appreciation of the Greek scene in both its aesthetic and its historical aspects.

Twelve years after the publication of the *Voyage Pittoresque*, the question of the picturesque became a matter of violent controversy in England. Both opposing views were defined in terms of the relation of the picturesque to classical landscape. Claude, was, after all, the model and founding father of all picturesque painters.[2] The two protagonists were Richard Payne Knight and Uvedale Price, and both published works on the subject in 1794. Knight's was entitled *Landscape: a didactic poem*, and Price's essay was 'On the Picturesque'. The poet Shelley later remarked that the whole controversy between them was no more than two men 'snarling at each other like two ill-trained beagles'.[3] Yet there was a point at issue. Though both might agree that the word picturesque 'is applied to every object, and every kind of scenery, which has been or might be represented with good effect in painting', they disagreed about the causes of our pleasure in the picturesque. While Price saw it as proceeding from a purely aesthetic response to nature, the product of intrinsic appreciation of beauty of line and colour, Knight argued that scenes acquired their picturesque quality largely from their intellectual associations.

The point is perhaps not easy to grasp in the abstract. Byron encapsulated it concretely and vividly in a letter to John Murray of March 1821:

Am I to be told that the 'Nature' of Attica would be more poetical without the 'Art' of the Acropolis? of the Temple of Theseus? and of the still all Greek and glorious monuments of her exquisitely artificial genius? Ask the traveller what strikes him as most poetical, the Parthenon, or the rock on which it stands? The columns of Cape Colonna or the Cape itself? the rock at the foot of it, or the recollection that Falconer's ship was bulged thereon?[4]

Why was the picturesque so intimately connected with the scenery of Greece? There is to begin with a simple historical answer. It was out of the traditional preoccupations of the young man on the Grand Tour – with landscape, history and antiquities – that the taste for the picturesque was born. But suddenly came the Napoleonic Wars. Most of Western Europe was now effectively inaccessible to Englishmen, who ran the risk of internment (like Edward Dodwell or Lord Elgin), or worse, at the hands of the French. New pastures had to be found for those artistic and lettered souls. Greece was the next step across the Mediterranean, and one hallowed already by the legends absorbed at school.

From an artist's point of view, the most significant recent visit had been that of Stuart and Revett (see Chapter 6). One of Stuart's earliest commissions thereafter had been to decorate the park at Shugborough in Staffordshire (1760–5) with a series of follies, turning it into one of the first neo-classical picturesque landscapes. From the start, Greek and picturesque were connected. For Horace Walpole, William Kent's introduction of the landscape garden in the 1730s had been responsible for the 'restoration of Greece'. Yet a garden like Shugborough was not really picturesque. For one thing, it was not composed enough: monuments were simply dotted down at convenient vantage points. Furthermore, Stuart's style of landscaping fell foul of both Richard Payne Knight and Uvedale Price. Knight was (by implication) forthright in his disapproval.

> Bless'd too is he, who midst his tufted trees
> Some ruin'd castle's lofty towers sees; . . .
> Still happier he, (if conscious of his prize)
> Who sees some temple's broken columns rise,
> Midst sculptur'd fragments, shiver'd by their fall,
> And tott'ring remnants of its marble wall; . . .
> But let no servile copyist appear,
> To plant his paltry imitations here;
> To show poor Baalbec dwindled to the eye,
> And Paestum's fanes with columns six feet high!
> With urns and cenotaphs our vallies fill,
> And bristle o'er with obelisks the hill!

No miniature copies of classical structures allowed, you see. Better a ruined castle (medieval); but best of all a ruined temple (classical). Price would have agreed with this:

A temple or palace of Grecian architecture in its perfect entire state, and with its surface and colour smooth and even, either in painting or reality, is beautiful; in ruin it is picturesque . . . Buildings of Grecian architecture, even where their prevailing character is grandeur, have yet an air of elegance mixed with it; so, likewise, when they become picturesque from being in ruin, the character of beauty still lingers about their forms and their ornaments, however disfigured – a circumstance which very essentially distinguishes them from the ruins of castles, and mere massive buildings. This may account for

the very few examples in Claude's pictures of ruins totally without
ornament, and with their broken parts strongly marked . . . It is not
a little remarkable, that of the two most celebrated of mere landscape
painters, Gaspar and Claude, the one who painted wild, broken,
picturesque nature, should have hardly any of those buildings which
we allowed to be most picturesque; and that the other, whose
attention to all that is soft, engaging and beautiful, is almost
proverbial, should comparatively have but few pictures without
them.

These lines might have been a prescription for all the painters
who now flocked to Greece and set about depicting the scenery
– never without a fragment of an ancient building, sometimes
distorted, relocated or invented to suit the painter, but still a
ruin – to give the picture focus, contrast and nostalgia. Fortified by a classical education, dimly aware of the beauties that
had already begun to be revealed by the works of Stuart
and Revett, and the lavish folios of Dalton and Le Roy,
supported by a generous train of servants and pack animals,
and strengthened by an English confidence that even a country
which already was flexing its muscles for a revolution less than
thirty years away would willingly act as their host, the young
men flocked to Greece. Painters, architects, poets and poetas-
ters all recorded their visions of the Ionian Islands, the Morea
and even the fastnesses of Epirus and Albania, fief of the
fearsome Ali Pasha of Ioannina. The islands of the Aegean and
the coast of Asia Minor drew them scarcely at all.

The painters, naturally enough, had their eye on the
pictorial possibilities of the scene. No melancholy here over
fallen beauty, no Turnerian sublime but the charm of ruin and
of pretty girls, of camels, and of exotically clad Greeks and
Turks to adorn the ruins and the hills.

From Thomas Hope in 1795 with his neat delineations of the
Aegean Isles, to the soft glow of Charles Eastlake in the 1820s,
there is a whole gamut of moods: William Gell's neat views or
his luminous, aqueous Vale of Tempe; the matter-of-fact
drawings of Michel-François Préaux or Sebastian Ittar;
the bright light of Dodwell; the limpid watercolours of
William Walker, the atmospheric scenes by Haygarth that
accompanied his poems, or the highly romantic landscapes
engraved for Thomas S. Hughes' *Travels*; the careful and
composed, studiedly picturesque drawings of Charles

Cockerell, the cool and precise Joseph Cartwright, the stippled mountains of William Page, or the golden glow that bathes H. W. Williams' renderings of the Temple of Aphaia or the Propylaea.

How far the appreciation of Greek landscape had come can be seen by comparing these luminous views with the rococo fantasy of Watteau's *Departure from Cythera* (1717). It is the difference between Stourhead or Stowe and the Temple of Aphaia on Aigina. It is the difference between Fénelon and the (at least attempted) grasp of social realities in Barthélémy's *Anacharsis* or Thomas Hope's *Anastasius*. It is the difference, too, between the false decorativeness that made Pope border Homer's river Xanthus with flowers, and the nostalgic pictorialism of the poetry of William Haygarth or W. R. Wright.

The gardens of Stuart and Revett are recognisably counterparts to the vision of Greece presented in the art of the first half of the eighteenth century. Fénelon's Greeks pursued their earnest virtues in a setting of tidy wildness and Arcadian abandon that owed as much to the rustic elegancies of Versailles as to the reading of Homer. Greece was an escapist's playground, and remained such, half a century after Fénelon, in the rococo novels of Wieland. But Watteau's painting is a work far too self-conscious – lingering in an infinite departure – to be dismissed as mere prettiness. Not for ever will these harlequins love or these columbines be fair: Arcadia is closed to modern pretence and pretension, and all one can do is go down for a visit. The painting signals the inadequacy of the rococo taste which was giving way to the harder nostalgia of the picturesque.

But the young Englishmen who visited Greece rejected the rococo not, like Goethe or Diderot, for its superficiality and irrelevance to deeper human concerns, but for its inadequacy towards the real landscape and their sense of history. It was the discovery of the Greek landscape that changed the understanding of Greek history. And it was the historical sense that gave the Greek landscape its especial importance in picturesque theory.

The painters were, to be sure, no more wedded than Le Roy to an accurate presentation of landscape. So essential did what Anthony Wood called 'the exemplary frailty of ruins' become to the landscape with architecture, that ruins might be imported where none existed. The meaning of ruin went far beyond a romantic frisson at the transitoriness of earthly things: it arose from an exercise of historical imagination. Where Diderot had liked ruins because they reminded him of eternity and of the smallness of our span in history,[5] these men liked them precisely because they were the products of time that must be recalled. The dawning of a historical consciousness went hand in hand with the desire to relate the heroic past to the landscape in which it had been enacted. 'Almost every rock,' wrote Edward Dodwell, 'every promontory, every view, is haunted by the shadows of the mighty dead. Every portion of the soil appears to teem with historical recollections; or it borrows some potent but invisible charm from the inspirations of poetry, the effects of genius, or the energies of liberty or patriotism.' (*Travels* I, iv)

But the travellers sought not only to read moral lessons in every stone (as the Renaissance had read them in such relics as coins or statues); many of them wished to put the stones to work in the service of a tougher historical enterprise. Goethe had asserted, and perhaps proved, that Greek forms could not be transferred without damage to a modern context. The travellers saw too that the real Greece bore little relation to the idyllic Eden of Renaissance and rococo art. The inconcinnity of heroic achievement with the crumbling glories of the landscape and the wretched condition of the contemporary Greeks, prompted the realisation that the past is indeed another country, and that the Greeks had indeed done things differently.

This sudden recognition of a real Greece of Turks, bandits, poverty, and ruins coincided with a new trend in scholarship, begun in Göttingen in the 1790s by F. A. Wolf, which was to transform the educated understanding of ancient Greece. For the first time people wished to know the Greeks as they really were. Far from the ahistorical antiquarianism of the seventeenth century, far even from the Dilettante enthusiasm which saw Greek forms as so much material for the use of English artists, the pendulum of understanding swung to an opposite viewpoint which made the ancients as foreign as the Red Indians and Pacific Islanders of whom explorers were beginning to send back their first fascinating reports.

If the past is indeed a foreign country, men with this

perception must have reasoned, it is necessary to visit a foreign country to find the past. The English were by far the most plentiful – and the most effective – of those who came to study the terrain of Greece, and the origins of this expertise are perhaps to be attributed to one of the more surprising features of the enthusiasm for the picturesque, namely the sudden interest in Pausanias (*fl* 150 AD), the Baedeker of ancient Greece, whose name has already occurred more than once. Pausanias, who lived in the time of Marcus Aurelius (121–180) and finished composing his *Description of Greece* about 176 AD, was the repository of the largest collection of topographical information about ancient Greece that was available to the modern world. His *Description* in ten books covered all parts of mainland Greece except Epirus, but omitted the islands and, more surprisingly, his native Ionia. It concentrated, in other words, on the Roman province of Graecia, describing buildings and monuments as they had stood in his day, with copious historical lore, in the manner of a modern guidebook.

The reading of Greek was always a rare accomplishment, though Johann Meurs consulted Pausanias in his writings on Athens. By 1762 Stuart was lamenting the non-availability of a translation of the work, so important to any who wished to study the topography and monuments of Greece. He, as we have seen, translated part of the description of Athens in the *Antiquities of Athens*, Volume I. In the last years of the eighteenth century two authors almost simultaneously stepped into the breach with their own versions of the long work. The first was by Uvedale Price (1780), and the second by Thomas Taylor the Platonist (1794).

Uvedale Price was also the author of the *Essay on the Picturesque*, and it is worth asking what common focus of enthusiasm could interest him in these two apparently so different topics. His commentator, J. G. Frazer, dismissed Pausanias as a landscape connoisseur but in the same passage shows his profound links with the 'associative' theory of the picturesque:

The plains which he traverses, the rivers which he fords, the lakes and seas that he beholds shining in the distance, the very flowers that spring beside his path hardly exist for him but as they are sacred to some god or tenanted by some spirit of the elements, or because they call up some memory of the past, some old romantic story of unhappy love or death. . . . If he looks up at the mountains, it is not to mark the snowy peaks glistering in the sunlight against the blue, or the sombre pine-forests that fringe their crests and are mirrored in the dark lake below; it is to tell you that Zeus or Apollo or the Sun-god is worshipped on their tops, that the Thyiad women rave on them above the clouds, or that Pan has been heard piping in their lonely coombs . . . The view of the sea from the Acropolis at Athens is noticed by him, not for its gleam of molten sapphire, but because from this height the aged Aegeus scanned the blue expanse for the white sails of his returning son, then cast himself headlong from the rock when he descried the bark with sable sails steering for the port of Athens.[6]

Pausanias, like the later artists, was highly susceptible to the melancholy of ruined cities and the forlorn relics of crumbled greatness. For him, as for the eighteenth century, classical antiquity was a lost world of godlike men and heroes, of strenuous beauty and sensuous intellect. He mourned at the ruined house of Pindar in Thebes; remarked on the prevalence of bandits around the ruins of Eleutherae; and of Megalopolis in Arcadia he wrote:

I am not astounded that [it] . . . should have lost all its beauty and ancient prosperity, or that most of it should be ruins nowadays, because I know that the daemonic powers love to turn things continually upside down, and I know that fortune alters everything, strong and weak, things at their beginning and things at their ending, and drives everything with a strong necessity according to her whim.

Not only Megalopolis fell prey to mutability, but also Mycenae, Egyptian Thebes, Minyan Orchomenos, Delos, Tiryns, Seleuceia on the Orontes and even the sunken island of Chryse near Lemnos (Pausanias 8, 33, 1–4). Lessons indeed in melancholy.

This was an aspect of his sensibility to which late eighteenth-century taste could respond. Contemporary life is there in Pausanias but little: Greece is a landscape whose meaning is its ruin.

Yet Pausanias was also intensely concerned to recover and describe every physical relic of the glory of Greece that was already six centuries old. A newly awakened historical interest could squeeze far more information out of his pages than

Strabo ever could provide. Not only history and legend, ritual and cult, but hard facts about the location of cities, fortifications, temples, treasuries and even individual works of art, were there to be used. And so beside the world of the painters and the poets there arose a new world of foot-weary students of the terrain: the world of Sir William Gell and François Pouqueville (to whom we owe the earliest description of the ruins of Mantinea – 1798); of Edward Dodwell and John Tweddell, Lord Aberdeen and John Cam Hobhouse, of Edward Daniell Clarke, above all of Captain William Martin Leake.

While the painters and tourists sought only for views and curiosities, the topographers were more serious-minded. Sextant and rule in hand, they paced out the Greek countryside, 'settling the geography' of Attica, identifying the site of Dium or Dodona, arguing and even coming to blows at the site of Troy, and seeing in every fountain a grotto of the Muses, in every grove a haunt of Centaurs. Rose Macaulay sneers: 'all this determining of positions must have been a very charming employment'; but certainly it seemed important to men whose education had centred on the classics of Greek history, and for whom the Peloponnesian War was more familiar than the history of England. In them the Greek past found its loyal servants.

Edward Dodwell and William Gell

Edward Dodwell first travelled in Greece in 1801, when he made a tour of the Ionian islands. A second journey, funded again from his own pocket (he never needed to look for paid employment), took him from Zante to Athens. In Attica he joined forces with William Gell and Sir Charles Monck: both Dodwell and Gell were to publish accounts of their journeys, Dodwell in 1821 and Gell in 1823. Dodwell's was extensively illustrated with his own picturesque (but truthful) drawings, while Gell specialised in watercolours. 'Every locality is shown as it really is', boasted Dodwell, adding that he had collected 600 drawings by Signor Pomardi of Rome, plus another 400 of his own. (Pomardi unfortunately distinguished himself on this tour by scribbling his signature on the Monument of Philopappus 'in half a dozen places'.)

In Attica he opened tombs and began to acquire a large collection of vases (all later to be sold to Ludwig I of Bavaria). It was just becoming fashionable, after Sir William Hamilton's finds in Etruria, to collect such items. But in the absence of any historical framework only a superficial connoisseurship was possible.

Pausanias, was, of course, Dodwell's constant companion as he tramped from Athens through Thessaly and back again to the Peloponnese. Early in 1806 he was at Mycenae: 'I approached the Cyclopian city of Pelops with a greater degree of veneration than any other place in Greece had inspired.' The lions on the gate fascinated him, though he wondered rather arbitrarily whether the column between them might represent a fire altar, and observed that lions symbolise water in Egyptian hieroglyphics – hardly the remark of a critical mind. He did however identify the Treasury of Atreus with the building mentioned by Pausanias. (Scarcely two years later it was ransacked by Veli Pasha, the governor of the Morea, as the 'tomb of Agamemnon'.)

On Mt Oeta it was the association with Greek tragedy that moved him: 'I much regretted my having omitted to examine the summits of Mt Oeta, as the origin of the story of Heracles might possibly be discovered.' (He thought it must be a volcano.) An exactly contemporary traveller, E. D. Clarke, was similarly fascinated by Mt Oeta, because its vegetation exactly corresponded (pine and oak) to the plants mentioned by Sophocles. Some forms of curiosity are easily satisfied.

If Gell and Dodwell were travelling companions, and destined alike to live out their days in Rome, a perhaps more congenial scene for the antiquarian endeavour, Gell was made of drier stuff than Dodwell. Not for him the fascination of literary association and comparatist speculation. His claims on our attention are considerably greater. Ten years younger than Dodwell, he likewise began his Greek travels in 1801, in this case with a journey to the Troad, where he had the company of other future members of the Society of Dilettanti, J. B. S. Morritt and James Dallaway. 1801 seems to have been an *annus mirabilis* for Greek travel; the steps of Thomas Hope, Lord Carlisle and Lord Aberdeen mingle their echoes on the plains of Greece. Every one was interested in the Troad, and many (including Gell and Dallaway) were to publish interpretations of its puzzling topography.

Two years later Gell was in Ithaca, this time on the track of Homer's Odysseus, and the results of his researches were published in 1807. Further trips to the Morea in 1804, and to Ithaca again (with Dodwell) in 1806 made him a veteran Greek traveller. So it comes as no surprise to find that when the Society of Dilettanti, in 1811, formed a committee for a second expedition to Ionia, they appointed Gell as its head. After devoting the year of 1812 to the study of a number of sites in Attica as well as the Ionian sites of Didyma, Cnidus, Aphrodisias and Magnesia (discovered by W. R. Hamilton in 1803), interspersed with requests for more money and assistance against privateers, Gell returned to find the Society too short of money to publish the results. Several schemes of publication were abandoned, partly because of disagreements among the Dilettanti, and it was not until 1817 that the *Unedited Antiquities of Attica* appeared. In 1821 came the first volume of the *Ionian Antiquities*. Volume II did not appear until after Gell's death, in 1840. The archaeological climate was already changing, and the volumes saw the light of day in a climate increasingly out of tune with such labours. Volume III appeared in 1860, IV in 1881, and V not until 1915.

Unsatisfactory though the Society of Dilettanti had proved, it was still an honour to belong to it. All the Grecian travellers of note (except Lord Elgin) were elected to it. Gell, who lived in Italy from 1806, was tied to the Society's apron strings for the rest of his life. Despite his complaints of neglect by his masters, he completed several works in these years, including his *Itinerary of Attica* (1810–11) and in 1817 that of the Morea.

The *Itineraries* are what they say they are – jejune catalogues of topographical notations with exact details of times and distances between each, and notes on the location of inns. This industrious work won sarcastic comment from Byron in a couplet which went through two revisions. He first wrote: 'Of Dardan Tours let Dilettanti tell, I leave topography to coxcomb Gell.' After meeting the man he changed 'coxcomb' to 'classic', and in the fifth edition Gell appeared, not unfairly, as 'rapid'. He did however also write 'That laudable curiosity concerning the remains of classical antiquity, which has of late years increased among our countrymen, is in no traveller or author more conspicuous than in Mr Gell.'[7]

Gell's more ambitious work was the 1823 version of his travels, which capitalised on the interest in Turkey aroused by the War of Independence. It was, he says, prompted by the remark of a lady: 'I wish you could give us anything but your dull maps and measures.' (It should be said that Gell's talk was clearly more sprightly than his pen.) Unfortunately the *Narrative of a Journey in the Morea* also makes for dull reading, and was ill received. A leitmotif is Gell's sarcastic attitude to the Greeks and Turks on whom he relied for assistance (or, not infrequently, obstruction), conveyed not only in words, but in a number of leaden cartoons that make one long for the sprightly pen of his younger compatriot Edward Lear.

Some moments of entertainment are offered by the antics of his companion, the unidentified Mr F – at Mantinea hurling himself from his horse to ensnare an interesting butterfly (which escaped), and landing flat on his face among the bushes; defending himself from dogs with the Englishman's usual weapon, the umbrella; being captured by bandits while collecting flowers, and amusing his captors by projecting animal silhouettes on the walls with his hands in the lamplight.

For all his industrious topographising, Gell has little of interest to say about any of the sites: a long walk to the ruins of ancient Methone is summed up with the remark, 'nothing worthy of observation', and the amazement of his native companions that a man should walk so far to see so little is noted without comment.

He was occasionally able to do some digging – itself a notable advance in 'archaeological technique' over previous travellers – by the assistance of 'a person of considerable fluency of speech, and talent of invention', who would detain the natives by 'pretended skill in magic or medicine', while Gell turned over the earth in the hunt for sculptures and inscriptions. Sometimes the pretence got out of hand and Gell had to play the doctor himself – with what results to the patient? – before the importunate Greeks would leave them.

One curious story concerns his usually half-hearted excavations. A rumour went round Paris some years after his journey that he had been engaged in the destruction of statues at Rhamnus in Attica. As Gell had never been there, he offers instead the true explanation of the destructions at Rhamnus, site of the ancient sanctuary of Nemesis, dread goddess of retribution. J. M. Gandy, the architect and draughtsman, who had been a member of the 1811 Dilettanti expedition, had found there a mutilated statue which he took to be Phidias' cult statue of the goddess. Scrupulous in his regard for antiquities, he drew it and then reburied it to preserve it from depredation.

But he had been observed. The next day he returned to the site, only to find that the statue had been dug up during the night and smashed to pieces. Evidently a local Greek or Turk had seen his interest and assumed, as was inevitable, that the stone must contain treasure. Hence the destruction. Gandy made the best of a bad job and hastily shipped the shattered fragments to London.

Gell's account is full of remarks on the likely outcome of the War of Independence which in hindsight make him look rather foolish. Though Turkish rule was universally reviled, few Franks could find much good to say of the Greeks, who so disappointed them by not being Homeric heroes that they regarded them as devoid of virtue of any kind.[8] Gell could see Greece only as a bone of contention for the European powers, and a quagmire for archaeologists if ruled by any power other than the Turks: anarchy would reign, and a foreign ruler would put in 'droves of prefects and commissaries' to hinder excavations. How wrong he was!

On this point at least Dodwell did not agree:

The remains [of Tiryns], that are as yet unknown, will be brought to light, when the reciprocal jealousy of the European powers permits the Greeks to break their chains, and to chase from their outraged territory that host of dull oppressors, who have spread the shades of dense ignorance over the land, that was once illumined by science, and who unconsciously trample on the venerable dust of the Pelopidae and the Atridae.

E. D. Clarke

Of greater moment was the tour of a young English don from Cambridge, Edward Daniell Clarke (1769–1822) whose Grand Tour in 1800–1 stretched from Egypt and the Holy Land to Russia, the Crimea and Northern Europe. He was a mineralogist by training (later to become professor of the subject at Cambridge), and mineralogical matters continually force themselves to the fore in the ten volumes of his travels – from his breakneck progress, shoe-soles smoking, across a fresh lava-flow of Vesuvius to the attention he paid to the marble of Paros. But like any good traveller in the Levant, he paid keen attention to the antiquities. He acquired a quantity of manuscripts, not least from Patmos, and had some success in buying medals, especially after he had dismissed the dragoman, Ibrahim, whose method of acquiring such items was to beat the owners about the head and demand them for nothing. He spent fourteen days measuring up the Plain of Troy, 'settled the geography' of the Attic coast; was severe on Elgin's depredations 'to adorn a miserable Scotch villa' (see Chapter 8) but with remarkable inconsistency was ready to remove any antiquities that appealed to him. (No doubt the University of Cambridge seemed a more worthy destination than Broomhall.)

He attempted no new identifications of monuments in Athens, though he allowed himself to hope that a tombstone bearing the name of Euclid, and now used as a horse-trough, might be that of the great mathematician. His name will for ever be linked with the 'Demeter' of Eleusis.

Eleusis is all but ruined now, as warships slumber offshore where once a king sat on 'the rocky brow That o'erlooks sea-borne Salamis', while cement factories and oil-refineries belch flame and black smoke far into the sky. There are plans to excavate the Sacred Way, that led from Athens to Eleusis, but these are bound up with that to extend the underground railway west from Omonia at least to Daphni: so the mechanical age remorselessly engulfs the stones even here. But perhaps this is after all an appropriate memorial of the spot where Persephone was seized – in a cloud of smoke – by the King of the Underworld and his chariot of black horses, and was plunged out of the light of day to eat the thin foodstuffs of Hades, leaving her mother Demeter to mourn her loss and wander in search of her. Demeter, goddess of the harvest, grieved so deeply that for a whole season the earth put forth no crops, and men began to starve. She came to Eleusis, and sat by the fountain called the Maiden Well, nursing her grief. Here the daughters of Celeus found her 'when they came to draw water and carry it home in bronze pitchers to their father's house.' Here she revealed the Mysteries, which became a sacrament celebrated here above all in Greece – a rite so secret that no one who witnessed it might tell of it for fear of Demeter's terrible retribution. Only a few echoes of august sanctity have survived to tinge, with a hint of *The Magic Flute*, these shining ruins.

Demeter's concern for the fertility of the land seemed to be exemplified in one of the most remarkable examples of continuity in Greek religion. In the village, half-buried in a dung heap, stood a statue of a buxom goddess bearing on her head a large basket evidently overflowing with fruits of the earth. Battered as it was, it was venerated by the peasants, who attributed to its magical powers the continued fertility of their land. Many travellers had noticed this 'Ceres', from Spon and Wheler onwards; it was in 1801 that Clarke finally contrived to remove it.

But the superstition of the inhabitants of Eleusis, respecting an idol which they all regarded as the protectress of their fields, was not the least obstacle to be overcome. In the evening, soon after our arrival with the firman, an accident happened which had nearly put an end to the undertaking. While the inhabitants were conversing with the Tchohodar, as to the means of its removal, an ox, loosed from its yoke, came and placed itself before the statue; and, after butting with its horns for some time against the marble, ran off with considerable speed, into the Plain of Eleusis. Instantly a general rumour prevailed: and several women joining in the clamour, it was with difficulty any proposal could be made.

'They had been always', they said, 'famous for their corn; and the fertility of the land would cease when the statue was removed.' Such were exactly the words of Cicero with respect to the Sicilians, when Verres removed the statue of Ceres: quod, Cerere violata, omnes cultus fructusque Cereris in hic locis interiisse arbitrantur. It was late at night before these scruples were removed.

Further hindrances, among them the fear of the Eleusinians that anyone who touched the statue would instantly lose his arm, and the need to bridge gaps in the quay, further delayed the transport of the statue, which the following day, 23 November, was eventually put on board a Casiot ship bound for Smyrna to begin its journey to England. The story receives its fitting conclusion in a remark Clarke adds in a footnote:

They predicted the wreck of the ship which should convey it; and it is a curious circumstance, that their augury was completely fulfilled, in the loss of the Princessa merchantman, off Beachy Head, having the statue on board.

The cargo was however recovered, and brought to Cambridge. It has alas long been recognised not as a representation of Demeter, but a cistophorus or species of Caryatid like those of the Erechtheion. Little attention is now given to the massive but faceless bust in the lower level of the Fitzwilliam Museum.

Clarke made more detailed, if erroneous, observations at the site of Epidaurus, the ancient healing sanctuary of Asclepius, where cures were effected by the epiphany of the god, perhaps supported by medical or therapeutic practice. Clarke was the first traveller to devote attention to the site, though Hugo Favoli had described its heaps of ruins in 1563, and Fourmont had copied a number of inscriptions here under the impression that he was at Hermione. It seems, indeed, to have been a difficult place to find. Clarke and his companions, having hired a boat from Aigina, instructed the pilot to head for Epidhavro; being assured by him, on arrival at a barren spot devoid of ruins, that this was indeed the place, they pressed him and eventually established that he had never heard of Epidhavro and had brought them to Piadha. (Dr Byron and Princess Caroline had similar trouble finding the place when they came in 1821.) Clarke and his companions promptly dismissed their caique and made inquiries among the locals, who told them that the Temple of Asclepius was to be found near Ligourio, though the palace of this great king was at Pidhavro.

They duly made their way to what Clarke describes as 'the Cheltenham of ancient Greece'. (Clarke was much given to such comparisons. Elsewhere he remarks on Epidauria as 'a region as easily to be visited as the County of Derbyshire, and where the traveller is not exposed to half the dangers encountered every night in the neighbourhood of London.' Tempe reminds him of Killiecrankie, and Thessaly of the Yorkshire Dales.)

He rambled round what could be seen of the site, guessing at the identity of the buildings. One at least was unmistakeable. The Theatre, as he rightly says, 'is one of the most remarkable in all Greece; not only from the state in which it remains, but in being mentioned by Pausanias as a work of Polycleitus, renowned for excelling all other architects in the harmony and beauty of his statues.'

But for Clarke the most remarkable relics were those in terracotta:

We discovered the ornaments of a frieze, and part of the cornice of a temple, which had been manufactured in earthenware. Some of these ornaments had been moulded for relievos; and others, less perfectly baked, exhibited painted surfaces. The colours upon the latter still retained much of their original freshness; upon being wetted with water, they appeared as vivid as when they were first laid on; resembling the painted surfaces of those 'pictured urns' (as they were termed by our English Pindar) upon which it is now usual to bestow the appellation of 'Grecian vases'.

It was forgivable in Clarke to be as blank as Dodwell on those vases, which, though their Greek origin had been established by Sir William Hamilton[9], did not come into their own until the efforts of Adolf Furtwängler and, above all, J. D. Beazley in the first decades of the twentieth century established a reliable chronology and typology.

Clarke had in fact misunderstood the layout of the sanctuary. The shortcomings of an archaeology that does not dig are now apparent; but digging was by no means an obvious activity at that time for the student of antiquities, and was also expensive and time-consuming. Gell dug, as we saw; Fauvel, like Dodwell, opened tombs in Attica; and even Princess Caroline dug a little at Piraeus. Hobhouse about the same time reported on tomb-opening (and faking) in the Troad; but to explore a tomb still seemed akin to desecration. The reverent tourist must admire the flesh, but it was not done to lay bare the privacy of the skeleton which time had slowly shrouded.

William Martin Leake[10]

Surely the most indefatigable of travellers and topographers, Pausanias only excepted, was the British army officer William Martin Leake, who, single-handed, established the location and name of almost every hitherto obscure site of ancient Greece, from the most famous and long-suspected sites to the minutest towns of Epirus, named fleetingly in Strabo, Livy or some obscurer author and otherwise lost to history. And he was almost always right.

His connection with Greece, a country which in the end held him in such honour that the Greek ambassador in London, Tricoupis, came to his funeral, came about quite by chance. In 1799, as a twenty-two-year-old artillery officer, he was sent to Constantinople with the British military mission to stiffen the Turks in their opposition to the French Republic, one of whose armies had occupied Egypt. He travelled with his commanding officer across Asia Minor in January and February 1800 with a view to joining the Ottoman army, then in Palestine. News of the convention of El-Arish turned them back in Cyprus, but this journey and Leake's subsequent solitary journey back to Constantinople formed the basis of his first published topographical account, not one of his best, as time was short for study and it contains too many guesses.

He established himself as an expert on the Ottoman Empire, despite the loss of all his papers containing the survey of Egypt, in the wreck off Cythera of the ship that was transferring some of the Elgin marbles to Malta. In 1804 he was sent to liaise with the local governor of European Turkey about putting their territories in a state of defence in anticipation of a French attack, following the expulsion of the French from Egypt. In addition he was required to make a military assessment of the topography and produce a study of 'the general geography of Greece'. How seriously he took his task can be seen in the seven thick volumes of *Travels in Northern Greece and the Morea*, plus two on the topography of Athens and Attica, and a later volume of addenda to the *Morea* volumes entitled *Peloponnesiaca*. A military duty developed into a labour of love. Pausanias was his bible: lamenting the continuing lack of an adequate translation of the periegete (he seems to have known only Price's), he translated very extensive portions of his author in the course of his own work. No indication by Pausanias was too small for him to investigate; though he complains (*Morea* 286) that the pressure of time prevents his checking every detail, this did not stop him, for example, from spending an hour or two attentively listening for the performance of the singing trout of Cleitor in Arcadia, mentioned by Pausanias. His assiduity and scrupulousness are clear too in the way he cites chapter and verse for the fertility of the plain of Orchomenos: 'the fertility of this plain is shown by its maize: I counted 900 grains in one cob.'

His topographical researches in Greece were conducted in two phases: February 1805–February 1807 and February 1809–March 1810, partly in the course of official travel, and partly at leisure. A military discipline kept him at his task day after day. Every morning finds him at a new site, and he usually began his journey before dawn, breaking after two or three hours for breakfast (except when a generous host would not allow him to leave without consuming a roast lamb), and forging ahead until noon or later when the heat dictated a halt. The rest of the day would be devoted to exploring the locality, and reporting on its customs, its produce and prosperity, its government and its antiquities.

Although the structure of his books was given by his original journals, the daily narrative is filled out with learned discussions of ancient topography based on subsequent study in the library. His careful attention to detail was not the least of the reasons why the books were not published until twenty-five years after the journeys were made. In a preface Leake states that in the first decade of the nineteenth century there was but little interest in Greek travels, while the War of Independence and its confused aftermath had brought it into the public eye in such a way that the appetite was insatiable in the 1830s. There was by this time a good deal of competition, from the books of Dodwell and Gell for example, but nothing to compete with the scale of Leake's undertaking. Much of the present book's discussion of the reliability of earlier travellers could not have been written but for Leake's dogged and pioneering labour.

So profuse is his information, it is hard to know how to illustrate his achievement briefly. Here was a man who surveyed the Peloponnese more thoroughly than any had done before; tried to identify the temples of Corinth (where he incorrectly took the great Doric temple of Apollo, already reduced to seven columns from the twelve Wheler had seen, for the Temple of Athena Chalinitis); discovered as much as could be discovered about this site, and that of Olympia, without actually digging (see Chapter 10); and made some of the earliest observations of the Temple at Bassae (see Chapter 8). Besides this he finally sorted out most of the outstanding

questions of the geography of Attica, including the problem of
the two agoras of Athens, the identification of Mt Anchesmus
with Mt Lycabettus, and the true nature of the Lysicrates
Monument and the Tower of the Winds. He made a thorough
survey of Attica which even Christopher Wordsworth could
scarcely add to. He speculated rationally on the site of the
temple of Apollo at Delphi. And, for the first time (and
anticipating Tozer by forty years) he explored minutely the
fastnesses of Northern Greece which few had penetrated
beyond Delphi. He conducted the first examination of Actium
(where the ruins of Nikopolis had been excavated to build Ali
Pasha's palace at Preveza); studied the Treasury of Minyas at
Orchomenos which had been explored by Elgin and was later
excavated by Schliemann; spent six hours copying a single
inscription at Karditsa in Boeotia; considered the problems of
the topography of Ithaca and Dulichium – reopening an old
scholarly sore that was to trouble future generations; identified
numerous sites that were little more than names in the historical record; and visited even Pella and Salonica where he was
imprisoned for several months, and where he copied an
inscription not published since Paul Lucas' visit one hundred
years ago, so remote was the area from travellers' concerns.

Leake's method comes out best in contrast with E. D.
Clarke's accounts. Both of them, for example, visited the
oracle of Trophonius at Levadhia. It was, Clarke averred, easy
to find though it had never been explored, for the entrance was
blocked. He treats his readers to an illustration of himself and
his companion, Cripps, before the entrance to the caves, and
devotes the rest of his account to fulmination against the
oracular mumbo-jumbo so circumstantially described by
Pausanias. Leake, by contrast, gives us a lengthy paraphrase of
Pausanias, and adduces Philostratus as well; describes the
niches and their inscriptions; asks himself which cavern contained the source of the Hercyna and concludes that excavation
was needed.

Or let us compare the two men again at another Boeotian
site, the natural pleasance of trilling water, odorous pine,
myrtle and oleander, which surrounds the quiet monastery of
S. Niccolo high in a recess of Mt Helicon. Yet this too was the
home of godhead.

E. D. Clarke had rested here on 9 December 1801, and

found that 'a more delightful retreat can hardly be found in the romantic passes of Swisserland. . . The air was filled with spicy odours, from numberless aromatic plants covering the soil. A perennial fountain, gushing from the side of a rock, poured down its clear and babbling waters into the rivulet below. A thick grove almost concealed the monastery . . . Nothing interrupted the still silence of this solitude, but the humming of bees, and the sound of falling waters.'

Clarke rightly surmised that this Christian retreat stood upon the site of an ancient sanctuary, and on finding an inscription on one of the pillars of a nearby church, referring to the Mouseia, Games sacred to the Muses, rightly divined that this was the very grove of the Muses, and fountain Aganippe, celebrated by Hesiod and described by Pausanias. Here the nine Muses had been nursed through infancy, and here every year offering was made to the hero Linos, murdered by Apollo for rivalling the god in song. The spring Aganippe was said to be the daughter of the River Permessus or Termessus. Here Hesiod had encountered the goddesses:

> where, with delicate feet
> Fast by Jove's altar, and the fountain, dark
> From azure depth, they tread the measured round;
> And bathing their soft bodies in the brook
> Permessus, or in that divinest spring
> Olmeius, or the well of Hippocrene,
> O'er Helicon's smooth topmost height they wont
> To thread their dances, graceful, kindling love,
> And, with fast feet rebounding, smite the earth.
> (Hesiod, *Theogony* 3–8: tr C. A. Elton)

The romantic frisson of such an association with a scene of such picturesque beauty was enough for Clarke, and he went on his way.

Not so for Leake, who passed by in December 1804, and made a longer halt in January 1806. He had not of course read Clarke's account; nor does he seem to have consulted it when he wrote up his account of Northern Greece for publication in 1835. It was Pausanias he had in hand; and having settled the site of Hesiod's Ascra, concluded that this fountain was Aganippe. No word on the picturesque setting; but he not only observed, but copied down and printed, the inscription mentioned by Clarke. His attention is all on the works of man and his needs:

St Nichola is a metokhi, or church and small convent dependent on that of Makariotissa, which is in the upper region of Helicon, towards its southern declivity. The metokhi is beautifully situated in a theatre-shaped hollow at the foot of Mount Marandali. The buildings stand in the midst of a grove of pine, walnut and plane, and olive, mixed with myrtle, bay and oleander, and adjoining to them are some gardens containing many hazel trees. A constant verdure is maintained here in summer by a copious source of water. The fountain Hippocrene, which was twenty stades above the Grove of the Muses, was probably at Makariotissa . . .

Pausanias, as Leake observes, saw many fine statues here: those of the nine Muses by Cephisodotus (fifth century BC), a bronze Apollo, a Dionysus by Lysippus (fourth century BC) and another by Myron (fifth century BC) – which Sulla stole from Orchomenos to dedicate here. There were figures of poets, including Hesiod and Arion; and of Orpheus surrounded by beasts in bronze and stone that harkened to his song. These had every one been removed by Constantine to his new capital, and were destroyed by fire in 404 AD. Nothing in truth remained here but the place's associations; and Leake's meticulous account is duller reading than the romantic Clarke's.

That is a contrast that could be drawn again and again in reading the two men. But their aims were different, and one should certainly not belittle Leake, whose achievement is far the greater.

After leaving Greece in 1810, Leake returned to England on a handsome pension to write up his researches, to receive academic honours from Berlin and Oxford, and to put in order his extensive collection of antiquities. The marbles (one of which was a present from Ali Pasha) he gave to the British Museum; the bronzes, coins, gems and vases were bought on his death for the Fitzwilliam Museum, the coins alone fetching £5,000. His last published work was *Numismata Hellenica* of 1854, and he died in 1860, in the satisfaction of having laid a firm foundation for the archaeologists, historians and geographers who would follow.

After about 1810 the topographers began to lose ground to the collectors (see Chapter 8). Then, the War of Independence put paid to antiquarian travel for some years. When peace returned to Greece, the copies of Pausanias were dusted off and operations resumed. (The painters, too, returned – chief among them James Skene and Edward Lear.) Christopher Wordsworth and Henry F. Tozer in the 1830s and '40s devoted themselves to the production of detailed and impressive accounts of Greek topography. They do not in spirit represent any advance on Leake, to whom they all paid tribute, and the palm of classical research had passed to the Germans, now numerous in Greece with its new Bavarian king.

An even more obvious contrast with the efforts of these hardy travellers is presented by the somewhat startling venture of the first package tour to a Greece still reeling from the war, a cruise on the Francesco Primo in the summer of 1833. This lasted three weeks and cost eighty pounds for the best places. The boat sailed from Naples via Zante, Patras and Navarino to Nauplia, allowing those who wished to do so to disembark at Patras and rejoin at Nauplia after travelling overland, just in the manner of Mark Twain's Innocents, thirty-odd years later. It went on to Constantinople, and then toured the Archipelago. Its passengers included, in the words of a fellow passenger:

A royal prince; Spanish nobles; Italian counts; French marquises; Dutch chevaliers, and, I may proudly add, English gentlemen. We had also a quack doctor from Paris; a gaming-house-keeper from Milan; a clergyman, poor as an Apostle, from Iceland, a grim looking student from the University of Göttingen; a Danish baron, music-mad; a singing count from Sienna [sic]; a crazy architect from Paris; and two Russian noblemen. There were only two ladies; – a Russian countess, who read nothing but Homer, and made classical mistakes; and a Bavarian lady; whose great merit was her inclination to render herself agreeable.[11]

Such was the complexion of those who interested themselves in Greek travel at this time. Gell's description offers a neat conclusion to a period in which Greek antiquities had become more or less public property, and the major difficulties of exploration had all slipped away:

The last news from the steam boat with 80 Grecian travellers, is from Nauplia. They have of course had constant disputes in so unruly a republic, but only two duels are as yet decided to be fought when the voyage terminates. The French on board unite into a club to bully the Captain in a body. Those who went by land across the Morea were furious at finding few people and no house with its roof on, though I told them how it was before they set out . . . Imagine them . . . at Vostizza [Aegium], Corinth, Eleusis or the Piraeus where they and all Europe expect operas, pianofortes, and billiards.

Even a free Greece could not instantly supply all the comforts to which less adventurous European travellers were accustomed.

Dodona

But the reader will perhaps be expecting an answer to Byron's question, posed at the beginning of this chapter. Where, indeed, was Dodona's sacred grove? Leake could write, in 1835, that 'Dodona is now the only Greek city of great celebrity, the situation of which is not exactly known by means of a comparison of ancient history with actual appearances.' It was frustrating that such a lacuna should be allowed to exist, that the word should remain mute which 'they went to hear On high Dodona mountain.'

Dodona, though perhaps not a large city, had its place in history as the site of the oracle of Zeus, whose answers were given through the rustling of doves in the sacred oak tree. Its priests receive one mysterious mention in Homer, who speaks of:

Dodona . . . about whose bow'rs
The austere prophetic Selli dwell, that still sleep on the ground,
Go bare, and never cleanse their feet
                              (Iliad, 16,234: tr George Chapman)

Aeneas was supposed to have visited it on his journey from Troy to Rome. It lay, to be sure, in Epirus, 'where the cattle-pasturing peaks slope down, begining from Dodona, towards the Ionian sea' (Pindar N 4,82), and Hesiod described the fertility of its fields (frag. 240).

Such descriptions should have been enough to offer a clue. Leake, knowing a lake had been close to the oracle, decided that the most promising site was Ioannina itself, and devoted some pages to visualising its ancient state:

Here, therefore, in place of the dirty street and bazars of the modern town, we may imagine a forest, through which an avenue of primaeval oak and ilex conducted to the sacred peninsula. Within the porticoes which inclosed the temple were ranges of tripods supporting cauldrons . . . which were so numerous and so closely placed, that when one of them was struck the sound vibrated through them all . . . the most remarkable of the anathemata was a statue dedicated by the Corcyraei, holding in its hand a whip with three thongs loaded with balls, which made a continual sound as they were agitated by the wind against a cauldron. In a picture of the temple of Dodona which has been described by Philostratus, the prophetic oak was seen near the temple, and lying under it the axe of Hellus with which he struck the tree, when a voice from it ordered him to desist. A golden dove, representing the bird of Egypt, which uttered the voice, was perched upon the tree; garlands were suspended from its branches, and a chorus from Egyptian Thebes was dancing around it, as if rejoicing at the recognition of the sacred dove from their own city.

Imagination with learning makes a worthy attempt to visualise a city already in decline when Augustus ruled in Rome, though the place remained important – and the seat of a bishop – until at least 516 AD. But Ioannina was not Dodona.

Christopher Wordsworth, the nephew of the poet and later Bishop of Lincoln, was in Greece only a few years after Leake, in the company of the bonhomous but somewhat vapid poetaster Richard Monckton Milnes. The pair echo the pattern of other Grecian duos, like Byron and Hobhouse, or Gell and Mr F: the one interested only in exercising sensibility and writing verses, the other labouring on a monument of learning. In this case it was the scholar whose achievement was the greater.

Wordsworth's *Greece*, published in 1839 (new edition 1853) was a summa of all that was known of the topography of Greece, handsomely illustrated with steel engravings – a collector's item. Wordsworth began his account of Dodona, 'to ascertain the site of Dodona would seem now to require a response from the oracle itself. The former dwelling of the spirit, which once guided half the world, is lost.' He went on however to dismiss his own scepticism, by drawing attention to some substantial ruins south-west of Ioannina, at a village named Dramisus. Small in extent, unusually situated in a plain rather than on an acropolis, and dignified by a considerable theatre and the partially standing remains of two temples, the site was clearly the most important of the area. Leake himself had remarked (*Northern Greece* I, 260) that it 'would be interesting to excavate these ruins'.

Arguing that the other features associated with the site might reasonably be some distance away if no landmark stood any nearer, Wordsworth allowed that the lake could be that of Ioannina, the spring that 'near the sulphuric mines worked by Ali Pasha, near Djerovini', and Mt Tomarus Mt Olitzka.

Wordsworth's intuition was certainly correct. Excavations were not undertaken until the 1870s when Constantine Carapanos, moved by the discovery of coins to dig here, explored the site and discovered certain proof of the identity of the place, in the form of inscribed bronze sheets. He failed to locate the temple of Zeus itself, however, and this most sacred precinct of Dodona was only found in the 1950s by S. Dakaris.

So by 1832 there was no cause to puzzle any longer over major questions of ancient Greek topography. The places were known. The task that presented itself was the deeper investigation of those places and the fuller understanding of their material remains. Scenes of romantic attraction had finally been metamorphosed into objects of scientific inquiry; and this was the task of succeeding generations in Greece. Who is to say whether this was gain or loss? But the unquenchable romantic spirit continued to seek to appropriate Greece in ever new ways; and the physical appropriations of pieces of ancient Greece will be the subject of the next two chapters.

CHAPTER EIGHT

A Tale of Three Cities:
London, Munich and Paris*

Antiquity is a garden that belongs by natural right to those who cultivate its fruits. (Captain de Verninac Saint Maur, commander of the expedition to bring the Egyptian obelisk to the Place de la Concorde.)

Picture Athens in the early years of the nineteenth century – a small shabby town of 1,300 houses, not much changed, bar a few collapsed hovels, from the description of Chandler a decade or two before:

The houses are mostly mean, and straggling; many with large areas or courts before them. In the lanes, the high walls on each side, which are commonly whitewashed, reflect strongly the heat of the sun. The streets are very irregular; and anciently were neither uniform nor handsome.

Antiquities were scattered everywhere, and funeral reliefs were often used to adorn doorways. Through it passed, 'with pen and palette', all the tourists we met with in the last chapter. Besides these, there were some more permanent residents, of whom the longest-standing was certainly Louis-Sebastien Fauvel (1753–1838).

Host and cicerone to nearly every foreign visitor to Athens, Fauvel had become one of the most familiar features of the Athenian scene. Born in 1753 at Clermont-en-Beauvais, he had acquired some distinction as an artist and draughtsman by 1780. In that year he departed with the architect Foucherot for a two-year tour in Greece. Four years later the Comte de Choiseul-Gouffier took him on as a professional artist to accompany his residence in Constantinople and to contribute illustrations to his *Voyage Pittoresque*. The Count allowed him a free hand and licence to travel – which he duly did, to the Peloponnese, to Athens and Marathon, and even to Santorini (where he found an inscription for which 'I knew enough Greek to work out what it was about . . . part of a portico repaired by Trajan.') But Choiseul-Gouffier's condition of this liberty was that anything Fauvel discovered should belong to him. His acquisitions included three verd antique columns from the Acropolis, one already displaced metope from the Parthenon, and two inscriptions from the Erechtheion. Delighted, Choiseul-Gouffier developed a yen for a relief from Sounion and a lion from the Mesogeia.

All this meant hard work for Fauvel. He was also busy on his own account, industriously making casts which got wet when he travelled by sea and had to be constantly redone. By the end of 1789 Fauvel was chafing under his master's yoke, demanding independence or at least recognition (he had received no acknowledgement of some busts he sent from Marathon). He soon retired to Greece; on his next return to Constantinople, in 1792, it was to find that Choiseul-Gouffier had fled to Russia to escape the consequences of the French Revolution.

He was now without employment, without salary, without prospects. It seemed best to retreat promptly to his beloved Athens, where he lived in poverty for the next nine years. He continued to make discoveries, and to increase his collection. To recoup some of the money Choiseul-Gouffier had owed him he sold some of his twenty-four cases of antiquities to the Directoire, and in 1795 the Institut des Arts agreed to provide a stipend.

Life was still far from easy. In 1799, after the French had invaded Egypt, Fauvel was imprisoned. He was visited in his confinement by John Tweddell, a talented artist and antiquary soon to die of fever and be buried in the Theseion; for safety Fauvel sold him forty or fifty drawings, which on Tweddell's death were sent to Lord Elgin in Constantinople and were never seen again. Tweddell interceded with the British chargé d'affaires to get Fauvel released. This took place in time for Fauvel to express his gratitude by arranging Tweddell's funeral.

In 1801 Fauvel returned briefly to France, where he secured from Talleyrand the post of sub-commissar at Athens. This he retained through war and revolution, destruction of property and illness, and most of all bitterness of heart and lack of recognition, until his death in 1838.

He had hoped in 1801 to obtain the privilege of excavating Olympia as the condition of his return to Greece; but deprived of any archaeological status he was forced to watch the activities of the foreign excavators blossom all around him. Instead he opened a number of tombs; explored dedicatory niches between Daphni and Eleusis; worked on his plaster scale model of Pausanias' ancient Athens; discovered the junction of the walls of Phaleron and Athens, and many other topographical details.

Generous always with his time and learning, his memoirs and his collections, Fauvel published nothing himself. Most of his notes and casts were lost in the rising of 1821. His museum was shut up in fifty-four cases in Athens, and much of it was broken up after 1825. What was left – 2,000 medals, some broken vases, terracottas, marble fragments, plaster casts and other items – was returned to France and sold.[1] The Bibliothèque Nationale acquired for 500 francs his manuscripts, maps and relief plan of Attica. 'Mince relique', says his biographer, 'd'une carrière si longue et vouée si complètement à l'archéologie.'

It is not surprising that he looked with bitterness on the activities of Lord Elgin's agents in Athens. Other explorers were to cause him frustration nearly as intense. For Fauvel was to see three great archaeological treasures slip through his grasp. A fourth was to come to France though not through his agency. Fauvel seems to have been doomed to stand on the sidelines.

It is the story of these four great discoveries that will occupy this chapter. The story marks a new stage in the position of Greek antiquities in European taste. Where previous generations had been content to draw and study, and even contemporaries would often find it enough to sketch and paint, and to pace out the topography and cautiously turn over a few stones, some travellers now began to be seized by a mania for acquisition. Clarke we have already met; Elgin and the other subjects of this chapter shared it in a considerable degree. The

mania was encouraged as often as not by the Turks who would
break off fragments of monuments as gifts or items of sale.

But the mania was not kleptomania, though its ends might
be various. Glory for the finder, glory for the subsequent
purchaser; the adornment of a national museum or an encouragement to the arts at home; the rescue of threatened
antiquities from the Turks – all these motives might come into
play. Museums had to develop to accommodate the new
works. The jumbled repositories of the seventeenth century,
even the Titanic collection of the Musée Napoléon, were
outstripped by the thoughtful principles on which the
museums of newly-proud states were designed. So what
began as rapacity ended as a large step forward for the scientific
study of antiquity. Not that the discoverers always benefited,
by any means; Lord Elgin least of all.

The Elgin Marbles

> Let Aberdeen and Elgin still pursue
> The shade of fame through regions of virtu;
> Waste useless thousands on their Phidian freaks,
> Misshapen monuments and maimed antiques;
> And make their grand saloons a general mart
> For all the mutilated blocks of art.
> (Byron, *English Bards and Scotch Reviewers*)

Lord Elgin has become the most notorious of those who
plundered Greek monuments to enrich their own dwellings or
to glorify their nations. His prize was after all the most
magnificent of any, and it was the only one to be prised stone
by stone from a still largely standing monument. But he
should hardly be tarred with a brush that leaves contemporaries scarcely touched; for who of the English travellers in
Greece could have refused the opportunity to acquire some
lovely memento of his journey to the Land of the Ideal? Few
indeed came back entirely empty-handed.

E. D. Clarke was only too ready, as we saw, to exert every
effort to acquire what he wanted, even as he penned his
memoirs condemning the activities of Elgin. Nor was he the
first. In 1785 Sir Richard Worsley and attendant artist had been
in Greece, collecting the marbles later to become famous as the
Museum Worsleyanum in the Isle of Wight. In 1794–6 J. B. S.

Morritt of Rokeby had travelled in Greece, and though he was interested in everything, and wrote about costume, manners, food and travel as well as antiquities in his letters home, one of his professed aims was to enrich Rokeby Hall with a few choice antiquities. The French government at one time formulated a plan for removing the Theseion to Paris in its entirety.[2] The 'juvenile and irresponsible, but far from wicked' Lord Sligo (as Byron described him), besides acquiring the columns of the Treasury of Atreus which have been in the British Museum since 1904, made a large collection of vases which 'according to the depreciation of Fauvel' were worth 150 piastres (£8).

Even Lord Nelson had a part to play, when he shipped home to England an altar from Delphi acquired by Sir William Hamilton: it is now at Castle Howard in Yorkshire.

One must remember, nonetheless, that many travellers genuinely believed themselves to be rescuing precious antiquities from certain destruction at the hands of the Turks:

A list of the principal objects thus barbarously levelled to the ground, may perhaps be neither uninteresting nor foreign to the present purpose.

At Athens, four ancient buildings have been entirely destroyed within these few years: a small Ionic temple in the Acropolis; another temple, supposed to be Ceres, near the Ilissos; a bridge over that stream, and the aqueduct of Antoninus Pius. Part of the Propylaean columns have been thrown down, with a mass of the architrave on the western front of the Erechtheion, and one of the columns of the Olympieion. At Corinth several columns of the Doric temple were destroyed a few years ago. The temple of Jupiter at Olympia has been reduced to its foundations. The remains of a temple at the eastern foot of Mount Lycaeon in Arcadia, have shared the same fate; and a Doric temple, of which several columns were standing at Apollonia in Epiros, were demolished only a few years ago, and the materials employed in repairing the seraglio of the Pasha of Berat; one column at present only remains. Chandler tells us that some of the columns of the temple at Sunium were destroyed by the Turks; and we know, from the same author, that the temple of Augustus, at Mylassa in Caria, was ruined by them a few years ago, and the materials employed for the construction of a mosque; and that great part of a magnificent temple at Mendelet, and another at Teos in Asia Minor had been converted into lime, the Turks having built kilns within the temples themselves! Many other examples might be adduced of the destructive influence of these tasteless barbarians over the splendid and interesting remains of Grecian architecture. (Edward Dodwell)

Such, then, was the position when Elgin began his embassy to Constantinople in 1799 at the age of 33. He was newly married to a vivacious but empty-headed girl, Mary Nisbet of Dirleton. On the Fife side of the Firth of Forth he had built a country house, Broomhall, to the designs of the Greek Revival architect, Thomas Harrison. It had cost him much of his money and he no doubt hoped that the Nisbet fortune would replenish his funds so that he could furnish it amply.

It was Thomas Harrison who suggested that his sojourn in the Levant would be a good opportunity to obtain casts of notable antiquities to adorn his classic home, or, as Elgin's secretary William R. Hamilton expressed it in 1815, 'to benefit the arts in England from the study of Greek architecture and sculpture'. Both aims were clear in Elgin's mind when he set off. He was anxious to adorn his house in a style befitting one who hoped to obtain a seat in the English House of Lords. At the same time, with a rich sense of the responsibilities of an ambassador, his plan for 'the improvement of the arts in England' was entirely genuine.

In this he followed the lead set not only by Stuart and Revett, but equally consciously by Sir William Hamilton, since 1765 British Minister at Naples. The latter's *Collection of Etruscan Greek and Roman Antiquities*, published with a text by P. F. Hugues d'Hancarville in 1766–7, had made the study of the Greek vases from the cemeteries of Etruria into a connoisseur's pursuit: Josiah Wedgwood owed all the success of his firm to Hamilton, for he had created the taste and provided the models that took the fashionable world by storm.[3]

Excavation offered many opportunities to the reformer of taste. Another example is the development of the Pompeian style for drawing rooms (every stately home should have one) in the years following the excavation of Herculaneum in 1738 and Pompeii in 1748.

A similar onslaught on English taste had been made by Elgin's older contemporary, Thomas Hope. He had inherited the fortune made by his father in business in the Netherlands, and embarked on a long tour of Greece and Ionia (1788–96), of which he produced a fictionalised account in his novel *Anastasius* (1819). (Byron said of it that his only two regrets were that he had not written it, and that Hope had.) He returned to England with the usual collection of marbles, determined to win the acceptance of the artistic world and to reform English taste in a neo-Grecian style. His important *Costume of the Ancients* was published in 1809. Like Schliemann later, and like Elgin himself, he was to find himself snubbed as an outsider by those he most wished to impress; but by degrees his chairs, fabrics and wallpaper designs – modelled largely on designs from Hamilton's painted vases – gained the favour of Regency England: he remains a notable figure in the history of taste.[4]

Elgin could hope for no less, though he was destined to achieve much more, at much greater cost. He set about finding a team of artists to work for him on the antiquities of Athens while he took up residence in Constantinople (where he built a second, smaller Broomhall as his ambassadorial residence). J. M. W. Turner, alas for posterity, proved too expensive at £400 per annum. It was not until he reached Naples that Elgin found a painter. Sir William Hamilton recommended a landscape artist named Giovanni Battista Lusieri, whom the ambassador engaged for £200 per annum.

Elgin's secretary, William R. Hamilton (no relation to Sir William), was to engage a cast maker and a figure painter to work under Lusieri. For the latter job he engaged a 'Calmuck' of savage appearance from Central Asia called Theodor Ivanovitch – 'the only man of taste his nation ever produced'. He also hired two draughtsmen, a hunchback called Balaestra and the young Sebastian Ittar, and not one but two cast makers.

It was also necessary for one who wished to impress the cultivated world to take a scholar to collect manuscripts wherever possible. Clarke could not be allowed to hold the field. Richard Porson was considered, but rejected as too drunken and unpleasant; instead Elgin engaged the Revd J. D. Carlyle, Professor of Arabic at Cambridge, a dreamy man with a taste for composing indifferent poetry at suitably impressive classical sites. Only on the plain of Troy in May 1801 was he moved to passion, when he and Hunt encountered E. D. Clarke and his companion J. M. Cripps. They could not agree on the site of Troy and the parties turned their backs on one another. The two Cambridge dons were enemies henceforth.

In May 1800 Elgin was presented with his team of artists, or 'Caro of Vertioso' (Carro of Virtuosi) as Lady Elgin called them in a letter home. Two Italians, two Germans, a Calmuck and two formatori of uncertain nationality, they must have presented a motley spectacle as they arrived in Athens three months later in the charge of Elgin's chaplain, Philip Hunt.

They began work at once – work which was to continue to occupy them for ten years. Among their equipment was the only cart in Athens. It had belonged to Fauvel, who was now in prison as an enemy alien. It was only the first of many pieces of assistance to his rivals. It was not until February that the party were admitted to the Acropolis – at a price of five pounds a day – but there were plenty of other monuments in Athens to be drawn, and casts to be taken. When the Acropolis was made available they set up their scaffolding and prepared to take the first casts. Abruptly and without warning the Disdar (military governor) of the Acropolis announced that the rock must be closed. A French fleet was gathering at Toulon, and the Porte, supposing it was directed against the Turks, had ordered that all military installations be closed to foreigners. Only for a firman signed by the Sultan would the Disdar open up again.

Thus did Elgin acquire the piece of paper on which a century of controversy and acrimony over the rightful ownership of the Parthenon Marbles has been based. The Turkish original is lost, and the Italian translation given to Hunt is crucially ambiguous. Hunt's recommendation (in July 1801) was that a firman be obtained permitting the artists to enter the Acropolis, to model the temples, to erect scaffolding and dig, and 'to take away any sculptures or inscriptions which do not interfere with the works of walls of the citadel'. No mention here of sculptures from the buildings. The firman itself informed the Voyvode of Athens (in St Clair's translation):

. . . it is our desire that on the arrival of this letter you use your diligence to act conformably to the instances of the said Ambassador as long as the said five artists dwelling in that place shall be employed in going in and out of the citadel of Athens which is the place of observation; or in fixing scaffolding around the ancient Temple of the Idols, or in modelling with chalk or gypsum the said ornaments and visible figures; or in measuring the fragments and vestiges of

An Amazon: a copy of the type from the
altar of Artemis at Ephesus, now at
Petworth House, Sussex

C.T. Newton with his lions at Halicarnassus. From his *Discoveries at
Halicarnassus*

Reconstruction view of the Mausoleum at Halicarnassus, by J.B. Fischer von Erlach

Reconstruction of the Mausoleum, Halicarnassus © British Museum

Jacques Spon. From his *Voyage en Italie,
Dalmatie et la Grece*

Carl Otfried Müller

William Martin Leake. Bust in the
Fitzwilliam Museum, Cambridge

Kyriakos Pittakis

Drawing after Cyriac of Ancona of the Parthenon
at Athens

'Hadrian and Sabina' (actually Cecrops and Pandrosos) from the west
pediment of the Parthenon. Plaster model in the Parthenon, Nashville,
Tennessee, after the drawing by Jacques Carrey

Greece in chains: the title vignette from Comte de Choiseul-Gouffier,
Voyage Pittoresque de la Grece

The remains of the gigantic Apollo on Delos in the seventeenth century

Interior of the Temple at Bassae, by O.M. von Stackelberg

'A Hermes in the guise of Caliban';
contemporary cartoon of Johann Martin
von Wagner

Reconstruction drawing of ancient Ephesus by Edward Falkener

Edward Falkener's imaginary view of the temple of Artemis at Ephesus

'The fight about Patroclus grew'. Dying warrior from the pediment of the Temple of Aphaia, Aigina

An 'owl' cup from Schliemann's *Trojan Antiquities*

other ruined buildings; or in excavating when they find it necessary the foundations in search of inscriptions among the rubbish; that they be not molested by the said Disdar nor by any other persons; nor even by you to whom this letter is addressed; and that no one meddle with their scaffolding or implements nor hinder them from taking away any pieces of stone with inscriptions and figures. In the aforesaid manner see that you behave and comport yourselves.

It was entirely with an eye to detail and ornaments that Elgin interpreted this permission:

Besides the general work (by which I mean that which had been begun at the departure of Mr Hunt) it would be very essential that the *Formatori* should be able to take away exact models of the little ornaments *or detached pieces if any are found* which would be interesting for the Arts. The very great variety in our manufactures, in objects either of elegance or luxury, offers a thousand applications for such details. A chair, a footstool, designs or shapes for porcelain, ornaments for cornices, nothing is indifferent, and whether it be in painting or a model, exact representations of such things would be much to be desired. Besides you have now the permission to dig, and there a great field is opened for medals, and for the remains both of sculpture and architecture.

But Hunt, it seems, had other ideas. When the Select Committee asked him in 1816, 'Do you imagine that the firman gave a direct permission to remove figures and pieces of sculpture from the walls or temple, or that that must have been a matter of private arrangement with the local authorities of Athens?', he replied, 'That was the interpretation which the Voyvode of Athens was induced to allow it to bear.' The inducements included presents of cut glass and firearms, and Hunt was permitted to remove the best of the metopes from the Parthenon. On 31 July it was removed. The first assault had been made, and by September 1803 100 cases were ready at Piraeus for shipment to London. Athens' chief glory had been reduced to a shell.

It was in this state that Elgin saw it when he arrived in Athens for the first time in April 1802. He could not be expected to feel the shock of the loss as did those travellers, like Edward Dodwell, who observed the spoliation in progress:

During my first tour to Greece I had the inexpressible mortification of being present when the Parthenon was despoiled of its finest sculpture, and when some of its architectural members were thrown to the ground. I saw several metopae at the south east extremity of the temple taken down. They were fixed in between the triglyphs as in a groove; and in order to lift them up, it was necessary to throw to the ground the magnificent cornice by which they were covered. The south east angle of the pediment shared the same fate; and instead of the picturesque beauty and high preservation in which I first saw it, it is now comparatively reduced to a state of shattered desolation.

Gell and Clarke were equally moved by the loss, sceptical though they were about the safety of antiquities in Turkish hands. But Elgin saw the results in wooden cases, not the shattered temple. Immediately he ordered further excavations in various parts of Athens, and departed again for Constantinople. Lady Elgin remained behind. She wrote in a letter of 24–5 May 1802 (by which time her husband was back in Constantinople):

Tuesday 25th May. – Know that, besides the five cases I have already told you of, I have prevaled on Captain Hoste to take three more; two are already on board, and the third will be taken when he returns from Corinth. How I have faged to get all this done, do you love me better for it, Elgin?

And how I have pushed Lusieri to get cases made for these last three packages!

I beg you will shew delight (lay aside the Diplomatic character) to Captain Hoste for taking so much on board. I am now satisfied of what I always thought – which is how much more Women can do if they set about it, than Men. I will lay any bet that had you been here, you would not have got half so much on board as I have.

As for getting the other things you wished for, down from the Acropolis, it is quite *impossible* before you return. Lusieri says Captain Lacy was, upon his first coming here, against the things being taken down, but at last he was keener than anybody, and, absolutely wished you to have the whole Temple of the Cari-something, where the Statues of the Women are.

It was the Cari-something, indeed, which caused native and foreign observers the greatest distress of all. Another young gentleman traveller, F. S. N. Douglas, recorded the following story:

An illiterate servant of the Disdar of Athens . . . assured me that when the five other κορίτσια (girls) had lost their sister, they manifested their affliction by filling the air at the close of the evening with the most mournful sighs and lamentations, that he himself had heard their complaints, and never without being so much affected as to be obliged to leave the citadel till they had ceased; and that the ravished sister was not deaf to their voice, but astonished the lower town where she was placed by answering in the same lamentable tones. We cannot refuse to acknowledge that the Athenians are not so indifferent as it has been sometimes represented to the wonders and monuments of their city.[6]

An even more elaborate version was that of Hobhouse:

A curious notion prevailing among the common Athenians, with respect to the statues, is that they are real bodies mutilated and enchanted with their present state of petrification by magicians who will have power over them as long as the Turks are masters of Greece, when they will be transformed into their former bodies. The spirit within them is called an Arabian, and is not infrequently heard to mourn and bewail its condition. Some Greeks in our time conveying a chest from Athens to Piraeus containing part of the Elgin Marbles, threw it down, and could not for some time be prevailed upon to touch it, again affirming, they heard the Arab (i.e. the enchanted spirit within the sculpture) crying out and groaning for his fellow-spirits detained in bondage in the Acropolis. The Athenians suppose that the condition of these enchanted marbles will be bettered by a removal from the country of the tyrant Turks.[7]

Clearly the statues still held the demonic powers that had haunted the antiquities of Byzantium, and made them objects of as much suspicion as veneration. Such perhaps was the source of the awe felt by the Disdar as he saw the metope fall, and let fall with it a tear accompanied by a sigh: 'Τελος! The end!' (At least he, or a successor, was not averse, ten years later, to bowling another metope over the cliff as a parting gift to his friend Cockerell.)

But the trials of the Marbles were only just beginning. The cases on board the Mentor sank with it off Cerigo (Cythera) and were not raised until October 1804. Other boats took more, up to a total of fifty; but fifty were left. These were finally got off on a ship commanded, by coincidence, by the brother of E. D. Clarke.

When Elgin left Constantinople on 16 January 1803 to return to England he had spent nearly £40,000 of his own money on all these works. Worse was to come. On his way home through France he was arrested, through an abrupt change of policy by Napoleon, as a prisoner of war and imprisoned in Paris, Barèges and lastly Pau until 1806. By this time Lady Elgin, who had returned to England nine months before, had taken up with one Robert Ferguson and Elgin had no alternative but to seek a – very expensive – divorce. He was almost ruined, he had no prospect of further political employment under the terms of the parole he had given Talleyrand for his release, and his cases of marbles were in large part still at Malta or in temporary storage in a shed in Park Lane. What future was there for the aspiring patron of the arts?

The first thing Elgin did was to arrange a public exhibition, in June 1807, in the Park Lane building. The artists flocked to see the marbles, and the effect was electric. Flaxman, whose style had been moulded in the economical linearity of vase painting to a spare classicism, was instantly converted by the richness of individual detail which in no way detracted from the sculptures' beauty. Fuseli strode about exclaiming 'De Greeks were godes!' De Greeks were godes! The protégés of Thomas Hope – Benjamin West, Benjamin Robert Haydon and Robert Westall – were overwhelmed. Haydon's reaction is famous:

The first thing I fixed my eyes on was the wrist of a figure in one of the female groups, in which were visible, though in a feminine form, the radius and the ulna. I was astonished, for I had never seen them hinted at in any female wrist in the antique. I darted my eye to the elbow, and saw the outer condyle visibly affecting the shape as in nature. I saw that the arm was in repose and the soft parts in relaxation. That combination of nature and idea, which I had felt was so much wanting for high art, was here displayed to midday conviction. My heart beat! If I had seen nothing else I had seen sufficient to keep me to nature for the rest of my life. . . .

I felt as if a divine truth had blazed inwardly upon my mind and I knew that they would at last rouse the art of Europe from its slumber in the darkness.[8]

He changed his style of painting forthwith. The arrival of the real thing showed what pale imitations the drawings of earlier travellers had been. (One must of course bear in mind the difficulty of drawing sculptures forty feet above the ground.) Dalton's rococo and Pars' lack of 'osteological truth' and hothouse Phidianism (as Quatremère de Quincy called it) became apparent; even the occasional obscurities of the drawings of Stuart and Revett were shown up.

But if the artists were enthralled, the connoisseurs or dilettanti did all they could to belittle the sculptures. For they demanded a rethinking of the most basic principle of Greek art, that of the Ideal. Goethe had already worked his way out of the impasse of the Ideal (see Chapter 6) and was enthusiastic about the marbles, decorating his home at Weimar with drawings of them by Haydon. Hazlitt puts his finger on the issue when he states that Phidias copied perfect but *real* human beings. No mathematical canon or Ideal, but human perfection such as Plato glorified lay at the root of Greek art. The frigid simplicity of the famous statues from Rome, the Apollo Belvedere and so on, was shown up as an evasion. No connoisseur would stand for this. It would strike at the roots of all their claims. The Townley Collection, to name no other, would be pushed into the shade. Further, what gentleman would wish to have one of those rugged and mutilated stones in his drawing room in place of an alabastrine Venus? The 'drawing room' criterion of art has a long history.

It was Richard Payne Knight who led the Dilettanti's attack on the marbles. He had already, it is probable, blocked in 1803 a proposed remittance by the Society to Lusieri. Now he made his position clear in a characteristically abrasive remark to Elgin at a dinner in 1806: 'You have lost your labour, my Lord Elgin. Your marbles are over-rated: they are not Greek: they are Roman of the time of Hadrian.' He had not of course seen the marbles; he had only misread Spon who stated that two heads, probably later additions, seemed to be portraits of Hadrian and Sabina (see p 76). Le Roy and Chateaubriand had been less circumspect and made the whole pediment Hadrianic. This was the opinion Payne Knight took over unexamined, and his opinion swayed the Dilettanti world; Elgin's chances of influence or even remuneration seemed to slip away.

He fought back with the Memorandum (composed by Hamilton), which detailed his purposes and his expenditure, and suggested that Parliament buy the collection. They offered £30,000, which was less than half what Elgin calculated as his total expenditure by this time, and he refused to sell.

To this hostility was added the public indignation of Byron, who with the publication of *Childe Harold* (March 1812) had become the darling of the British public. He had already condemned Elgin before ever seeing Athens (see Epigraph) and he now returned to the attack. Five stanzas of *Childe Harold* were devoted to Elgin's crime. A cancelled stanza links Elgin and Hamilton (who had died in 1803) with Aberdeen and also with Hope.[9] But both these latter, already established in English society, were better placed to withstand the assault than Elgin. The most vigorous attack came in *The Curse of Minerva*, written like *Childe Harold* in Athens in 1811, but published a little later. This attacked not only Elgin's desecrations but the alleged gullibility and foolishness of the marbles' admirers:

> Round the throng'd gate shall sauntering coxcombs creep,
> To lounge and lucubrate, to prate and peep;
> While many a languid maid, with longing sigh,
> On giant statues casts the curious eye;
> The room with transient glance appears to skim,
> Yet marks the mighty back and length of limb;
> Mourns o'er the difference of *now* and *then*;
> Exclaims, 'These Greeks indeed were proper men!'
> Draws slight comparisons of *these* with *those*,
> And envies Laïs all her Attic beaux.
> When shall a modern maid have swains like these!
> Alas! Sir Harry is no Hercules!
> And last of all, amidst the gaping crew,
> Some calm spectator, as he takes his view,
> In silent indignation mix'd with grief,
> Admires the plunder, but abhors the thief.
> Oh, loath'd in life, nor pardon'd in the dust,
> May hate pursue his sacrilegious lust!
> Link'd with the fool that fired the Ephesian dome,
> Shall vengeance follow far beyond the tomb,
> And Eratostratus[10] and Elgin shine
> In many a branding page and burning line;
> Alike reserved for aye to stand accurs'd,
> Perchance the second blacker than the first.

The end result was ignominy for Elgin.

As St Clair writes (see p 202):

He fell, undefended, from Byron's onslaught. Had it not been for Byron, his ambition of improving British taste might have been quietly fulfilled and the honours he so ardently desired might have been bestowed; the present-day Greeks might feel as little passion that the Parthenon Marbles are in London as they do at the Venus of Melos being in Paris. Such considerations could, of course, provide very little comfort at the time.

He retired to a modest existence in a wing of Broomhall, while his sculptures, now moved from Park Lane, stood, many of them in the open courtyard, at Burlington House.

Meanwhile Lusieri was still busy in Athens, and even obtained from Veli Pasha an agreement by which he could dig at Olympia. But Elgin had no spare cash and was not willing to lose his labour a second time. All he could afford was a recompense to the city of Athens in the form of a clock, which was placed on a pedestal near the Tower of the Winds. It survived less than ten years before being destroyed in the War of Independence. (Edmond About neatly characterised the exchange as 'a glass necklace for a gold ingot'.)

Lusieri himself remained in Elgin's employment until his death in 1821. In all that time he completed two drawings. He was buried in the Capuchin convent in Athens.

The Temples of Aigina and Bassae

Statues are what I want above all, and for my collection to shine with their excellence.   (King Ludwig I of Bavaria, to Johann Martin von Wagner)

And we come at last in the marbles of Aigina to a monument, which bears upon it the full expression of . . . humanism, – to a work in which the presence of man, realised with complete mastery of hand, and with clear apprehension of how he actually is and moves and looks, is touched with the freshest sense of that new-found, inward value; the energy of worthy passions purifying, the light of his reason shining through bodily forms and motions, solemnised, attractive, pathetic.   (Walter Pater, *The Marbles of Aigina*)

There is more to Elgin's story, but to set the scene for its conclusion we must first return to Athens and to the activities of another group of young enthusiasts for Greek art and architecture. Young Englishmen of *haut ton* hardly moved in the same circles as Elgin's shaggy crowd of artists, though they inevitably met through the pivotal figure of Fauvel.

The first of the lordly trippers to come specifically to study archaeology was 'the travell'd thane, Athenian Aberdeen', as Byron called him. Born in 1784, endowed by the death of his father at twenty-seven in 1791 with a fortune he could not inherit until his majority, he filled in the interim after taking his degree at Cambridge (to obtain which, as a peer, he did not need to sit an examination) in travel to the Continent. Travel had been eased by the Peace of Amiens of 25 March 1802, and on 19 November Aberdeen set off for Greece, landing at Piraeus on 1 April 1803. The rest of the year was devoted to travel in Greece and Asia Minor; in Athens he saw the conclusion of Elgin's work on the Parthenon, and he may have been one of the 'two English gentlemen' who offered Lusieri 50,000 piastres (£4,000) for the Parthenon frieze.[11] In the end he got a single foot from a metope: this is now lost.

He also had the Pnyx restored, and conducted excavations in Attica and at Amyclae (see p 105). At Messene he got a head, now in the British Museum (no 1600); but Olympia had been already 'pretty well explored' and he guessed there was nothing further to find. How wrong he was!

After his return to Scotland in 1804, his political career absorbed much of his attention. But he was able to enlarge his understanding of the antiquities he had seen in Greece, reviewing publications on archaeology and in May 1805 being elected to the Society of Dilettanti, in which he remained active until he became Foreign Secretary in 1828. In 1811 he was chairman of the committee which financed Gell's third expedition of the Eastern Mediterranean – the one which resulted in the *Antiquities of Eleusis* and *Antiquities of Attica*. In 1812 he wrote a long introduction to William Wilkins' translation of Vitruvius, which was later revised as the *Inquiry into the Principles of Greek Architecture*. He argued strongly that the appreciation of beauty is spontaneous and aesthetic, not intellectual, which put him on the side of Richard Payne Knight against Uvedale Price and perhaps made his resistance to the arguments for the merits of Elgin's marbles the more obdurate.

This honourable work, like that of the Revd Robert Walpole, whose impressive collection of *Memoirs Relating to European and Asiatic Turkey* was published in 1817, deserves to be sharply distinguished from the more rapacious acts which command the centre of the stage – even though the same men might often engage in both.

If such was the archaeological climate in Athens, the social tone, at least among the English, was certainly set by Lord Byron, who arrived in autumn 1809. From Athens, Byron would explore the vicinity with his friend Hobhouse, making excursions to favourite spots such as Sunium (where the party was once attacked by bandits) and to Marathon. It was Hobhouse who investigated the antiquities of the places, which Byron roundly dismissed as 'antiquarian twaddle'. While Hobhouse was opening tombs in the Troad, Byron was shooting snipe. And in Athens a romantic adventure like saving an adulteress from forcible drowning was more to his taste than examining statues and inscriptions. That is not to say that he was indifferent to the fate of the antiquities, but 'the improvement of the arts in England' meant nothing to him: his aim was to honour the glory that was Greece, but to do through poetry and action what archaeologists did through study.

Byron in fact liked a mixed portion of experience. Besides his famous swim from Sestos to Abydos, and his less well-known climb up the Symplegades, his adventures included 'a few alarms from robbers, and some danger of shipwreck in a Turkish galliot six months ago, a visit to a Pacha, a passion for a married woman at Malta, a challenge to an officer, an attachment to three Greek girls at Athens, with a great deal of buffoonery and fine prospects . . . Hobhouse rhymes and journalises; I stare and do nothing.' (To F. Hodgson, off Abydos, 5 May 1810.) A planned experimental leap, like Sappho's, from the promontory of Leucas (*Letters* I, 276) was abandoned, as was the idea of buying the island of Ithaca (*Letters* I, 305).

But it was through Byron that the next major archaeological event of these years came about. By November 1810 his circle included, besides the poet William Haygarth and the novelist John Galt (who was trying to start a business on Mykonos), 'the French consul and an Italian painter [Lusieri] and . . . five Teutones and Cimbri, Danes and Germans, who are travelling for an Academy.' (To F. Hodgson, 10 November).

These Northerners were Baron Haller von Hallerstein (1774–1817), an architect from Nuremberg, Jakob Linckh

(1786–1841), a painter from Württemberg, Baron Otto Magnus von Stackelberg of Estonia (1787–1857 – later the victim of a hair-raising kidnap by bandits),[12] and two Danes, Peter Oluf Brøndsted (1780–1842) and G. H. C. Koes (1782 –1811), of whom the latter was to die only a year later at Zante. All of these were busily engaged on the study of the antiquities, following a plan they had formed while students together in Rome. Parties, excursions, boat trips were the order of the day when they were tired of their studies.

Like attracts like, and when a month later two young English architects arrived in Athens, they quickly formed part of the band. The dominant figure was Charles Robert Cockerell. Twenty-two years old, he was travelling like the architects of the two preceding generations to enlarge his repertoire of classic forms, and was destined to become one of the best known architects of his generation: chief among his triumphs is the Ashmolean Museum in Oxford. He had just come from Constantinople where he had fallen in with John Foster, another apprentice architect from Liverpool.

Both the Englishmen enjoyed the merry cosmopolitan society of Athens, and lost their hearts at least temporarily to Greek girls. But it was only Foster who allowed himself to be permanently ensnared, at Smyrna some time later; even now his romances deflected him from his studies to an extent that Cockerell thought excessive.

Cockerell and Haller became the closest of friends and also shared their serious working habits, measuring and sketching all day. 'As a true German,' Cockerell wrote of Haller, 'he naturally borders on the phlegmatic and in fits of melancholy which occur sometimes moralizes and sometimes worse is as dull as a Tombstone. His spirits never rise above the Tenor . . . Gropius [see p 191] introduced me on my arrival here to Haller and we have worked together ever since. I have found Gropius a most excellent and agreeable man.' (His view of Gropius was to change over the next months.)

After a winter in Athens, spring brought the desire for change. An easy move was across the Gulf of Aigina. While Stackelberg, Brøndsted and Koes set off for Constantinople, the other four took a boat to Aigina. That was on 22 April. They had not got far before they overtook the ship *Hydra*, on board which was Byron, holding a farewell party with Lusieri,

Nicolo Giraud and some of the Elgin marbles. The four came on board, drank port and punch deep into the night and only retired to their boat when the *Hydra* was ready to sail.

That was the last they saw of Byron, who reached England a few months later. When Byron returned to Greece, it was for the last time, to die in the War of Independence.

The party of architects reached Aigina at break of day on the 23rd, and immediately set off to find the famous temple that overlooked the Gulf from its glorious pine-clad eyrie. Aigina, home of some of the most famous heroes of the Trojan War, and by the fifth century so serious a commercial rival to Athens that Pericles called her 'the eyesore of the Piraeus', celebrated its prosperity by frequent entries in the great atheltic contests of Greece, and by the creation of a temple which is still one of the glories of the Greek landscape; set on an eminence overlooked by Mt Hellenion, and overlooking the bay of Agia Marina as well as the twenty miles of sea that separate it from Athens, its pine-surrounded columns still catch the mariner's eye as they did at the turn of the nineteenth century.

Many travellers had visited it, and had uniformly supposed it to be the famous temple of Zeus Panhellenios, situated on the highest peak of the island. But although it was clear that this was by no means the highest mountain on Aigina, few challenged the identification. It was not until 1901 that Adolf Furtwängler established its identity with the temple of Aphaia described by Pausanias. (Aphaia was a Cretan goddess, identified with Athena). Some thought it a temple of Aphrodite; W. M. Leake actually puzzled himself as to why Pausanias never mentioned this temple, though he had so much to say of the supposedly insignificant Aphaia!

The date of the temple's construction is uncertain, though the east pediment is later than the west; current opinion would put the west pediment in the 490s, the east in the 480s.

The temple was a natural target for this group of young men. Much of the stonework had already been broken down by Aeginetans in the search for bronze and lead.[13] They pitched camp and began to excavate the shallow covering of earth:

We got our provisions and labourers from the town, our fuel was wild thyme, there were abundance of partridges to eat, and we bought kids of the shepherds, and when work was over for the day, there was a grand roasting of them over a blazing fire with an accompaniment of native music, singing and dancing. On the platform was growing a crop of barley, but on the actual ruins and fallen fragments of the temple itself no great amount of vegetable earth had collected, so that without very much labour we were able to find and examine all the stones necessary for a complete architectural analysis and restoration. At the end of a few days we had learnt all we could wish to know of the construction, from the stylobate to the tiles, and had done all we came to do.

But meanwhile a startling incident had occurred which wrought us all to the highest pitch of excitement. On the second day one of the excavators, working in the interior portico, struck on a piece of Parian marble which, as the building itself is of stone, arrested his attention. It turned out to be the head of a helmeted warrior, perfect in every feature. It lay with the face turned upwards, and as the features came out by degrees you can imagine nothing like the state of rapture and excitement to which we were wrought. Here was altogether a new interest, which set us to work with a will. Soon another head was turned up, then a leg and a foot, and finally, to make a long story short, we found under the fallen portions of the tympanum and the cornice of the eastern and western pediments no less than sixteen statues and thirteen heads, legs, arms &c. all in the highest preservation, not 3 feet below the surface of the ground. It seems incredible, considering the number of travellers who have visited the temple, that they should have remained so long undisturbed.

A contemporary painting by William Turner shows the debris of arms and heads, where the altar has since been uncovered.

Cockerell was quick to recognise the unique value of these works for the history of art, representing as they did a period of sculpture hitherto unrepresented in any known monuments:

. . . the figures are abo. 5 to 5.6 high in very powerful action evidently in combat, the Costumes are of the most antique kind I have ever seen, the Helmets are made to cover the nose & face as those you remember in Hope's book, Grieves to protect the skin & large bucklers. There are two in high preservation which draw a bow, the hands pulling the string & arrow are wonderfully beautiful, some are clad in a leathern coat & a costume something resembling the Roman, I have seen such at the Parthenon, in general how they are without drapery of any kind, & the anatomy & contour I assure you are equal to anything I have yet seen. Our council of artists here considers them as not inferior to the remains of the Parthenon & certainly in the second rank after the (Belvedere) Torso, Laocoon & other famous statues.

The Aeginetan school of sculpture was spoken of with unusual reverence in ancient authorities, and it was clear that this was a find of the highest archaeological, artistic and commercial value.

The excitement of the friends must soon have been soured as they realised that each would wish his own country to have the honour of possessing the unique works. Nonetheless they continued to work together for three weeks, until 4 May, when all the marbles were uncovered. It was less than a week before the local officials of Aigina arrived, at 10 am on 27 April, and laid formal claim to the antiquities of the site. Linckh had foreseen this; he had been up since four, getting the marbles ready to ship. While the argument was still going on, the boat arrived at the bottom of the hill, and by one o'clock they were off to Athens.

The natural course the next day was to go to Fauvel and tell him of the find. His amazement was much mixed with acquisitive envy. Linckh, efficient as ever, squared the Aeginetan officials by buying the excavation rights for 800 piastres. But what was his astonishment when Fauvel himself appeared with two pickaxes, borrowed four of their labourers and began to dig in the self-same spot!

We could not restrain our distaste at this and told him directly that it would not do. He was very angry at that, and began in his rage to measure superficially what Haller and Cockerell had already measured with the greatest precision. We found today [28 April] another figure which is armed with a leather breastplate and a leather cap over the helmet, two prone torsoes, the figure of Minerva, the great fleuron and the frontispiece [acroterion] with two small female figures, which are dressed in the style of the Etruscan sculptured columns. We found today five more heads and fragments of a griffon [?].

Cockerell, meanwhile, was quite pleased with himself. By 13 May he had the sculptures ensconced in a large house and was busy piecing them together. Fauvel, he admitted, was disappointed, but 'is too good a fellow to let envy affect his actions, and he has given us excellent help and advice.' In fact he had, at Linckh's urging, got the four to draw up a contract stating their joint ownership of the marbles. Cockerell had no cause to be too sanguine.

At present the excitement of the task must be to restore the scene that had adorned the gables. What legend was here portrayed? Cockerell formed no opinion – but Leake and Dodwell, who were among the first people to see the sculptures, recognising the figures of Athena and of a dead or dying warrior, both took it for the moment when:

> Another bitter fight about Patroclus grew,
> Tear-thirsty, and of toil enough, which Pallas did renew
> Descending from the cope of stars
> (*Iliad* 17, 543ff: tr George Chapman)

In fact the Aeginetans had no need to go to Homer for their myth: local tradition provided the theme both of the west gable, the second (Homeric) siege of Troy, and of the east gable, the first expedition of Telamon and Heracles against Laomedon King of Troy. Of that venture Pindar wrote in 480 BC, perhaps less than ten years after the completion of the temple:

> There is no nation so barbarous
> So perverse of tongue, it has not heard
> Of the renown of Peleus, hero, blest son-in-law of gods,
> or does not know the fame of Aias,
> son of Telamon, or of his father
> whom Alkmena's son [Herakles]
> brought with the Tirynthians
> to bronze-loving war, an eager ally
> aboard the ships for Troy,
> that toil of heroes, to avenge the treacheries of Laomedon.
> (Pinder *Isthmian* 6)

Heracles is easily recognised with his bow and his lion-head helmet. So, in the earlier composition (of the later siege) are Paris with his Phrygian cap and Telamon (formerly taken for Ajax) with his lion-blazoned shield.

The next great question was, what was to become of the marbles? At first Cockerell hoped Lord Sligo would offer to buy the marbles, but the Germans would not take less than

£6,000 for the lot. Soon after this two English travellers, Henry Gally Knight and a Mr Fazakerley offered to buy out the two Germans for £2,000 (a profit of 10,000 per cent each) and present them to the British Museum. This proposal too was rejected. Bound by their contract, the four decided to hold an auction of the marbles at Zante, to take place on 1 November 1812. In the meantime they were stored at Malta, to be safe (unlike Zante) from possible French attack.

Though the adventure of the Aigina marbles naturally steals the limelight, it represented only a small part of Cockerell's and his friends' activities in Greece that winter and spring. Cockerell and Haller had devised a plan to produce a book together on their return. This plan was tragically aborted when Haller died of a fever in the Vale of Tempe in September 1817. Cockerell, disheartened and busy with commissions in England, let the plan slide and did not publish his book, *The Temple of Jupiter Panhellenius at Aigina and of Apollo Epicurius at Bassae* until 1860. It was only then that an important and brilliant discovery about Greek architecture that he had made as early as 1814 was made public.

This was the observation of the entasis, or curvature of Greek Doric columns, in which Cockerell anticipated the findings of both John Pennethorne (1837) and F. C. Penrose (1845). A letter to Robert Smirke of 23 December 1814 incorporates a sketch of one of the columns of the Parthenon which shows 'how a rod or line stretched down from the top of the columns begins to depart from the shaft at the height of 17'7" and leaves 2" at the base of the column. Similarly, a line stretched from the underedge of the last fillet of the capital to the base touches at 11' and leaves ¾" at the base.'[14]

I have just returned [he adds] from a trip to Egina whither I took also my ladders. The ancient Temple of Jupiter Panhellenius has also the entasis in precisely the same proportion with Minerva, i.e. in a co. 17.2 the swelling is half an inch at 6 ft from the base. In Theseus I have not been able to ascertain it from the ruined state of the columns: it is the case with the Corinthian columns of Hadrian, and I have no doubt that it was a general rule with the Greek architects.

Even Stuart, he remarked with pride, had failed to observe this interesting property, which is now generally recognised as being responsible for the airy quality of the massive columns of the Parthenon: dead straight lines would produce a bulging and earthbound effect.

Cockerell also collected a good quantity of inscriptions. His manuscript copy was given by a descendant to C. T. Newton, and on publication in 1885 it was clear that he was a good copyist and had made several additions to the corpus.[15]

With the marbles safely out of the way for the time being, Cockerell and his friends tried their hands at a dig at Eleusis, but found no sign of the Temple of Demeter. (Gell and the Dilettanti, the following year, had better luck.) Then they went on to the Peloponnese and had another desultory dig at Olympia, where the deep silting prevented them finding anything more than had already been observed by Leake.

Their next piece of serendipity was more successful. They made for another magnificent and lonely site, the Temple of Apollo Epicurius, the Helper, at Vassai in Arcadia, high in the mountains above Andritsaina. Positioned with that unerring eye of the ancient Greek for a site of unparalleled magnificence, in a dell of the hill which overlooks all the mountains of Arcadia and south to the tableland of Ithome, it had been erected by the citizens of Phigaleia in the fifth century BC as a thanks-offering for deliverance from plague. The architect was Ictinus, who had built the Parthenon for Pericles. Unusual in several features – a cella-door positioned at the side, perhaps offering a direct view for the cult statue to the holy mountain opposite, and engaged Ionic columns rather than free-standing Doric ones within – it probably reflected the design of an earlier sanctuary on this somewhat cramped site.

The capital of one free-standing column at the back of the cella is of interest as an early version of the full-blown Corinthian of later columns: it embodies elements of Ionic, combined with acanthus leaves. Unfortunately, all our knowledge of it derives from Cockerell's drawing, since the capital has since disappeared. (The capitals of the engaged Ionic columns were copied by Cockerell in the columns of the Ashmolean Museum.)

Situated high among savage mountains where even now only goatherds go, and the one bus daily will deliver the tourist to pass the night as best he can before offering its return service on the following day, it had remained undiscovered by Western travellers until 1765 when the French architect Joachim Bocher, engaged in the erection of villas on Zante, came upon it in his quest, which resembled that of Stuart and Revett, for a new architectural language. Unfortunately he was murdered soon after this and so was unable to introduce the proto-Corinthian capital to the aristocracy of Zante.

But the word spread. It soon became a point of honour to visit the grey temple in its arid solitude, and of course Leake had been there – on 7 May 1805, making his usual early start at 5.50 am, from Tragoi. After quoting the whole of Pausanias' account, he concurred in his judgement of the temple's *harmonia* – an ambiguous word which he takes to mean precision of masonry jointing, but which may mean harmony in our sense – but remarks that the immense conglomeration of rubble will make the site unintelligible until it is cleared. He was not immune to its glory, though:

Nothing in Greece, beyond the bounds of Attica . . . is more worthy of notice than these remains [we must remember that Olympia, Delphi and Epidaurus were all as yet unexcavated]; though Aigina be more picturesque, many persons will prefer the severe grandeur, the wildness and variety of this Arcadian scene . . . in which there is no want of objects interesting to the spectator by their historical recollection.

Wilderness, the picturesque, and history: it is the taste of his generation in a nutshell! Stackelberg's reaction looked forward rather to romanticism: 'There rests still a Genius in this natural scene, which did not fade with the cheerful world of the gods.'[16]

The story of Cockerell's discovery of the first fragment of the frieze is dramatic. The Greeks had tried to hustle them away, for fear of reprisals from the Turkish authorities, but the companions pretended they had firmans and continued with their scrambling and poking. Suddenly a fox, disturbed by all the unwonted activity, bolted from where it was lying under a mass of stone. Cockerell immediately dived down where it had come from and saw, to his amazement, a sculptured bas-relief – Lapiths and Centaurs again fighting out their eternal battle in stone. Hanging upside down as he was, he sketched it hastily and withdrew, concealing his tracks, lest others take the prize that was to be theirs alone.

The native labourers, however, had by this time deserted, and the work of digging was proving too rough for the young gentlemen, even before the owner of the land arrived (with four armed attendants) to forbid further digging. They had no option but to stop and seek formal permission from the Turkish authorities. This meant a visit to Veli Pasha, son of the formidable Ali Pasha, in his jewels-and-velvet court at Tripolis, where John Galt, visiting him a few years earlier, had found him 'free and urbane, with a considerable tincture of humour and drollery.'[17] Veli, who had some pretensions as an archaeologist, scented saleable antiquities, and duly provided a firman permitting them to dig on condition that he received half of whatever was recovered. The primate of Andritsaina was obliged to provide men, tools and food for the undertaking.

The party assembled at Andritsaina in July 1812, and consisted of Foster, Haller, Linckh, Stackelberg, Brøndsted and the Austrian consul Georg Christian Gropius. Koes had died in Zante a year before; Cockerell was absent in Sicily after a tour of Asia Minor, but was to be given the free use of all Haller's own drawings. Sometimes as many as 100 men were working on the site, spurred on by the sound of drums and pipes uttering the shrill wail of a Peloponnesian dance. Gradually, to the usual accompaniment of quarrels and petty theft among the workmen, attacks from bandits and so on, the whole of the frieze and metopes was brought out, though no pedimental sculptures were ever found.

The team dutifully sent half the finds to Veli Pasha. He was mortified to find nothing among them of obvious commercial value. He gazed uncomprehendingly at these lively figures with their short swords and oval convex shields. The Turkish eye was not attuned to figural representation: he sent them back again, merely commenting on the excellence with which the artists had portrayed the tortoises.

Veli now became the victim of the intrigues of Constantinople; ousted from his pashalik, he was willing to sell out his share in the finds for £400. Quickly they got from him the documents necessary to remove the stones from the country. As they left their camp among the ruins a fire broke out, and like Adam and Eve pursued by the flaming sword they left their troubled paradise behind. One hundred and fifty men carried the antiquities alongside the River Neda to the sea at Bouzi: here they were hastily shipped to the British-ruled safety of Zante.

Cockerell wrote of the dramatic embarkation of the marbles, and described how everything was loaded on to the boat except the Corinthian capital from the cella, when the new Pasha's troops arrived to stop the shipment. Hastily the ship put to sea, and the Turks hacked the capital to bits in a fury. But Cockerell had not been present; and Haller later wrote to Cockerell asking him if he should visit Bassae again, to re-record its details. The venomous fury of the locals was to become a leitmotif of such accounts. In fact the capital never left the temple site: a few fragments of it were found there by Kavvadias in 1902–8.[18]

At Zante the marbles were installed in a rented room and arranged in a probable sequence – though even today their arrangement is uncertain – and offered for sale in May 1814.

Though the friends now had two magnificent collections to sell, the disposal of the Aigina marbles was the first priority. As the friends undertook their various travels through 1811–12, they had appointed Georg Christian Gropius (?–?1845) as their agent in the sale. Gropius was a North German painter from Brunswick who had accompanied Wilhelm von Humboldt to Paris and then in the early years of the century, when he was perhaps twenty-five or so, had been sent as agent for Lord Aberdeen from Italy to Athens. Since then he had remained in Greece, engaged in commercial activities. In 1816 he became Austrian consul, and from 1840 acted for Britain and Prussia as well. He became almost as prominent an Athenian figure as Fauvel, and knew every traveller of note. He survived the War of Independence despite or because of his connections on both sides: everyone, Ross tells us in 1835, recognised his 'strict sense of justice, his good heart, his cosmopolitan education, his rich experience and accurate topographical knowledge.' At this time Cockerell would have shared his good opinion.

Cockerell, through his friend Hamilton, had persuaded the Prince Regent to put in a bid of £6,000 to £8,000 for the Aigina marbles. Somewhat prematurely, the Prince Regent, besides agreeing, had sent a warship to collect the marbles from Malta. Taylor Combe, the Keeper of Antiquities at the British Museum, went with it to make the formal bid. Cockerell felt secure of their future.

He did not worry much about the interest of the good Fauvel in the works: though the latter had written and described them with cautious enthusiasm to Visconti, the Keeper of Antiquities at the Louvre, the maximum French bid was to be £6,000, and transport to Marseilles to be at the risk and charge of the vendors. There was no other way the French could be sure of the goods, while the English fleet controlled the Mediterranean; but of course it reduced the value of their bid.

But something went wrong with the plan. It should not be laid to the charge of Haller, though since November 1811 he had had responsibilities to Crown Prince Ludwig (later Ludwig I) of Bavaria. The Crown Prince, a keen amateur of archaeology, who once said he would rather be a citizen of ancient Greece than King in Bavaria, was anxious to set his future kingdom on an equal footing with the great powers, and the acquisition of a collection of antiquities rivalling those of London and Paris was an important goal – the only exception to his habitual parsimony. He had already acquired by purchase the whole of Dodwell's collection of vases, and his appetite was whetted. Haller was provided with credits and it was suggested that he might remove the remaining horse's head from the Parthenon, or perhaps two more Caryatids from the Erechtheion.

This was too much for Haller, who instead excavated graves in Attica, sites in Ithaca and Megara, and in 1816 the Theatre of Melos which he bought for twenty pounds plus a quarter share of the finds to the ex-proprietor. He reported promptly and optimistically to Ludwig on the finds at Bassae.

Perhaps realising that an extra effort was needed to secure such major prizes as the Aigina and Bassae marbles, Ludwig sent a special agent. This was Johann Martin von Wagner (1777–1858).

Wagner had, since 1810, been the agent in Rome of the Bavarian king. He was a well-respected painter and architect who had already been in Rome for six years. In his first twelve months as Ludwig's agent he had acquired numerous Roman statues from princes, dukes and cardinals who were only too ready to sell. It was an expensive business, and Wagner often had to bid against Denon who was buying for the Louvre. When the first reports were published of the finds at Aigina, and it was known that they were to be offered for auction, Ludwig lost no time in despatching Wagner to Zante with a credit of 70,000 gulden and strict instructions to be at Zante by 1 November. He must assure himself that, although the works were pre-Phidian, they were superlative of their kind. The seventeen statues must be bought as a complete lot. Ludwig gave detailed instructions on how he should calculate the instalments for different prices, and on the transport back to Munich.

Wagner was hardly enthusiastic about his lot. A squat and grotesque figure, a Hermes in the shape of Caliban as contemporary cartoonists were wont to depict him, he hardly seemed suited to the role of bringing home the glories of Greece. The forests of Germany would have suited him better. Certainly he would have been better fed there – a matter which was to be a sore point on his journey.

His journey from Otranto began on 30 September 1812, but on reaching Corfu the following day he found himself facing a ten-day wait for further transport. Food, he complains, was far from plentiful – 'nothing but old mouldy bread, which at home would hardly be given to pigs.' Two days later there was nothing but eggs, which he helped down with some more of the same bread (after first breaking it up by hammering at it with a stone). At Nikopolis they got some grilled goat, and when on 26 October they reached Sta Maura (Lefkas) there was finally a good breakfast to be had. Wagner was heartily relieved to arrive on Zante – only to find himself compelled to seven days in quarantine, shut in a damp lazaretto without light, food or water.

His mind was finally taken off these privations when Gropius arrived on 30 October to explain the situation. Haller and Linckh, he told him, were very keen that he should buy, and had even offered to contribute to the price in order to secure the sale for the German Prince. Wagner duly put in his bid on 1 November and easily outbid the French. The English agent, however, was still in Malta under the impression that the sale would take place there. Gropius was eager that Wagner should sign a contract at once; not surprisingly Wagner was reluctant when he had not even seen the marbles, in Malta as they were. He could not, he forcefully stated, buy for his Prince a 'cat in a sack'. In the end he signed a 'provisional contract' and set off for Athens to see Fauvel's casts of the finds. The sight of even three or four broken torsos was enough to assure him that here was a prize of the first order, and he ratified the contract at once.

In the circumstances it is hardly surprising that Cockerell did not think much of Gropius' behaviour. He suspected in fact that Wagner had bribed him not to inform Taylor Combe at Malta that the sale would take place at Zante. This seems unlikely since Wagner too remarks with contempt on Gropius' level of honesty: even after the sale was agreed Gropius tried to make a little extra out of cheating the insurers, and made difficulties in Wagner's shipping the marbles, in the hope of winning a further contract for the freight.[19] Fauvel by contrast was very helpful. The gentle fellow was really absorbed in his six-feet-long scale plaster model of the Acropolis of Athens.

Wagner was of course able, while at Zante, to see the Bassae frieze. Rightly finding it of far inferior artistic quality, he declined the opportunity to buy it. Ludwig had indeed only empowered him to buy it if he could be sure it was of the school of Phidias, which of course it was not. A more straightforward auction took place on 1 May 1814, where the bidding was concluded in the Greek manner by the blowing out of a candle at nightfall. The English government was anxious not to be upstaged again, and the Governor of the Ionian Islands bid £15,000 on their behalf, easily outstripping the French offer through Fauvel of £8,000.

But it was Ludwig who had secured the real prize, and at scarcely half the price of the inferior Bassae frieze. He was delighted with Wagner's work:

Like Odysseus, you have suffered much, Wagner, and that on my account, which I shall remember all my life. I am extremely pleased with you. It was not possible to carry out this purchase better than you have done. In all and every detail you have thought of my advantage more than a man can of his own. Honesty, spirit, connoisseurship, and astuteness – all are united in Wagner.

When the marbles were finally shipped from Malta in July 1815, they went straight to Rome where they were restored by the Danish sculptor Bertel Thorvaldsen. It had been conventional since the time of Bernini to 'restore' all ancient statues, though as we shall see, Canova refused to do so to the Elgin marbles. Cockerell objected to many of Thorvaldsen's restorations; the purer taste of this century has removed his work, as well as several times rearranging the order of the figures.

Since that time the archaic grace of these statues has been variously estimated. It was too soon for the medievalism of Victorian taste to clothe them in the glow of Walter Pater's unbridled enthusiasm: Dodwell's appraisal was more circumspect:

They were evidently made prior to the introduction of the beautiful ideal in Grecian sculpture. The muscles and the veins, which are anatomically correct, exhibit the soft flexibility of life; and every motion of the body is in scientific harmony with that of nature. The limbs are strong, though not Herculean, and elegant, without effeminacy; no preposterous muscular protuberance, no unnatural feminine delicacy, offends the eye. They are noble, without being harsh or rigid; and are composed with Doric severity, mingled with the airy grace of youthful forms. The perfection of the finish is quite wonderful; every part is in a style worthy of the most beautiful cameo. . . . The most extraordinary circumstance however in these statues is, the want of expression, and the sameness of countenance, which is to be observed in all the heads. This approximation to identity is certainly not fortuitous: for the artists, who were able to throw so much varied beauty into the forms of the bodies, were no doubt fully able to infuse a similar diversity of expression into the features. Their talent was probably confined to one style of countenance, by some religious prejudice. . . .

All the figures have been painted; the colour is still visible, though nearly effaced. The colour on the aegis of Minerva is very distinguishable. The white marble of which the statues are composed has assumed a yellow hue, from the soil in which they were buried.

Their broken limbs have been judiciously united at Rome; and some extremities, which were not found in the excavation, have been so well restored and imitated, as to be scarcely distinguishable from the originals. They are destined to render the cabinet of Munich one of the most interesting in the world.   (*Travels* I, 570f)

So proud was Ludwig of his marbles that a large set of table porcelain was commissioned (1834–6) from the Nymphenburg works, in dark red and gold with a meander surround, in the centre of each piece of which was painted one of the statues from the temple. The set joined other series adorned with Roman Emperors, scenes from Livy, and works from the Pinakothek. (The dinner service is now beautifully displayed at Schloss Nymphenburg in Munich.)

At least as important as restoration was display. A fitting home must be built for these glorious antiquities, which should be at the same time a 'temple to the German genius'. Such was Ludwig's idea. His first plan was that Haller should produce a design for a building to be at once a museum and a ballroom with illuminations for nocturnal festivities. But in the end the task fell to Leo von Klenze, Ludwig's architect in residence. Though Klenze had not at this stage of his career yet visited Greece (see Chapter 10), he made good use of those who had. The Glyptothek he designed for the Aigina sculptures and the rest of Ludwig's collection, quite apart from its Greek appearance, set standards for museum design which put it way ahead of its contemporaries and was to influence successors like the Berlin Museum to a marked degree.

It is worth quoting at length from Wagner's letter to the King of 11 October 1815, as it is the first outline of a museum on modern lines, spaciously planned for purposes of study and use rather than private gloating:

In contemplating the manifold Museums or collections of ancient statues, and as a result of the observations which I have in that way had the opportunity to make, I have come to the opinion or fundamental ideal that a quantity of statues tumbled together in one hall tend to arouse an unpleasant sensation in the spectator – the educated man – and tend also to the disadvantage of the exhibited antiquities themselves. It must arouse a negative sensation in the spectator for this reason, that too many and various demands are made on his imagination in quick succession, and his spirit does not have enough time to contemplate the beauties of any one in particular. He is rushed from one object to another and in this way loses the true flavour which such elevated works of art are capable of arousing in the human spirit, and which can only be achieved through calm and undisturbed gazing. . . .

The majority of ancient statues, especially the idealising ones, have a various character, and at the same time quite various styles or treatments. To appreciate the various handling and achievement of each work with equanimity and taste it is necessary, I believe, that one see such works in isolation one from another. I would therefore make the following proposal, to introduce sub-divisions into the general division of Gods or Ideal works. I.e. I would bring together 3 or 4 statues of similar treatment or style and similar mythological content in one room, and exhibit all the works in this way in numbers of 2 or 3 or 4 as they require by their own nature.

In this way it will more readily be possible to give the statues the most suitable lighting, which is not possible if they are all exhibited together in a hall: for some will of necessity receive good, and others bad lighting.

It will be observed that Wagner's stylistic criterion does not extend to a genuine chronological division; but the proposals he made were of the first importance. In fact he went on to specify that the Aigina marbles, as being obviously a stylistic and mythological unity, be exhibited together. One need only compare this to the almost picturesque arrangement of the Parthenon marbles in Elgin's shed in Park Lane to realise the leap in scientific understanding that has been taken.

The tale of this second city can conclude with some remarks of Leo von Klenze in an address to the Bavarian Academy of Sciences of 31 March 1821, entitled 'On the removal of works of plastic art from contemporary Greece, and the latest undertakings of this kind.' Many Westerners were uneasy about the despoliation of the country whose past they revered above all others. Klenze took one of the most coherent stands of the time on the controversy.

Greek art [he said], is the highest art known to man; the Western world had at last reached a level of intellectual and spiritual maturity [*Bildung* was his word] in which it could properly appreciate that art, in the recognition that, as Plato said, individual beauty reveals the highest ideal. Yet the remains of that art were dispersed in a 'tragically desolate land, guarded and mocked by barbarians'. The works were subject to daily destruction, and those who removed them were not worse than the Goths; rather they should be likened to a Perseus, rescuing their beautiful Andromedas from a threatening monster. All power to their arms!

Already hands were at work on Olympia where Winckelmann had first and rightly cast his eyes. If the Germans should continue their glorious task:

The works of Phidias and Myron will willingly rise out of their moist graves and emigrate hither, where, as Pindar's hymn once received the returning victors from Olympia, our jubilation will welcome these conquerors of the centuries.

Such was the task and duty of the coming age of German Imperialism.

The affair of the Aigina and Bassae marbles had a profound effect on the position of Lord Elgin. An insignificant kingdom had become the possessor of statues widely acknowledged as masterpieces of classical art, and England had been baulked of the opportunity to acquire a treasure which at least some of its discoverers had anxiously intrigued for her to obtain.[20] The mission of the West to save Greek marbles was being undertaken by other hands, and the nurture of art was being effected in museums abroad.

It is hard indeed to see why Elgin's collection was looked at with such unique disfavour in these years. Was it one man, Richard Payne Knight, who could hold back the taste and glory of a nation to such a degree? No doubt Elgin's insistent and pompous protestations of injustice did him little good – for no one loves a failure. Byron's charges of theft could not seriously cut much ice, when the Prince Regent would bid for other marbles, and Aberdeen would boast no less of depredations.

In 1814 Elgin was still working at public opinion. Then Napoleon abdicated, and Elgin set off at once to Paris to obtain the opinion of Ennio Quirino Visconti, the Keeper of Antiquities at the Louvre. Visconti came to London to see the marbles, at Elgin's expense, and produced a letter full of enthusiasm. He pointed out that the Elgin marbles, with the Laocoön, were the only surviving *original* Greek works (as opposed to Roman copies) of those sculptors singled out by the ancients for admiration.

Further negotiations with the Government were begun. The Trustees of the British Museum set up a committee to consider Elgin's overtures: it consisted of Charles Long, Lord Aberdeen and Richard Payne Knight, hardly a favourable conjunction from Elgin's point of view. Though Byron had tarred Aberdeen with the same brush as Elgin, Aberdeen was a member of the Dilettanti, a disciple of Payne Knight, and a former member of the Athenian Club which had (apparently) declined to admit Elgin as a member. Though Long talked of a maximum price of £35,000, Payne Knight wished to draw the line at £15,000 (the price paid for the Bassae marbles) or £20,000, and also declared that an Act of Parliament should be passed to prevent Elgin from trying to sell his collection abroad.

Clearly the bait was now taken. The spectacle of the loss of the Aigina marbles to Bavaria had alerted the English connoisseurs to the prestige value of sculptures found in Greek lands. Prince Ludwig was known to be willing to offer cash for Elgin's marbles. But the English were prepared to bargain hard for what they wanted.

Elgin's petition came to Parliament on 15 June 1815, but a decision was deferred until February. Three days later the Battle of Waterloo changed the face of Europe, and with it that of the Louvre. All the works of art Napoleon had looted were to be dispersed. Though at first it seemed that each of the conquering powers might get a share, it was eventually decided that all the works should be returned to their original homes. England, whose museums would receive no enrichment from this source, could look still more favourably on Lord Elgin's marbles.

The Roman sculptor Canova, delighted at the return of Rome's treasures, had added his voice to the campaign for Lord Elgin. If the Bassae marbles had been worth £15,000 the year before, Elgin's must surely be worth £100,000:

. . . As to the taste of those who hesitated to acknowledge the beauty of the Elgin Marbles and decided at once without hesitation on the Phygaleian ones, nothing need be said . . . There are one or two groups very fine in these Phygaleian Marbles but still approaching to manner; and in most instances they are entirely mannered. United with the Elgin collection their errors will do no injury to the student and both together will form the finest museum in Europe.

Canova's intervention was important in another way too, for his categorical refusal to contemplate their 'restoration'. By the time the Select Committee of the Government began its hearings of Lord Elgin's case, on 29 February 1816, his position seemed much stronger. One member of the previous year's committee was on the panel of 1816, Charles Long:

there were also F. S. N. Douglas and J. H. Fazakerley. Elgin's
estimate of his expenses, increased by interest and by the
arrival of eighty further cases since 1811, now came to
£72,240.

The hearing lasted two weeks and took evidence from a
number of sculptors and painters. Haydon was not called lest
his presence offend Payne Knight. The questions posed seem
now curiously beside the point: 'Were the Elgin marbles as
good as, eg, the Apollo Belvedere and the Laocoön? Did they
exhibit Ideal Beauty or was their naturalism a defect? Would
they be of more value if restored?' The artists could hardly give
direct answers to questions couched in such leading terms; but
they suited the connoisseurs who were called. The third of
these was Lord Aberdeen, who now changed his tune to extol
the merits of the sculptures and attribute them firmly to the
age of Phidias. He again suggested a price of £35,000, low but
not outrageously low in relation to the £15,000 for the Bassae
marbles, and this was eventually agreed. Elgin received
£17,000, since the rest went to pay off a creditor who had
cunningly transferred his debt to the Government. He was still
a poor man. But he had, to a considerable extent, won. Artistic
taste was permanently altered.

The fall of Richard Payne Knight was swift and sure. Artists
exulted, and the Royal Academy omitted his name from its
invitation list for the year. An Act of Parliament transferred
the marbles to the Government, and Lord Elgin and his heirs
were made trustees of the British Museum. Most important of
all, the wished-for impact on European taste had been made.
The death-knell of the Ideal was sounded. Since 1816 most
artistic taste has recognised the marbles of the Parthenon as the
supreme surviving achievement of Greek art and perhaps one
of the greatest works of art in the world. The British Museum,
too, was established in the first rank of museums at a time
when museums were coming to be an important symbol of
national prestige. Lord Elgin had served his country well.

This is not the place to enter into the controversy that has
raged intermittently over the propriety of the marbles' remaining in England, particularly since in this century they
have become a symbol of Greek national pride and unity. We
have already seen that the removal of the marbles was widely

received as an act of barbarism. An Athenian teacher, Ioannes Benizelos, wrote to Philip Hunt in January 1803:

I am sure if you saw Athens today you would be very happy. One thing only would make you sad as it does all those who have some understanding of these things – the last deplorable stripping of the Temple of Athena on the Acropolis and of the other relics of antiquity. The temple is like a noble and wealthy lady who has lost all her diamonds and jewellery. Oh, how we Athenians must take this event to heart, and how we must praise and admire those ancient heroes of Rome, Pompey and Hadrian, when we look on these things.[21]

The Parthenon, now a noble and wealthy lady, had come a long way from the painted tart of Plutarch! What had been built as a triumph of imperialism and extortion, as a gaud to delight the proud populace of Athens, had become an emblem of all that was best in Greece, in Greek art and in modern Greek aspirations. An aged Albanian remarked to Hobhouse one day soon after the removal: 'Guard them well – one day we shall ask for them back again.' (*Travels* I, 299f)

   Even as the Act of Parliament was passed, transferring the marbles to the nation, one MP was bold enough to propose an amendment by which the Government would commit itself to return the marbles at any time to the then government of Greece, if it should ask for them. It was not, of course, passed.

The Venus de Milo

> What the art of Greece created
> Let the Frank with conquering weapons
> Carry to the banks of Seine,
> And in glorious museums
> Let him show his victor's trophies
> To the wondering Fatherland.
>
> Ever will they keep their counsel,
> Never step down from their platforms
> Into fresh and vigorous life.
> He alone can own the Muses
> In whose bosom they are warmed;
> To the vandal, they are stones.
> (Friedrich Schiller, *On the Marbles at Paris*, 1800)

The French government in the first years of the nineteenth century had no such delicate scruples as the Bavarian architect or the British MP about its right to remove to Paris what works of art it pleased. Napoleon's plan was simple: Paris was to be the artistic Mecca of Europe, and all the continent was to be made tributary to its glory. Italy was naturally Napoleon's first hunting ground. Rome and Florence were stripped of their treasures. From Venice came the bronze horses that the Venetians had taken from Constantinople, and Constantinople from Rome, to adorn the Arc du Carousel; thence came vast Tintorettos, so vast they had to be cut in half to transport them. The most famous classical statues were brought from Rome. Many were not even unpacked, the paintings not unrolled: the important thing was that they should be within the walls of the Musée Napoleon. One Tintoretto was too high to fit the walls of the gallery: Napoleon blithely suggested docking it to fit, but luckily this was too much for the Director of the Museum, Baron Vivant Denon. But he too was more acquisitive than discriminating. Pure glory was the Imperial aim; scholarship and the arts were scarcely thought of.

Nonetheless, a lone voice spoke against the plunder as early as 1796. The voice was that of Quatremère de Quincy (1755–1849). Quatremère, the sculptor and connoisseur, and mentor of Jacques Louis David, was later to be secretary of the Académie des Beaux Arts. He had been artistic director for the construction of the Pantheon in 1791, but had come close to the guillotine in 1793. No doubt this influenced his attitude to the depredations of Napoleon.

In his *Lettres sur l'enlèvement des ouvrages de l'art antique à Athenes et à Rome* of 1796, Quatremère argued first that the idea of conquests by a republic was in itself subversive of liberty. In particular the plunder of arts was an offence to civilisation, for mankind's cultural achievements were the property of mankind. Rome – for example – could never be moved wholesale to Paris, and removal of its treasures could only result in a divided and diminished splendour. 'The antiquities of Rome are a great book, of which time has destroyed or dispersed the pages.' In another image, Rome itself was a museum: and you would not break up a museum to give every château an item. It was the concentration of antiquities in Rome that had enabled Winckelmann to achieve what he did. Nothing, he argued, echoing Schiller, is so dangerous as an ignorant friend – a pregnant apophthegm which Klenze had specifically to rebut when he claimed that the West was now fit to receive ancient art.

Quatremère's was a voice crying in the wilderness. But by 1814 the great rape was over, and with the conclusion of the Napoleonic Wars most items had been restored again to their homes. The Louvre (as it now was) was looking somewhat empty. The success of Lord Elgin and of Prince Ludwig turned the eyes of the French government to the Aegean as a source from which to replenish it. Instructions went out to the Consul General at Smyrna that any available antiquities should be purchased by the local consuls for the benefit of the Museum in Paris. It seemed a return to the methods of Colbert and the days of Paul Lucas; but taste would enthuse over items very different from Lucas' star exhibit (see p 89ff).

Such was the position when, in the spring of 1820, a peasant named Yorgos on the island of Melos, removing an old tree stump that was in the way of his plough (another story said he was rescuing a sheep that had fallen into a hole), came upon a buried marble figure. It was situated about 500 yards from the theatre (unfortunately for Prince Ludwig, who at once hoped to claim it as coming from his own land). In the hole were the two halves of a nude female figure, two stelae and various fragments including a hand holding an apple.

Yorgos informed the French consul, one Brest, of his discovery, no doubt reasoning that Brest might be able to ensure a sale at a good price to the French government through one of the ships, *Estafette* and *Lionne*, at present anchored in the harbour.

From here the course of events is quite uncertain. Brest himself told two different versions of the discovery; Voutier, an ensign on board the *Estafette*, who later distinguished himself fighting on the Greek side in the War of Independence, produced another. What is certain is that the French ships departed, some time after 8 April, to report the find to the consul at Smyrna. Brest felt unable to take any decisive action, being quite uncertain of the value of the statue. On 16 April another French ship, the *Chevrette*, arrived, commanded by Lt Dumont Durville. With him was his second-in-command Lt Matterer. In the meantime events had taken a further turn, for an Armenian priest had bought the statue from Yorgos, with a view to presenting it to the dragoman, Prince Nikolaki

Morusi, whose favour he wished to regain. The two Frenchmen were rightly impressed by the figure, but like Brest they
did not trust their own judgement. They in turn set sail, this
time for Constantinople where they intended to inform the
ambassador, the Marquis de Rivière, of the find. Almost
immediately the *Estafette* returned, this time with the twenty-
five-year-old Count Marcellus aboard. Here let the absent
Matterer take up the tale:[22]

After our departure for Constantinople, several days elapsed, and the
priest had time to buy his charming Venus Victrix, which he did,
buying it from the Armenian for 2000 piastres or twelve hundred
francs. When M. de Marcellus arrived at Melos, this statue was
wrapped up, and had been brought down from the Castro, and was
on the shore ready to be loaded on to a merchantman sailing to
Constantinople to return it to the pasha who had paid for it.

I cannot resist remarking here that if by a miracle this beautiful
Venus had been able to transform herself in a flash into a living
Venus, she would have groaned and wept hot tears to see herself
dragged over the beach, jolted and rolled by men furious with anger;
for she must have fallen into the sea, for the following reason.

M. de Marcellus was on the gangway of the *Estafette*, ready to
disembark, when he saw a great crowd of men on the shore, and was
afraid that there would be a fight, since the Armenian priest had a
rather high standing among the Greeks of his religion: so he said to
M. Robert, 'We must arm ourselves with rifles and swords, and take
twenty sailors similarly armed', which he did on the spot.

They got into the boat, and reached land where there was an
uproar around the case containing the Venus de Milo, and the Greeks
appeared determined not to let the statue be removed; but at a signal
from the captain of the *Estafette*, who cried out, 'Here, men, take that
box and put it in my boat', the battle began. Sticks and swords rained
blows, many of them on the head and back of the poor Armenian
priest, and on those of the Greeks who uttered cries of despair and
commended themselves to God. The consul was there, armed with a
sword and a thick staff, which he plied very vigorously; an ear was
cut, blood flowed, and during the battle, some of the sailors got hold
of the case which was being knocked from side to side in the mêlée,
got it on to their boat and took it to the *Estafette*, which at once set sail
for Constantinople.

This version of things was not unnaturally contested by the
Comte de Marcellus. According to him, the statue was already
embarked for Constantinople, whither Morusi had de-

spatched it, when the *Estafette* arrived. Only the prevailing north wind prevented the ship leaving Melos at once. Marcellus began to argue and haggle, and after two days he obtained the statue for a price of thirty pounds. He was filled with deep emotion as 'my goddess, my glory, my Venus' was hoisted on to his ship.

Matterer's story is a good one, and it may be true; but it explains rather neatly the absence of the statue's arms. It is undoubtedly true that several smaller fragments got lost before the statue reached the Louvre, including the hand with the apple, and an inscription from the base naming the sculptor as Alexander of Antioch.

This was one of the most intriguing parts of the find. Apart from the punning echo of the name Melos (mélon=apple), which suggested this *chef d'oeuvre* might really have been made for the island where it was found, it raised the possibility that the Venus was part of a group representing the judgement of Paris, where the shepherd boy presented the apple to the fairest of the three goddesses. Be that as it may – and it sounds a bit like literary fantasy – no other figures were found in the cache. The remark of Fauvel was equally apposite: the goddess, he said, no longer held the apple because it was the apple of discord, thrown among the parties to the discovery to ensure that no two of them should agree.

Joke as he might, there is no doubt that Fauvel was delighted with the find. Marcellus took his Venus with him on the rest of his voyage through the Mediterranean and finally brought her to show to Fauvel at the Piraeus. When the young Count revealed his goddess, first by moonlight, then by the light of torches, the aging Fauvel knew that at last France had acquired a masterpiece. It was, he judged, as good as the Capitoline Venus and worth 100,000 écus (1,200–1,500 francs). 'I came to Greece,' he said to Marcellus, 'young like you along with other passionately devoted antiquarians; we grew old in our investigations. But never did any of us meet on our way such a piece of good fortune as you in obtaining this Venus.'

No more of the statue was ever found. Colonel Rottiers tried to dig on Melos in 1825 but the government of Greece, embroiled with the Greek Revolution, was no longer friendly to such activities and he was stopped. Nor has Melos since yielded any fragments that could give a clue as to the pose or the date of the statue. Opinion would now put the Venus in the late second or first century BC.

More important was the question of restoration. A goddess without arms cried out for new ones. Fortunately Quatremère de Quincy, who in his new role as Secretary of the Academy now had no objection to foreign works arriving in France, held the view that Canova had already expressed (21 April 1821):

I think that, without excluding any of those little records of detail which parts require, the statue must remain in the mutilated state in which it was found. I think that in this state it will not fail to reveal to us the style and taste of one of the most celebrated schools of antique sculpture; that it will not be less instructive for artists, nor less precious to true amateurs, who perhaps will see in it the rarest and most precious morsel in our museum, where she will continue to deserve, in her new circumstances, the title of Venus the Victorious.

As is well known, this title did not stick, any more than other suggestions such as Venus Rivière. After some moving round, from the 'Hall of Diana' to the 'Hall of Apollo Belvedere', she ended up in the 'Hall of the Tiber', with the sobriquet Vénus de Milo. Here she was to engage more hearts than any other single piece of antique sculpture in Europe, the vanished Cnidian Venus only excepted. Heine[23] and Leconte de Lisle[24] were just two who were devoted to her. Perhaps in no other city could she have been more highly honoured. It was perhaps the last onslaught of the gods of antiquity on the hearts of the general public.

> Marbre sacré, vêtu de force et de génie,
> Déesse irrésistible au port victorieux,
> Pure comme un éclair et comme une harmonie,
> O Vénus, ô beauté, blanche mere des Dieux! . . .
>
> Salut! a ton aspect le coeur se précipite.
> Un flot marmoréen inonde tes pieds blancs;
> Tu marches, fière et nue, et le monde palpite,
> Et le monde est à toi, Déesse aux larges flancs! . . .

CHAPTER NINE

The Lions of Asia Minor

> High towers, fair temples, goodly theatres,
> Strong walls, rich porches, princely palaces,
> Large streets, brave houses, sacred sepulchres,
> Sure gates, sweet gardens, stately galleries,
> Wrought with fair pillars and fine imageries;
> All these (O pity!) now are turned to dust,
> And overgrown with black oblivion's rust.
> (Edmund Spenser, *The Ruins of Time*)

The seaboard of Asia Minor is spread with the skeletons of magnificent cities. From Troy in the north to Xanthus in the south, the names are a roll-call of the proud origins of Western thought and of the wealth that Roman rule brought to Anatolia. Ephesus, Miletus and Colophon, where philosophy was born; Cnidus of the Aphrodite, most beautiful of ancient statues; Didyma of the oracles, Priene of the town planners, Pergamum the capital of the cultured Attalid dynasty: all these cities rose in the fifth century, flourished first modestly and then, under Rome, magnificently; the rivers silted up the sea, landlocking their harbours and burying their buildings; Christians superseded pagans, despite flurries under philhellenes like Hadrian and Julian; the cities declined into medieval villages, the victims for a millennium of Sassanians and Saracens, Seljuk and Ottoman Turks, Gauls and Goths. Crippled by the onslaught they sank into reedy desolation about their towering temples and theatres, until travellers came from Europe to redeem them from oblivion.

Spon and Wheler were the first to pay attention to Ionia,

correctly identifying the sites of the Seven Churches of Asia and other cities. When Chandler and his companions came, the charm of Christian associations had become attenuated, and it is the classical past (always contrasted with the wretched present) that is in the forefront of his attention. As the sites became familiar through Chandler's books, those interested in antiquities realised that here were sources at least as plentiful as the sites of Greece itself.

That interest was strongest, now, in those who had charge of the great European museums. The days of private, and even royal, acquisition had passed. The number of museums was increasing rapidly; in Britain, from 12 to 59 between 1800 and 1850 (and to 240 by 1887); and the development in other countries was comparable. Museums were run, like the British Museum, by trustees with a strong sense of responsibility alike to their masters and to their public, and to the collections themselves. The British Museum had come a long way since Robert Cotton's grandson had settled the Cottonian library on the nation in 1700. The biggest single augmentation had been the collection of Sir Hans Sloane which he bequeathed to the nation in 1749, and it was at this time that the Museum was moved to Montagu House, on the site of the present Museum. Horace Walpole neatly, if sarcastically, summed up the character of the collections:

You will scarce guess [he wrote to Horace Mann] how I employ my time; chiefly at present in the guardianship of embryos and cockleshells. Sir Hans Sloane is dead and has made me one of the trustees to his museum, which is to be offered for twenty thousand pounds . . . he valued it at fourscore thousand; and so would anybody who loves hippopotamuses, sharks with one ear, and spiders as big as geese! It is a rent-charge to keep the foetuses in spirit![1]

The voyages of discovery in the reign of George II had brought many new treasures, of a more conventionally antiquarian kind; and the Museum had acquired the collections of other great connoisseurs: the vases of Sir William Hamilton (in 1766; most of a second shipment from Naples in the 1790s was sunk off the Scilly Isles), the sculpture collection of Charles Townley and the coins of Richard Payne Knight; and, greatest of all, the Elgin marbles which were at last appreciated at their true value. In 1825 came sculptures from Persepolis. At last the

British Museum had the edge over the Louvre, which had ceased from major acquisition after Napoleon's brief attempt to gather all the artistic products of Europe under one roof. The trustees' appetite was whetted, and as adventurous Englishmen plunged deeper and deeper into Anatolia they were eager to make what contribution they could to bringing back the spoils for Britain.

The new building for the British Museum, designed in 1823, was finally completed only in 1852 (though the entrance hall and staircase were opened to the public in 1847). The architect was Robert Smirke, another veteran Grecian traveller. The British Museum was the last and greatest of the buildings in the Grecian style in London: its exterior laid uncompromising claim to the inheritance of the classical tradition, and the collections had to match the frame.

The Monuments of Xanthus

The first enterprising explorer in Asia Minor was Charles Fellows (1799–1860). Freed from financial cares by the fortune of his father, a banker, he indulged a passion for travel which led him further and further afield: in 1820 he moved from Nottingham to London; in 1827 he tried a new route up Mont Blanc; and in 1832 he departed for ten years' travel in Italy and the Levant. By February 1838 he had reached Smyrna; it was in April of that year that his first discoveries were to be made.

For an inveterate traveller, he seems to have made heavy weather of Turkish conditions. Of course he carried the usual supplies of every Englishman abroad at this period – a mattress, hammock, canteen, arrowroot and plenty of tea – and usually travelled in a party of about seventeen, including horses. He also carried useful items as gifts to the natives: writing paper, pencil-leads, pocket compasses, mosquito nets and pictures of Queen Victoria. Yet after all these preparations to secure the goodwill of his hosts, he was unable to stand their company. Page after page of his journal is devoted to the agonies of entertainment by Turks to whom it could be the height of impoliteness to leave a guest alone to get on with his diary. In the end he was driven to feigning illness to preserve his peace and, it seems, his sanity.

Most travellers previously had penetrated no further East
than Bodrum. An exception was Charles Cockerell, who had
been at Myra in 1812.

While examining some statues (Captain Beaufort, inventor
of the Beaufort scale, recorded), one of the mob exclaimed, 'If
the infidels are attracted here by these blasphemous figures,
the temptation shall soon cease; for when that dog is gone, I
will destroy them.' The story is indicative of the dangers from
which English travellers conceived it to be their duty to
liberate the ancient works of art they found.

Captain Beaufort himself had been occupied in 1811 and
1812 with a hydrographic survey of the south coast of
Anatolia: his brief was to study and report on the naval
resources, 'yet the venerable remains of former opulence and
grandeur, which everywhere forced themselves into notice,
were too numerous or too interesting not to have found some
admission among the more strictly professional remarks.'[2]
But Beaufort had to confine his investigations to the coast,
and, as Leake in 1800 had observed, there must be numerous
inland cities to be discovered. These were a lure for a man like
Fellows.

Fellows' great discovery was Xanthus, the capital city of the
Lycians. Here the Cyclopean and Greek walls were clearly
visible, and the site was too vast to survey adequately. But
many of the monuments were easily to be examined and
explored, though they carried with them an air of mystery.
Even now little is known of the Lycians beyond the topographical facts and what can be deduced from the monuments
discovered by Fellows. The French excavations begun in 1950
have not turned up major sculptural or architectural finds – for
Fellows removed them all.

An Indo-European race, perhaps calling themselves
Termilae, the Lycians have left as their relics a few inscriptions
of their kings, and quantities of funereal and memorial monuments. For miles along the cliffs at Xanthus stretched rows of
these extraordinary tombs, dug out of the rock and fronted
with pedimented doorways so that each resembled a neat little
house. Deeply buried in rubble stood other monuments,
scarcely visible but so alluring that Fellows could not leave
them lie. The Lycians certainly admired Greek art, and
perhaps imported Greek artists to work on their ceremonial

tombs; but the iconography remains resolutely Near Eastern. Battle scenes and city scapes follow precedents closer to those of Assyria or Achaemenid Persia, though the figures have all the vivacity of fourth-century Greek art. The silence of history is extraordinary, for Xanthus remained a famous city – expecially for its schools – at least until 412 AD when Proclus visited it and found it in ruins, due probably to earthquake.

For the first time an archaeologist faced a site without a literary record to assist him: it was to lead to some interesting interpretations. But it was also to be seven years before Fellows could give the monuments the attention they deserved – for first they must be unearthed.

Such was the interest aroused by the published account of Fellows' tour of Lycia that the Foreign Secretary, Lord Palmerston, at the request of the trustees of the British Museum, applied to the Sultan for a firman permitting the removal of some Lycian works of art. The Museum asked Fellows to provide them with a list of the sculptures to be removed. But Fellows was not to be held back from his adventure, and insisted on going himself to supervise the removal of whatever stones he chose. He promised to pay his own expenses, and asked only for a free passage and rations. This was agreed, but the journey was abortive since the firman could not be obtained. Fellows was in Lycia from late 1839 to 1840, and made good use of his time, since, although he could not remove any stones, he could travel freely, and in fact discovered the remains of thirteen hitherto unknown ancient cities.

It was not until a third trip, which began in October 1841, again with the backing of the British Museum on similar terms, that some progress was made. There were a number of monuments that Fellows had set his heart on obtaining. One of these was the Harpy Tomb (now in the British Museum), which was erected about 480–470 BC to house a member of the Xanthian ruling family. It is nearly nine metres high including the pedestal, and is decorated with reliefs of winged females or 'harpies', holding small human figures in their clutches. They are the spirits of the dead carrying souls to the underworld, but to Fellows they recalled some famous lines of Homer, about the unfortunate daughters of Pandarus:

The ravishing Harpies snatched the maids away
And gave them up, for all their loving eyes,
To serve the Furies who hate constantly.
                              (*Odyssey* 20, 76–78)

Still, the interest of ancient stones was above all in the echoes
they gave of ancient literature. It was hardly to be conceived
that the stones could portray a scene unknown from the
literary tradition.

Other structures to be removed included one which sports
the longest known inscription in the still undeciphered Lycian
language. On a platform of rock above the plain stood a group
of 'temples', and one of them, adorned with friezes and
statues, was also to be removed stone by stone for the British
Museum.

This is the structure which is now the glory of the Xanthus
room, the Nereid Monument, a temple-like edifice of Parian
marble in airy Ionic on a tall platform, erected about 380 BC,
again as a monument to a Lycian ruler. Its weightless female
spirits soar at the threshold of the colonnade; others have
swooped down, headless all but full of the wind's grace, to
greet visitors at floor level. All around the platform stretch
friezes representing the battles of Greeks against alien tribes –
perhaps the dead king's battles against his own enemies.
Fellows, always willing to take any literary assistance he
could get, immediately decided that they represented the
resistance to the Persian General Harpagus in 547 BC, told of
in Herodotus. The assumption put the date of the monument
over a century too early.

Fellows did not have an altogether easy time removing these
massive quantities of stone from where they lay strewn over
the scene. In October 1841 he got the news that his firman
from the Sultan, permitting their removal, was waiting with
the English consul at Smyrna. On arrival however at Smyrna
in mid-November, he found not a firman but a letter dated 7
June which simply asked for details of what it was proposed to
remove. Fellows determined to go to Constantinople himself
and make clear exactly what he wanted. On 30 November the
redoubtable Englishman had his firman in his hand. It stated
that the Sublime Porte, because of its friendship to the English,
was ready to allow the removal of the 'sculptured stones, lying
down, and of no use, at a place near the village Koonik

[Kınık]'. The terms seemed unambiguous; Fellows was wary of Turkish official pronouncements, which were liable to be interpreted all too literally. He remembered with misgiving the permission given to the Revd F. V. J. Arundell nine years before to 'take down' some sculptures on a gate at Ephesus: the local authority had decided that his remit did not extend also to taking the stones *away*; and so they were left to crumble on the ground.[3]

Fellows hastily purchased spades, picks and crowbars at Constantinople (when the expedition was over these were given away to the grateful peasantry), and embarked again two days later for Rhodes. A journey which should have lasted thirty hours took sixteen miserable days to accomplish, but at least the Pasha of Rhodes allowed the party to pass on without further delay.

On reaching the mouth of the Xanthus, Fellows and his team began to sail their equipment upstream. In December, the Xanthus was swollen by rain and was wider than the Thames at Westminster, a 'powerful, wild and unmanageable river' running at about five miles per hour. It took them four days to cover the nine miles upstream to Xanthus.

But now there were further troubles. No funds had been given to Captain Graves of the *Beacon* on which he sailed, and Fellows had to find all the workmen's wages from his own pocket. This was not quite what he had meant by 'paying his own expenses'. Graves, indeed, was a source of considerable and continued frustration. It was the bureaucrat pitted against the explorer, a battle of will against obstinacy.

Another group of travellers, Captain T. A. B. Spratt, Edward Forbes and Edward Daniell arrived in January 1842, while the excavations were at their height.

While we were there [wrote Spratt] these sculptures were daily dug out of the earth, and brought once more to view. The search for them was intensely exciting; and, in the enthusiasm of the moment, our admiration of their art was, perhaps, a little beyond their merits. As each block of marbles was uncovered, and the earth carefully brushed away from its surface, the form of some fair amazon or stricken warrior, of an eastern king or a besieged castle became revealed, and gave rise to many a pleasant discussion as to the sculptor's art therein displayed, or the story in the history of the ancient Xanthians therein represented, – conversations which all

who took part in will ever look back upon as among the most
delightful in their lives.

Eventually, Fellows had piled up on the quay seventy-eight
cases of marbles for the British Museum.

The labourers, though enthusiastic, were not skilled. The
Horse Tomb was removed 'in a way more sailor-like
than scientific'; the top was hauled off and the centre fell in
pieces. Destruction was still very much a part of these
errands of mercy to neglected ruins. The impatience of the
adventurer easily dominated the minute precision of the
archaeologist.

During January, Fellows had most of his finds ready for
transportation to the coast. Besides the Nereid monument,
there were the Chimaera Tomb from Tlos, the Harpy Tomb,
the Winged Chariot Tomb, the Lion Tomb, and a pedestal
with a god and a goddess. Fellows asked Captain Graves to
provide some flat-bottomed boats to convey the stones down-
stream. Graves' answer was that he would apply to Captain
Beaufort at Malta, and they could expect an answer by March!
Fellows was speechless. His rage at the pointless and expensive
delay was exacerbated by Graves' incapacity even to produce
an adequate supply of nails: the 300 he sent at the first request
were 'scarcely a day's supply'.

However, the expedition managed to pass its time, com-
fortably lodged in a peasant's house (after some protests, they
had succeeded in persuading the peasants to move elsewhere).
One diversion was cricket. This, Fellows solemnly conjectures, was now played in Lycia for the first time in history. 'At
all events the wonder expressed by the living generation
showed that it was not a game known to the present inhabitants.' So the wild rocks and still flowerless plains of Xanthus
resounded alternately to the bangs of the carpenters' hammers
and the thumps of ball against bat, interspersed by yells of
'How's that!'

One caller had been the solitary Augustus Schönborn
of Posen. (Fellows miscalls him Schönbrunn.) Augustus
Schönborn (1801–57) had, in 1841, obtained an eight-month
leave of absence from the Gymnasium (grammar school) in
Posen (modern Poznan) and departed, accompanied by the
geographer Heinrich Kiepert, for Smyrna. Early in October of
that year they set off into the interior. Schönborn rapidly

acquired the reputation among the Turks of 'a man with a beard who picks up stones and puts them down again.' Indomitably he copied inscriptions and acquired coins, though dogged by asthma and fever. His leave was extended by five months on application to the Prussian Minister for Education and Medicine, and in 1843 he was rewarded by a reception by the King himself, at which he was given the title of Professor.

A second journey in 1850 was undertaken alone, except that he had to take two servants to carry the heavy photographic equipment he had just learnt to use. The combined hazards of this burden, of poor food, attacks from robbers, drought and rheumatism brought him an early death in 1857 in his native Posen. But his publication of the Lycian inscriptions was a model of its kind – and an example of a scholarly and arduous venture undertaken with no thought of fame or reward. His work was to have repercussions twenty years later when the Austrian archaeologist Otto Benndorf set out to rediscover a site first described by Schönborn, the ancient tomb monument at Gölbaşı (see Chapter 11).

But we have leapt ahead of our story. Fellows' fourth expedition in 1844 had the assistance of a party of a hundred sailors, Maltese stonecutters, casters, carpenters, etc, and an additional twenty-seven cases were obtained and removed to London. The Museum refunded all Fellows' expenses and thanked him most heartily in writing for his zeal and public spirit. In 1845 he was knighted, and he retired for the remaining fifteen years of his life to the Isle of Wight, 'occupying his time with agricultural pursuits'. (DNB)

Even in 1842 there was not much left to admire at Xanthus. Spratt, Forbes and Daniell investigated a number of other sites, including Antiphellus, Tlos and Oenoanda (though the great inscription, containing an entire philosophical treatise, erected here by one Diogenes, was not found until two French scholars, Holleaux and Cousin, came here in 1884). Spratt allowed himself some regret for the tomb of Payava, wrenched from its site at Xanthus: 'If it could not be transported without mutilation to England, it had been better left where it stood, the ornament of the fallen city, and an object of pilgrimage to the Oriental traveller.' Such travellers are still few, admittedly, in comparison with those who visit the

British Museum, but a site of ancient association has been despoiled of its individual beauty.

But Lycia took its toll of its violators. In May, Daniell left his companions to make an independent tour. He got frequent news of, though he never met, the lone 'man with a beard', and missed him only narrowly at Selge. After Selge he went his solitary way to Aspendus, where he contracted a fever. He travelled on to Antalya to recuperate, and to write what was to be his last letter to Spratt. A fortnight later he was dead. A lonely death in the cause of topographical exactitude.

The Lions of Halicarnassus

> In vain do earthly princes, then, in vain,
> Seek with pyramidës to heaven aspir'd,
> Or huge colosses built with costly pain . . .
> To make their memories for ever live;
> For how can mortal immortality give?
> Such one Mausolus made, the world's great wonder,
> But now no remnant doth thereof remain . . .
> But Fame with golden wing aloft doth fly,
> Above the reach of ruinous decay,
> And with brave plumes doth beat the azure sky.
>   (Edmund Spenser, *The Ruins of Time*)

When Spenser wrote those words, it might indeed have been supposed that the Mausoleum of Halicarnassus, one of the Seven Wonders of the World, had vanished into oblivion as thoroughly as the Hanging Gardens of Babylon, the Colossus of Rhodes and the Temple of Artemis at Ephesus.

Mausolus, the ruler of Halicarnassus, who died in 353 BC, had planned for himself one of the most spectacular of ancient tombs, bequeathing a name to architectural history. The building was never finished. The architect Pytheos was working on it at Mausolus' death; his widow Artemisia kept the work going, but she too died only two years later. When Alexander the Great invaded Persia in 334, he set off a chain reaction of local rebellions; one, that of Orontobates and Memnon in Caria, resulted in the burning of Halicarnassus. Still the Mausoleum survived the fire. The encyclopaedic Roman, Pliny the Elder, incorporated a detailed but perennially puzzling description of it in the thirty-sixth book of his *Natural History* (36, 4, 30–31).

Pliny stated that its perimeter was 440 feet, though the long sides were 63 feet each. He further stated that it was 25 cubits high, and that the pyramid above the colonnade was as high as 'the lower structure' and was topped with a quadriga; and that the total height was 140 feet. As 25 cubits is approximately 37.5 feet, to make up the full height a high plinth must be assumed to be included. This has been the basic form of all reconstructions: the latest, by K. Jeppesen[4] who excavated the area in the 1960s and '70s, assumes a plinth, colonnade and pyramid of 42 feet each, plus a quadriga 14 feet high – a solution neat in its proportions (3:3:3:1) as well as its arithmetic. The friezes were on the podium and on the quadriga base; statues stood between the columns, and the lions topped the entablature of the colonnade.

Pliny's description had engaged the imagination of the Renaissance: among those who produced draughtsmen's versions of the edifice from this description were Maarten van Heemskerck and Johann Bernard Fischer von Erlach – though Heemskerck, with his array of arches, niches and obelisks, seems hardly to have been trying. Hawksmoor imitated it in the steeple of St George's, Bloomsbury. What a triumph it would be if enough fragments from the building could be found to satisfy the learned curiosity of these often fantastical architects.

The building had remained substantially complete throughout antiquity, and the learned bishop Eustathius saw it in the twelfth century. In 1404 it was shattered by a tremendous earthquake, so that when, eleven years later, the Knights of St John began to build their castle of St Peter on the headland, there was a plentiful supply of building materials lying ready to hand. It seems that the first blocks of the Mausoleum were built into the castle in 1494, and it was finally dismantled by 1522.

Several centuries were to pass before attention to the remains was renewed. The castle was closed to Europeans after 1600. Richard Dalton in 1749 recognised and drew several pieces of the Mausoleum frieze where they lay or were embedded in the castle wall; but access was generally hard. Early in the nineteenth century a party of antiquarians had been frustrated by a too literal reading of their permission to 'go round' the castle. Another had obtained a firman permitting him to enter the castle, but declined to exercise the privilege when it was pointed out that the firman made no mention of his coming out again.[5]

In 1844 the pieces of the frieze were observed by the ambassador to the Porte, Stratford Canning (1786–1880); but it was only in 1846, through a 'triumph over Turkish procrastination', that he was able to have twelve of the seventeen slabs removed, at a cost to himself of three or four thousand pounds, and shipped to the British Museum.

Canning was himself an enthusiast for archaeology. Among his subordinates at Constantinople he numbered Layard, the discoverer of Nineveh, and Rawlinson, the father of Assyriology. He had provided both with funds to pursue their researches, until Nineveh was unearthed and the British Museum was willing to take over the expense. He would have bought the stones of Bodrum but Abdul Medjid made him a gift of them.

Captain Harry Edgell, who was responsible for the removal of the frieze to London, wrote of the Amazon figures: 'one could sit and gaze on them for hours, and still find new beauties, but when cleaned and properly set up their attractions will be tenfold. . . We have christened them the Canning marbles, and thanks to him, England may now boast of possessing some of the most exquisite specimens of sculpture in the world, and a fine field is opened to the antiquary and historian in searching out their history.' Canning, perhaps mindful of his predecessor Elgin's opprobrium, declined the honour of having the marbles named after him in favour of the Sultan whose gift they were, but their impact was no less for that.

The assistant curator at this time at the British Museum was Charles T. Newton (1816–94). He was much excited by the frieze and in 1852 (the year in which Canning was created Lord Stratford de Redcliffe), the Museum secured for him the post of vice-consul on Lesbos: a sinecure which allowed Newton to devote most of his time to the securing of new treasures for the Museum. He was a man well suited to the task – of great strength and stature, with a massive Victorian beard which gave him the appearance of 'a weather-worn antique Zeus'.

Full of the Victorian's confidence of superiority and of achieving whatever he wished eventually, – which secured him some enemies[6] – his account of his travels is full of humour: amusement at the problems caused by the natives (*Travels* II, 88–90), and a ready answer, namely to buy up all the houses on the site he wished to excavate; exasperation that never daunted his persistence, as in the matter of the lions (below); and a capacity to laugh at his misfortunes that compares well with Fellows' bouts of anger and despair (*Travels* I, 124).

His first visit to Bodrum was made in 1855, though he did not begin to excavate there until April 1856. Before this he had identified and visited the Amphiareion at Oropos in Attica, where the healing hero Amphiaraus, struck into the ground by a thunderbolt at Thebes, had re-emerged and had in classical times been honoured by coins thrown into a well by his grateful patients. Newton had also visited the Troad, of which he gives a vivid description, and remarks that 'the untravelled scholar can form no conception' of the geographical realities necessary to the understanding of Homer. Prophetic words! On Mytilene the archbishop had demanded of him 'Are you come like another Curzon, to rob us of our antiquities?' On Calymnos in October 1854 he had acquired inscriptions, collected coins, and dug at the Temple of Apollo between Pothia and Linaria, breaking up Byzantine walls to extract the fourth-century inscriptions. Tiring of dull Calymnos, he returned to Mytilini (while Canning borrowed a steamer from the fleet in the Crimea to convey his marbles away), and thence to Constantinople. Here he dug around the serpent column, and acquired among his assistants the sobriquet of 'the wise man who digs holes in the ground'. By the time he reached Bodrum he was a seasoned excavator as well as a man of learning.

He had seen Lord Stratford's Amazon from the Mausoleum in Constantinople in 1852, and pronounced it 'finer than any of the slabs in the British Museum'. He had applied at this time for a firman to excavate in the Sultan's dominions; this had still not arrived in April 1856, but in mid-December 1855 Newton got tired of waiting and set off for Bodrum to do what he could.

By April 1856 he was exploring Bodrum but unable to dig. His covetous eye was fixed on five stone lions, formerly observed only by Ludwig Ross (see Chapter 10). He suggested to Panizzi at the British Museum that a firman be obtained to remove them, an enterprise which resulted in one of his most entertaining adventures. Panizzi, not troubled with legal niceties, arranged for the departure of HMS *Gorgon*, which arrived at Bodrum in November 1856: but Newton's attention was for the time distracted from the lions by his discovery of the site of the Mausoleum.

On 10 April 1857 he recorded, 'After months of anxiety and weary labour I am at length able to say that the main object of the expedition is fulfilled, for the site of the Mausoleum is no longer a matter of uncertainty.' He had found it in the town centre, where architectural fragments lay thick and were built into the masonry of the houses. There was also a fragment of a lion. The field in question, however, turned out to be *vakıf* (land held in trust under Islamic law for charitable purposes); nonetheless Newton instantly obtained permission to dig from the *vakıfcı* – 'my good friend Salih Bey'. He soon came upon a pavement (the basement of the Mausoleum), column bases and a marble beam with ultramarine blue paint still visible on its underside. There were also two portions of lions.

Unfortunately his trench came up rapidly against a house which barred his way: 'It was evident that this house must be bought.' But:

. . . the old Turk whose house stood in my way had a termagant wife, who objected strongly to our proceedings. One day when we were engaged in an experiment how near to the foundations we could venture to dig without undermining the house, a long gaunt arm was suddenly thrust through the shutters from within, and a discordant female voice screeched out some unpleasant Turkish imprecations on our heads.

Mehemet Chiaoux, who happened to be standing close to the window, with his back to the house, beat a hasty retreat, with a very discomposed and uncomfortable expression of countenance. It was only after some days that he told me that the old lady had taken this opportunity of dropping some burning cinders down his back, between his shirt and his skin.

Eventually the bargain was concluded for twenty pounds in gold. Further digging ensued, until one day one of his work-men, 'on probing the roof of a gallery where the rock had been replaced by masonry, . . . detected a soft place, and his crowbar suddenly finding its way upwards, lifted up the hearthstone of a grave sententious Turk, who was sitting quietly smoking his chibouque in his own house.'

But all this task of uncovering one of the Seven Wonders of the World was so much idling compared with the real desire of C. T. Newton's heart:

While we were making these discoveries on the site of the Mausoleum, we were anxiously waiting for the firman empowering me to take possession of the lions which I had discovered in the Castle last year. Unavoidable delays prevented the granting of this document; and in the mean time the Commandant of the Castle suddenly received orders from the Turkish Minister of War to remove the lions from the walls and send them to Constantinople. He lost no time in putting this order in execution, and before many days had elapsed two of the finest lions were extracted from the walls. It was not a pleasant sight for us to see this operation performed under our very eyes, after we had brought spars for scaffolding and all manner of means and appliances for the express purpose; however I gulped down my mortification as well as I could, and despatched two letters, one by sea, the other by a swift overland runner, to Smyrna, to apprise Lord Stratford that the Turkish Minister of War was trying to steal a march on us. My messenger sped on night and day; and the Commandant pushed on with his work no less expeditiously. Two more lions were soon dug out of the walls. The extraction of two of my eye-teeth could not have given me so great a pang. When the Commandant had removed four lions, he paid a formal visit to my diggings, accompanied by all the principal Turks in Budrum.

'You have found nothing but little fragments I see,' he said, with an air of triumph. At that time we were digging up small fragments of lions' tails, with an occasional leg or hind-quarter, but no heads. I endured his civil impertinence for about a quarter of an hour, till at last my inward chafing found vent in a strong expression or two in English, addressed to Captain Towsey. The Turks did not understand what I had said; but guessed from the expression of my countenance what was passing in my mind, and withdrew with many ironical compliments. That same day, the lions having been duly swathed in raw sheepskins, were placed on board a caique to be sent over to Cos, where they were to be transhipped by steamer to Constantinople. I had a photograph made of two of them, and took a last fond look at these precious remains of the school of Scopas. The caique, as the Commandant informed me, was to sail that night, and I went to bed sick at heart. It was the end of a great hope.

LAND OF LOST GODS

At 4 a.m. the next morning I was suddenly roused from my sleep by the voice of a midshipman from the Gorgon. 'The Swallow is come in from Constantinople, and the officer of the watch thinks that the firman is on board.' I had had so many disappointments about the firman, that I received this news with sceptical indifference, and doggedly fell asleep again. At 6 a.m. another messenger from the Gorgon woke me up. 'The captain wants to see you immediately.' I hurried on board, and found Towsey pacing the quarter-deck impatiently, his gig alongside, ready manned.

'Why have you been so long?' he said, 'the firman is come.'

'Of what use is the firman now?' I answered, very sulkily; 'the lions are gone.'

'The caique is still in the harbour,' he said, 'waiting for a fair wind to come out, and we are yet in time.'

I jumped into the boat without a word more: a few vigorous strokes brought us into the harbour. The captain of the caique was drawing in his little mooring lines in a lazy, sleepy sort of way. On the pier-head stood the doctor of the Quarantine, an Italian, who took great interest in our diggings.

'Don't let that caique go,' I cried out; 'I have a firman for the lions.'

'It is all right,' he replied; 'I have his papers still, and he cannot leave without my signature.'

We walked straight into the Castle, and asked to see the Commandant. Very much astonished he was at so early a visit from the Captain of the ship of war and the Consul. He had evidently just emerged from his *yorgan*, and his *narguileh* was hardly lit. We had boarded him with that indecent haste with which mad Englishmen occasionally invade the *kieff* of an Oriental when any real emergency occurs, without waiting for the due interchange of compliments. After hastily wishing him good morning, I put the firman into his hand with that air of cool satisfaction with which a whist-player trumps an ace on the first round. Turks are seldom astonished; but my friend the Commandant was really discomposed. He read the firman through several times. The document was duly signed and sealed; the wording of this writ of *habeas corpus* was so precise that there was no evading it. The lions were to be delivered to me whether still in the walls or already embarked. Suddenly a bright thought struck the Commandant.

'The firman,' quoth he, 'makes mention of lions, *aslanlar*; but the animals in the walls of the Castle are leopards, *caplanlar*.'

'Come, come, *dostoum*, my friend,' I said, 'aslanlar or caplanlar, you know very well what are the beasts meant by the firman, and where to find them. I claim those beasts, and no others.'

'But,' said the Commandant, suddenly shifting the ground of his objections, 'who is to pay me for the expenses I have incurred? The allowance made to me by the Porte is so small that the outlay for removing the lions has been made in a great measure out of my own pocket.'

'Make your mind quite easy on that subject,' I said; 'I am ordered to pay all the expenses incurred.'

'And the caique, who is to pay that?'

'I pay the caique too.'

The lions were forthwith handed over to me, and the Commandant reimbursed.

At last the British Museum had its lions. It is a mere postscript that in June, Newton found the statues commonly said to be those of Mausolus and Artemisia (though the explorer took the latter for his 'goddess-charioteer').

Newton might have been able to use the Lion Tomb he studied at Cnidus in July as evidence for the plan of the Mausoleum. This likewise consisted of a peristyle with pyramid, topped in this case with a lion. It does not, however, have the massive plinth that belongs to the Mausoleum. It was probably erected in the early fourth century BC, perhaps to celebrate Conon's defeat of the Spartans.[7]

But even Praxiteles' Cnidian Aphrodite herself could not have deflected Newton. He was not really interested in architectural reconstruction, still less in topographical study. He had eyes only for the coping sculpture of this tomb. This gigantic lion, weighing eleven tons, was at length removed with a crane using gigantic pincers. His reverence is overwhelming:

While he had been lying grovelling on the earth we had never seen his face at all; so that, when we had set him on his base, and our eyes met for the first time his calm, majestic gaze, it seemed as if we had suddenly roused him from his sleep of ages. . . When I stood very near the lion, many things in the treatment appeared harsh and singular; but on retiring to the distance of about thirty yards, all that seemed exaggerated blended into one harmonious whole, which, lit up by an Asiatic sun, exhibited a breadth of chiaroscuro such as I have never seen in sculpture; nor was the effect of this colossal production of human genius at all impaired by the bold forms and desolate grandeur of the surrounding landscape. The lion seemed made for the scenery, and the scenery for the lion.

So perhaps it is hardly best housed in the grey and even light of the British Museum where it now rests.

Having relieved this structure of its most alluring element, as well as making off with the fine statue of Demeter of Cnidus, Newton moved on at once to pastures new, and by the end of August was at Didyma with a firman to remove the statues from the Sacred Way, eleven miles of a fine Roman road built from Miletus to Didyma by Q. Julius Balbus in 100 AD. It took sixty Turkish workmen one day to move a single statue the three miles to the coast. Newton sent to the British Museum in all ten seated figures, a sphinx and – a lion. It will come as something of a shock to the reader to learn that one fine lion still stands near a corner of the Temple at Didyma. (More lions from Halicarnassus remain in the Archaeological Museum in Istanbul.)

But the malarial season was setting in, and Newton ceased his labours. In May next year came the shock of an order to cease all excavations; having paid off his workmen, he despatched his 218 cases of sculptures home to London, only noting in passing that leopards were still to be found between Cnidus and Didyma. In 1859 he became consul in Rome. The antique Zeus had done well by the infant museum. He was to be the witness of the unearthing of another of the Seven Wonders before his work was done.

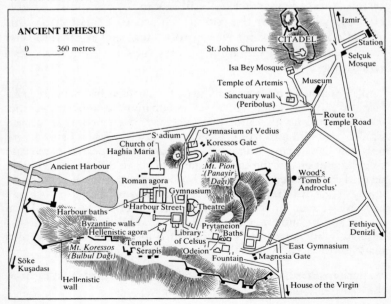

Diana of the Ephesians

> I've seen Babylon's walls wide enough to take traffic.
> I've seen the statue of Zeus on the banks of the Alpheus.
> I've seen the Hanging Gardens and the Sun's Colossus,
> The enormous labour of the Pyramids towering upwards,
> The immense tomb of Maussolus, but once I'd set eyes on
> The temple of Artemis with the clouds almost touching
> It put all other marvels into the shade. Except for Olympus
> I'd say the Sun shed its light on nothing sublimer.
>   (Antipater of Thessalonica (*c* 508 BC – *c* AD 20).
>   in *Anth Pal* 9, 58: tr Tony Harrison)

Soon after Newton's triumphant return from Halicarnassus and Cnidus, the trustees of the British Museum were given another opportunity to gamble with the marshy soil of Ionia and its hidden treasures. Early in 1864 they received a letter from one John Turtle Wood, describing himself as an engineer on the Smyrna–Aidin railway. He asked for £100 to enable him to excavate the Theatre and Odeum of Ephesus in the hope of finding a clue to the site of the great temple of Artemis. A Levant lunatic? He had no credentials, and nothing to show for a previous season's excavation at his own expense except seventy-five deep holes in the ground on a plateau south-west of Ayasolouk. What reason had they to place confidence in him? And what was the special lure of these extensive but shattered ruins, that swayed their decision?

Ephesus, like most of the cities of Ionia, has a long history. Almost all that stands now is from its Roman imperial splendour, and not of the classical age. And that age was a colourful age, vividly reflected in the stories told by Philostratus about Apollonius of Tyana, who chose the city as the scene of some of his most striking miracles. The Emperor Vespasian's private magician was also an Ephesian. But the city's fascination for the Christian ages had been quite as great as for that melancholy laudator of *les neiges d'antan*, Antipater of Thessalonica, because, of course, St Paul staged here one of the best recorded showdowns with pagan cult. Here was the temple of Diana of the Ephesians, Artemis the Mother-Goddess with her grape-cluster of breasts, the fashioning of whose images kept the Ephesian silversmiths in work.

The Temple of Artemis, as one of the Seven Wonders of the World, naturally attracted Westerners eager to recover the traces of a past at once gloriously pagan and resoundingly Christian. But where was it? In the marshes of the Cayster delta, not a trace was visible.

When Wood wrote his letter to the Directors of the British Museum, he had already spent a season in pursuit of this elusive temple which had captured his imagination. The Otto-man Government employed him to run a team of workmen on the railway, and this engaged his time fully. But there was little to do in his leisure hours in the marshy and – in summer – malarial plain. A classically educated Victorian, he knew of the reports of the Wonder of the World in Pliny, Pausanias and Philostratus. With the energy and taste for exploration equally characteristic of the Victorian, he had decided to find it. He had some money saved, and resolved to spend it on the search. So he applied, with the help of the British Ambassador, for a firman from the Turkish authorities in Constantinople. Its terms were generous, for they allowed him to export any antiquities he might find in the course of his dig.

But where was he to begin? The ruins of Ephesus were vast. It was not as if there had been just one temple. The cult of Artemis stretched back into legendary antiquity, and if tradition was to be trusted, no fewer than eight temples had been built successively on the same site. The cult of the goddess was supposed to have been introduced by the Amazons, the warrior women who inhabited the region before the coming of the Greeks.

The truth of the matter was that the pre-Greek inhabitants had worshipped the mother-goddess generally called Cybele. When the Greeks came, probably in the tenth century or earlier, they smoothed the transition to the new order by identifying the old goddess with their own Artemis. Of the eight temples of the legend, only two are mentioned in the literary tradition, though the archaeologists have found traces of five. The first great historical temple belonged to the great period of temple building in the early sixth century, when the temple of Hera on Samos and of Apollo on Chios were also created, as well as that of Apollo at Naucratis in Egypt and another at Didyma (burnt down in 494 BC).

The two near neighbours were inevitably rivals, and the Ephesians could not allow the Samians to upstage them. As soon as they heard that Rhoecus and Theodorus had begun work on Samos, they sent for Chersiphron and his son Metagenes from Cnossus in Crete to build a temple for them. In addition they persuaded Theodorus to come and advise them on the technique of building on swampy ground. The dimensions of their temple were 52.5 by 105 metres, and it was the first monumental building in the world made entirely of marble.

Pliny explains how it was constructed:

It was built on marshy soil so that it might not be subject to earthquakes or be threatened by subsidences. On the other hand, to ensure that the foundations of so massive a building would not be laid on shifting, unstable ground, they were underpinned with a layer of closely trodden charcoal, and then with another of sheepskins with their fleeces unshorn. . . . The architect in charge of the work was Chersiphron. The crowning marvel was his success in lifting the architraves of this massive building into place. This he achieved by filling bags of plaited reed with sand and constructing a gently graded ramp which reached the upper surfaces of the capitals of the columns. Then, little by little, he emptied the lowest layer of bags, so that the fabric gradually settled into its position. But the greatest difficulty was encountered with the lintel itself when he was trying to place it over the door; for this was the largest block, and it would not settle in its bed. The architect was in anguish as he debated whether suicide should be his final decision. The story goes that in the course of his reflections he became weary, and that while he slept at night he saw before him the goddess for whom the temple was being built: she was urging him to live because, as she said, she herself had laid the stone. And on the next day this was seen to be the case. (*Natural History* 36, 21)

The Temple's double colonnade comprised a forest of 127 columns, 19 metres high. One of the most remarkable features of the Temple were the thirty-six sculptured columns on the west front adorned with sculptures. It was said that each one of them was the gift of a different king, the gifts of Croesus of Lydia being preeminent. One surviving fragment is inscribed 'presented by King Croesus'. After a century or so of intermittent hostility between the Ionian cities and the Lydian kingdom, his accession in 560 BC had ushered in a period of calm. He concentrated on strengthening his eastern frontiers, and preferred friendship with his western neighbours to a continual struggle for dominance. One of the expressions of this friendship was the munificence with which he endowed the

Temple of Artemis. He also endowed the Temple of Athena at Sardis and made regular tributes to other Greek shrines, notably Delphi. It was Lydian money that had created the world's Wonder.

The temple, begun in 560 BC, was never completely finished. Work stopped on it for over sixty years in 546 BC, the year Croesus fell from power. A period of insecurity followed his fall. Forty years later, the Ionian Revolt against Persia ushered in the Persian Wars against Greece. When these finally ended in 479 BC with the repulsion of the Persians from mainland Greece (though not the Asian coastline), work on the temple was resumed. Pliny tells us that the construction of the temple lasted 120 years; if we begin those 120 years from the accession of Croesus we would have a completion date in about 440 B.C. The dedication of the temple was marked by an ode by the poet Timotheus who died in 439 B.C. This is the temple which Herodotus saw and which he mentioned in the same breath as that greatest of Wonders, the Pyramids of Egypt.

But one night in 356 BC it was burned down by a madman called Herostratus who conceived (rightly, alas) that this would be an effective way to make his memory immortal. Legend said that the deed took place on the same night that Alexander the Great was born; and when that young man reached maturity, he too, mindful of his immortal fame, proposed to sponsor a new temple. The Ephesians, jealous of their independence, replied that it was not fitting for one god to build a temple to another. Instead they gathered all their resources to build a new temple on the same plans as the first. The main difference was that it stood on a podium 2.68 metres high, with 13 steps. This neutralised the instability of the marshy ground, and also echoed the style that had become traditional for monumental buildings in Ionia, such as the high-stepped Mausoleum. The architect was Cheirocrates, some of the sculptures and reliefs were provided by Praxiteles and Scopas. The carved-relief columns reproduced the scenes shown on the earlier ones, though their style was contemporary. The huge altar surround of the fifth-century temple was re-used as the foundation for the altar of the new temple, and this was adorned with sculptures of Amazons: five sculptors competed to produce the finest figures they could, and several copies of the original type exist.[8] The building was still a Wonder of the World, and the proud Ephesians illustrated it on their coinage. If the gods were said to have built the first temple, anyone who looked at the latest one (wrote Philo the Jew in about 40 AD) 'would believe that the gods had left their immortal regions to come down to live on earth'.

This was the temple that Antipater saw in all its splendour, and which when the Empire became Christian fulfilled its fate instead as a quarry. Many stones were taken for the Basilica of St John, and pillars and marbles came to adorn the Church of Hagia Sophia.

How this would all have delighted the heart of that censorious father of the Church, Clement of Alexandria (late second century AD)! For him all marble images were 'plainly stamped with the characteristic nature of demons'. He was pleased to discover and retail the prophecy of the Sibyl of Cumae, that the temple of Ephesian Artemis would be engulfed by earthquakes and rents in the ground. 'Prostrate on the ground: Ephesus / Shall wail, weeping by the shore, / And seeking a temple that no longer has an inhabitant.'

Those who travelled to Ayasolouk could not believe that all trace of the temple had been lost. No fewer than seventeen of them, from Spon and Wheler onwards, confidently identified it with the ruins of the Great Gymnasium, which overlooks what was in ancient times the harbour. The complicated vaults below recalled the name of Labyrinth that was often attached to ancient temples.

Chishull in 1699 thought he found some of its walls between the port and the city, and Tournefort thought he had found four or five columns of it standing in January 1701, while the Comte de Caylus thought the ruins on the entire plain were those of dependencies of the temple.

The travellers should have paid more attention to Pliny, who said that the temple had been built on a marsh, than to the Sibyl who vaguely placed it 'on the shore'. There were several other clues to be found in the ancient authors too. Xenophon had written that the River Selinus ran past the temple. Vitruvius emphasised the marshiness of the site by stating that wagons could not be used in the construction because they sank. Strabo (14,640) placed the temple at a distance of one to two javelin throws from the city (which Falkener makes about

900 or 1,800 feet); Herodotus however made it 4,200 feet from the Old Town. Most significantly, Pausanias (7, 2) stated that the tomb of Androclus, the legendary founder of Ephesus, stood by the road which led to the temple from the Magnesian Gate. And along this road, according to Philostratus (*Lives of the Sophists* II, 23), a wealthy Roman had constructed a sheltering stoa 600 feet in length.

It was not a matter of finding just the temple; the gate, road and stoa should also have left remains. In 1862 Edward Falkener published a book on Ephesus. He had visited Asia Minor in 1844–5 and spent two weeks at Ephesus, exploring the whole of the city and making detailed plans of the major buildings on the basis of the remains he found. It was only after his return to England that his reading led him to a new theory of the site, so that he longed to go back and explore again. He identified the Magnesian Gate with the major remains where the cleft of the valley between Mt Pion and Mt Coressus broadens out to the inland plain, just beyond the East Gymnasium (which he called the Opistholeprian Gymnasium). He surmised that the temple would lie in a straight line from this point along the valley. In fact he was not so far wrong.

It was a pity that Wood, isolated in the shack that housed the management of the railway works, had not seen Falkener's book when he began his own search. Indeed, the coincidence of dates is so striking that one cannot help wondering if he had seen it, but deliberately chose to dig elsewhere. If so, the enthusiasm of the amateur would have been employed to much more profit if preceded by proper scholarly preparation for the job; but the trustees of the British Museum were in no position to know this, any more than Wood was. For the first time one sees the enthusiastic amateur falling short of his own reach; hereafter professionalism was to assert its sway in archaeology as in other pursuits.

At any rate, Wood states that he was unable to locate the Magnesian Gate mentioned by Pausanias. Instead he looked at the terrain with an architect's eye, and decided that in Chersiphron's place he would have built his temple on a low plateau to the west of the city, overlooking the flat area which in antiquity had been the Great Harbour, before the silt of the Cayster had moved the shoreline several miles out to sea.

In spring 1863 he hired five labourers recently laid off from the railway works and began the excavation. Wood did not like to abandon his lodgings in Smyrna for a second home nearer the site. So every day he travelled from Smyrna to Ayasolouk. This journey of fifty-odd miles began with a walk of one and a half hours to the railway station. Here he took the train which covered the distance to Ayasolouk in three and a half hours. He would arrive when the day was well advanced, and force himself and his men to dig through the hottest period for six hours until he had to leave for his return journey of five more hours. In June the workmen refused to continue and he suspended excavations until September. At this point he determined to take a leave of absence, and rented a room in Ayasolouk itself, from the goods manager of the Smyrna-Aidin railway. 'The whole tenement was so dilapidated that it threatened to tumble down whenever I walked across the room.' (In fact it did fall down soon after he left.) At least his landlord, an Armenian from Scala Nova (Kuşadası) did not trouble to collect any rent.

He now resumed excavations by exploring the Great Gymnasium which Chandler had taken for the temple, and some of the harbour works. He found a few inscriptions, but no sign of the temple. It looks as if he was digging at random to keep his spirits up.

It was at the end of this season that he determined to apply to the British Museum for help. Luckily it was Charles Newton, the excavator of Halicarnassus, who now held the purse strings. Having a taste himself for adventure-archaeology, he agreed to a grant to finance a further season, renewable on the basis of results. The discovery of a second Wonder of the World by agents of the British Museum would be a true feather in the cap of the trustees. He knew, too, that Wood's credentials were not as flimsy as they seemed. Scientific excavation was in its infancy. Luck and persistence could still be as important as learning; and if the care lavished on every scrap of earth in a modern dig was unimaginable then, there could be no better recommendation for an excavation than experience of engineering. Much of the problem would be one of logistics. In the heavily silted plain, countless tons of earth would need to be removed to uncover fifth-century levels.

Wood got his grant. By this time, however, he was back at

his job as an architect in Smyrna. He could not visit the
excavation every day, but hired a superintendent for his forty
labourers. They cleared the Odeum, which lay under soil in
some places twenty-three feet deep. They discovered a number of inscriptions, which would count as a rich haul today but
then seemed a meagre consolation for the frustration of the
devouring passion to find the temple. He and Mrs Wood spent
their evenings reconstructing, like jigsaw puzzles, the fragmentary inscriptions that were found. He began to acquire
some notoriety, and the dig was visited by celebrities from
Britain and America, and even the Pasha's secretary. One day
Wood was mistaken for the English consul; unfortunately the
error was made by an assassin, and Wood spent some time in a
hospital near to death.

Years went by. His health deteriorated under the strain
and ' frustration coupled with the malaria endemic to the
marshes. Further advances from the British Museum enabled
him to dig the theatre in the years 1866–68. The summer of
1867 he spent in England to improve his health. Early in 1868
his finds were removed by HMS *Terrible*: the Museum was
getting its money's worth out of the indomitable explorer.
But if Wood wanted his temple, the Museum was more
pleased with the individual finds which they could add to
a fine display, than in any increase of topographical knowledge.

The work there 'was undertaken', said the Rt Hon Robert
Lowe in 1873 'by the Trustees of the British Museum, not for
the purpose of ascertaining the site or form of the Temple,
objects quite beyond the scope of the duties of the Trustees,
but for the sake of such relics of ancient art as might be found
buried among the ruins. The ascertainment of the site was
a mere incident, the main object was the acquisition of
specimens of ancient statuary and architecture.'[9]

Wood found it increasingly difficult to get workmen. One
of the team was murdered, but after the arrest of thirty of his
fellows the matter was declared unsolved and they were
released again. Wood's fever returned. Further attempts were
made on his life, this time deliberately. Brigands were rife.
The walls of the holes he dug fell in. The landowners were
becoming increasingly tired of their small plots being made
useless for cultivation, and their demands for compensation

rose higher and higher. One demanded fifty pounds for
permission to dig in his field, but Wood beat him down to
three pounds. Mice ate his squeezes.

But suddenly all these troubles paled. He found a clue. In the
theatre there was uncovered, late in 1867, a series of slabs
inscribed with decrees concerning the gold and silver images
given to the Temple of Artemis by a wealthy Roman, C
Vibius Salutaris.[10] This long inscription not only described the
images and the procession that took them from the city to the
temple, but indicated quite clearly that it left the city through
the Magnesian Gate. Wood had reached the point Falkener had
reached, by pure reflection, five years before.

Through the 1868 season Wood worked at uncovering the
road that led through the Magnesian Gate. After 140 feet it
forked, one branch heading for Magnesia, the other round the
hill towards the modern Turkish town of Selcuk. Wood
excavated both roads and after 500 yards found remains of the
Stoa, stated by Philostratus to be 600 feet long, on the road
leading to Ayasolouk. But he found no sign of the temple. It
was May; the season was over, his money was exhausted and
he returned to England.

But the British Museum still had confidence in his search.
Next autumn he was back with a further grant. He was
rewarded with success, for in February 1869 he discovered
among numerous tombs the remains of the Tomb of Androclus – 2,600 feet from the Magnesian Gate. This was further
proof that he was on the right track. He dug another 600 feet,
and found the road, 45 feet wide, which led away from the foot
of the mountain and was lined with marble sarcophagi. But he
could dig no further, for the barley was full-grown and he
could not afford to compensate the landowners for fields of
grain. He walked disconsolately home to his lodgings, and
decided to gamble the last of his funds on an olive grove
that caught his eye. But at this critical moment his firman
ran out.

He rushed to Constantinople where he was luckily able to
get the firman renewed with speed. The workmen sunk their
spades again and immediately uncovered part of a thick wall of
massive blocks of stone. But the trip to Constantinople had
exhausted his funds and he could not afford to dig another day.
He persuaded the Museum to make yet another grant, which

they did with the warning that if he did not find the temple this time no more money would be forthcoming.

At last their trust was rewarded, for in this wall they uncovered two large inscriptions stating, in Latin and Greek, that this wall had been built by the Emperor Augustus to surround the Temple of Diana, in the year 6 BC.[11] At the eleventh hour Wood had discovered the site of the temple that had dazzled the centuries.

This put the whole expedition on a different footing. In autumn 1869, after six years of labour with only his own faith as his impetus, Wood returned to Ayasolouk empowered by the Museum to buy the entire site and excavate it fully. Wood was to spend a further four years at this task. The foundations of the temple were twenty feet down, and below the water table of the plain, which had risen since antiquity. The water-logged soil made digging dangerous, and once a hole collapsed and killed a workman. Earthquakes, incessant rain, fever and the continuing intrigues of the locals as well as the crimes of the workmen made the task a dreadful one.

But they worked down to the pavement of the temple *before* the archaic one endowed by Croesus. They found a mosaic pavement, which was taken up in a wooden frame by a skilled carpenter called Long Wilson; six fluted column drums; a column base (now in the British Museum) which Wood took for that of the archaic temple, and a capital. By the end of 1870 they had shifted 4,000 cubic yards of soil. (This heap of detritus was to be a problem when excavations were briefly resumed by the English in 1904.)

In December 1870 Heinrich Schliemann, fresh from his first season at Troy (Chapter 11), arrived and was 'kindly enthusiastic in his congratulations'. In January Newton finally arrived: this was the first visit of any Museum official to the site whose excavation they had been paying for for six years.

The next season began on 5 September 1871, with the site under several feet of water. In ten days they found part of the Amazon frieze. The slab weighed eleven tons, and the road collapsed under it. It was mid-November before they could move it to the coast for shipment. Another column base soon came to light. Many smaller finds were certainly pilfered.

Visitors in spring 1872 included the Duke and Duchess of Mecklenburg-Schwerin, Prince Frederick Charles of Prussia and the Roman Catholic Archbishop of Smyrna. By now 44,000 cubic yards had been cleared, and Wood applied to the trustees for £6,000 – a vast sum – to clear the entire site. Luckily the Chancellor of the Exchequer was a classical scholar, and in the autumn the money was forthcoming. In spring 1873 nearly sixty tons of sculptural remains were shipped from Ayasolouk to London.

The final season began in autumn 1873 after the obtaining of a fresh firman. The first aristocratic visitor this time was the Princess de la Tour d'Auvergne, who begged Wood for some 'nice little bits' of the temple as souvenirs. Luckily Wood was used to this kind of request and kept a pile of valueless fragments for the purpose. One he did not give away was a moulding with two astragals, between which ran a strip of lead folded over a strip of gold – a curious echo of the mysterious 'gold thread' mentioned by Pliny in the Temple at Cyzicus (see p 33).

At this point Wood conceived a desire to tear down the Great Mosque because some of the blocks appeared to be taken from the temple. This was too much for the Turks however, and the Mudir stood guard over the entrance with pistol and sabre. When Newton arrived for his regular visit on 2 January he saw that little was to be achieved by further digging and advised the abandonment of the excavation. After a final vain exploration of a few drains, Wood agreed, and packed his bags for the last time to bid farewell to the site that had been the focus of all his endeavours for over ten years. He sold his carts and his horses to a Belgian engineer; did his last calculation – they had removed 132,221 cubic yards of soil – and discharged his workmen in tears. He planted eucalyptus trees on the spoil banks and, with his wife, turned towards Smyrna with wandering steps and slow. 'And as we left the spot slowly and lingeringly we looked back frequently at the beautiful scene, which had had such a fascination for us, and which had been for so many years associated with our united labours.'

The postscript to Wood's work is a short one. The British Museum sponsored a further excavation under D. G. Hogarth from 1904–5 which explored the archaic stratum. Pumps were constantly at work to keep the site exposed, but the expedition found little, and least of all the altar which was the chief lost prize remaining.

In 1895 Carl Humann had bought the adjoining plot for Austria; a season in 1897 revealed little, but later Austrian digging at Ephesus (including the site of Wood's dig which they bought from the British) was more successful. Many finds are housed in a special museum in Vienna.

Since 1966 Fritz Eichler and then Anton Bammer have again worked on the temple site, and finally succeeded in finding the remains of the great altar. Bammer's reconstructions are highly instructive, but the temple itself will never stand again. The one re-erected column stands in a green pool surrounded by flowers, a forlorn reminder of the 127 columns there once were. Atop it nests a family of storks, the only inhabitants now of the home of Great Diana of the Ephesians, whose worship with her temple is buried for ever in the marsh. She dwells now in the British Museum, which she shares with other relics of verdant Ionia. The storks fill the home of the ancient goddess of childbirth.

CHAPTER TEN

The German Kingdom

To celebrate the day of your arrival
and to mark the day of your bright procession
Greece throws before you her mountains and valleys, making
    them leap for joy,
She sends the Naiads with cheerful laughter into the branches of
    the trees to behold you
And hurls the dolphins against their liquid gates. . . .
Come now, establish Academies of wisdom
Delight your ears with innocent harmonies!
And thou, O aged Korais, thou light who extinguish
And thereby illumine every lamp in Greece
– Even if age, far away, rules over you –
Take us by the hand and erect for us Museums!

(Alexander Soutsos, *Letter to King Otho*, 1833)

'The snow lay from last night low down the slopes of Hymettus; by evening it was gone, except on the highest part, and the wind was excessive . . . At four o'clock I determined to go for a walk, and it was really very nice.'

The date was 20 February 1842, and the writer a German classical scholar, no longer young, by the name of F. G. Welcker (1784–1868). He, and the German archaeologist Ludwig Ross, were bidden to dinner at the Royal Palace at seven o'clock. From Welcker's lodgings near the Tower of the Winds to the newly completed palace was a short walk, but the signs at once of building and of demolition were evident at every step.

Chandler, or even those who like Byron had seen Athens

while it was being ravaged by the War of Independence, would not have recognised the city. The national pride of newly liberated Greece had demanded as a priority the creation of a fitting capital. Even before it had been determined that the state capital should be Athens, the Provisional Government had engaged Stamatis Kleanthes and Eduard Schaubert of Breslau as the architects of a new Athens. In 1833, after a brief period as a Republic, Greece became a kingdom with the accession of Otto, the son of Ludwig I of Bavaria, to the throne. The expense of the Kleanthes-Schaubert plan forced its abandonment, and a revised plan was produced by Leo von Klenze (1784–1864), architect to Ludwig, whose work on the Glyptothek in Munich had been so important for the display of the Aigina collections.

It was Klenze's Royal Palace that Welcker would see before him, a tasteful pink box adorned with classical palmettes. An earlier plan of the King of Prussia to situate the palace on the Acropolis had been wisely abandoned, even as the Acropolis and the surrounding area were cleared of houses too scruffy to be endured. A sweeping grid plan was devised for the city, with the Acropolis at its southern point and the Palace at the easternmost. In 1835–6 Stadiou, Athinas, Ermou and Eolou Streets were developed with series of monumental and distinguished buildings. The most notable survival of this period is the University of Christian Hansen (1839). The style was maintained in the Academy of 1859 and Library of 1887–91, by Theophil von Hansen, and the Polytechnic of 1862–80 by Kaftanzoglou. In the 1840s arose in succession a school, an agricultural school, a botanic garden, a library; everything but a museum.

As Ross and Welcker came up to the door of the palace, they were received in a friendly manner by the Queen herself, 'in the simplest of pale silk dresses'; there were no other guests but four ladies of the court, two adjutants and the marshal. Welcker took advantage of this intimacy to discuss at length with the King his eagerness to undertake excavations in the Theatre of Dionysus, which would surely bring to light information that would illuminate much that was hitherto obscure in the history of Attic drama. The King promised to think about it; but it was not until 6 June, when Welcker was on the point of leaving Athens, that he professed himself willing to allow a four-week dig. Nevertheless, Welcker wrote, 'no court could be more lovable or more generous'.

That evening was an exceptional one. More often there would be a grand affair like the ball at the Prussian ambassador's on 6 June. After that intimate dinner with the King and Queen, it was a contrast to enter on what seemed like the setting of Thomas Mann's *Royal Highness* transplanted from its Alpine fairyland to burning Athens. Here were distinguished ladies, the wives of French and Russian diplomats; here was the Austrian ambassador Prokesch von Osten, himself the author of a fine topographical account of his classical travels. Welcker talked long with him.

But Welcker did not need to move in the most elevated circles to find congenial company in the Athens of the 1840s. Martin von Wagner had found Greek conditions odious and the uncertainty of breakfasts distressing. Winckelmann's friend Riedesel and the mis-hellene Bartholdy were scarcely honourable exceptions to the dearth of German travellers. But the country was now comfortable for Germans. The King spoke scarcely any Greek, and besides had imported his court, his advisers and even his ministers. George Brandis, for example, his scientific adviser, had arrived in March 1837 with his entire family and household including the maid and the house-tutor, a young philologist called Ernst Curtius (of whom we shall hear more).

Welcker himself had been assured of hospitality by a former student, the councillor Constantine Schinas. But that movement in philological study to which Welcker's own work was central, and which had begun with F. A. Wolf, had sent many other Germans to match their linguistic and literary learning with the topographical and architectural evidence.

Of course much of the ground work had been done. Welcker struggled dutifully with the many volumes of Leake as he made his inspections of the Acropolis; but his friend Ludwig Ross had also written, and was still writing, valuable and detailed accounts of the Peloponnese and the islands. H. N. Ulrichs too, of whom he saw a good deal, and Friedrich Thiersch had done much to elucidate the topography of Delphi.

But Welcker did not often contribute anything to the minutiae of archaeological endeavour. Frequently he seems satisfied simply to be on a site of ancient renown: his appreciation is a philologist's rather than an archaeologist's.

When he moved out of Athens he found a world that had scarcely changed since before the war, or indeed since Wheler's day. The conservatism of the Peloponnese, and the lack of interest in agricultural improvement, ensured that conditions in the country, though liberated, were still uncomfortable. Despite a lame foot, diarrhoea and insomnia, he was thrilled by Mycenae where 'the Pelopids surged up' before his eyes, though he found the lions of the Lion Gate stolid and unnatural. The Argive Heraion was fascinating, Sparta a disappointment. A seven-hour ride over Taygetus was closed with a night of 'fleas and topographical dreams'. The road to the Styx was impassable in April; at Lerna he failed to find a monument referred to by Ross. Things became more cheerful at Argos where he was entertained by an Englishman, Mr Major, who showed him his collection of half a million silk-worms. But all in all he was glad to get back to Athens after six weeks on the road.

In Athens, Welcker was not short of other companions. So crowded was his social life that on his first arrival he stayed forty-eight days, and came away from one of those glittering but cosy balls swearing he never wished to leave Athens. Still the mainstay of German society in Athens, aged as he now was, was the Austrian consul Gropius. Less popular with the Greeks must have been J. P. Fallmerayer, who became notorious for his belief that the modern Greeks were entirely of Slavic origin and had no classical blood in their veins.

It was Ludwig Ross (1806–59) of whom he probably saw most. Ross' career had progressed hand in hand with the establishment of the German kingdom in Greece, and his work had been central to the care for antiquities exhibited by the new kingdom. Schooled in a system of classical education perhaps even more taxing than that of England, Germans could not look at Greece without seeing ancient Greeks. It was the classical culture of Greece, not the Byzantium of the Empire or the Phanariot and expatriate intelligentsia, that was to be the keynote of regenerate Greece. Ross was the ideal man for the job.

Born in Altekoppel in Holstein in July 1806, he had attended school and university in Kiel, after which he went to pursue postgraduate work in Copenhagen. Here he saw an art gallery for the first time. The Danish government at that time offered a regular travel grant for students from Schleswig-Holstein; Ross won this and determined to use it to visit Greece.

He arrived on Hydra on his birthday, 22 July 1832. His delight at setting foot for the first time on the 'sacred soil' of Greece was only slightly marred by the surroundings he stepped into ashore – a morass of rubbish, dead fish and rotting vegetables, among which pigs rooted, grunting, and naked children played. Capodistria had been assassinated ten months previously, and the Provisional Government was doing its best to avert a Civil War. Ross' timing was superb, for two weeks after his arrival, on 8 August, the assembly in Nauplia voted for the appointment of Otto as King of Greece. The event was not unexpected, and Ross had arrived with a lithograph of Otto in his luggage, which duly took its place in the government building in Nauplia. Ross had started off on the right foot.

Ross stayed at Athens in a house on the north slope of the Acropolis which he shared with two other German architects and the Greek architect Kleanthes. (It later became the first University of Athens.) One of the Germans, Lüders, caused a sensation as the bitter winter set in by building out of some pieces of metal the first stove ever seen in Athens.

Ross knew a number of the foreign residents, and there was a regular table d'hôte at the house of the Italian philhellene Casalis. He soon got to know the architect and doyen of German philhellenes, Friedrich Thiersch, the Austrian consul Gropius, Welcker's old pupil Schinas (the first rector of the University, later to be ambassador in Munich); met Lamartine when he passed through Nauplia on 17 August; and travelled to Athens with Professor Black who had married Byron's Maid of Athens. He thus met the husband of her sister, Kyriakos Pittakis, who claimed the broadest archaeological knowledge of any Greek living.

At this time he joined forces with the Cambridge scholar Christopher Wordsworth and his effete poetical friend Richard Monckton Milnes, on a tour of Attica. With them came also some English friends of Milnes. Ross must have found the company of the diligent Wordsworth congenial. 'Wordsworth never believes he has gloated long enough on any antiquity whatever, and loves an old wall with a passion more intense than that with which any of Rio's Italian heroines burnt for their unseen lovers.' (Milnes) The excursion was not all pleasure, despite their meeting at the Euripus with a number of Greeks professing eager anticipation of their shortly-expected new King; for it was on this journey that Wordsworth was stabbed in the neck by brigands and was in danger for some time. He recovered however, and published a useful account of Attic topography.

In February 1833 the King arrived, amid great jubilation. As he made his triumphal entry into Nauplia he was conducted to the old Friday mosque, which had been fitted out as a festival hall for the purpose. The lintel of the main door was made from a column removed from the Treasury of Atreus at Mycenae. As Otto stepped beneath it, the Germans believed, he entered on the heritage of Atreus' son Agamemnon. If that single column could speak, of how many thousand years of history could it tell!

In May the site of the capital remained undecided, but the King made a visit to Athens to assess its possibilities. Ross, with Forchhammer and Lassaulx, showed the royal party round the antiquities. At this point Ross' tour seemed to have reached a fitting conclusion. He was on the point of leaving when, in August 1833, he was offered the post of *Unterconservator*, or deputy keeper of antiquities. He accepted without hesitation, and was at once immersed in the intrigues and rivalries of the court. For the next year he worked with Klenze on the plans for Athens, and the construction of the Royal palace proceeded apace. Such was the rapidity of growth of the city that builders could get a twenty to thirty per cent return on their work in less than a year. In August 1834 the King entered Athens: a service was held in the Theseion and the King proceeded to the Palace. This was the last time the Theseion was used as a Christian church; in the next spring it was turned into a museum.

In August 1834 the excavation and restoration of the Acropolis began, under the direction of Ross, now created *Oberconservator*. After some disagreement with the military, who were accustomed to use the mosque in the Parthenon as a garrison house, Ross got sole control of the great rock. Here, after his day's end, he could climb with a visiting colleague to the west gable of the Parthenon and admire the matchless view as sole possessor:

It was a hot and enervating summer, the atmosphere oppressive and thick; only the morning and evening hours on the Acropolis provided some relief . . . when the heat of the day was over, we used to climb towards sundown on the ramparts of the Parthenon, sit down on the western gable and let our gaze and our thoughts wander over the miles wide panorama, which contained, from Troezen and Aegina to Corinth, Megara and Marathon, many of the most celebrated localities of Greece. My servant brought a bowl of coffee and pipes, and we enjoyed ourselves here till dusk.

The first task was the destruction of the Byzantine, Frankish and Turkish fortifications, at which Ross began work with eighty labourers on 4 January 1835. This work released all the blocks of the temple of Wingless Victory, which was briskly reconstructed in its original spot on the south-west tip of the Acropolis. So many other building blocks were turned up that, although Ross spent 50,000 drachmas on the excavations, he was able to recoup forty per cent of this by selling the blocks to builders.

In this work Ross's right-hand man was Leo von Klenze, the architect of Ludwig I who had begun as early as 1816 to transform Munich into a neo-classical city. His many buildings in the Greek style included the Valhalla near Regensburg (begun 1827), and made him the natural choice for official architect to Otto's kingdom. His work was by no means confined to the stones of Athens: like many Germans who travelled at this date, he drew both real and imaginary or restored views of Greece (one cityscape of ancient Zante is a complete fantasy). On his return he built several more major edifices for central Munich, if possible even more Greek than before – the Ruhmeshalle, the Propylaea and the Monopteros of Nymphenburg. He also built in Athens – notably the church of St Dionysus, and of course the Royal Palace.

But his work at the Acropolis was vital.[1] The Parthenon was restored as far as possible, beginning with the re-erection of all the columns on the northern side, because it was the side visible from the city and it was therefore of importance to create a picturesque (*malerisch*) effect.

His reconstructions were famously precise, and won him academic honours in all the cities of Europe – Leipzig,

London, Milan, Madrid, Paris. He returned to Munich a celebrity.

Ross's lordly manner with his antiquities did not make him altogether popular. In spring 1835 an English fleet anchored in Piraeus. Swarms of teenage midshipmen flocked up to the Acropolis, climbing all over the Parthenon and other ruins, overturning blocks, burrowing in foundations and carving their names. In the end Ross had the gates locked against them, after which, as he charmingly relates, they would gather outside and yell insults at him, of which the most frequent was 'son of a witch'. (One cannot think he got this quite right.)

But Ross did not spend all his time in Athens. Several volumes, evidently intended for popular consumption despite their considerable length and their heavy Gothic type, recount his journeys to the islands of the Aegean, and to various parts of mainland Greece – in the latter case as the official archaeologist with the royal party. The first excursion, of September 1834, through Boeotia and Phocis to Mt Oeta, included beside the king, Colonels Tzavellas and Vassos, Colonel Brandt, Makryannis and Mamouris, the Court Marshal, the Court Doctor and the Cabinet Secretary, two Greek ordnance officers, Lt Baron Würzburg and Ross himself. This inconspicuous party made its way through the dry autumnal landscape, followed everywhere, Ross tells us, by troops of peasants trying inarticulately to express their love for their King. At Thebes one of the dangerous brigand brothers Chondroyannis came to prostrate himself in a demonstration of loyalty. Ross's vision of Otto's kingly presence seems like that of one of the magical princes of Grimm's fairy tales, by now widely known in Germany.

The King was interested in antiquities and insisted on seeing everything, even climbing to the Corycian cave above Delphi, a feat the colonels were not keen to emulate. Ross must have been kept busy satisfying the intellectual appetite of his royal charge.

By 1836 Ross's reputation had deteriorated, largely owing to growing Greek hostility to the *xenokratia* (foreign rule), and to unfounded allegations that he had given away antiquities (which were now confined by law to Greece) to Prince Pückler-Muskau on his visit in 1836. Then the Minister of Culture announced that henceforth Ross would be forbidden to publish any of his archaeological discoveries abroad: all Greek artefacts were the property of the Ministry, and his reports were to be made to the Minister alone. It was a particularly sore point that Ross published his work in Latin, a language no Greek could read. In this intolerable situation he offered his resignation. It was accepted.

Ross wrote to the King, who was abroad for his wedding. When Otto returned in February 1837, Ross learnt that scholars in Germany had mounted a campaign for his re-instatement. But instead he was offered a post as Professor of Archaeology at the newly-founded University of Athens. This post he held for six years, until the further anti-foreign upsurges of 1843 forced him to leave the country for good.

After travelling for some time in southern Turkey, he returned to Germany to find himself out of touch with the latest trends in scholarship. (Even Welcker had found him difficult to argue with.) His naturally conservative and abrasive temperament found its outlet partly in vigorous altercations with other scholars, and partly in an extraordinary series of articles in the *Allgemeine Zeitung*, which occupied him until he became crippled by ill-health in 1849. (He died in 1859.) These articles must have been highly intriguing to the members of a German nation still fragmented and looking for its identity. Ross had gone beyond the Kingdom of Greece to explore the semi-deserted southern coast of Anatolia. If Germans could make a home in Athens, he reasoned, why not also in Lycia, Caria and Ionia? Their desolation was distressing, the inhabitants apathetic. Surely a programme of systematic immigration from Germany would bring the area a new prosperity and open its gates to world trade; at the same time of course it would bring honour and a sense of common purpose to the colonising nation, and answer its perennial lust for *Lebensraum*. If the editors of the rival paper, the *Rheinische Beobachter*, thought his ideas crazy, it was only because they favoured German colonies in the New World, Russia or the Dutch East Indies. The first moves to German unification in 1848 strengthened Ross's resolve. German naval power, he wrote, should be made to match that of England and France in the Mediterranean; the disgrace of the fact that Prussia's consul in Ragusa (Dubrovnik) was a master baker should be obliterated; and the black, red and gold flag should fly over Smyrna instead of

those of the Empire, the Kingdom of Prussia, the principalities
of Hamburg, Hanover, Mecklenburg and the rest. All that
would be needed, he wrote, was *Macht und Geld*, power and
money. If a fleet was too difficult, the conquering army could
march via Bulgaria to overwhelm the *yailas* of Lycia. War is a
fact of life, and the German nation should turn it to its
advantage.

And, he added, research commissions could be sent at the
same time. Had you thought scholarship was altogether forgotten? (In fairness one should point out that Newton, too, in
1865[2] suggested that the British government buy up all of
Turkey in order to bring it under proper cultivation.) Ross's
ideas were scarcely consonant with the international situation
which made the two western protecting powers supporters of
Turkish interests against Russia. Austria too feared Russia and
should have set the tone for a pan-German policy. But Ross
was little in tune with Western thought, in scholarship or in
politics: his outlook was that of the Germans in Greece, and
would have gone down better with his King in Athens than
with his countrymen.

Germans were still coming thick and fast. The most important might have been Carl Otfried Müller (1797–1840),
who had become Professor in Göttingen in 1819 at the age
of twenty-two, and had set off in September 1839 on the
longed-for tour of Italy and Greece. He had already published
important work on Greek mythology and literary history, but
perhaps his most notable contribution had been his study of
the ancient Dorian races and his history of the island of Aigina.
On 4 April 1840 he could write to his wife in transports, 'At
last, at last in Athens.' He collected a hundred inscriptions
illustrating the tribute levied by classical Athens on its allies,
and was in ecstasies at being able to check his queries simply by
going to look at stones on the Acropolis itself. A celebratory
dinner was held for him by the other German scholars then in
Athens, on a summer evening in the Academy Garden.
Kyriakos Pittakis, the doyen of Greek archaeologists, and
John Gennadius were also there.

The snow in Arcadia made further travel impossible until
mid-May; then Müller set off for the traditional tour, un-
marred except by Curtius' contriving to lose Müller's precious
measuring rod at Sparta. They visited the usual sites and

returned to Athens on 17 June. On the 16 July he was at
Delphi, hunting eagerly for the temple sculptures, which he
was sure must be buried somewhere there. Would he really be
able to compare the originals with the suggestive description
in Euripides' *Ion*, and with the text of Pausanias? To his wife he
wrote:

I felt really excellent as I engaged in this hunting around for
antiquities; physically, too, strong and cheerful. My digestive
troubles are of no significance; others suffer worse in this climate;
a cloth wound firmly round my body and a little dieting give me
complete protection.

On 26 July, from Levadia:

I trusted in my ability to endure the sun and undertook to copy the
inscriptions on a stone that lay upside down; my head was hanging
and the sun shone in my eyes. I paid for it dearly. I got such a heat in
my head, headache, nervous irritation, that I could do no more
thereafter at Delphi, as every similar exertion renewed the sickness,
which I have not even now shaken off with the increasing heat.

Six days later Carl Otfried Müller was dead. The love of
Greece had claimed its latest victim.

When Welcker visited Delphi in May 1842, his delight in
arriving at that fantastic site by the clear light of the moon was
sensibly marred by thoughts of his lost colleague and the
blight of a promise that was yet in early bloom.

But it was not just Germans who flocked to the newly
independent Greece. There were the American missionaries –
poets, George Hill and Julia Ward Howe; the painter James
Skene, who when Welcker arrived had just shipped 400
paintings of Greek scenes home to Scotland; there was George
Finlay, the historian of the *Tourkokratia* and the Revolution,
'looking like Shelley's ghost' and telling racy tales of Lord
Byron; and the travellers who passed through, like Fellows,
Tozer and Pashley.

There was the Duchess of Plaisance, who owned Mt Penteli
and was building what is now the Byzantine Museum; she
achieved a fame second only to Lady Hester Stanhope. Not
least among her eccentricities, she kept the body of her
eighteen-year-old daughter pickled in brandy, and was
accustomed to recite at length from Boileau and Racine.

The Greeks had no wish to be outdone in zeal for their own

antiquities. It might seem that these relics had little place in Ottonian Athens; yet this unsatisfactory solution to the demands of nationhood had many advantages for archaeology. From the first stirrings of the movement for independence, the antiquities of Greece, with what they reflected of the glorious past, had been central to nationalist ambition. The great exiled intellectual focus of nationalism, Adamantios Korais (1748–1833), had raged at E. D. Clarke's removal of manuscripts from Patmos, and had devised a set of rules which were supposed to ensure that any antiquities found were handed in to the Holy Synod who would create with them a Hellenic Museum, with elaborate catalogue and details of provenance. The best site for it, he averred, would be his birth place, Chios. Needless to say this remained in his lifetime a pipe dream; but the scholarly soundness of the plan was a good omen for more favourable times.

In 1813 a group of Greeks inspired by the ideals of Korais founded the Philomousos Etaireia, whose aims were to uncover and collect antiquities, assist students and foreigners who loved Greece, and publish books. (Cockerell, Haller, Stackelberg, Foster and Linckh were all members.) Their headquarters is now scarcely noticeable in a square in Plaka given over to cafés, restaurants and souvenir stands, but again it augured well for the future.

Leake had written in the early 1800s that, once the Greeks should become free, they would not lack for enthusiasm in the excavation and conservation of their antiquities. And so it was to prove. Nationhood demanded a respect for the nation's past, and the Greeks were not averse to the Germans' attention to their classical heritage.

Even under Capodistria some care had been shown for antiquities. The scattered stones of the temple of Apollo ('Aphrodite') on Aigina were collected in 1828–9 to build an orphanage in the town; late in 1829 this was made into the first Greek archaeological museum, a role which it filled until 1834 when the collection was moved to Nauplia and then to Athens.

Some digs were allowed, for example that of Friedrich Thiersch at Delphi, but it was insisted that finds should stay in Greece.

With Otto's arrival, the Greeks quickly followed up the

establishment of the German-led archaeological service with the all-Greek Archaeological Society (*Arkhaiologiki Etaireia*), instituted in 1837 'for the discovery, recovery and restoration of antiquities in Greece'. Their first meeting took place in the Parthenon on 28 April – a symbolic setting, for 'these stones are our heritage' as it was stated in the opening address – a cry to be echoed throughout the history of independent Greece.

The founding fathers of the Society were Alexander Rangavis (1810–92) and Kyriakos Pittakis (1798–1863). Though Welcker, Ross and Fallmerayer – and even Rangavis – displayed considerable contempt for Pittakis' learning and judgement, his importance as the father of archaeology in Greece can hardly be overestimated. Furthermore, many of the criticisms levelled at his scholarship and accuracy have been shown to be unfounded.[3] His book of 1835 on the topography of Attica was a respectable contribution, and the inscriptions he published in the *Arkhaiologiki Ephemeris* from 1837–1860 became the basis of the Attic collection in the *Corpus Inscriptionum Graecarum* (completed in 1877). Klenze described Pittakis' unrelenting though often frustrated passion to protect his antiquities:

If he saw anyone approach them, he leapt in the greatest anxiety over stick and stone to the place where the greatest danger threatened. . . . Only the greatest love for his subject and an enthusiasm such as this genuinely interesting man possessed, could endure an office so arduous to fulfil – the more so, as daily events showed the insufficiency of his efforts. How far this was so, I often saw for myself. Shortly before my arrival, half a figure from one of the newly recovered, magnificent frieze sections of the Parthenon was knocked off by an Englishman before Pittakis' very eyes and taken away; and once I found myself in the Parthenon, Pittakis came up to me, calling for help, because some officers of an American frigate in Piraeus were on the point of hacking down the magnificent ornaments of the Erectheion and carrying them off. The traces of this situation were, alas, only too clearly, and increasingly, to be seen on these magnificent monuments, to the extent that the eventual result would be the complete disappearance of all their sculptured forms. But the more Pittakis, Ross and I bemoaned the situation, the less it seemed to trouble the foreign powers. One of them told me in Nauplia, as a delightful item of news, that a brig under an Austrian flag had recently landed thirty or forty men on the island of Delos, which is known to be now uninhabited, and that they, supplied with the necessary tools and means of transport, had taken everything they could find on board ship and made off with it.[4]

Pittakis' passion for antiquities went back to his youth during the War of Independence, when he had used his topographical studies to solve the problem of lack of water during the siege of the Acropolis by the Turks, by finding the ancient Clepsydra. He had also prevented his fellows from removing lead from the monuments for shot.

The all-Greek Archaeological Society, once founded, had to find itself a role. Its funds were too low at first to permit any excavations, but over the next four years it managed to undertake several digs in Athens – at the Theatre of Dionysus (1840–1), which they made their first objective, at the Tower of the Winds (1838–9), the Thrasyllos Monument, Propylaea and Erechtheion, gate of the agora, and also the lion at Chaeronea (all 1839–40).

At least as important was the Society's propaganda role. Even in the 1830s antiquities were still being burnt for lime, and Pittakis was responsible for putting an archaeologist in charge of every quarry (1838). He also instituted a law that no ancient sites were to be given as dowries. Such pressure was effective in decisions like that of the Austrian ambassador Prokesch von Osten to present to the Greek state the Pnyx, which was his private property (1857). But it was too much to expect that looting and quarrying, and the tendency to treat Greece as a German fief, should stop at once (see below).

A financial crisis in the 1840s was resolved in 1848 when the Society sold its shares in the National Bank and set up the first Cast Gallery. A prime motive was to obtain from London casts of the Parthenon sculptures, and of the friezes from the temple of Nike, and that of Apollo Epicurius at Bassae. It must have been a considerable humiliation to have to pay to obtain mere reproductions of what many Greeks considered theirs by right of inheritance.

Further financial crises led to the collapse of the Society after 1854, the year of the cholera in Athens, and it was not reconstituted until 1858, with twenty-seven of the original members. To these were quickly added another 376 – an impressive total. From now on the Society dug continuously, almost every year, mostly in Athens, until 1894. Their work was of major importance in turning excavation in Greece into a scientific procedure consonant with that being developed in Mesopotamia; but in 1850 it looked as if the archaeological palm had passed to another institution. This was the French School in Athens.

The French School in Athens was incorporated on 11 September 1846, as the culmination of a long period of discussion and manoeuvring in the French Academy and the diplomatic service. Sainte-Beuve attributed to himself the key role in effecting its establishment, but he was building on the foundations of his older contemporaries Adamantios Korais and Philippe LeGrand. Korais had throughout the eighteenth century been the standard bearer of Greek nationalism in Paris; and LeGrand was the doyen of Greek topographical study. They had envisaged at Athens a cultural institution, in French hands, which would bring to Greece the benefits of French language and culture while encouraging the appreciation of the Greek heritage. Enthusiastic young Frenchmen would flock to Greece to learn Greek and to study the art and literature. As Sainte-Beuve put it:

Every year . . . there would be a journey devoted to explorations in art or living commentary on an ancient author. The choruses of *Oedipus* read at Colonus; those of *Ion* at Delphi; the odes of Pindar studied in the presence of the sites he celebrated; a great historian pursued step by step through the theatres of wars he described; Arcadia traversed, Xenophon in hand, in the train of the victorious Epaminondas – these would be speaking researches which would resolve more than one geographical problem detected at one's desk.

LeGrand's vision had been almost exactly that of the Ecole as it became by 1900, an Académie des Beaux Arts to conserve monuments, house a library and cast gallery, and to conduct excavations and explore the islands. It should build on the work of the *Expédition Scientifique de la Morée* of 1829. Le Bas who, with Bory de St Vincent, led the expedition was to see it as a challenge to the 'pacific crusade' of the Germans in Greece.

But when the School was first founded it was with a much less precise aim. Its purposes were to be humanist, philhellenic, artistic, archaeological, philological and political. The last was of no little importance. Its foundation was largely the result of the good relations between the Greek Prime Minister Ioannes Kolettis (1784–1847), the ex-brigand and physician to

Ali Pasha, and the French Minister Theobald Piscatory. Politics at Athens in the first twenty years of Otto's reign were controlled by the rivalries of the three 'parties': the Russian party under Metaxas, the French under Kolettis and the British under Mavrokordato. The astute French minister E. A. Thouvenel, who came to Athens in December 1845 and succeeded Piscatory in June 1848, summed them up: neither Kolettis nor Metaxas could run a respectable government, and the English party had no power. It was the war of the ministers for Otto's ear that determined events. Though Otto increasingly leaned to the Russian party with its irredentist promises of Orthodox unity, and cast his eyes on the throne of Constantinople, it was the French who knew how to manipulate him. Sir Edmund Lyons, the British minister, represented Palmerston's intolerant foreign policy with a personal truculence and ferocity that endeared him to none. Small British grievances were bones of contention for years, and neither Palmerston nor Lyons would let Greece forget her obligation to repay the Powers' loan. Little wonder that Kolettis should favour the foundation of an educational institution designed not least to counteract what the School's historian calls the 'brutal hypocrisy' of English policy in Greece. Piscatory believed the foundation would help to forestall the British aim of obtaining dominance in the Levant, and keep the Mediterranean a French lake. It was a conflict over which France nearly declared war when Palmerston blockaded the Piraeus in 1849.

The seven founder members of the School were housed in the Gennadius House and quickly acquired a large number of eager pupils – over 150, from all walks of life. But, if the educative role of the School was clear, its scientific role was less so. Edmond About was scathing about the School, as about most things in Greece, in his account of his stay in 1852, as one of the only two members of the School. One member, Grenier, has left a sardonic picture in a letter of 27 April 1847, of the Athenian excursionist with 'a long broad tin box, painted green, in which he collects flowers, plants, pieces of marble, shells, medals, old nails, pieces of scrap iron, tortoises and other curious beasts.' Hardly a rival to the Archaeological Society!

The years immediately following brought some improvement. The excavations of Charles Beulé on the Acropolis

(1852) made the School renowned, and in the next twenty years there was a 'transition from romanticism to erudition' (Radet) in its members. From 1856 they were able to work closely with the *architectes-pensionnaires* who had been rewarded for winning the Prix de Rome with a trip to Greece, and were housed now in the same building, the Maison Lemnienne (now Hotel Grande Bretagne).

Both groups were interested in antiquities, especially architectural antiquities, and their interests thus coincided closely. The drawings and plans produced by the young architects are still of great interest for the history of architecture, and real discoveries were made. The first of these young men had come to Greece in 1845, the year of the retirement of Quatremère de Quincy who, although he believed that architects should study Greek buildings, had refused to countenance any of the *architectes-pensionnaires* visiting the country. Those who came now concentrated almost entirely on temples, the best preserved and most imitated exemplars of Greek architecture. It was at this time that the argument over hypaethral temples reached its height. Had Greek temples all been roofed, or had some been open, courtyard-like, in the centre? The case for the latter was argued by Pennethorne in 1837 and by F. C. Penrose (to become the first director of the British School at Athens in 1886) in 1846–7; Quatremère de Quincy had suggested perforation as early as 1805–7. Gradually it became clear that, as Vitruvius had implied, some were and some were not.

Another thorny issue was the question of whether Greek buildings had been painted. Again, Quatremère in his *Jupiter Olympien* of 1815 had provided convincing evidence at least that sculptures were, and Cockerell's observations of the Parthenon in 1810–11 corroborated him; but many were unable to accept their conclusions. It was left to the young architects to make observations of the temples, on some of which fragments of paint were still clearly visible, and to prove the matter beyond a shadow of doubt.

Now every sketch of a Greek temple to come from a draughtsman's hand was brightly coloured in the chromolithographic tones of gaudy red, blue and yellow, poor approximations to the earth-based hues of the Greek painter's palette. Countless are the names of the now forgotten

architects who produced immaculate and gorgeous restor-
ations of temples from every corner of the Greek world from
Pergamum to Selinus.[5] The discovery of polychromy had a
direct effect on the style adopted for the decoration of the
interior of the British Museum (1852) and the Greek
Court of the Crystal Palace (1851), as well as the University of
Athens. In 1844 Charles Lock Eastlake published his study,
Methods of Painting adapted to Mural Decoration; and it was the
encaustic whose use he expounded which was used in the
British Museum.[6]

The extremity of the passion for temples is evinced in Ernest
Renan's *Prière sur l'Acropole*, conceived in 1865 and written
down in 1876:

O Archegetis [i.e. Athena], ideal which the man of genius incarnates
in his masterpieces, I would rather be the last in your house than the
first elsewhere. Yes, I shall attach myself to the stylobate of your
temple; I shall forget all discipline except your own, I shall become a
stylite on your columns, my cell shall be upon your architrave . . . I
will love none but you . . . I will exalt, I will flatter, the present
inhabitants of the land you gave to Erechtheus. I will try to love them
even to their faults; I shall persuade myself, O Hippia [goddess of
horses], that they are descended of those horsemen who celebrate up
there, on the marble of your frieze, their eternal festival . . . Support
my firm intent, O goddess of Salvation; assist me, thou who savest!

But the French were to find themselves upstaged in the 1870s
by the Germans, who had managed to retain their influence
despite the unsatisfactory conclusion to Otto's reign.

Greece had undergone remarkable political developments
since 1834. It was not destined to remain for ever an agreeable
playground for the German intelligentsia. Otto, though he
had begun his reign in a wave of popularity, had hardly been
an unmitigated success. Forced to concede a constitution in
1844, he had lost the unpopular chancellor Armansperg, to be
replaced by Kolettis, whose pro-French leanings we have
already seen. Though Otto subscribed to the Great Idea of
a unified Greek state for all Greeks, he had notably failed
to achieve any extension of Greece's boundaries. Thoughts
of incursions against the Ottoman Empire were quelled by
the protecting powers, especially Britain and France who
were mainly concerned, in the years leading up to the Crimean
War, to keep the Ottoman Empire intact. It was left to loyal

figures like the poet Soutsos to represent Greece and Russia as 'sisters' and to pray for their 'unity' as the culmination of Christian progress. The presence of Stratford Canning in Constantinople, and the replacement of Lyons by the scholar-diplomat Thomas Wyse in June 1849, led to greater sympathy between Greece and Britain (Wyse's son came close to succeeding Otto as king of Greece), but this did not stop the British blockade of Piraeus in that year, or the joint British and French occupation of the port from 1854–7.

The King was eventually toppled by a rising in October 1862. He returned to Bavaria, where Klenze's Propylaea in Munich, built to celebrate his reign, had been completed on the day of his overthrow. He died seven years later, a patriot without a country or a cause.

The new King chosen by the protecting powers was the Danish prince who became George I of the Hellenes. A new constitution gave considerably more power to the Greek people than they had had under Otto; the goodwill of the protecting powers was further marked by the cession of the Ionian Islands to Greece in 1864. The Greek ministers made sure of their own power and their responsibility, chiefly for our purposes, for their country's antiquities. Though no such unreasonable stipulations were made as had been placed on Ross, the law prohibiting export of antiquities was strictly enforced.

The accession of a Dane to the Greek throne by no means entailed the dissipation of the German presence or influence in Greece. Though French visitors increased in number,[7] and several Britons did important work, it was through German work that the greatest of discoveries in the new Kingdom was to be made. The architect of this triumph was Ernst Curtius (1814–96), whom we met earlier as the private tutor to the family of George Brandis, travelling to Athens in 1837. Curtius had remained in Greece until 1840, travelling with C. O. Müller and obtaining books for him for the preparation of his journey (Müller had written that he would be glad to find an abridged version of Leake's eight or nine volumes!), and described his response to the Greek landscape in letters and poems. In 1843 he published his *Anecdota Delphica* and in 1851–2 his major work, *Der Peloponnes*. In 1884 he had become Professor in Berlin and been called to act as tutor to the Crown

Prince of Prussia (later Friedrich Wilhelm IV), and had 'stood by him in his darkest hour' of 1848. Friedrich Wilhelm had reciprocated that support when on 10 January 1852 Curtius lectured in Berlin on the subject of Olympia:

Again the grit and sand of the Alpheus runs over the holy soil of art, and we ask with increased longing: When will that womb be opened again, to bring the works of the ancient to the light of day?

What lies there in the dark depths is life of our life. If other messengers of the gods have gone about the world and announced a sublimer peace than the Olympian war-truce, yet still Olympia remains for us sacred soil, and we should carry over into our world, lit as it is by a purer light, the impetus of enthusiasm, the love of fatherland that joys in self-sacrifice, the dedication of art and the strength of the joy that outlasts all the troubles of life.

As Friedrich Wilhelm commented, 'I would willingly stand at the door myself with a collecting box!' after such a lecture.

Olympia had indeed acquired a unique importance in the modern mythology of ancient Greece, which however was only equal to its unique status among the Greek cities in antiquity. Its excavation was the greatest achievement of Germany in Greece.

Olympia

> If, my soul, you yearn
> to celebrate great games
> look no further
> for another star
> shining through the deserted ether
> brighter than the sun, or for a contest
> mightier than Olympia
>   (Pindar *Olympian* 1)

Olympia was a city that transcended political boundaries and rivalries. Like the oracle at Delphi and a few other sites, it was a centre for all Greeks. Every four years the Olympic festival was held – a religious celebration accompanied by Games which stretches far back into the mists of antiquity and the legendary past, for it was supposed to have been founded by Heracles, when he celebrated his victory over Augeas and 'fenced the Altis and marked it off in a clean space . . . To Kronos' Hill he gave a name; for before it was nameless when

Oinomaos ruled, and drenched with many a snowstorm. . . .
The evening was lit by the lovely light of the fair-faced moon.
All the holy place was loud with song in the glad feasting
like the music of banquets.' (Pindar, *Olympian* 10) Ancient
chronographers put the historical foundation of the Games in
776 BC, which has some approximate plausibility; and from
that date a chronology of Greek history was in antiquity
devised, on which we still depend.

It was in the sixth century BC that the Olympian Games
developed into more than a local religious festival. With the
new prosperity of Greece, won from its trading and its
colonies, the wealthy classes of all the Greek states began to
compete for the prestige of Olympic victory in one or other of
the athletic contests: boxing, wrestling, the foot-race, the
javelin and the discus, or in the *pankration* which demanded
best in all five for an outright win. But the *crème de la crème*
sought victory in the chariot race, where their purebred horses
would be shown off and, in addition, they need not soil their
clothes with the dust of the stadium, since a charioteer would
do the work. Now victors began to receive the honour of
statues and dedications; some were even accorded cult status
as heroes; and by the early fifth century elaborate choral
songs were composed which would bring the victors' glory
back to their native cities when they were performed at the
homecoming. Olympia was becoming big business.

The city drew wealth to itself from the flocks of contestants
and spectators. Huge temples were erected, one of which, the
temple of Zeus, contained the gold and ivory statue of the god,
many times life size, which was regarded as one of the
Wonders of the World. Even the solemn-minded Stoic,
Epictetus, said that it should be regarded as a misfortune
to die without having seen this masterpiece of the sculptor
Phidias. The temple, too, was adorned with elaborate sculptures, now the glory of the Olympia Museum. The metopes
showed the twelve labours of Heracles; one pediment showed
the god Apollo stilling the indecorous battle of the Lapiths and
Centaurs, while the other represented the more familiar
legend of the foundation of the Olympic Games, in which
young Pelops won his bride Hippodameia from her father
Oenomaus in a chariot race.

But all these mighty statues had lain underground since the

earthquake of the sixth century. The Olympic Games had last been celebrated in 393 AD, and then abolished, along with other operations of paganism, by the Emperor Theodosius I. The great statue of Zeus was taken to Constantinople, where it perished in one of the repeated fires of the crowded wood-built city. The Emperor Nero had already plundered Olympia of its choicest statues and valuables to adorn his Golden House, after contriving to win every competition at the Games with ease; but when Pausanias came, half a century later, there were still to be seen countless statues and dedications, rows of small treasuries, and all the bric-à-brac of a pilgrimage centre, a fair and a sports meeting rolled into one. Pausanias devoted one-sixth of his whole long book to the treasures and legends of Olympia. But, as Leake wrote:[8]

Of the immense number of brazen statues, which had accumulated in all these countries in the course of ages, none have been dis-covered, except such as had been buried by convulsions of nature, or some other cause of sudden ruin, or such as had been hidden, to protect them from plunder. . . The cause could have been no other than the ignorance and insecurity which accompanied the decline of the Roman empire, the gradual extinction of Paganism, and with it the cessation of all respect for such productions of art, either as sacred or beautiful; soon followed by Christian persecution, the authors of which were not displeased to find the objects of their hostility possessing a considerable metallic value. When such a feeling became general, and when Christianity became the religion of government, a few years may have sufficed to convert all the best monuments of an art which had required ages to be brought to perfection, and which we have hitherto tried in vain to imitate, into objects of common utility; and we may still, perhaps, have the material of some of those works in the form of the hideous coinage of Constan-tine and his successors.

Curtius achieved what his country had aspired to for over a century. Winckelmann, lured as much by the thought of the naked boys exercising in the palaestra as by the possible gains to the history of classical art, had set his heart on the excavation of Olympia as the main purpose of his never-accomplished journey to Greece.[9] His older contemporary, Bernard de Montfaucon, had attached a similar importance to the likeli-hood of finding a store of treasures at this, the richest of all Greek sanctuaries: he had put much effort into a vain attempt to persuade Cardinal Quirini, who became Bishop of Corfu in 1723, to initiate a dig by the Alpheus. Stakelberg too had dreamt of digging here.

The Renaissance perhaps centred its moral idealism on Sparta, the seventeenth century on Athens; but once Winckelmann had established the congruence of the Greek and the physical ideal, Olympia, symbol at once of the physical and spiritual perfection of man, was the lure for every visitor.

Scarcely anything was visible above the ground when Chandler visited the site in 1766. In 1787 Fauvel, still prospecting for the Comte de Choiseul-Gouffier, had recognised with delight some fragments of the sacred enclosure. He

arrived upon the banks of the Cladeus . . . It runs in a bed, or rather in a deep ravine, to join the Alpheus, after having watered a plain to the north, in which are some fine ruins. Perceiving on this river the relics of an ancient bridge, I examined the nature of its banks both to the right and to the left, and I remarked every where, at the depth of about six feet from the surface of the ground above, relics of pottery, of bricks and of antique tiles; I also perceived some fragments of marble. These discoveries, joined to that of the bridge, convinced me that I was among the ruins of some town noted in antiquity . . . Some men, sent by the aga of a neighbouring village to seek materials for building, were at this moment turning up the ground. What was my surprise, when on inquiry I found that they called their village Andilalo, or *the Village of the Echo*! I could not then forbear calling to mind, that the Greeks who assisted at the Olympic Games were accustomed, as Pausanias relates, to listen to a remarkable echo, which repeated sounds seven times over. This discovery impressed me still more strongly with the idea that I was upon the very ground where once stood Olympia.

He had been followed by Gell and Dodwell in 1805, but when Leake came it all still lay underground. Despite this, by using the indications of Pausanias and the few vestiges that were visible, especially of the Temple of Zeus, in a site much silted by the combined actions of the Rivers Alpheus and Cladeus which met here, Leake was able to produce a map which is accurate in most details. His main error is in placing the stadium on an axis NNW/SSE alongside the hill of Cronos; it was left to the excavations ordered by Adolf Hitler, in pursuit of topographical celebration of the Aryan ideal of manhood, to discover its true alignment parallel to the Alpheus, to the east of the sacred enclosure.

Having done all this work, Leake was understandably put out to see, in the publication of the *Expédition Scientifique de la Morée* (1831–8), that his visit had gone totally unremarked by them and that they had failed to read his account, published in 1830. The French tome is surely one of the least interesting of works of Greek topography. It records the mission sent early in 1829 by the French government, as a successor to the Commission on Egypt, to survey the physical aspect, archaeology, architecture and sculpture of Greece, to 'paint the portrait of a country reduced to a skeleton', and to rectify the travesty of geography provided by the Abbé Barthélémy. The expedition claimed that, on their visit to Olympia in 1829, 'nothing had been ascertained beyond the existence of a temple,' and 'all was conjecture until their excavations'. They had in fact spent about six weeks in the early summer of 1829 digging in the ruins, but had turned up but little. What they did get was removed to the Louvre. Leake wrote (in 1846) that the site would well repay excavation, and stated his conviction that the Greeks would do so, 'when they have shaken off the deplorable state of poverty' resultant from the struggle for freedom. (He compared their eagerness favourably with Italian apathy in matters archaeological.)

The French had paid more attention to careful plans made of the site by Spencer Stanhope[10] in 1813; these had a considerable influence on Quatremère de Quincy's magnificent folio *Le Jupiter Olympien* (1815), which offered perhaps the most plausible reconstruction so far of the great chryselephantine Zeus of Phidias.

In 1836 the project had seemed to come as close as ever it might to fulfilment. This was the core of a plan propounded to the King's Chancellor Armansperg by the wandering dilettante Prince Pückler-Muskau. We have met Pückler-Muskau already as the figure unwittingly responsible for Ross' dismissal from the archaeological service. He had spent his youth travelling in Europe, Greece, Asia Minor and Moscow, acquiring as well as an education and a number of antiquities (including inscriptions) an African mistress named Machbuba who did little to impress Prussian society when he returned in 1839. (Ludwig I once suggested to him that he should try an

expedition to the moon, and drop a line thence to Munich.)
Like Ross later, Pückler-Muskau's first thought on arrival in
the Levant in 1835 was that it might provide a suitable setting
for German colonies. His plan was to put them in Greece itself.
So it was entirely in character when, a year later, he proposed
to the King's Chancellor Armansperg that he should buy some
land at Sparta to build a park, and also, more important,
should buy the site of Olympia.[11] The gardener would tread in
the steps of the excavator and turn Olympia into a modern
paradise. Ross was all in favour – even with the suggestion that
the park should be used as a site for a new Olympic festival
based on the Munich Oktoberfest (founded not long before to
celebrate the marriage of Ludwig I). There was however to be
no horse racing 'in the English style' – just athletic pursuits
fitting to noble young men, shooting, wrestling and foot-
races, as well as competitions in singing and dancing. Those
whose stomachs revolt at the thought of the shady, cicada-
haunted Altis resounding to the oompah of brass bands, the
splash of steins of beer and the slapping of leather-clad thighs,
will be glad that the Greek government no longer allowed
foreigners to purchase land in Greece.

This scarcely credible suggestion was fortunately the final
fling of individual arrogance towards Greek antiquities. But
thirty-nine years later, the Emperor Wilhelm I continued the
enthusiasm of his elder brother. He sent Curtius to Athens as a
special representative of the Empire to arrange a contract for
the excavation of Olympia. This was a remarkably disinterested act for the ruler of the three-year-old Empire, since his
collections and museums stood to gain nothing to enhance
their prestige. All antiquities excavated must by law now
remain in Greece. What the German Empire would display
was the power and capacity of its authorised intellectuals. (It
was as representative of that authority that Curtius was to
make life so difficult for Schliemann (see Chapter 11), the
outsider, who craved above all recognition from the profession.) It was accepted that no new texts would now be found
to feed the mills of science: instead, epigraphy and art history
were to be the beneficiaries. For a nation now at peace, and
with a profound and long-standing spiritual engagement with
Hellas, the excavation of Olympia would be a uniquely
appropriate task.

The enthusiasm of the Emperor for classical archaeology was shown in another way too. While Curtius was in Athens in 1874 he took the first steps towards setting up the German Archaeological Institute in Athens (there had been one in Rome since 1828, when the patron was the Crown Prince of Prussia). Library and printing types were acquired, and by the following year regular fortnightly sittings could begin. The first of these took place, like that of the Roman sister institution, on 9 December, Winckelmann's birthday. The first volume of *Mitteilungen* appeared in 1876. How the lean connoisseur from Stendhal would have rejoiced to see what Curtius achieved in the site on which he had set his never-satisfied heart!

On 25 April 1874 Curtius, the German Ambassador, the Greek Foreign Minister and the Keeper of Antiquities signed the Olympia Convention. This was the first legally explicit excavation agreement between two governments and became the prototype for countless others all over the world, in the following century.

The key provisions were[12] that each government should appoint a commissar to ensure adherence to the agreement; the Greek government should provide police to enforce it; the German government should pay all expenses including compensation to landowners and should have the exclusive control over choice of excavation areas at Olympia and over the workers; *all finds should remain in Greece* (though at its discretion the Greek government might give the excavators any duplicates as 'souvenirs'), while Germany had the right to make copies and casts; all finds were to be published simultaneously in Greek and in German.

The Reichstag approved Curtius' application for the sum of 57,000 talers. Curtius chose as his assistant Friedrich Adler; and work began, with 450 labourers. The site consisted of two square miles between the Hill of Cronos and the River Alpheus: much of it lay under eighteen feet or more of mud, silt and sand. When the excavators arrived, the intervening years since 1829 had covered up much of what had been visible to Leake and the French expedition; only one corner of the Temple of Zeus was visible. This was supposed by the local inhabitants to be the remains of a king's son's palace. 'Effendi,' the villagers asked, 'you who know everything – why did the

King's son build his palace here among these wretched houses?'

In the circumstances the progress of the excavation was extraordinarily successful. The first spade was sunk into the ground on 4 October 1875. Just over two months later (14 December) began the disinterment of the statues from the east pediment of the Temple of Zeus. Six days later appeared the Winged Victory which had stood before the temple. Week by week, limb by limb, the heroic bodies resumed the form they had been given 2,000 years ago. Adolf Boetticher, who described the excavation, allowed himself a pang of regret that these forty-two magnificent figures should be doomed to stay in Athens 'which is so difficult to get to', rather than adorning the museums of the Empire; but the Germans observed their contract scrupulously.

Curtius, as befitted a scholar, wrote 'it is the written word which speaks most clearly', and valued the more than 400 inscriptions, illustrating uniquely the range and development of the Greek dialects, above the statues, terracottas, statue bases and even the bronzes of which Olympia produced the richest collection in the world.

Perhaps most enthusiasm was evinced by the discovery of the Hermes described by Pausanias, at once taken for a work of Praxiteles (fl 364 BC), one of the two most famous sculptors of antiquity. But the recovery of the pedimental sculptures was · of equal importance for its revelation of the power of the early classical style at an intermediate stage between the grinning fixity of the Aigina marbles and the sublime naturalism of the Parthenon frieze. These works put the Germans in the forefront of the illumination of the archaic style (to be further illustrated by Kavvadias' discovery of the series of korai from the Acropolis in the 1880s). Hegel had understood as well as Lord Elgin that the day of the *beau ideal* was over; with the discovery of Greek classicism, the road was opened for the appreciation of its immediate predecessor. As Humann (see Chapter 11) was at the same time revealing the greatest work of the latest florescence of Greek art in Pergamum, the German Empire could claim real precedence in the study of the art of antiquity.

Olympia was the first site to be excavated on recognisably modern scientific principles. Careful but lavish presentation of the results made the finds available to the learned world for study, and opinion was not slow to recognise the achievement. Once again, as the whole complex was laid bare, the scene of Greece's greatest and most peaceful glories seemed to live again – its ancient sanctuaries of the Mother and of Hera below the shapely hill of Cronos, the magnificent temple of Zeus with its dignified pediments, the rows of dedicatory statue-bases of famous victors, the dedicatory weapons, the hotel, the gymnasium, the palaestra, even the workshop of Phidias, now a ruined Byzantine church. Only Phidias' seated Zeus of gold and ivory, one of the Wonders of the World, was gone for ever, live though it might in reconstructions based on Pausanias' description. The stadium was left for the Germans to excavate between 1936 and 1942.

But the most enduring and familiar legacy of the excavation to the modern world was the re-establishment of the Olympic Games by Baron Coubertin in 1896. In this he tried to bring to his own world some of that enjoyment of peaceful competition, isolated from the shocks of war and political strife, which the Games had meant to ancient Hellas. How far that noble dream still lives is a matter for personal opinion; but it bore already no real relation to the concerns of the learned excavators. This new Ideal of Greece was a distraction from the task of understanding the old Greece. Knowledge was all the quarry now.

CHAPTER ELEVEN

The Race of Empires

Homer composed a tale, offered and accepted as such: for no one ever doubted that Troy and Agamemnon had never really existed any more than the golden apple . . . Any history that is not contemporary is suspect.   (Pascal, *Pensées* 436)

'Father . . . if such walls once existed, they cannot possibly have been completely destroyed: vast ruins of them must still remain, but they are hidden away beneath the dust of ages.' He maintained the contrary, whilst I remained firm in my opinion, and at last we both agreed that I should one day excavate Troy.   (Heinrich Schliemann, *Ilios*)

Heinrich Schliemann and Troy

> High barrows without marble or a name,
> A vast, untilled, and mountain-skirted plain,
> And Ida in the distance, still the same,
> And old Scamander (if 'tis he) remain.
> The situation seems still formed for fame.
>   (Byron, *Don Juan* IV, 77)

In the same year that Ernst Curtius began his excavations at Olympia, another German archaeologist had begun work that was to make his name a household word for a century and more to come. Heinrich Schliemann was fulfilling a lifelong ambition – to discover Homer's Troy.

Troy, the setting for the first great poem of Western literature, Homer's *Iliad*, had exercised a fascination over all succeeding ages from classical Greece onwards. Homer, Plato said, was the teacher of the Greeks, and his *Iliad* and *Odyssey* occupied a place in Greek consciousness analogous to that of the Bible in the early modern world. Homer's heroes – Achilles, Odysseus, Ajax, Hector, Agamemnon, Helen – had become the object of religious cult by the fifth century BC, and their sagas formed the subject of most of the tragedies of classical Athens as well as of poetry, vase-painting and narrative sculpture.

Yet by the nineteenth century, the site of Troy had become quite uncertain. That point of scepticism had not been reached, as it now has in the late twentieth century, when one might question whether Troy ever existed, and whether the Trojan War ever took place (though Blaise Pascal in the seventeenth century had uttered the unconventional opinion that Homer's work was pure fiction). Few had questioned the existence of Homer's Troy; but where was it to be found? Opinions differed violently, and by the eighteenth century, lifetime enmities might be formed by differences over the question.

Until the Christian era no one had doubted that Troy was identical with the 'Village of the Ilians' at the hill of Hisarlik, which became the Roman Novum Ilium. (Ilium was the common Greek name for the city of Troy as opposed to the region.) The only dissenting voice was a local writer called Demetrius of Scepsis, who insisted that Homer's topographical indications did not fit that site. In particular, Homer mentioned two springs close together, which were not to be found in this vicinity, though such a phenomenon was to be found at nearby Callicolone. The site at Callicolone became canonical through its adoption by the geographer Strabo. (Pausanias, alas, never described the Troad.)

In the seventeenth and eighteenth centuries, an impressive group of ruins near the coast attracted most of the votes of travellers; many travellers from Britain, France and Italy revelled in the supposed Homeric associations of what was actually Alexandria Troas, the foundation of Alexander the Great. By the time of Edmund Chishull (1699), a sense of architectural period had developed sufficiently to enable him to reject this identification, but it was not until 1750 that Robert Wood published his book in which he argued for the

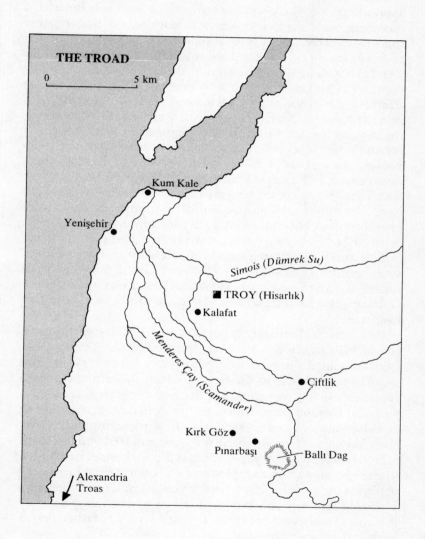

THE TROAD

0   5 km

Kum Kale

Yenişehir

Simois (*Dümrek Su*)

■ TROY (Hisarlık)
● Kalafat

Menderes Çay (Scamander)

● Çiftlik

Kırk Göz●
    Pınarbaşı ●   Ballı Dag

Alexandria
Troas

site at Pınarbaşı (which he spelt Bunar bashi), the modern name for Callicolone.

This vindication of Strabo's view was somewhat disappointing since there was next to nothing visible at Pınarbaşı; travellers could no longer attach famous names to evocative ruins. Nevertheless, it was accepted by all the turn of the century travellers, being argued for in fullest detail in 1791 by J. B. Lechevalier, who had been in the Troad with Choiseul-Gouffier. Clarke, who was also there in 1801, proposed an alternative location near Çiplak, not far from Hisarlik; and in 1822 Charles Maclaren published an argument reviving the arguments for Hisarlik. His arguments were cogent if Homer's text was taken as gospel: it would have been impossible to run, as Achilles did in pursuit of Hector, three times round Bali Dağ at Pınarbaşı in heavy armour; Pınarbaşı was invisible from the crest of Mt Ida where Zeus was said to have sat to watch the progress of the fighting; and there were two springs at Hisarlik too, which furthermore was at a more appropriate distance from the coast for the action of the *Iliad*.

The question was rejected as insoluble by George Grote, who began his monumental *History of Greece* with historical times – the first Olympiad of 776 BC. Homer was mere legend, and legend had no place in the discussions of a scientific historian.

Heinrich Schliemann, however, was not a scientific historian. Nor was he a professional archaeologist. (This fact was to make Curtius unremittingly hostile to his endeavours and singularly grudging in the recognition of his achievements.) No, Schliemann had spent his life as a merchant, creating a personal fortune from commerce in America, St Petersburg and elsewhere. When, in 1866, the already greying millionaire abandoned his first (Russian) wife and children and his commercial career to enrol as a student at the Sorbonne, he claimed that the passion to discover Homer's Troy had been implanted in him at the age of seven when he was given Dr G. L. Jenner's *Universal History*. This book contained an engraving of Troy in flames, and Aeneas fleeing the city with his father on his back and his son at his side.

'Father,' he said, 'if such walls once existed, they cannot possibly have been completely destroyed: vast ruins of them must still remain, but they are hidden away beneath the dust of ages. He maintained the contrary [Schliemann goes on, in the preface to *Ilios*], whilst I remained firm in my opinion, and at last we both agreed that I should one day excavate Troy.'

It is hard to know whether to believe this tale as literal truth. As Irving Stone has written:

In his excavating, in the books he published about his work, he was scrupulously honest, trustworthy. In his private life he was an epic poet whose personal Odyssey was based more on invention than on memory. He had the talent to rewrite the past, to make its strands fit harmoniously into the present fabric of his life. He did not lie, he recreated, he took an eraser to the blackboard of his younger years, wiped out the gritty chalk marks of actuality and, with a firm, bold hand, wrote a more lyrical version of his past.

Two years after his enrolment at the Sorbonne he embarked on the trip that was to change his life. This was the tour of Greece which he described in his sentimental journey *Ithaca, the Peloponnese and Troy* (1869). Corfu, which was commonly identified with the Phaeacia of the *Odyssey*, struck him like a revelation. Everything corresponded exactly, in his enthusiastic mind, to Homer's descriptions. The world of Homer lay before him as sun-drenched fertile earth, glorious vegetation, fruit and crops, the limpid water of the stream Cressida. It assumed even more tangible form when he crossed to Ithaca, the home of Odysseus, in the company of a guide who 'on the way retold the adventures of Odysseus from beginning to end. The ease with which he recited them proved to me clearly that he had told the same story thousands of times' – though he could not satisfy Schliemann's anxiety to identify Mt Aetos, the harbour of Phorcys, the grotto of the Nymphs and the field of Laertes. This remarkable exhibition of the oral tradition may be believed by those to whom Greece is an Ithaca as romantic as it was for Heinrich Schliemann.

Schliemann's aim now was to make himself completely a part of the Greek scene until it and his achievements were one. Did ever an archaeologist's career belie more thoroughly Rose Macaulay's dictum that archaeology is 'the sacrifice of beauty to truth'? For truth he did indeed uncover, though the world was slow to accept it; yet truth resulted only from his beautiful imaginings and intuitions.

The extraordinary story of his acquisition of a Greek wife by choosing from a selection of photographs the one most closely corresponding to his vision of Helen of Troy is scarcely part of the archaeological story. But of course it is another facet of the way Schliemann made the Homeric world as immediate as here and now. Sophia has the distinction at least of being the only woman in this book to receive recognition as an archaeologist in her own right. She was fêted by London for her assistance at Troy and her independent work at Mycenae.

Schliemann's plan to dig at Hisarlik was already formed at the end of that first tour in 1868. It was not after all so odd to expect archaeology to confirm the literary record, to seek for a city where Homer appeared to have placed it. That was what the antiquaries had been doing for centuries, and Charles Newton accepted it as one of the main functions of excavation. What is more striking is that Schliemann was the first to excavate to test a hypothesis, rather than simply to see what would turn up.[1] He wished to prove the reality of Homer's Troy, and to prove that it had been where he believed it to be. It is this use of what might be called experimental method which makes him the Father of Archaeology. By comparison, Curtius was a traditionalist. Curtius did not believe that excavation could prove anything new – only that it could fill out a picture, provide data for philologists to work on.

It was a difference in the value attached to Homer's poems, then, that lay at the root of the irreconcilability of the two men. Homer stood on a pinnacle in England. Since 1711 his supremacy had been unchallenged. Matthew Arnold's writings of the 1860s testify to his towering stature. But his position was less secure in Germany. The analytic criticism of Wolf and Lachmann cast doubt on Homer's very existence, let alone his historical value. German culture was preconditioned to reject Schliemann's belief in a historical Troy. So Schliemann had to make a legend himself. Not surprisingly, support came more readily from England than from Germany.

Long before 1859, when he became High Commissioner of the Ionian Islands, William Gladstone had become firmly convinced that Homer, 'the point of origin from which all distances are measured', enshrined recoverable historical reality. One year before the publication of *The Origin of Species*, Gladstone argued in his *Studies in Homer and the Homeric Age* (1858) that the poet represented an accurate record of the way of life of early Greece. Gladstone was to receive Schliemann's discoveries at Troy with enthusiasm and to offer much real support.

The excavation of Hisarlik began after his marriage to Sophia had been solemnised on 23 September 1869.

A spring campaign in 1870 without permission of the Turkish government only made the obtaining of a firman to continue work in autumn the more difficult. Part of the land belonged to the American consul Frank Calvert, but his Turkish neighbour was reluctant to sell his half. Eventually, the Minister of Public Instruction, Safvet Pasha, ordered the local governor to buy the land, and then to make it available to Schliemann for purchase – a transaction effected for 3,000 piastres. It was cheap at the price since it was, as Schliemann said, 'not a commercial matter, but one of solving the most important historical problem ever solved.' (*Briefwechsel* I, 80)

In October 1871 he was still waiting for his firman. When it at last arrived it had three main provisions: all finds were to be divided, half going to Schliemann and half to the Turkish government for its new Museum; uncovered ruins must be left in the state in which they had been recovered; and all expenses were to be borne by the excavator himself. But even before the firman arrived Schliemann had begun digging again, convinced that if he should find the real Pergamus of Troy, the German Emperor or the British Museum would do the rest. He reckoned without the Berlin opposition. On 13 September, Curtius had visited the Plain of Troy with several other Berlin scholars – and they had settled firmly for Pınarbaşı. Curtius' convictions were no more easily shaken than Schliemann's. 'Berliner's Infallibility' was a catch phrase – and no one was more a Berliner than Curtius. Who, after all, was this ignorant millionaire who had decided to swoop into a subject to which they had devoted a lifetime, and aim to overturn everything? The English had ever loved the amateur – but not so the Germans.

Schliemann broke through the entire mound with a massive trench in order to penetrate as fast as possible to the bottom or oldest stratum – for naturally he assumed that Priam's Troy must be the oldest. It came as something of a shock, then, to find, quite high up in the mound, strata of sherds quite obviously older than anything that could be associated with the period of the Trojan War. We can now surmise what had happened. The mound had been levelled off in antiquity, and as the top layers had been removed they had come to the bottom of the outer part of the slope, leaving older strata on top – at the sides – while in the centre the lower part of the stratigraphy remained undisturbed. It is to Schliemann's credit, again, that we can extract from his puzzlement a realistic picture of the situation. Of course, many provenances are destroyed for ever.

This setback almost drove Schliemann to despair. But a second, longer season in 1872 produced fine things: a Hellenistic relief of Helios, and the foundations of a tower which Schliemann at once named the Great Tower of Ilium (in fact it was a section of the circuit wall of Troy II).

More evidence came in some further finds:

> Athens, 1 January 1873.
> I have just made the important discovery that all the owls heads with helmet which I find on the trojan gobelets from 2 to 12 meters depth and all the owls faces which I find with the 2 female breasts and navel on the vases as well as the 2 female breasts and navel with which a vast number of vases are decorated and finally all the owls faces which I find on the numberless idols of hard white stone and on 2 of terracotta together with the never missing female girdle represent the ilian Minerva the protecting divinity of Troy and that consequently the common epithet of this goddess in Homer 'γλαυκῶπις' does not signify with blue, sparkling or firy eyes, as it has been translated by scholars of all centuries, but it signifies 'with the owls face'. The natural conclusion is that Homer knew very well that Minerva with the owls face was the protecting divinity of Troy and that consequently Troy existed and that it existed on the sacred premises which I am excavating

All these finds were reported with promptitude and enthusiasm to Curtius, who promised to 'use' anything Schliemann sent in the *Archäologische Zeitung*; in fact he published not a single article, and reproduced Schliemann's photographs with his own comments. On hearing of the Helios metope, he raised Schliemann's hopes that the government might now support him. In ten days a cast was on its way to Curtius. It was not the financial aspect, but the need for scientific recognition, that drove Schliemann. And his Berliners constantly rejected him.

He had found walls; a city; he had found sherds of pottery apparently portraying owls, the special birds of Athena the protectress of Troy; what more could be demanded as proof? Schliemann was desperate. In May 1873 came something which should give him world-wide recognition: treasure.

The Treasure of Priam has aroused suspicion ever since it was found. Schliemann's reports of the position of the find seemed inconsistent; he was even accused of having bought the pieces in separate transactions from the dealers of Istanbul, and planted them on the site. This would, after all, be no more than an Odyssean ploy from one who could claim, straight-faced, that Pallas Athena stood by him as he conducted his excavations (*Briefwechsel* II, 382). The suspicion was strengthened when it was discovered recently that the report of the find had actually been inserted in his diary at a date subsequent to that of the alleged find – further pointers to a less than *bona fide* provenance for the finds. Another recent suggestion has been that he concealed all items of value as they were made in order to avoid the Turk's taking his daily quota: he assembled them all and smuggled them out of the country before announcing his find. But certainly Schliemann's underhand ways got him into trouble later.

The treasure, which finally came to rest in Berlin, went missing at the end of the Second World War, so no chance of autopsy remains to check Schliemann's claims. But study of the photographs has led modern scholars to believe that the treasure is probably all of a piece, and certainly of the right period for its provenance). Schliemann himself noted the resemblance of the style of a second treasure (found three months before the great treasure, and stolen by his workmen, whence it came into the possession of the Turkish authorities), to gold vases and beakers found in Hungary in 1844 (*Briefwechsel* I, 252 and 377). Modern research has confirmed a number of interesting links between Troy and Thrace:[3] again Schliemann's adviser Eugène Piot had not let him down.

This is no place to settle once and for all the authenticity of the treasure. It aroused extreme interest, and in November 1873 Alexander Conze invited him to exhibit it at the Museum of Art and Industry in Vienna, of which he was director. Schliemann insisted, however, that it only made sense to

exhibit it in the context of all his finds at Troy – more than
300 baskets and chests-full! (*Briefwechsel* I, 242). If Vienna
could not offer that, he would build himself a museum in
Greece, or perhaps Campania, where it could be exhibited
properly. Here the amateur sets his scientific concern for a full
conspectus against the, perhaps surprising, desire of the professionals for something more sensational. This was of course
the first move in Austria's plan to acquire a collection of
antiquities to rival the glories of London and Paris.

When C. T. Newton visited Schliemann at Troy a month
later he was overwhelmed and convinced by the enthusiast's
finds of two-handled cups exactly like those described by
Homer. There seems to have been a natural affinity between
the two men. Like Schliemann, Newton believed that a
collection should be exhibited entire rather than a selection
being made: reasonable enough, since any selection reflects the
presumptions of the selector, but a little hard on the public in
search of archaeology as entertainment.[4]

Newton's support, and assistance in publishing Schliemann's finds in *The Times*, was followed by that of Gladstone.
Perhaps after all Schliemann was getting somewhere.

At this point it is convenient to assess Schliemann's
methods, procedures and assumptions. Digging was by the
1870s, hardly something new. But there are ways and ways of
digging. Schliemann has been much criticised for his procedures at Troy – smashing through the entire mound to get to
the lowest and presumably earliest level, and destroying
valuable evidence in the process. But, crude as his understanding might be, he did take seriously the principles of
stratigraphy established by Curtius, and not even first by him.
Stratification and the accurate recording of find spots had
become an accepted part of a proper excavation as early as
1869, when Richard Popplewell Pullan completed seven years'
work at the behest of the Ionian Committee of the Society of
Dilettanti in the excavation of Priene. Though his primary
purpose was to deepen knowledge of the forms of Ionic
architecture, he anticipated Curtius in the introduction of a
grid system for recording find spots. He was also, like Schönborn, a photographic pioneer.

An equally important practitioner of scientific recording
methods was Alexander Conze, who had made a point of

visiting Schliemann, in a spirit of something like homage, on his way to his own excavation of the Sanctuary of the Great Gods on the island of Samothrace in April 1873. He too was a photographic pioneer, and was the first to benefit from the technology which allowed photographs to be printed in the published excavation reports without being re-engraved. But like Curtius, Conze was excavating data to enlarge the historical record; not, like Schliemann, creating a new area of study.

Conze's expedition makes a piquant contrast with that of Schliemann. He had behind him not only the authority of the Imperial Museum in Vienna, where he had recently been appointed to the first chair in archaeology, but all the resonant panoply of the Imperial-Royal Ministry for Culture and Instruction. He had the assistance of the State Railway, the Southern Railway, Austrian Lloyd and, last but by no means least, the Donaudampfschifffahrtsgesellschaft or Danube Steamship Company. His expedition represented the first flurry of the race of nations for archaeological glory; a race which did not interest Schliemann and from which Curtius, proud of his own Olympia, did his best to exclude him.

A second important contribution of Schliemann was in the method of classification of his finds. The new science of comparative philology had induced a mania for typological classification, so that when Schliemann came to arrange his finds for exhibition he had them arranged strictly by type and provenance, with no attempt at a chronological series. Not everyone agreed even then with this rejection of the historical, but it was a respectable system at the time. Like many of Schliemann's scientific techniques he had learnt it not from intuition but from discussion with a sympathetic colleague, the anthropologist Rudolf Virchow (of whom more below).

A third arm of Schliemann's achievement must be deferred to an appropriate moment in the story; this was his employment of a trained architectural expert, Wilhelm Dörpfeld.

The next year, 1874, was a bad one. The reviews of *Trojan Antiquities* criticised the layout as unsystematic, the photographs as inadequate. Curtius read one of the reviews publicly to the Berlin Archaeological Society, an underhand thing to do when Schliemann was not present to reply. He abandoned Troy in discouragement and moved his attention to Athens.

Here he spent £465 on demolishing the Venetian tower on the
Acropolis, and was about to excavate the Propylaea when
King George rescinded his permission. The Turkish government brought a lawsuit against him in Athens to obtain their
half of his Trojan antiquities. He turned his eyes to Olympia,
only to be upstaged by Curtius. It was not surprising that by
the end of the year he was attacking even his former ally Frank
Calvert for 'libel'. He had made his dream come true, had
found Troy and proved it to his satisfaction, and none of his
countrymen believed him.

He spent a year marking time in southern Italy before
returning to Greece in 1876 to conclude the excavation of his
Homeric dream with an attack on Mycenae. It was the finds of
December 1876 that finally made his reputation. He seemed to
have a nose for treasure. Simply by following what Pausanias
said, and in despite of other archaeologists, he uncovered circle
'A' of the shaft graves and the wonderful gold ornaments that
are now the glory of the National Archaeological Museum in
Athens. There seems to be no documentary authentication of
the legendary telegram to King George of Greece, 'I have
gazed on the face of Agamemnon'; but who will believe he did
not exclaim those very words as his intuition uncovered
another hitherto unsuspected glory of Greece?

Mycenae was the book of the year. Never had an archaeological study received such acclaim, or sold so widely
(*Briefwechsel* II, 272: 10 April 1878). The Trojan treasure was
now brought to London and exhibited throughout 1876 at the
South Kensington Museum. In 1877 the Royal Archaeological
Society bestowed its medal on Heinrich and Sophia
Schliemann, and Sophia delivered a speech herself, in English,
describing their labours at Mycenae. At the time she was six
months pregnant. Their son would be called Agamemnon.

Yet still the German scholars were sceptical, declaring
Mycenae to be Celtic, Hellenistic or even medieval. But
Schliemann did manage to elicit the support of Rudolf
Virchow (1821–1902), a physical anthropologist and pathol-
ogist, whom he had first met in 1875. In 1877 he became a
member of the German Anthropological Society, founded by
Virchow. In 1879 Virchow accepted an invitation to join
him at Troy, along with Emile Burnouf (1821–1907) who
had also supported Schliemann's Trojan campaign from the

beginning. Burnouf established the seven layers of Troy and drew maps, Virchow devoted attention to the geography of the Troad and to the systematising of Schliemann's own labours. The result of their co-operation was *Ilios*, a far finer book than *Trojan Antiquities*.

At last receiving recognition, Schliemann, as usual, pushed his luck. Virchow nearly lost Schliemann's friendship through a plan to publish an article which Schliemann thought would anticipate his own publication. Virchow harboured no hard feelings (though it was Schliemann who had the more to lose), but sought an interview with Bismarck to convey to him the conditions on which Schliemann would consent to let the Trojan finds come to Berlin. Accommodation was on offer in the new Ethnological Museum. Schliemann insisted that he must have five halls specially set aside and marked for all time with the name SCHLIEMANN. In September 1888 Schliemann received a letter from Bismarck himself, announcing the transfer to the Ethnological Museum and expressing gratitude and honour to Schliemann. In the same year the German Archaeological Institute in Athens was opened. Prussia's presence in archaeology was assured.

But in the meantime, Berlin settled, Schliemann had turned back to Asia Minor. A further Trojan campaign of 1882 was conducted with the assistance of a man Schuchardt characterised as 'Schliemann's greatest find' – Wilhelm Dörpfeld. Schliemann had observed him at work at Olympia with Curtius, and had made him his own. Dörpfeld was to become one of the greatest archaeologists of the new century, and as much of a Grecian as Schliemann himself. (He made his home, and ended his days, on Homer's Ithaca.)

In a letter to Gladstone, Schliemann expressed very clearly Dörpfeld's achievement at Troy:

Troy near the Dardanelles 3d May 1882
For this year's exploration of Troy I had engaged the two very best German architects I could get hold of, Dr Höfler of Vienna and Dr Dörpfeld of Berlin; both of them had gained the great prize in the academies of Vienna and Berlin and the latter had been for 5 years chief architect in the German Empire's exploration of Olympia. These two architects have found out, and proved to me, that the *first* city, whose ruins are 23 feet deep, has been succeeded by a *large* city, which used Hissarlik merely as its acropolis and sacred precinct of its

temples, as well as for the residence of its king and family. They have
laid bare the ruins of two very large buildings in this city, each of
which was ab^t 33 f^t broad and 100 f^t long; the roofs were sustained by
pillars, of many of which the lower part remains. The walls of these
buildings consist of raw bricks, and are 10 f^t thick. These walls have
been burnt by a fire put on both sides; this is proved by their vitrified
surfaces, over which we see a vitrified coating of clay 1 inch thick.
The foundations of this buildings are 12 and 13 f^t deep and consist of
large blocks. The blocks of bricks marked H on plan I and III in my
Ilios, which we had mistaken for remnants of the city wall, are parts
of the buildings. For these two buildings, probably temples, there
was a separate gate of large dimensions on the S. side, flanked by two
stone towers, which we are now excavating; probably stairs led up
from the gate to the temples. The other gate, on the S.W. side, which
I excavated in 1873, was built by the people of this 2^d city, but it was
then only single. Before this gate and *below* the house N: 188 (in Ilios)
we see the foundations of a *large* building, probably that of the king;
to the north of them are the ruins of 4 or 5 other houses. The 10
treasures I found belonged, except one, to this 2^d city, for they were
contained in the *débris* of the 2^d settlers between the royal house and
the walls for the *débris* had *not* been removed by the latter. In the
trenches I dug to the S. and W. on the plateau outside Hissarlik I
found a great deal of pottery of this 2^d city. There are besides distinct
marks that the walls extended to the plateau on which must have
stood the lower city. The Pergamos and no doubt also the lower city,
were destroyed by a fearful conflagration. This large city, which is
no doubt the Homeric *Ilios*, was succeeded by another city with
lilliputian houses such as you see on Plan I in my *Ilios*; these houses
were built on the ashes and had no foundations; this city had *no* lower
town and occupied only ab^t ⅔ of the hill of Hissarlik. This second
brick-city was likewise destroyed by a general conflagration. In both
these burnt cities the pottery is identical in fabric and shape, and as I
can not now find out what was found in the 2^d and what in the 3^d
city, I shall be obliged to allot to both conjointly all the objects
represented on pp. 305–517 of *Ilios*.

I regret not having had such architects with me from the
beginning, but even now it is not too late.

But in his Trojan work now, as in his digs at Orchomenos
(1880), Tiryns (1884) and Alexandria (1888), Schliemann was
simply consolidating. He cast his eyes to Crete: but perhaps it
was as well that a young man waited in the wings of history for
the glory of uncovering another pre-Hellenic civilisation. For
what could have been only a tailpiece to Schliemann's work

became a new world of discovery for the new century, and the life's labour of Arthur Evans.[5]

Established and assured as he at last was, Schliemann was still insecure enough to fly into a panic at concerted opposition like that of Stillman, Penrose and Farnell, who claimed that Tiryns was Byzantine, or of the eccentric General Boetticher, who claimed that Troy was really a necropolis (a form of claim revived eighty years later by Wunderlich in the case of Knossos).

. . . I thought my work at Troy had been done and intended to excavate on the site of Knossos in Crete; when I was forced by a libeller of mine, Captain Boetticher, to recommence the exploration of Ilium. This man had been libelling me for more than 6 years, pretending that my collaborators Dr. Dörpfeld, Profr Virchow, Emile Burnouf, Dr. Hoefler had *falsified* the plans of Troy and that we had made a large fortified *Acropolis* with towers, gates and [walls] . . . out of a mere *fire-necropolis* and all that without having been here. As we disdained to answer him he became so impertinent as to publish soon a book against me and lots of pamphlets with venomous attacks, which he sent to all and every professor of the German universities and which he read in every scientific congress. Seeing the impossibility of stopping his mouth in any other way, I solicited from the Sublime Porte another *firman*, built in this desert, a small village of wooden houses and begged the Academies of Berlin and Vienna to send Delegates to a Conference to be held on the ruins of Troy at the end of November. I also forced our libeller to appear; to each of the delegates and to Boetticher I paid fr 1250 – $ 250 for travelling expenses. I send you to-day a copy of the protocol, from which you will see that all our libeller's theories were rejected by the delegates of the Academies.

History exacts its own judgement on such theories.

The controversy over Troy is far from dead. Schliemann's achievement in discovering the ruins of a great city and powerful civilisation cannot be denied, but the hypothesis which led to his discoveries continues to be disputed. This city stood in a place which fits the details given by Homer about Troy. But was it called Troy? What language did its inhabitants speak? Was there ever a Trojan War? Does that saga of the war go back to first-hand accounts of the city's fall, or was it invented in later years, perhaps even to explain the existence of a mighty ruin about which the Greeks knew nothing? If this city was that of the legend, which of its many successive levels of habitation should be identified as that of the great war? Schliemann thought Homer's Troy was the earliest level but one; Troy II. Dörpfeld argued rather for Troy VI, a view which long held sway, until the American Carl Blegen argued instead for Troy VIIa, now perhaps the dominant view among believers. Two books published in 1985 take opposite extremes of the argument, the one proposing a return to the identification with Troy VI, the other asserting that all the evidence for identifying Hisarlik with Troy is purely circumstantial and that the Trojan War, to say the least of it, need never have taken place.[6] Schliemann's legacy will be with us for a long time yet.

Whatever one makes of his specific interpretation of Troy, it is not in dispute that Schliemann, the last of the amateurs, was also the first of the professionals. He blended his own romanticism with the scientific methods of his contemporaries in an amalgam that has characterised the layman's perception of archaeology ever since. His scientific achievement, as well as his historical contribution, were far greater than those of his coeval discoverers who joined in the Race of Empires for archaeological glory. It is that, as well as the fact that he added a millennium of prehistory to the Greek world, which makes him a pointer forward beyond the true theme of this book. It is the foreground which makes the labours of his contemporaries seem old-fashioned: but they were no less important to their rulers on that account.

It is significant that it was in the Ethnological Museum that his finds were housed, not in the great Museum built by Schinkel to house the artistic treasures of Prussia. It is in the context of the establishment of that Museum that the achievements and adventures of Schliemann's German contemporaries must be seen. Conze, who had offered to house Schliemann's Trojan finds in Vienna, would not take them for the Museum in Berlin of which he became director in 1877. What, then, was it destined to receive?

The Berlin Museum

> As Gods once descended to men,
> So let mankind become noble, like to the Gods,
> The rules which art invented will be victorious

In reason, just as in the realm of Forms.
And everything will beautifully merge
To a single work of art, resembling itself alone.

(J. G. Herder, *Pygmalion*, 1801)

The growing German national consciousness which Ross had
fanned with his extraordinary articles of 1844, and which was
finding its most extensive expression in the overwhelming
music dramas of Richard Wagner, had by now set its focus on
the Prussian State. Bismarck had made Prussia synonymous
with Germany, by diplomacy or guns directed against lesser
German states. Berlin was entering its heyday as a world
capital the equal of Paris, Rome or London.

It comes as no surprise to find its imperial dream expressed
as much in its museums as in its military affairs. Under the
hands of Ludwig I and Leo von Klenze, Germany had come to
know, in the Munich Glyptothek, what a museum might be.
J. M. von Wagner, as we saw (Chapter 8), had been deeply
involved in the correct disposition of the Glyptothek, ap-
plying to the display of the collection a degree of thoughtful-
ness which has kept the German museums ahead of their
European competitors ever since. Yet German states were
small and disunited, and could not muster funds for great
works. They had to be content largely with what they had.
Munich still remained an isolated example, advanced and splendid though it was; the other great German collections, those
made by Augustus the Strong (1670–1733) at Dresden (where
there had been a Kunstkammer since 1587), by the Landgrave
Friedrich II (1760–86) at Kassel (whose Fridericianum was the
first public museum on the European continent), as well as
lesser collections like that of the Elector of Mannheim (where
Goethe first studied Greek art) and of Gotha, Brunswick,
Stuttgart and Karlsruhe – all these remained stuck in the
eighteenth-century mould. A new attitude to art and antiquities demanded new museums.

It was not that there had been no pressure for change, least of
all in Berlin. In 1797 Professor Aloys Hirt had invited Friedrich Wilhelm III to form a single collection of his antiquities. In
a memorandum of 1798 he wrote: 'It is below the dignity of an
ancient monument to be displayed as an ornament'.[7] Instead,
museum collections should be for study, for 'public instruction and the noblest enjoyment' of mankind's achievements.

The collection, he proposed, should be open all week to artists, 8–4 at weekends to the public. He anticipated Wagner's plan for the Glyptothek by suggesting a series of small rooms, and a typological arrangement of exhibits.

The hesitancy of the cultivated but indecisive Friedrich Wilhelm III ensured that the plan got nowhere. It was not until 1815, with the return of Napoleon's loot and Friedrich Wilhelm's new acquisitions of painting collections, that designs were invited from Karl Friedrich Schinkel, a protégé of Wilhelm von Humboldt, who had met him in Rome in 1803 and in 1810 had secured him a post in the Prussian buildings administration. He had cut his teeth on the competition for the Valhalla, won by Klenze, and on the Neue Wache in Berlin (1816). He had acted as artistic agent for the Prussian Chancellor Hardenberg, and from 1818 to the end of the 1820s he was engaged on numerous plans for the refashioning of central Berlin. Not all were executed, but despite that Berlin is essentially his city.

He might have made Athens his own too if his plan for a Royal Palace on the Acropolis (see p 238) had been approved by Otto; but fortunately it was not.

In 1823 his plans and site for a new Museum at Lustgarten, on the island in the Spree, were approved. The cost was estimated at 700,000 thalers, and this was accepted by the 'thrifty king in frugal times'. A massive Ionic colonnade of eighteen columns rose up, topped by flying deities and reliefs, and containing a series of domes and sky-lit halls, to be the home of Prussia's collections.

The head of the committee on the Museum was Wilhelm von Humboldt, now nearing the end of his long life in the service at once of Prussia and of the cultivation of human perfection. Herder's cry to bring art out of the lumber room of museums and into the heart of man had been echoed in Humboldt's thought and in that of scholars like F. G. Welcker (tutor to Humboldt's children and always a close friend), who had been keen to ensure that the interplay of museums with artistic creation should be maintained and enhanced.[8] The link of the two went back to Goethe and Winckelmann, and had been encouraged alike by scholars such as Christian Gottlob Heyne and archaeologists like J. Zoëga (whose biography Welcker wrote). Wilhelm von Humboldt wrote to the

King of Prussia on 21 August 1830 in terms which echoed Welcker's words of three years earlier, 'Nothing seemed to me more important than that the Museum [in Berlin], whose exceptionally generous foundation is a permanent memorial of the protection and elevated support which your Royal Majesty has allowed to grow up on the arts and those who devote themselves to them, should be given over as soon as possible to the public use for which your Highness intended it.' The museum was there for the public, the artist and the scholar – in that order: a temple of art which only by the way, as it were, glorified its royal patron.

Scientific display was not the first concern, and the monumental style proved ill-adapted to that purpose when it became dominant.[9] It might not be far-fetched to see in the German museum of the 1820s a moral programme as strong as that which dominated the English landscape gardens of a century earlier.

Humboldt had again an ancient collection to work with as a basis. A Kurfürstliche Sammlung of coins had been begun in 1686; Friedrich II had built up the collection by acquiring the collection of Cardinal Polignac in 1742, that of Stosch, and in 1767 a number of statues restored by Cavaceppi. In 1770 an Antikentempel had been erected in the Potsdamer Park. But Humboldt completely refashioned this unhistorical and unsystematic hotchpotch. He had infected Schinkel with the ideas and ideals that he and Thorwaldsen already shared, on ancient art and its display. Humboldt was opposed to the kind of scholarship that delights in the amassing of minute detail to the detriment of deeper, broader understanding. Scholars – or collectors – should make it their aim to become 'profoundly aware of the "divine Sehnsucht" that had animated [the Greeks] and to make it part of one's own being.'[10] So an exhibition should be designed above all for spiritual impact on the observer. And it should be open to all.

The statues were to be erected on pillars (as in Munich) instead of being placed against the walls, and good lighting was of the first importance. Only genuine works (no casts) were to be admitted. A complete range of all types and periods of art was to be obtained. Acquisition of new antiquities by purchase was desirable: 'Every piece which is genuinely antique, provided it is of artistic beauty, must be welcome here.'

The catch is in that parenthesis, 'provided it is of artistic beauty'. This echoed the strictures imposed by the trustees of the British Museum on the finds made by J. T. Wood at Ephesus. The improvement of the arts was the primary aim, however illusory, of archaeology through most of the nineteenth century.[11]

Yet it was to be fifty years before any major new finds came to enhance the Museum's collections. And when they did, the scientific study of the past had gained the upper hand over Humboldtian aestheticism. It was a matter for chagrin that the finds from Olympia could not be brought out of the country. But Curtius, after all, rejoiced more over one inscription than over ninety and nine statues or pieces of jewellery. What Berlin eventually acquired was infinitely more in keeping with the grand visions of a temple of art. And it was the austere and scientific Alexander Conze who oversaw the arrival of one of the most romantic finds of the century.

Carl Humann and Pergamum

And to the angel of the church in Pergamos write 'I know thy works, and where thou dwellest, even where Satan's seat is; and thou holdest fast my name, and hast not denied my faith, even in those days wherein Antipas was my faithful martyr, who was slain among you, where Satan dwelleth.'   (Revelation 2.13)

Men say that Giantes went about the Realme of Heaven to win
To place themselves to raigne as Gods and lawless Lordes therein.
And hill on hill they heaped up aloft into the skie,
Till God almighty from the Heaven did let his thunder flie,
The dint whereof the ayrie tops of high Olympus brake . . .
                (Ovid *Metamorphoses* 1, 150 ff: tr Arthur Golding)

The thunder of those clashes in heaven seems an appropriate metaphor of the thunderous clashes of nation against nation in the fight for the last removable scraps of ancient civilisation.

Pergamum had been one of the great cities of the Hellenistic world. Of little significance in the classical period, it rose to prominence after the death of Alexander the Great, when the latter's successor to the rule of Asia Minor, Lysimachus, made it his capital and treasury. When Lysimachus died, his treasurer Philetairos became ruler of Pergamum, and kept it independent despite the attempts of Antiochus of Syria to annex the kingdom. In 263 BC his successor Eumenes established a dynasty which soon made Pergamum one of the wealthiest and most cultivated cities of Asia. Under the patronage of Eumenes' successors, three Attaluses and one more Eumenes, a distinctive culture developed.

Bibliophily was one of the Attalids' obsessions. They assembled a library of 2,000 volumes (which vanished when Antony gave it to Cleopatra as a little present). The collection roused the jealousy of Ptolemy, King of Egypt, who at once prohibited the export of papyrus; so the Pergamenes introduced the use of skins as writing material instead. Animal skin treated to be used for writing is now called parchment, from its place of origin.

There were many fine buildings, not least of course the library. There was a Temple of Demeter, a huge ceremonial hall and a sanctuary of the Egyptian gods, as well as a notable healing sanctuary of Asclepius. Perhaps the most important cult was that of Athena; but the glory of the city was the Altar of Zeus on the topmost peak of the hill.

This altar was built by Eumenes II, perhaps in 184–3 BC, as part of the celebration of a new agreement with Rome, grateful for his support against Antiochus of Syria, and to honour the defeat of the Galatians. (Tournefort's ancestors of Ancyra, it will be remembered.) The altar became celebrated in its own time for the magnificence of its sculpture and friezes in the distinctive 'high-baroque' Pergamene style that also characterises the Laocoön. In the third century Ampelius described it to his friend Macrinus as one of the Wonders of the World: 'a marble altar 40 feet high with very large sculptures; and it portrays the Gigantomachy.' This Battle of the Gods and Giants was the most notable of the several friezes.

'Terrible of aspect did they appear,' the mythographer Apollodorus wrote of the Giants, 'with long locks drooping from their head and chin, and with serpents for feet . . . And they darted rocks and burning oaks at the sky . . . Surpassing all the rest were Porphyrion and Alcyoneus.' The gods gathered to quell the Giants' insurrection. Athena and Heracles finished off Alcyoneus, and Zeus struck Porphyrion with a thunderbolt: 'Ephialtes was shot by Apollo with an arrow in his left eye and by Heracles in his right; Eurytus was killed by Dionysus with a thyrsus, and Clytius by Hecate with torches, and Mimas by Hephaestus with missiles of red-hot metal. Enceladus fled, but Athena threw on him in his flight the island of Sicily; and she flayed Pallas and used his skin to shield her own body in the fight.'

This savage war in heaven was often used by classical artists as a prototype of the war of civilisation against the barbarians. It was particularly appropriate in the context of a cultured kingdom beleaguered by barbarian tribes such as the Galatians.

With the waning of paganism, this huge altar, 36.4 by 34.2 metres, with its frieze 120 metres in length, might well seem one of the greatest seats of the old religion, a throne of Satan. The snake-legged Giants only added to its sinister splendour. Inaccessible as it was, it was allowed to fall into ruin while a village arose below the hill. In the tenth century many of the plates of the frieze were used to build a Byzantine fortification wall. By the fourteenth century no sign remained of the altar and its sculptures, and its beauty was forgotten; the other buildings of the Attalid capital could only evoke the sighs of a future Emperor (see p 19).

In 1820, when the Revd Pliny Fisk from Boston made a pilgrimage to the site, on his way to establish a Protestant mission in Palestine, the city had already been built and ruined a second time:

Vast walls are still standing, composed principally of granite, with some fine pillars of marble. The castle includes five or six acres of ground, and about half way down the hill is a wall which includes several times as much . . . Most of the walls are evidently not very ancient, and are said to be the work of the Genoese. The foundations, and a part of the wall, seem more ancient, and are said, perhaps with truth, to be the work of the ancient Greeks. Noticed several Corinthian capitals, and copied one Greek inscription.[12]

Only nine years earlier Cockerell had been able to see 'considerable remains of the temple, but they are rapidly disappearing, for the Turks cut them up into tombstones.'[13]

But the throne of Satan was to be restored almost to its former glory in Lutheran Prussia, through the agency of one sickly enthusiast. His name was Carl Humann.

Born in 1839 in Steele near Essen, Humann had been trained as an engineer at the Berlin Academy of Architecture (1860–1). But even at that time ancient sculpture fascinated him as much as architecture: he spent half his time drawing after the antique in the museums. When he graduated, his poor health led him, on doctor's orders, to fix his residence in the south, and he moved to the Levant in 1861. There he spent the next six years travelling in Turkey, sending geographical information to Kiepert in Berlin, collecting antiquities, and from time to time carrying out an architectural commission such as the construction of a palace for the English ambassador.

In 1862 his elder brother Franz became minister on Samos, and in 1867 acquired from the Sultan the concession for five road and rail routes in Asia Minor, including one from Constantinople to Smyrna.[14] Carl soon joined Franz's team of engineers, and took on general responsibility for 2,000 labourers, 500 pairs of oxen, and camels, as well as mules and machinery.

Yet these vast concerns did not deter him, any more than they did J. T. Wood in the same years, from indulging his antiquarian interests. He had done some digging on Samos. From Samos he visited Smyrna, where he gazed in sorrow at the fallen Corinthian capitals of the Trajaneum (which he took for the Temple of Athena Polias); and in 1864 he made his first visit to Pergamum. The craggy city fascinated him and he thereafter could not keep away. His enthusiasm was mingled with anxiety, for Pergamum was used as a source of supply by the lime burners (who, of course, had plenty to do where roads were being built).

It was not until 1871 that he found time to explore Pergamum more carefully. His work at Samos had already attracted the attention of Ernst Curtius, by now the foremost professional archaeologist in the Greek world. Curtius came to visit him at his work on 27 September 1871. The excitement was great as it became clear that he had begun to uncover a magnificent series of sculptures. Many years before, his friend and host Nicholas Rallis in Smyrna had unearthed a slab with a lion on it, and had sent it to Constantinople. These sculptures seemed to be in series with it. 'No one then realised that it was a piece of the famous Gigantomachy; for years it lay neglected, until the Greek Society for antiquities took pity on it.' (But that was not until 1879.)

It was not long before Humann was uncovering more slabs. One demanded two days' work to unearth; then Humann returned the day after to study it, only to find one of his workmen had sawn it up to make a stairtread. Humann's response was swift: he identified the culprit and had him put in prison. Thereafter there was no talk of vandalism or theft.

In December 1871 Humann wrote to Curtius with a report of some further finds:

When I had blasted the wall down so far that we were close up to it I personally carefully removed stone after stone and found the neck and chin, then the left cheek and the eye. When I saw the eye I cried out: 'That's a dead man!' For this statue, although completely and beautifully sincere, definitely had the emaciated and stark look of death. I am telling you this because it shows that one can set no great store by my artistic critical faculty. Eventually the statue was completely excavated and turned out to be a beautiful youth with curly hair, stretched out, the breast high and drumlike (25 cm), the right arm, unfortunately broken, raised, the left hanging down, the head slightly inclined to one side, the mouth half open, not distorted by pain, but rather by fatigue, as though asleep; only the wide-open rolled back eyes showed that we were looking at a man killed in battle. Strength and beauty were here united in most marvellous harmony.[15]

Several other slabs were also brought to light. They were of the same bluish marble as the foundations of the temple identified by Curtius. Everything Humann could unearth was hastily despatched to Berlin. In 1877 Alexander Conze was appointed director of the sculpture gallery: one day, while pondering on the fine reliefs Humann had found, he came upon the passage of that obscure author Ampelius, quoted above. Surely Humann had got hold of the great Gigantomachy itself! Another of the world's Wonders was within the grasp – this time – of the Berlin Museum.

Immediately Conze wrote to Humann (July 1877), who at this time was considering an offer of the directorship of a Turkish salt-mine. 'Everything is in doubt, if you do not act as my personal representative. The Ministry would give its trust and favour only to you personally.' Humann was delighted.

At once he entered the employ of the Museum. With a draft of 2,700 marks, work could begin.

By August 1878 the German government had secured a firman permitting excavation. One-third of the finds were, as was now customary, to go to the diggers, one-third to the landowner, and one-third to the Turkish government. The imperial ambassador in due course got permission for the excavators to take the first two-thirds; and by a combination of circumstances they were eventually able to take it all.

On 9 September 1878 Humann began a new trench between the Byzantine walls and the third Attalid wall, on a plateau with a view to east, south and west. It was a solemn moment, and Humann signalled it as such with a little speech:

In the name of the Protector of the Royal Museum, the fortunate and universally loved Man, the never conquered warrior, the heir of the most beautiful throne in the world – in the name of our Crown Prince, may this work grow in happiness and good fortune.

The workers supposed him to be reciting a magic formula; nor, admits Humann, were they entirely wrong.

His success was astonishing. By 24 September they had revealed seventeen relief slabs, including the lovely Helios and Selene groups. 'We have found an entire artistic epoch,' wrote Humann, 'the greatest surviving work of antiquity is now under our hands.' Perhaps not everyone would have shared, even then, the implied rating of Pergamene art above that even of classical Athens; but in the circumstances he could be forgiven. And after all, what a coup for the greatest museum of what was surely the greatest nation!

Humann was in haste to pack the finds, and anxious for Conze to buy the site outright. He had to keep this quiet; even his letter to Conze was signed simply 'Carl', lest the Turkish postal authorities discover his secret.

At this time Humann's first son was born in Smyrna: but the demands of the dig would not permit him to leave even to see his child. The work went on until the end of December, when they had unearthed thirty-nine slabs of the Gigantomachy, four slabs of the Telephus series, seven to eight hundred fragments, ten free-standing statues and thirty inscriptions. They had removed 1,800 cubic metres of earth.

Permission was secured from Constantinople to keep the

collection together. The bankruptcy of the Turkish state made
a sale of the Sultan's share for 20,000 marks an attractive
proposition. The slabs were packed in cases to begin their
descent seven hundred feet down the mountain. From here
they had to be got across the plain to Dikeli, on the road
Humann had built ten years before. (It had never been repaired.) They built wagons; it took them five days to cross the
plain, which with the winter rains had become little less than a
lake.

In January HMS *Comet* came to Dikeli to ship the sculptures
to Constantinople; the lighter was grounded once in a storm,
but in four weeks all was loaded and the task was done.

Humann's doctor ordered him to bed, where he stayed for
three weeks. But work was far from over. By 1 May another
twenty-five slabs of the Gigantomachy had been found, plus
thirty-seven statues. On 21 July Humann's wife came to visit
the dig, with Dr Boretius from Berlin. As they climbed up to
the altar, seven eagles wheeled above their heads. Just as they
reached the excavation, a new slab fell forward: it represented
Zeus with his Giant opponent. Was there no end to the divine
blessings on the Prussian government? Wilhelm I was in
favour with Zeus – or with Satan.

The Greeks of Smyrna were not as ready as the Sultan to see
the sculptures leave the country. Many, Humann admitted,
would have preferred to see them stay on their own site,
restored to their former splendour; but others were glad to let
them go where the educated world could more easily see and
study the great works of their ancestors. The marbles were put
on display in 1880, but reached their present situation in the
Pergamum-Museum only in 1930.

Curtius had made Humann a fellow of the German
Archaeological Institute for his achievements, amateur
though he was. In 1884 he was to become an official employee
of the Royal Museum; but his work in Asia Minor was far
from done. He returned for two further seasons, 1880–1 and
1883–6. It was in the last season that the young archaeologist
Carl Schuchardt came to work with him at Pergamum, and his
account brings the forty-seven-year-old archaeologist vividly
to life. If he knew he was no scholar or connoisseur, he knew
too what his own value was.

'Are you a philologist?' was his greeting to Schuchardt. The latter, sensing a trap, hastily assured the older man he was an archaeologist. This was as well, when he heard Humann's definition of a philologist – 'a man with two left hands who when he comes here falls off the fortifications'. It was indeed not long before Schuchardt fell over and hurt his knee; you may imagine he kept quiet about it.

If Humann was often rude – no doubt as a result of his always delicate health – he was also devoted to the German card game skat, and would play it with Schuchardt for hours, staking trifles. Schuchardt's year with Humann was 'the happiest of my life'. The 'Bismarcklies' – as the Germans were called among the Turkish country people – had reaped their reward from Anatolia. Humann's would be a hard act for another museum to beat. Yet already his achievement was being eclipsed in archaeological circles everywhere except the strongholds of Berliner infallibility ruled by Curtius.

One of the young officers on the *Loreley* which took the second shipment from Dikeli to Berlin wrote to his father: 'We are now in Pergamum, and are transporting the marbles which Mr Humann has found here on the citadel.' By the next post came the reply: 'My dear son, you must not say Pergamum, but Pergamos, for that is what Homer calls the citadel of Troy; and you must not say Humann either, but Schliemann, for it is he who has unearthed so many things there.' No doubt Curtius, if he had read this letter, would have been quite un-mortified.

Otto Benndorf, Georg Niemann and the Heroön of Gölbaşı-Trysa

The Royal Museum in Berlin under Conze had suddenly gained an overwhelming lead in sculptures and treasures from Greek lands. Archaeologists from other lands – particularly German-speaking ones – were not willing to let the position go unchallenged. More explicitly than ever before, national prestige and international competition became the primary motive of archaeological endeavour. It might be thought that competitive acquisition was hardly the best way to ensure reliable work on the understanding of ancient sites; yet the stimulus proved in fact remarkably effective.

In 1883 Otto Benndorf (1838–1907), who had worked with

Conze on Samothrace and had succeeded him as Professor of Archaeology at the University of Vienna, wrote of the 'Race of the Nations' that had led him, as representative of the Austrian archaeologists, to turn to the still only superficially explored regions of Southern Anatolia.

When Conze's results were finally published in 1880 the Austrian intelligentsia had begun to look around for another area to study. Austria had not done particularly well out of that excavation. All finds had to be shared with the Turkish government and its own new museum in Constantinople – one of the products of the Tanzimat (Reform) following 1871, and since 1882 under the vigorous direction of the father of Turkish archaeology, Osman Hamdi Bey (1842–1910). So some of the materials went to Vienna, where they were included in the World's Fair of 1873 that set the coping stone on the glories of Franz Josef's Vienna; and they were eventually housed in the Kunsthistorisches Museum when it was completed in 1883. Most of the rest was lost *en route* to Istanbul. (What is in the museum on Samothrace today is largely the result of the American excavations begun in 1938.)

But where was the Empire to turn? The Greek mainland and islands were already bespoken by the French and German schools; Schliemann and Humann were at Troy and Pergamum; the Americans had Assos in the Troad, and other Turkish sites; Magnesia and Didyma were being investigated by the French; while the new British School at Athens was flexing its muscles in Greece itself. South was the only way to go.

The obvious destination was Gölbaşı, where the German Augustus Schönborn (see pp 214–5) had in 1842 already noted the existence of interesting buildings with relief decoration. Benndorf enlisted the co-operation of a colleague, Georg Niemann. After a period spent studying the Lycian monuments in the British Museum, they set off on 6 April 1880. Official support was easily come by. Humann and the geographer Kiepert gave practical advice; the Austro-Hungarian branch of Lloyds gave them free passage to Smyrna; the Southern Railway was also quick to proffer its services. The Royal and Imperial Fleet provided them with a paddle-steamer. Besides the consuls in Smyrna, the Royal and Imperial Minister of the Exterior and the Royal and Imperial

Minister for Education and Culture evinced strong interest. Benndorf was a gifted fund-raiser, and would use his talent again fifteen years later when a new expedition to Ephesus was mounted.

Once in Lycia, the site was far from easy to find. Schönborn had come upon it by chance, and his description of the location was vague. Schönborn had also noted the danger of destruction, by earthquake or by Moslem piety. What would Benndorf and Niemann find, forty years on?

In the end they were not disappointed. Following their noses, and as much by luck as judgement, they found themselves suddenly facing the saddle of a steep hill – unmistakably that described by Schönborn. The hill was thick with ruins of buildings and sarcophagi. Above them loomed a long and highly decorated wall with a monumental gateway in its centre:

Rushing ahead, I worked my way through thick thorny underbrush and shale, arriving breathless at the entrance gate, which opened in the wall an appreciable distance above the precipitous slope. Without waiting at the first structure, the curious nature of which increased my expectation, I climbed excitedly up the masonry of the wall to the lintel of the gate, and found myself suddenly opposite an abundance of sculpture in the interior of the ruin, enchantingly concealed in part by the tall trees nearby and the vegetation that had grown up among them. In the glow of the setting sun the sight was marvellous. I confess that these first moments of contemplation at the long sought and now successfully achieved destination, in the noiseless and solemn silence and desolation of a magnificently expansive Nature, stone desert all around, with a view on to the mountainous landscape deeply gullied and adorned with chains of snow and to the high vaulted and endless sea, count among the deepest impressions of my life.

They had only a month to explore this forgotten paradise of untouched ruins, and no permission to dig. All they could do, therefore, was to photograph the remains. But what remains they were! Terraces of massive stone houses, often with their own cisterns; over thirty colossal sarcophagi with pointed roofs and stepped bases, in the Lycian style now familiar from Fellows' pieces in the British Museum; and above all the great heroön or hero-shrine, a vast enclosure with relief decoration on all four sides, in some cases on both inner and outer walls, undamaged by quarrying but severely weathered. The frieze belonged to the same period, it was clear, as the sculptures of the Nereid monument at Xanthus; and its subject was no less than a complete conspectus of the whole legendary past of Greece: the story of the Seven against Thebes; the local saga of Bellerophon and the Chimera; the war of the Greeks and Amazons; the rape of the daughters of Leucippus at Sparta; the stories of Meleager and of Odysseus' slaughter of the suitors; and a few figures remaining from what seemed to be a Theseus cycle.

Who in this stony wilderness, so far from Greece's Ionian epicentre, had immortalised in stone the great heroes of Greece? Why? What scion of Bellerophon was housed in the pillar tomb? Benndorf and Niemann could only guess at the answers as they made their way reluctantly back to the coast (getting lost near Cardamyla) via the Temple of Hecate at Lagina. Surely they must return to study the site more closely. These questions were never to be answered; but the importance of the albeit battered work of art was evident.

The results of their four months' absence aroused great interest in the learned world of Vienna. It seemed self-evident that the originals of these intriguing photographs must be secured for the Vienna Museum. A Society was promptly formed, the 'Society for the Archaeological Exploration of Asia Minor', under the auspices of his Excellency Count Edmund Zichy, Nicholas Dumba, Baron von Wansberg, and numerous other Barons and Freiherrs, as well as several ministers and the professors Löwy and Studniczka. They had the direct assistance of an engineer, Gabriel Knaffl-Lenz, Ritter von Fohnsdorf, and last but not least, of the vice-consul at Rhodes.

This gallery of Royal-Imperial pomp and dignity secured them from the Sultan a firman allowing digging at Gölbaşı and Lagina, and permitting them, as usual, to keep one-third of the finds. It was in April 1881 that the expedition departed, pausing at Trieste to hire a smith, three masons, three carpenters and four labourers. They also had as foreman Jani Samothrakis of Tinos (recommended by Humann), an interpreter, a kavass or consular guard, two cooks, three grooms, a zaptieh or gendarme and a Turkish commissar. The yailas of Gölbaşı had not seen such an army in millennia.

Their first act on pitching camp was to erect a large wooden hut with the double-headed Hapsburg eagle painted on the front. After this they could turn to the problem of commissariat. There was of course no grocery store in these wild mountains. All that was regularly available was milk and eggs. The nearest village was half an hour away, and bread had to be got from Dembre, a four hour journey. Luckily for the party a Greek opportunist from Castellorizo noticed their problem and set up an oven in a nearby medieval ruin. Water, however, had to be got from cisterns as there were no wells; and wine and other luxuries had to be brought from Rhodes.

Nonetheless they remained the entire summer; and by offering good wages they raised their local workforce from an initial sixty to three times that number. Most of the time these were engaged in building a road to the coast (an hour and a half's journey) to remove the spoils. Dr Felix von Luschan took more photographs; Schneider made drawings and Tietze studied the geology.

Despite their privations, the scene had its compensations for one with the Austrian's gift for drawing romantic meanings from the scenery:

The earth did not yet glow and hum, the cool nights were refreshing, even in the grilling sun of day one felt the mildness and pleasant gentle movement of the air; eye and senses were open to every enchantment which spring with its fresh lines could spread over the melancholy-beautiful solemnity of the surroundings, across which we gazed from our camp site. Never was it more impressive than at evening, when the sun quickened its relief in every farthest corner, and drew deep shadows over the low bushes nearby, which showed green over and between the grey stone blocks and hillocks; when the workers came home weary in the twilight, handed in their tools and, after a quick meal, struck up their cheerful Italian melodies, until night darkened and the moon rose large beyond Cape Chelidonia, pouring out its light, bright as day, over all the heights and clefts of the landscape, and over the sea that gleamed like a silver shield.

Schubert should have set it to music.

Nonetheless, the expedition achieved its objective (though Lagina had to be forgotten). To speed the work, all the relief blocks were chiselled off twenty to twenty-five centimetres from the surface, numbered, and moved by stages to the coast. A last minute order of two waggons from Vienna alone made the task possible. At last came a telegram from Constantinople conceding the discoverers the Sultan's share in this treasure he had never set eyes on; and by early October they were all installed in the Künsthistorisches Museum in Vienna. Due to lack of space they had to be cut up and stored in the basement courtyard. They are still there.

If national prestige was enhanced by the acquisition of great artistic treasures of Greek antiquity, that is not to say that the arts at home were any longer enriched by the availability of the classical models.

It has to be admitted, archaeology was now in the hands of the professionals. That pendulum swing between the love of Greek antiquity for what it could teach us of the Greeks, and for what it could do to enhance our own lives, had become firmly arrested at the intellectual end of its parabola. Our story began with the use of Greek statues to enhance national prestige – that of Rome, then Constantinople; later the courts of the Renaissance princes and ultimately the Sun King himself – and its last trajectory is through the glory of the German Empire. We saw taste shift to the antiquarianism of the seventeenth century which attempted to gather and – a century later, in the hands of a Caylus or a Paciaudi – to sort and organise the data on classical art and life; we saw the swelling dominance of the Ideal which subdued all artistic endeavour to its imperious sway, sometimes enlivening but more often deadening or trivialising; we saw the tension between the aims of the topographers who aimed to identify sites and explicate ancient texts, and the picturesque artists who wished to compose ruins into pleasing landscapes, often with little thought of accuracy. Yet that picturesque imagination fostered the romantic understanding of the otherness of the Greeks that was the precondition of scholarly insight and endeavour. Archaeology came of age in the 1870s – a romantic science whose aims are historical.

CHAPTER TWELVE

Conclusion: Return to Ithaca

The excavations of Troy, Olympia and Samothrace set a tone in the exploration of Greece that has not changed essentially in the last hundred years. Archaeologists search not for works of art to glorify their patrons or their countries, not even in the first instance for inscriptions to illuminate the historical record; they seek for evidence of the past of a kind only archaeology can provide.

That is by no means a simple aim. The evidence can be of many kinds, and even a decision on what is evidence is affected by the archaeologists' preconceptions. New discoveries come about because the discoverer's goal, his Ithaca, is always changing. Sherds, pins, seeds and mouldy fabrics are all valued by today's excavators; how that would have startled Joseph Pitton de Tournefort, who despised even inscriptions if the persons they referred to were of excessive obscurity. Greek vases were long ignored, and when they became of interest it was as objects of vertu, models for art not evidences of the past. Sir William Hamilton could not have expended so much love on the broken sherds that now determine our chronology.

Even in the mid-nineteenth century some people had begun to doubt the value of amassing the lumber of the past. When Nathaniel Hawthorne visited England in 1855[1] he felt the burden of tradition represented by the museums and such items as the Elgin marbles to be so oppressive that he suggested their contents should all be burnt. Cool heads by the 1890s had realised that the use being made of ancient art by

contemporary artists was negligible: the Elgin marbles had
served their purpose, but they were now of no further use and
should be sent back.[2]

If you cannot destroy the past or use it creatively, you can
exorcise its burden by studying it.[3] A corpse is no threat,
and to prove it you may dissect it. This, to a jaundiced eye,
might seem the controlling purpose in the development of
archaeology after 1870.

Yet the proto-archaeologists of the past all foreshadowed
one or other of the interests of present-day scholars. The
location of sites known from history interested Spon, Leake,
Schliemann. The antiquarian taste valued inscriptions, which
now are scarcely a part of archaeology: the successors of
Cyriac, Spon, Wordsworth, Müller, Curtius and Ulrichs in
this area are the historians. The interest in buildings for their
value as architectural models seems to be dead, as is the interest
in collecting for the encouragement of artists, though
museums will still pay large sums to acquire choice items,
valued for their beauty rather than their historical importance.
Here archaeology comes closest to entertainment – a tendency
the austere archaeologist will deplore at his peril.

It was those who dug who showed the way forward. The
English antiquaries of the seventeenth century already did this,
but the practice never became common in Greece until the
nineteenth century, with Gell, Fauvel and even Princess Caroline delving beneath the earth to reveal its secrets. Too often it
was assumed the rewards would be minimal, as with the
French at Olympia. It took Schliemann at Troy to prove
otherwise.

Schliemann's understanding of stratigraphy has been combined with the recognition of the importance of pottery series,
first made possible by Adolf Furtwängler, and with the other
techniques developed by archaeology for areas and periods
where literary records are non-existent – ground surveys,
resistivity metering and the like. What is new in the twentieth
century is the interest in cultural process; but inevitably that
has concentrated on periods where the literary record is scant
or non-existent. Classical Greece is too well organised already
to yield much here. It is a province, rather, of art history.

And that, too, is the province of academe, not a live
presence at the centre of artistic practice. The Ideal was

perhaps a straitjacket, the Greek Revival often frigid; the Renaissance princes made their collections available to the artists with astounding results, but Humboldt could only dream of a similar centrality for classical art in nineteenth-century Prussia. No one even tries now. Yet love and scholarship must surely, as for Humboldt, always go hand in hand. We must both gaze upon the light and peer into the dark; admire what is left and seek for what is lost.

What art lost, scholarship gained. The romantic science that thrives on the recognition of ancient otherness has added new dimensions to our understanding of the Greek past, which Spon or even Curtius could scarcely have dreamed of. The classical world had become so familiar that the search for otherness had to plunge through millennia, or eastwards to Mesopotamia. After Schliemann's work at Troy, Evans' at Knossos added another millennium of civilisation to Greek prehistory. That picture has been enriched by the work of Marinatos on Santorini, and lately Andronikos has taught us to estimate afresh the Macedonian kingdom where Alexander was born.

The first major dig of the British School of Archaeology at Athens (founded in 1886) at Phylakopi on Melos revealed important aspects of Aegean prehistory. The English excavations at Perachora uncovered something of the Geometric Age and the recent work at Emborio has made the Dark Ages glimmer a little less opaquely. For the historically minded, the scope for extending knowledge of the early Mediterranean increases all the time.

The recovery of major classical sites, too, has proceeded apace. The religious sites were to the fore in the excavations of the 1880s and 1890s: the healing sanctuaries of Asclepius at Epidaurus and of Amphiaraus at Oropos, of the Great Gods at Samothrace, as well as the oracular site at Delphi, finally cleared and excavated by the French, and published in a series of which thirty-six volumes have not yet brought it to a conclusion, and the site of the Mysteries of Eleusis. Major civic sites have also been uncovered: Corinth and the Athenian agora are the jewels in the crown of the efficient and well-endowed American School of Classical Studies in Athens. The developments of the last century would alone furnish material for a long book.

For the non-specialist, it is Classical Greece, Greece of the fifth and fourth centuries and of the Roman Period, that exercises the greatest fascination. The hordes who descend in buses, planes and boats, equipped with the most exiguous backgrounds of history, thrill spontaneously to the glory Greece still offers to every visitor. It is not, perhaps, the great secular excavations of the twentieth century that excite the most appeal. Great civic centres have been unearthed at Corinth, the Athenian agora, Thera, Priene, Megalopolis; but now as ever it is the temple sites, the homes of the heroes, which draw the crowds, and scenes of ancient secular bustle and rowdy market cries are quieted to a bee-loud haunt of a few determined wanderers, prepared to grapple with the lesser mysteries of wall-foundations, pavements and gutters.

I like my archaeologists romantic. Few of them, now, care to be such, except in Greece where national honour can still be enchanced by a great find like Santorini or Vergina. Yet there is no understanding without love. There is, I believe, a healthy romanticism, a sense of the need to fight against the frailty of mortal things, in the increasing interest in the restoration or reconstruction of ancient buildings. The Parthenon was re-built to mark Greece's new status as a kingdom; the new Republic will be glad further to enhance its greatest building, and smiles too on the exciting plan of the American School for the reconstruction of the Temple of Zeus at Nemea. Yet the biggest issue confronting the Greek Archaeological Service is one not so much of restoration as of conservation. The pilfering lords have gone, but the hungry clouds of pollution do damage in Athens nearly as bad. We must be grateful that Leake's prophecy has been fulfilled: there are responsible guardians of the ancient past in Greece, and in Turkey too.

Wilhelm Dörpfeld, the successor of Schliemann at Troy, made Homer's tale as real as Schliemann had for himself. He lived out his years on the island of Lefkas, which he identified as Homer's Ithaca. (The identification of Ithaca was almost an archaeologists' parlour game in the early years of the twentieth century.) He, I think, epitomises the archaeologist as lover. Everyone has his Ithaca, his goal, perhaps ill-defined, which nonetheless directs every step of his life. Cavafy's version of the symbolic Ithaca is well-known:

Do not hurry the journey at all.
Better that it should last many years;
Be quite old when you anchor at the island,
Rich with all you have gained on the way.
Not expecting Ithaca to give you riches.
Ithaca has given you your lovely journey.
Without Ithaca you would not have set out.

There must be something of Ithaca in the romantic traveller's view of Greece, the impetus that has driven him there for over five hundred years now. The ideal of Greece no longer holds sway, yet Greece, somehow, for better or for worse, will not go away. It is the seeking for our own roots, our own reflection, in that landscape of spectacular beauty and fierce nakedness, that draws us back. It is the feeling that drove Otto Benndorf as he mounted the col which concealed the mausoleum of Gölbaşı, or Spon as he ascended the temple at Corinth with his measuring line; that drove Dodwell as he visited the haunts of centaurs among the picturesque beauties of Mt Oeta, or Cockerell as he scrambled about the fallen debris of Bassae; that drove even Cyriac to envision sea-nymphs cavorting around his ship as he sailed the Aegean in search of the past. Those of us who can travel can see all these things (except perhaps the sea-nymphs) without needing to uproot the buildings and statues from their surroundings. The totality of landscape that gave birth to the Greek gods, to Western art, philosophy and politics, to our dreams and passions and our incurable nostalgia, will always lure us on to discovery and reflection.

We who set out on this pilgrimage
looked at the broken statues
we forgot ourselves and said that life is not so easily lost
that death has unexplored paths
and its own particular justice;

that while we, still upright on our feet, are dying,
become brothers in stone
united in hardness and weakness,
the ancient dead have escaped the circle and risen again
and smile in a strange silence.

(George Seferis, *Mithistorima*)

Bibliography

The first section of the bibliography is a list of general works, arranged by subject, which will provide background and further detail on the themes of this book. The second is arranged according to chapters, and for each chapter gives the original sources on which the account is based, followed by the most useful modern general works, or discussions of controversial points.

General

1 ARCHAEOLOGY

V. Hausmann, *Allgemeine Grundlagen der Archäologie*, Munich 1969

A. Kokkou, *The Care for Antiquities in Greece and the First Museums* (in Greek), Athens 1977

A. Philadelpheus, Archaeology in Greece, in *Panhellenion Leukoma Ethnikes Hekatontaeteridos* vols, Epistemai, 1925, 75–88 (in Greek)

G. A. C. Rumpf, *Archäologie I: Einleitung, historischer Überblick*, Berlin 1953

M. Wegner, *Altertumskunde*, 1951

2 THE TRAVELLERS

F. L. Bastet, *Naar palaeizen uit het slik. Wandelingen door de antike wereld*, Amsterdam 1983

C. W. Ceram, (ed), *The World of Archaeology*, 1966

D. Constantine, *Early Greek Travellers and the Hellenic Ideal*, Cambridge 1984

J. Grant, *A Pillage of Art*, 1966

F. W. Hasluck, Notes on MSS in the British Museum relating to

Levant Geography and Travel, in *Annual of Brit Schl at Athens* 12, 1905–6, 196–215

Rose Macaulay, *Pleasure of Ruins*, 1953

F. H. Marshall, *Discovery in Greek Lands*, Cambridge 1920

Karl Meyer, *The Plundered Past*, 1973

Adolf Michaelis, *A Century of Archaeological Discoveries* tr B. Kahnweiler, 1908

Adolf Michaelis, *Ancient Marbles in Great Britain*, Cambridge 1882

J. M. Paton, *Chapters on Medieval and Renaissance Visitors to Greek Lands*, Princeton 1951

Pausanias, *Guide to Greece* tr Peter Levi, Harmondsworth 1971

Terence Spencer, *Fair Greece Sad Relic: Literary Philhellenism from Shakespeare to Byron*, 1954

Richard Stoneman, *A Literary Companion to Travel in Greece*, Harmondsworth 1984

F. M. Tsigakou, *The Rediscovery of Greece*, 1981

3 THE FATE OF GREEK ANTIQUITIES

Michael Ashley, *The Seven Wonders of the World*, 1980

Diana E. E. Kleiner, *The Monument of Philopappus*, Rome 1983

L. and R. Matton, *Athènes et ses Monuments, du XVIIe siècle à nos Jours*, Athens 1963

Adolf Michaelis, *Der Parthenon*, 1871

M. Patelarou, *Athens from the end of the ancient world to the foundation of the Greek state* Exhibition catalogue, Athens 1985 (in Greek)

J. M. Paton, *The Erechtheum*, 1927

4 HISTORY OF SCHOLARSHIP

Joan Evans, *A History of the Society of Antiquaries*, Oxford 1956

Sir Henry Lyons, *The Royal Society 1660–1940*, Cambridge 1944

J. E. Sandys, *History of Classical Scholarship*, Cambridge 1906, 2nd edition

W. B. Stanford, *Ireland and the Classical Tradition*, Dublin 1976

Ulrich von Wilamowitz-Moellendorff, *History of Classical Scholarship* ed Hugh Lloyd-Jones, 1982

5 MUSEUMS AND COLLECTING

Joseph Alsop, *The Rare Art Traditions*, Princeton 1982

Germain Bazin, *The Museum Age*, Brussels 1968

Kenneth Hudson, *A Social History of Museums*, 1975

Oliver Impey and Arthur MacGregor, ed, *The Origins of Museums*, Oxford 1985

Sir David Murray, *Museums, their History and Use*, 1904

Nikolaus Pevsner, Museums, in *A History of Building Types*, Princeton 1976

Volker Plagemann, *Das deutsche Kunstmuseum 1790–1870*, Munich 1968

F. Saxl and R. Wittkower, *British Art and the Mediterranean*, 1948

Valentin Scherer, *Deutsche Museen*, Jena 1913

H. Seling, The Genesis of the Museum, in *Archit. Review* 141, 1967, 103–114

F. H. Taylor, *The Taste of Angels*, 1948

A. S. Wittlin, *The Museum. Its History and Tasks in Education*, 1949

6 HISTORICAL BACKGROUND

Ferdinand Gregorovius, *Geschichte der Stadt Athen im Mittelalter*, 1889

F. W. Hasluck, *Christianity and Islam under the Sultans*, Oxford 1929

A. E. Vacalopoulos, *Origins of the Greek Nation: The Byzantine Period 1204–1461*, Brunswick, NJ 1970

A. E. Vacalopoulos, *The Greek Nation 1453–1669*, Brunswick, NJ 1976

D. M. Vaughan, *Europe and the Turk*, Liverpool 1954

D. A. Zakythinos, *The Making of Modern Greece. From Byzantium to Independence*, Oxford 1976

Bibliography to Chapters

CHAPTER ONE

The major works of Greek observers are:

Ps-Codinus, *Patria Constantinopoleos*

Anonymous, *Parastaseis Syntomoi Chronikai*

These two works, which overlap considerably, were edited by Th. Preger in *Scriptores originum Constantinopolitanarum* I–II, Leipzig 1907. The *Parastaseis* have been edited in A. Cameron and J. Herrin, *Constantinople in the Eighth Century*, Leiden 1984

Constantine of Rhodes, *Description des oeuvres d'art et de l'église des Saints Apôtres de Constantinople* ed E. Legrand, Paris 1896

Nicetas Choniates, *Ravages committed in Constantinople by the Christian Armies* tr in E. D. Clarke, *Travels* VIII, 424–438

Theodore II Lascaris, *Epistulae* ed N. Festa, 1898; also in Migne, *Patrol. Graeca* vol. 144, 777 f.

Accounts by foreigners include:

Ogier Ghislain de Busbecq, Observations of the Columns of Constantine and Arcadius, in *Itinera*, 1582

Peter Coeck van Aalst, *The Turks in 1533. Drawings made at Constantinople published from woodcuts* ed Sir W. S. Maxwell, 1873, from the original Antwerp edition of 1533

G. Dousa, *De itinere suo Constantinopolitano epistula*, Leiden 1599

Evliya Celebi Effendi, *Travels in Europe, Asia and Africa in the Seventeenth Century* tr J. von Hammer, 1834–50

Pierre Gilles, *The Antiquities of Constantinople* tr John Ball, 1729, from the original Lyon edition of 1562

Modern discussions:

R. G. Austin, Quintilian on Painting and Statuary, *Class. Quart.* 38, 1944, 17–26

A. Cutler, The *de signis* of Nicetas Choniates: a reappraisal, in *Amer. Jnl. Arch.*, 1968, 113–18

J. H. D'Arms, *The Romans on the Bay of Naples*, 1970

Ch. Diehl, Quelques croyances byzantines sur la fin de Constantinople, in *Byz. Ztschr.* 30, 1930, 192 ff

J. Ebersolt, *Constantinople byzantine et les voyageurs du Levant*, Paris 1918

C. Mango, *The Brazen House: a study of the vestibule of the Imperial Palace of Constantinople*, Copenhagen 1959

C. Mango, Antique Statuary and the Byzantine Beholder, in *Dumb. Oaks papers 17*, 1963, 53–76

D. A. Miller, *Imperial Constantinople*, New York 1969

Magrit Pape, *Griechische Kunstwerke aus Kriegsbeute und ihre öffentliche Aufstellung in Rom*, diss Hamburg 1975

Jean B. Pappadopoulos, *Theodore II Lascaris: Empereur de Nicée*, Paris 1908

J. J. Pollitt, *The Ancient View of Greek Art*, New Haven 1974

C. Vermeule, Graeco-Roman Statuary: Purpose and Setting I–II, in *Burlington Mag.* 787, Oct 1968, 545–58 and 788, Nov 1968, 607–13

CHAPTER TWO

The works of Cyriac of Ancona are almost entirely lost. The surviving scraps and derivatives are not altogether easy to locate. They can be found as follows:

Itinerarium ed L. Mehus, Florence 1742; reprint under name of Kyriaci, Bologna, 1969

R. Sabbadini, *Fontes Ambrosiani* II, 1–53 Ciriaco d'Ancona e il Peloponneso, trasmessa da Leonardo Botta

Epigrammata reperta per Illyricum a Cyriaco ed C. Moroni, Rome 1664. No complete copy of this work exists, and the date is uncertain.

Cyriacus of Ancona's Journeys in the Propontis and Northern Aegean 1444–1445, ed E. W. Bodnar and C. Mitchell, Philadelphia 1976

F. Scalamonti's biography of Cyriac is in G. Colucci, *Delle Antichitè Picene* XV, Fermo 1792, 45–155. There is also an edition by Charles Mitchell

Modern discussions:
The most important are two papers by Bernard Ashmole: Cyriac of Ancona, *Proc. Brit. Acad.* 45, 1959, 25–41; and *Jnl. Warburg and Courtauld Inst.* 19, 1956, 179–99

Also:
F. Babinger, Notes on Cyriac of Ancona and some of his friends, in *Jnl. Warburg and Courtauld Inst.* 25, 1962, 321–3

E. W. Bodnar, *Cyriacus of Ancona and Athens* Coll. Latomus 43, Brussels 1960

E. W. Bodnar, Athens in April 1436, in *Archaeology* 23, 1970, 96–105, 189–99

C. C. van Essen, *Cyriaque d'Ancone en Egypte* Mededel d. kon. nederlands akad. d. wetenschapen, afd. letterkunde, n. reeks deel 21, 12, Amsterdam 1958

E. Jacobs, Cyriacus von Ancona und Mehemmed II in *Byz. Ztschr.* 30, 1929, 197–202

P. and K. Lehmann, *Samothracian Reflections*, Princeton 1973

Paul MacKendrick, A renaissance Odyssey: the life of Cyriac of Ancona, in *Classica et Medievalia* 13, 1952, 131–145

C. Mitchell, Ciriaco d'Ancona: fifteenth century drawings and descriptions of the Parthenon, in V. J. Bruno, *The Parthenon*, New York 1976

C. Mitchell, Ex libris Kiriaci Anconitani, *Ital. Medioev. ed Umanistica* 5, 1962, 283–99

F. Pall, Ciriaco d'Ancona e la crociata contro i Turchi, in *Bulletin de la section historique de l'académia Roumaine* 20, 1938, 9–68

C. G. Patrinelis, Kyriakos o Ankonites, *Epeteris tes Etaireias Byzantinon Spoudon* 36, 1968, 152–62 (in Greek)

Fritz Saxl, The Classical Inscription in Renaissance Art and Politics, in *Jnl. Warburg and Courtauld Inst.* 4, 1940–1, 19 ff

M. Vickers, Cyriac of Ancona at Thessaloniki, in *Byz. Mod. Gk. Stud.* 2, 1976, 75–82

Cf. also R. Harprath, Giulio Romano und die Kenntnis der Korenhalle des Erechtheion, in *Boreas* 6, 1983, 212–6 (further influence of Athenian monuments on Renaissance art: was Cyriac the intermediary?)

Historical background:

Roberto Weiss, *The Renaissance Discovery of Classical Antiquity*, Oxford 1969

Lauro Martines, *The Social World of the Florentine Humanists, 1390–1460*, Princeton 1963

Francesco Filelfo, *Epistulae*, 1506

F. Babinger, *Mehmed the Conqueror and his Time*, Munich 1953; tr Princeton 1973

F. Masai, *Plethon et le Platonisme de Mistra*, Paris 1956

C. M. Wodehouse, *Gemistus Plethon*, Oxford 1986

S. G. Xydis, Medieval Origins of Modern Greek Nationalism, in *Balkan Stud.* 9, 1968, 1–20

On Buondelmonti:

C. Buondelmonti, *Descriptio Cretae*, in F. Cornaro, *Creta Sacra*, 1755, I, 1–124

C. Buondelmonti, *Description des Iles:* a French translation from a Greek version, ed E. Legrand, Paris 1897

R. Weiss, Un Umanista Antiquario: C. Buondelmonti, in *Lettere Italiane* 16, 1964, 105–116

The Labyrinth:

A. M. Woodward, The Gortyn 'Labyrinth' and its vistors in the fifteenth century, in *Annual of Brit. Schl. Athens* 44, 1949, 324–5

M. Guarducci, The earlier visitors to the 'Labyrinth' of Gortyn (in Greek), in *Kretika Chronika* 4, 1950, 527–8

CHAPTER THREE

The Arundel Marbles:

Denis E. L. Haynes, The Arundel Marbles, in *Archaeol.* 21, 1968, 85–91 and 206–11; and booklet of the same title, Ashmolean Museum, Oxford 1975

Mary F. S. Hervey, *The life, correspondence and collections of Thomas Howard, Earl of Arundel*, 1921

David Howarth, *Lord Arundel and his Circle*, 1986

F. H. C. Weitens, *De Arundel-collectie*, Utrecht 1971

The letters of Sir Thomas Roe were edited by the novelist Samuel Richardson, 1740, and printed also by Michaelis in *Ancient Marbles*, 1882

Sir Kenelm Digby:

Sir Kenelm Digby, *Journal of a Voyage into the Mediterranean* (1628), ed J. Bruce, 1868

J. F. Fulton, *Sir Kenelm Digby, Writer, Bibliophile and Protagonist of William Harvey*, New York 1937

Peiresc and the Antiquaries:

C. T. H. Wright, *N. Fabri de Peiresc*, 1926

L. van Norden, Peiresc and the English Scholars, in *Huntington Lib. Qtly* 12, 1948–9, 369–90

W. E. Houghton, The English Virtuoso in the Seventeenth Century, in *Jnl. Hist. Ideas* 3, 1942, 51–73, 190–219

A. Momigliano, Ancient History and the Antiquarian, in *Jnl. Warburg and Courtauld Inst.* 13, 1950, 285–315 = *Studies in Historiography*, 1966, 1–39

C. Vermeule, Aspects of Scientific Archaeology in the Seventeenth Century, in *Proc. Amer. Philos. Soc.* 102, 1958, 193–214

Rubens:

P. P. Rubens, *De imitatione statuarum*, c 1608

J. M. Muller, Rubens' theory and practice of the imitation of art, in *Art Bulletin* 64, 1982, 229–47

Wolfgang Stechow, *Rubens and the Classical Tradition*, Cambridge, Mass 1968

CHAPTER FOUR

Spon's works are:

Voyage d'Italie, de Dalmatie, de Grèce et du Levant fait aux années 1675 et 1676 par Jacob Spon et George Wheler I–II, Amsterdam 1679

Miscellanea Eruditae Antiquitatis, 1679

Recherches curieuses, 1683

Réponse à la critique publiée par M. Guillet, 1679

See also: A. Molliere, *Une famille medicale Lyonnaise au XVIIe siècle – Charles et Jacob Spon*, Lyon 1905

Guillet's works are:

An Account of a late voyage to Athens, 1676; from the French edition of 1675

Lacédémone ancienne et nouvelle, Paris 1679

Lettres écrites sur une dissertation d'un voyage de Grèce, publié par Mr Spon, médecin antiquaire, 1689

Francis Vernon's only surviving published work (his MS diary is in the Royal Society library) is the Letter to Mr Oldenbourg, *Philos. Trans.* XI, April 24 11676, 124 and 575–82; reprinted in John Ray, *Collection of Curious Travels and Voyages* (1693), II 19–29. There is a French translation in Spon's *Réponse*. His work is favourably assessed by B. D. Meritt, *Hesperia* 16, 1947, 58–62 and *Hesperia* suppl. 8, 1949, 213–227

On the other dramatis personae:

Albert Vandal, *Les Voyages du Marquis de Nointel*, Paris 1900

M. Collignon, Le consul Jean Giraud et sa relation de l'Attique au XVIIe siècle, in *Mem. Acad. des Inscr.* 39, 1913

T. Bowie and D. Thimme, *The Carrey Drawings of the Parthenon Sculptures* Bloomington, IN 1971

Cornelio Magni, *Relazione della città d'Atene*, 1674; publ 1688: on Nointel in Greece

J. R. Wheeler, Coronelli's Maps of Athens, in *Harv. Stud. Class. Phil.* 7, 1896, 177–89

On Athens in the seventeenth century:

M. Collignon, Documents du dix-septième siècle relatifs à Athènes, *Comptes rendues de l'Académie des Inscriptions* 25, 1897, 56–71

Comte de Laborde, *Documents inédits ou peu connus sur l'histoire et les antiquités d'Athènes*, Paris 1854

Comte de Laborde, *Athènes au XVe, XVIe et XVIIe siècles*, Paris 1854

A. Mommsen, *Athenae Christianae*, Leipzig 1868

Th. E. Mommsen, The Venetians in Athens and the Destruction of the Parthenon in 1687, in *Amer. Jnl. Arch.* 45, 1941, 544–56

H. Omont, Athènes au VIIe siècle, in *Revue des Etudes Grècques* 14, 1901, 271

On ancient Athens:

I. T. Hill, *The Ancient City of Athens: Topography and Monuments*, Cambridge, Mass 1953

J. Camp, *The Athenian Agora*, 1986

CHAPTER FIVE

The fundamental source is H. Omont, *Missions archéologiques françaises en Orient aux XVIIe et XVIIIe siècles* I–II, Paris 1902

The other travellers:

J. Pitton de Tournefort, *Voyage into the Levant* tr John Ozell, 1718. There is an abridged version of the original French, edited by S. Yerasimos, Paris 1982: it omits most of the archaeological material

Fourmont: *Relation abrégée du voyage littéraire . . . fait dans le Levant par ordre du Roy dans les années 1729–30*; *Memoires de litterature tirez des registres des assemblées de l'Académie depuis 1726–1730*, in *Histoire de l'Académie Royale des Inscriptions et Belles Lettres* vol. VII, Paris 1733, 344–59

Remarques sur trois inscriptions trouvées dans la Grèce, in *Hist de l'Acad. des Inscr.: Mem de Litteraire tirez des registres* XV, 1743, 395–419

Further references in my article, *Boreas* 8, 1985, 190–198. See also

A. Spawforth, Fourmontiana, in *Annual Brit. Sch. Athens* 71, 1976, 139–45

Caylus: Comte de Caylus, *Recueil d'Antiquités égyptiennes, étrusques, grècques, et romaines*, Paris 1756, 8 vols

F. Sevin, *Letters to Comte de Caylus from Constantinople*, Paris, an X 1802

Paul Lucas, *Voyage du Sieur Paul Lucas au Levant*, 1704; *Voyage . . . fait par ordre du Roy . . .*, 1712; *Voyage . . . par ordre de Louis XIV . . .*, Rouen 1710 (sic); Amsterdam 1720

Xavier Scrofani, *Voyage en Grèce fait en 1794 et 1795* I–III Paris and Strasbourg An IX, 1801

CHAPTER SIX

General works:
J. Mordaunt Crook, *The Greek Revival*, 1972

Lionel Cust and Sidney Colvin, *History of the Society of Dilettanti*, 1898

Th. Kraus, *Die Aphrodite von Knidos*, 1957

Nicholas Penny and Francis Haskell, *Taste and the Antique*, 1981

Marcus Whiffen and Frederick Koeper, *American Architecture* I, 1607–1860, Cambridge, Mass 1981

The travellers:
Richard Chandler, *Travels in Asia Minor* Oxford 1775 and *Travels in Greece*, Oxford 1776: an abridged version of the former is edited by Edith Clay 1971

Earl of Charlemont, *Travels in Greece and Turkey* ed W. B. Stanford and E. J. Finopoulos, 1984

Edmund Chishull, Iter Asiae Poeticum, in *Antiquitates Asiaticae*, 1728

Edmund Chishull, *Travels in Turkey*, 1747

Edmund Chishull, *Inscriptio Sigea antiquissima*, 1721

Richard Dalton, *A Series of engravings . . . Greece*, 1751–3

Richard Dalton, *Antiquities and Views in Greece and Egypt . . .*, 1791

Society of Dilettanti, *Ionian Antiquities*, 1769

J. B. Fischer von Erlach, *Entwurf einer historischen Architektur*, Vienna 1721; reissued Dortmund 1978

W. Inwood, *The Erechtheion at Athens*, 1831

J. D. Le Roy, *Observations sur les édifices des anciens peuples*, 1767

J. D. Le Roy, *Ruines des plus beaux monuments de la Grèce*, 1758; 1770

John Montague, Earl of Sandwich, *A voyage . . . round the Mediterranean in the years 1738 and 1739*, 1799

Charles Perry, *View of the Levant*, 1743

Willey Reveley and Sir Richard Worsley, *Museum Worsleyanum*, 1794

James Stuart and Nicholas Revett, *The Antiquities of Athens*, 1762–1816

On the dramatis personae:
B. F. Cook, *The Townley Marbles*, 1985
B. Fothergill, *Sir William Hamilton, Envoy Extraordinary*, 1969
F. J. Messman, *Richard Payne Knight: the Twilight of Virtuosity*, The Hague and Paris 1974
David Watkin, *Athenian Stuart*, 1982
Humphrey Trevelyan, *Goethe and the Greeks*, Cambridge 1941; reissued 1981

CHAPTER SEVEN

The Picturesque:
The fundamental treatment is still Christopher Hussey, *The Picturesque*, 1927
See also E. T. Webb, *English Romantic Hellenism* (Manchester 1982); Christopher Thacker, *The Wildness Pleases*, 1983; Rose Macaulay, *Pleasure of Ruins*, 1953

Pausanias:
Christian Habicht, *Pausanias' Guide to Greece*, Berkeley, California 1985
James G. Frazer, *Pausanias and Other Greek Sketches*, 1900
A. Diller, The Manuscripts of Pausanias, in *Trans. Amer. Philol. Assn* 88, 1957, 169–89
R. E. Wycherley, Pausanias in the Agora of Athens, in *Gr. Rom. Byz. Stud.* 2, 1959, 21–44

Choiseul-Gouffier:
M. G. F. A. Comte de Choiseul-Gouffier, *Voyage Pittoresque de la Grèce*, Paris 1782
L. J. J. Dubois, *Catalogue d'Antiquités . . . formant la collection de . . . Choiseul-Gouffier*, Paris 1818
B. Dacier, *Notice sur la vie et les ouvrages de M. le Comte de Choiseul-Gouffier*, Paris 1819

E. D. Clarke:
E. D. Clarke, *Travels* I–VIII, fourth edition 1818
William Otter, *Life and Remains of Edward Daniell Clarke*, 1825

Dodwell:
Edward Dodwell, *Classical and Topographical Tour in Greece*, 1819
Edward Dodwell, *Views in Greece*, 1821 (The plates are reproduced in E. Dodwell, *Klassische Stätten und Landschaften in Griechenland*, ed U. Sinn, Dortmund 1982)

Edward Dodwell, *Views and Descriptions of Cyclopian or Pelasgic Remains in Greece and Italy*, 1834

Gell's works are:
The Itinerary of Greece, 1819
Narrative of a Journey in the Morea, 1823
The Topography of Troy, 1804
Society of Dilettanti, *Unedited Antiquities of Athens*, 1817
Society of Dilettanti, *Antiquities of Ionia*, I–V, 1821–1915
See also F. W. Hasluck, *Annual Brit. Sch. Athens* 18, 1911–12, 272, on his drawings and notebooks; A. M. Woodward and R. P. Austin, Some Notebooks of Sir William Gell I *ibid*. 28, 1926–7, 107–127

Leake's works are:
The Topography of Athens, 1821; 2nd ed. 1841
Journal of a Tour in Asia Minor, 1824
Travels in The Morea, I–III, 1830
Travels in Northern Greece, 1835
Peloponnesiaca, 1846

Other travellers:
John Cam Hobhouse, Baron Broughton, *Travels in Albania and the Provinces of Turkey in 1809 and 1810*, I–II, 1855
François Pouqueville, *Travels 1798–1800*, 1820; *Voyage de la Grèce*, 6 vols, 1826
Dr Byron, *Voyages and Travels of Princess Caroline*, 1821
Elizabeth Craven, *Memoirs of the Margravine of Anspach*, 1826

CHAPTER EIGHT

Fauvel:
Louis François Sebastien Fauvel, Lettres d'Athènes, 1806–1811 (MSS in Gennadeion Library, Athens)
P. E. Legrand, Biographie de LFSF, antiquaire et consul, in *Rev. Arch.*, I, 1897, 41–66, 185–201, 385–404; II, 1898, 94–103, 185–223
C. G. Lowe, Fauvel's First Trip through Greece, in *Hesperia* 5, 1936, 206–224

The Elgin marbles:
The bibliography on this subject is enormous. Orientation can be made through William St Clair, *Lord Elgin and the Marbles*, Oxford 1967; 1984. Other works I have found useful are:
Canova, *A Letter from the Chevalier Antonio Canova and Two Memoirs . . . on the Sculptures in the collection of the Earl of Elgin, by the Chevalier E. Q. Visconti*, 1816

I. Gennadios, *Lord Elgin and the Previous Archaeological Invasions of Greece especially Athens*, 1930 (in Greek)

William R. Hamilton, *Memorandum on the Subject of the Earl of Elgin's Pursuits in Greece*, 2nd edition 1815

Jacob Rothenberg, *Descensus ad terram. The Acquisition and Reception of the Elgin Marbles*, New York 1977

Theodore Vrettos, *A Shadow of Magnitude. The Acquisition of the Elgin Marbles*, New York 1974

Cockerell:

C. R. Cockerell, *Travels*, ed Samuel Pepys Cockerell, 1903

C. R. Cockerell, *The Temples of Jupiter Panhellenius and Apollo Epicurius*, 1860

David Watkin, *The Life and Work of C. R. Cockerell*, 1974

Haller:

Carl Haller von Hallerstein, *Bemerkungen über das Jupiter Panhellenius Tempel zu Aegina, und über die darinnen gefundenen Bildhauereien*, 1811

Hans Haller von Hallerstein, *. . . und die Erde gebar ein Lacheln. Der erste deutsche Archäologe in Griechenland, Carl Haller von Hallerstein 1774–1817*, Munich 1983

Georges Roux, *Karl Haller von Hallerstein. Le Temple de Bassae*, Strasbourg 1976

Stackelberg:

Otto Magnus Baron von Stackelberg, *Der Apollotempel zu Bassae in Arcadien*, Rome 1826; *Costumes et usages des peuples de la Grèce moderne*, 1825, and *Vues Pittoresques et Topographiques*, 1834; posth

Gerhardt Rodenwaldt, *Otto Magnus von Stackelberg: Der Entdecker der griechischen Landschaft 1786–1837*, Munich/Berlin n.d. but after 1945

Wagner:

Johann Martin von Wagner, *Bericht über die Äginetischen Bildwerke . . . mit einem Vorwort von Schelling*, Stuttgart/Tubingen 1817; *Reise nach Griechenland* ed Reinhard Herbig in *Wurzburger Stud. z. Altertumswissenschaft* 13, (Festgabe H. Bulle), Stuttgart 1938, 1 ff.

Winfrid von Pölnitz, *Ludwig I von Bayern und Johann Martin von Wagner*, Munich 1929

The rest of the Aegina/Bassae team:

K. Brøndsted, *Voyage dans la Grèce*, 1825–30; *Reisen und Untersuchungen in Griechenland*, 1826

Peter Goessler, Jacob Linckh, ein wurttembergischer Italienfahrer, Philhellene, Kunstsammler und Maler, in *Münch. Jb. d. Bildende Kunste* 12, 1937–8, 137 ff

Richard Gropius, *Genealogie der Familie Gropius*, 1905; Görlitz 1919

Leo von Klenze, *Über das Hinwegführen plastischer Kunstwerke aus dem jetzigen Griechenland und die neuesten Unternehmungen dieser Art*, Munich 1821

Description de la Glyptothèque de Louis I roi de Bavière, 1835

The Venus de Milo:

J. Aicard, *La Vénus de Milo. Recherches sur l'histoire de la découverte*, Paris 1874

J. P. Alaux, *La Vénus de Milo et Olivier Voutier*, Paris 1939

Comte de Clarac, *Sur la statue antique de Vénus victrix découverte dans l'île de Milo en 1820*, 1821

Cecil Gould, *Trophy of Conquest. The Musée Napoleon and the Creation of the Louvre*, 1965

E. Michon, La Vénus de Milo: son arrivée et son exposition au Louvre, in *Rev. Etudes Grècques* 13, 1900, 302–370

E. Michon, *Le Marquis de Rivière et la Donation de la Vénus de Milo*, Paris 1906

Quatremère de Quincy, *Lettres sur l'enlèvement des ouvrages de l'art antique à Athènes et à Rome*, Rome 1818; also *Lettres sur le projet d'enlèver les monuments de l'Italie*, Paris An V/1796

R. Schneider, *Quatremère de Quincy et son intervention dans les arts*, Paris 1910

R. Schneider, *L'esthétique classique chez Quatremère de Quincy*, (1805–1823), Paris 1910

CHAPTER NINE

The British Museum:
Edward Edwards, *Lives of the Founders of the British Museum*, 1870

Charles Fellows:
A Journal written during an excursion in Asia Minor, 1838
An Account of Discoveries in Lycia, 1841
The Xanthian Marbles, their acquisition and transmission to England, 1843
Travels and Researches in Asia Minor, 1852 (contains the preceding works with some other material)
On the finds at Xanthus see also P. Demargne, *Fouilles de Xanthos* I, 1958
William A. P. Childs, *The City-Reliefs of Lycia*, Princeton 1978

Schönborn:
C. Schoenborn, *Life of J. A. Schoenborn*, 1868

Of Fellows' other visitors, T. A. B. Spratt is the author of *Travels in Lycia*, 1847, with Edward Forbes, and *Travels and Researches in Crete*, 1865

Newton:
Charles T. Newton, *Discoveries at Halicarnassus, Cnidus and Branchidae*, 1861 and *Travels and Discoveries in the Levant* I–II, 1865

On Stratford Canning, the most recent life (with bibliography) is L. G. Byrne, *The Great Ambassador*, Ohio State UP 1964

Ephesus:
Edward Falkener, *Ephesus and the Temple of Diana*, 1862
J. T. Wood, *Discoveries at Ephesus*, 1877
D. G. Hogarth *Artemisium. Excavations at Ephesus*, 1908

Useful modern works include:
Anton Bammer, *Die Architektur des jungeren Artemision von Ephesos*, Wiesbaden 1972 and *Das Heiligtum der Artemis von Ephesus*, Graz 1984
Clive Foss, *Ephesus after Antiquity*, Cambridge 1979
F. Miltner, *Ephesus*, Vienna 1958
Wolfgang Oberleitner *et al*, *Funde aus Ephesos und Samothrake*, Kunsthistorisches Museum, Vienna 1978

CHAPTER TEN

Historical background:
Leonard Bower and Gordon Bolitho, *Otho I, King of Greece. A Biography*, 1939
E. M. Church, *Sir Richard Church in Italy and Greece*, 1895
Jon V. Kofas, *International and Domestic Politics in Greece during the Crimean War*, Boulder CO 1980
Wolf Seidl, *Bayern in Griechenland. Die Geburt des griechischen Nationalstaats und die Regierung König Ottos*, Munich 1981
Edouard A. Thouvenel, *La Grèce de Roi Othon*, 1890

The German archaeologists:
F. G. Welcker, *Tagebuch einer griechischen Reise*, 1865; and see R. Kekulé, *Das Leben F. G. Welckers*, 1880
Ludwig Ross, *Reisen des Königs Otto und der Königin Amalia in Griechenland*, Halle 1848. A second edition of 1851 has the title *Wanderungen in Griechenland im Gefolge des Königs Otto und der Königin Amalia*
Ludwig Ross, *Reisen nach Kos, Halikarnassos, Rhodos und der Insel Cypern*, Halle 1852
Ludwig Ross, *Kleinasien und Deutschland*, Halle 1850
Ludwig Ross, *Erinnerungen und Mitteilungen aus Griechenland*, Berlin 1863
See also O. Jahn, *Biographische Aufsätze*, Leipzig 1866, 133–64 on

Ross; this essay also appears as the introduction to Ross, *Erinnerungen und Mitteilungen*

Carl Otfried Müller, *Ein Lebensbild in Briefen an seine Eltern mit dem Tagebuch seiner italienisch-griechischen Reise* ed Otto and Else Kern, Berlin 1908

The Bavarian connection and Leo von Klenze:

Norbert Lieb and Florian Hufnagl, *Leo von Klenze: Gemälde und Zeichnungen*, Munich 1979

Oswald Hederer, *Leo von Klenze*, Munich 1964

Egon Casar Conte Corti, *Ludwig I von Bayern*, Munich 1937, 1979

Glyptothek München Exhibition catalogue, Munich 1980

Ein Griechischer Traum: Leo von Klenze, Exhibition Catalogue, Munich 1985

The French connection:

G. Radet, *L'Histoire et l'Oeuvre de l'Ecole Française à Athènes*, Paris 1901

M. C. Hellmann and P. Fraisse, *Paris–Rome–Athens*. Travels in Greece by French architects in the nineteenth and twentieth centuries, exhibition catalogue: Houston, Tex. 1984

Edmond About, *Greece and the Greeks at the Present Day*, Edinburgh 1855

Sainte-Beuve, *Sur l'Ecole française à Athènes*, in *Portraits Litteraires* III 478–84, n.d.; ?1901

Charles Garnier, *A Travers les Arts: Causeries et Mélanges*, 1869

E. Beulé, *L'Acropole d'Athènes* I–II, 1853–4

E. Beulé, *Etudes sur le Peloponnese*, 1855

Philippe Le Bas avec E. Landron, *Voyage archéologique en Grèce et en Asie Mineure fait par ordre du Gouvernement Français*, Paris 1847–53; plates vol. ed S. Reinach 1888

Philippe Le Bas, *Dissertation sur l'utilité qu'on peut retirer de l'épigraphie pour l'intelligence des auteurs anciens*, 1829

J. B. G. M. Bory de Saint-Vincent, *Relation d'un voyage scientifique de la Morée*, 1837–8

The Germans in Greece:

Adolf Michaelis, *Geschichte des deutschen archäologischen Instituts 1829–1879*, Berlin 1879, 171 ff. on the Athens Institute

Alfred Richard Meyer (ed), *Fürst Pückler in Athen*, Berling 1944

August Ehrhard, *Fürst Pückler. Das Abenteuerliche Leben eines Künstlers und Edelmannes*, Berlin and Zurich 1935

Anton Berger, *Prokesch-Osten. Ein Leben aus Altösterreich*, Graz 1921

F. W. von Thiersch, *De l'état actuel de la Grèce, et des moyens d'arriver à sa restauration* I–II, Leipzig 1833

H. N. Ulrichs, *Reisen und Forschungen in Griechenland* I, Bremen 1840, II, Berlin 1863

J. P. Fallmerayer, *Reise von Thessaloniki nach Larissa*, 1841

The English in Greece:
Sir Thomas Wyse, *An Excursion in the Peloponnesus in the year 1858*, 1865; see also James J. Auchmuty, *Sir Thomas Wyse*, 1939

F. M. F. Skene, *Wayfaring Sketches among the Greeks and Turks*, 1847

H. F. Tozer, *Researches in the Highlands of Turkey* I–II, 1869

The Greek archaeologists:
S. Kastorchis, *Historical account of the activities of the Archaeological Society in Athens from its foundation in 1837 until 1879*, Athens 1879; (in Greek)

P. Kavvadias, *History of the Archaeological Society from its foundation in 1837 until 1900*, Athens 1900; (in Greek)

K. S. Pittakis, *L'ancienne Athènes ou la description des antiquités d'Athènes et ses environs*, Athens 1835

Olympia:
John Spencer Stanhope, *Olympia; or Topography illustrative of the actual state of the plain of Olympia, and of the ruins of the city of Elis*, 1824

Ernst Curtius, *Olympia*, Berlin 1935

Curtius' other works on Greece include: *Peloponnes*, 1851–2; *Anecdota Delphica* 1843; *Ein Lebensbild*, 1903

Quatremère de Quincy, *Le Jupiter Olympien*, 1815

Adolf Boetticher, *Olympia* (2nd edition Berlin 1886; first edition 1883)

CHAPTER ELEVEN

Historical background:
F. E. Bailey, *British Policy and the Turkish Reform Movement*, Cambridge, Mass 1942

R. A. H. Bickford-Smith, *Greece under King George*, 1893

On the Victorians:
Richard Jenkyns, *The Victorians and Ancient Greece*, Oxford 1980

Frank M. Turner, *The Greek Heritage in Victorian Britain*, 1981

Heinrich Schliemann:
Schliemann's own works are: *Ithaka, der Peloponnes und Troja*, Leipzig 1869; French version Paris 1869; *Trojanische Altertümer*, Leipzig 1874; *Mykenae* (Leipzig 1878, New York 1878); *Ilios* (Leipzig 1881, London 1880); *Orchomenos* (Leipzig 1881); *Reise in der Troas im Mai 1881*, Leipzig 1881, *Troja*, Leipzig 1884; London and New York

1884; *Tiryns*, Leipzig 1886; New York 1885, London 1886; *Bericht über die Ausgrabungen in Troja im Jahre 1890*, Leipzig 1891. His Troy diaries are in the Gennadeion in Athens, and there is a microfilm in the Ashmolean in Oxford. His letters have been edited by E. Meyer, *Briefweschsel* I–II, Berlin 1953–8
The bibliography on Schliemann is vast; the works I have found most useful are: Carl Schuchardt, *Schliemann's Excavations* tr E. Sellers, 1891
Irving Stone, *The Greek Treasure* (a fictionalised biography), 1975
Hartmut Döhl, *Heinrich Schliemann: Mythos and Argernis*, Munich/ Lucerne 1981
Donald F. Easton, Schliemann's Discovery of 'Priam's Treasure': two enigmas, in *Antiquity* 55, 1981, 179–83; Schliemann's Mendacity: A False Trail?, in *Antiquity* 58, 1984, 197–204
W. M. Calder III, Schliemann on Schliemann: a study in the use of sources, in *Greek Rom. Byz. Stud.* 13, 1972, 333–353
D. A. Traill, Schliemann's Discovery of Priam's Treasure: a re-examination of the evidence, in *Jnl. Hell. Stud.* 104, 1984, 96–115

On the Troad and the Trojan War:
J. M. Cook, *The Troad, an archaeological and topographical study*, Oxford 1973
Michael Wood, *In Search of the Trojan War*, 1985
Lin Foxhall and J. K. Davies (eds), *The Trojan War: its Historicity and Context*, Bristol 1984
Donald F. Easton, Has the Trojan War been Found?, In *Antiquity* 227, 1985, 188–96

Conze:
A. Conze, *Reise auf den inseln des thrakischen Meeres*, Hanover 1860
A. Conze, A. Hauser and G. Niemann, *Archäologische Untersuchungen auf Samothrake*, Vienna 1875; same authors with O. Benndorf, *Neue Arch. Unters. auf Samothrake*, Vienna 1880 and *Reise auf der Insel Lesbos* (Hanover 1865)

Pullan:
J. C. Carter, *The Sculpture of the Sanctuary of Athena Polias at Priene*, 1983

The Berlin Museum:
P. O. Rave, *K. F. Schinkel*, Darmstadt 1981

Humann:
Carl Humann and Otto Puchstein, *Reisen in Kleinasien und Nord-syrien*, Berlin 1980
Eduard Schulte, *Carl Humann, Der Entdecker des Weltwunders von Pergamon*, Dortmund 1971

Theodor Wiegand, *Der Entdecker von Pergamon, Carl Humann*, Berlin 1930

Philipp Vandenberg, *Das versunkene Hellas. Die Wiederentdeckung des antiken Griechenland*, Munich 1984

Benndorf and Gölbaşı:

O. Benndorf and G. Niemann, *Das Heroön von Gjölbaschi-Trysa*, Vienna 1889–91

Otto Benndorf, *Vorläufiger Bericht uber zwei Öesterreichische Archäologische Expeditionen nach Kleinasien, Arch.-Epig. Mittheil. aus Öesterreich Jahrg.* VI Heft II, Vienna 1883

F. Eichler, *Die Reliefs des Heroön von Gjölbaschi-Trysa*, Vienna 1950

Notes

Works referred to in abbreviated form receive a full entry in the bibliography to the Chapter.

Chapter one

1. Villehardouin, *Conquest of Constantinople*, tr M. B. Shaw, Harmondsworth 1962, 108 f
2. S. Runciman, *A History of the Crusades*, 1954, III 130. See also E. Bradford *The Great Betrayal*, 1967
3. Polybius 39. 2f, Strabo 8.6.23
4. Pliny *Nat Hist* 36.45 f; H. Abramson *Calif. Stud. in Class. Archaeol.* 7, 1974, 1–25
5. J. Grant 1966, 19–22
6. K. Lehmann, *Hesperia* 14, 1945, 259–69
7. Pliny *Nat. Hist.* 34.8; cf Leake, *Athens* 44 f
8. According to Edmund Chishull, 1699. Tournefort also saw them gone in 1700, so it is odd that Lady Wortley Montagu claims to have seen them in 1717. Hobhouse (II. 325) said it was Murad IV who removed them, Evliya that it was Selim II, and Thevenot that it was Mehmed II
9. C. Mango 1959, 101
10. The gift from Tiridates is the version of Thomas Coryat and Petro Giustinian. Marino Sanudo said they were Persian. See J. F. Crome, *Bull. Corresp. Hellenique* 87, 1963, 209–228; V. Galliazzo, *Boreas* 8, 1985, 49–80; exhibition catalogue, *The Horses of San Marco*, Thames and Hudson, 1979
11. A. Cameron and J. Herrin, *Constantinople in the Early Eighth Century*, 1983
12. N. Wilson, *Scholars of Byzantium*, 1983, 138; A. S. F. Gow, *The Greek Anthology: Sources and Ascriptions*, 1958; A. Cameron, *Porphyrius the Charioteer*, 1973, 109
13. Migne, *Patrol. Graeca* 156. 45 ff

Chapter two

1. Paton 1951
2. It is notable that Buondelmonti makes no mention of Hippocrates' Plane Tree, which is now one of the sights of Cos town and is reputed to have been standing since Hippocrates' time. The earliest allusion to this massive tree that I have found is from the Earl of Sandwich in 1738 (but he does not associate it with Hippocrates)
3. The Mausoleum had in fact been destroyed by an earthquake in the twelfth century, and its remains were not unearthed until 1846. See Chapter 9
4. It was in fact underneath them: Chapter 4
5. See Elizabeth Rawson, *The Spartan Tradition in European Thought*, Oxford 1969
6. Cf Stoneman 1984, 62 f
7. Tim Severin, *The Jason Voyage*, 1985, 117
8. The reconstructions are in F. W. Hasluck, *Cyzicus*, Cambridge 1910. Covel's account is in BM Add. MSS 22. 914 ff
9. Ashmole 1959, 27
10. P. and K. Lehmann, *Samothracian Reflections*, 1973
11. Babinger 1973, 497; and *Byzantion* 21, 1951, 136 ff

Chapter three

1. F. Picot, *Rev. Arch.*, 1902, 223–31
2. C. Vermeule, *European Art and the Classical Past*, 1964, 95, 63 (Raphael), 75 f. (Giulio Romano), 81 (Bronzino)
3. M. Vickers, *Burl. Mag.* 883, Oct. 1976, 680–7
4. S. de Castiglione, *Ricordi* 1549 contains instructions on the use of antiquities as ornaments
5. John Evelyn, *Numismata* 1697
6. Accounts of the Louvre gallery of antiquities are in Peter Mundy 126 f., Coryat *Crudites* I. 173 f
7. D. Howarth 1985, 80
8. Haynes 1975
9. F. L. Bastet 1983; see now D. Howarth 1985, 156 f. and 196 on further use of the Arundel Marbles by Rubens and others
10. The Museum Age p. 136; cf J. M. Crook, *The British Museum*, 1972, 63.
11. Letters, ed. P. Tammizey de Larroque, VII 791–2

Chapter four

1. The very importation of a fictitious building, the Pantheon, (though it may be a garbled allusion to Hadrian's Temple of Olympian Zeus, sometimes called Hadrian's Pantheon), which Burton must have got from his reading of Martin Crusius' *Turcograecia* of 1584, shows how little was known of the present state of Athens
2. The Dutch culprit in question was probably David de Leu de Wilhem, who while living at Aleppo in the 1620s acquired many antiquities for the

nascent museum at Leiden: see H. Schneider ed *Rijksmuseum van Oudheden*, Haarlem 1981

3. Probably that at 97 on the Blue Guide map – which collected the waters of the Inopus!

4. Covel, *Diary* ed J. T. Bent, 1893, 79

5. J. Meursius, *Fortuna Attica* 1622, *Cecropia* 1622, *Athenae Atticae* 1624, *Areopagus* 1624, *Ceramicus Geminus* 1663. Francis Rous, *Archaeologia Attica*, 1675 (completed in 1637), could only base his topographical statements on the work of Meursius, with an admixture of information from the Latin itinerary of Hugo Favolius 1563

6. His account, 'Examen reliquiarum antiquitatum Athenarum', is edited by A. Michaelis in *Mitteil. d. Deutsch. Arch. Inst. Athen* 1876

7. W. B. Dinsmoor, *Hesperia* suppl. 5 (1941), 16

8. *Relation de l'état present de la ville d'Athènes*, Lyon 1674

9. The fictitious inscription 'To the Unknown God' on the Parthenon gained a surprising currency, featuring not only in the pious fantasies of the Capuchins, but in the *Turcograecia* of Martin Crusius, who had his information from the learned Greek Simeon Kavasilas in a letter of 1578. Had some pious soul in the 1570s erected such an inscription, which had survived until the Capuchins' arrival and thereafter been torn down? The matter is a mystery. Crusius also took from another Greek, Theodore Zygomalas (1573?), the incorrect name of Pantheon for Parthenon, and placed before it – or on the pediment? – two marble horses – not a lion

10. Mylonas, *The Eleusinian Mysteries* (Princeton 1961), J. Travlos, *Pictorial Dictionary of Ancient Athens*, 1971, fig 379 (no. 152)

11. Cited in V. J. Bruno, *The Parthenon*, New York 1974

Chapter five

1. Chateaubriand, *Travels in Greece, Palestine, Egypt and Barbary* tr F. Shobel, 1811, 39

2. A hundred years later, both C. R. Cockerell and F. S. N. Douglas actually did take string

3. A more detailed account of Fourmont is in my article in *Boreas* 8, 1985

4. His general reliability is shown by L. Robert, *Rev. Phil.* 18, 1944, 19 n. 2

5. *Monumenta Peloponnesiaca*, 1761

6. *L'histoire et le secret de la peinture en cire*, 1755

7. L. F. Maury, *L'Ancienne Académie des Inscriptions et Belles Lettres* (1864), 213

8. Dident, *Salons* (1765) II 207; P. Gay, *The Enlightenment*, 1966 I 70, 120; D. Lowenthal, *The Past is a Foreign Country*, Cambridge 1985, 65

Chapter six

1. *Anecdotes of the Arts in England*, 1800; cf A. S. Wittlin 1949

2. Wittlin 1949, 88

3. Omont 48 f

4. T. B. W. Spencer 1954, 145; W. B. Stanford 1976, 133

5. J. M. Paton 1929, 606
6. W. B. Stanford, *Lord Charlemont in Greece and Turkey*, 1985, 179
7. Letters of Lady Mary Wortley Montagu (Everyman ed.), 119, 181
8. Letter to Horace Mann, 14 April 1783
9. It was the difficulty and expense that deterred Robert Adam, who might have anticipated their work. But he settled on the more convenient site of Diocletian's Palace at Split. See D. Yarwood, *Robert Adam*, 1970
10. Dalton's book, in the style which had become familiar from Caylus, Fischer and Pococke, includes Egyptian antiquities in its purview. Both books represent the taste of the age for highly detailed topographical renderings of ancient sites. In artistic accomplishment they go far beyond the functional sketches of Spon and Wheler. Le Roy, in fact, seems to have produced his book expressly to cash in on the very taste which had inspired Stuart and Revett's journey, and to rival their own work, which in the end only appeared some years after his. A bibliographical curiosity is represented by the set of twelve engravings of Greek scenes by one Robert Sayer, *Ruins of Athens and Other Valuable Antiquities in Greece*, published in Augsburg in 1764 by G. C. Kilian (who five years later published a similar volume on Baalbec). Most of Sayer's illustrations are direct copies of Le Roy's, even to the groups of figures, though in several cases the scenes are reversed, presumably as a result of copying the plate directly on to the steel. In other cases Sayer leaves out portions of the buildings to make room for others: for example plate 8 represents the temple at Sunium with the far row of columns omitted and the Monument of Philopappus added at the left! Sayer's is a portmanteau Greece, with monuments crowded together in invented locations; it was presumably a cheap 'pirate' edition of Le Roy produced to gratify a taste few could afford to indulge with the originals
11. Cf Robert Adam, *Letter to Lord Kames* March 1763. It was Sir John Soane who first decreed that Greek architecture be stripped of ornament which was only functional in its original setting: his aim was a 'naturalistic' architecture based on Greek principles
12. Homeric Hymn to Dionysus 80–88, tr George Chapman
13. Oliver St John Gogarty, *Rolling down the Lea*, 1950, 5; W. B. Stanford 1976, 119
14. Cited in T. Webb, *English Romantic Hellenism*, 1982
15. T. Wiegand, *Didyma* II, 1958
16. Cited in T. Webb 1982, 146

Chapter seven

1. E. Lecky – de Dedem, *Un general hollandais sous le premier Empire*, 1900
2. Claude was to such an extent a model for the Picturesque artist that many painters carried with them a piece of equipment called a Claude glass: a dull reflecting surface, often oval, which could be tilted and turned before the artist to produce a natural yet Picturesque composition, already in soft focus, which he could proceed to copy more or less directly
3. Shelley *Letters*
4. The reference is to William Falconer's poem, *The Shipwreck*
5. J. Seznec 1957, 109

6.   J. Frazer, *Pausanias*, 1900, 32–4
7.   Monthly Review, August 1811
8.   D. Constantine 1984, 150f
9.   Cf Chapter 8, note 3
10. Particular thanks are owed to Dr J. M. Wagstaff for his comments on this section
11. Cited in E. Clay, *Sir William Gell in Italy*, 1976, 162

Chapter eight

★   Special acknowledgement needs to be made in this chapter to two books which cover portions of its story: William St Clair, *Lord Elgin and the Marbles*, Oxford 1967, 1983, and C. P. Bracken, *Antiquities Acquired* (Newton Abbot 1975). At many points I have been able to do little more than summarise their full accounts

1.   The grave stele shown in a famous painting of Fauvel at home was however excavated by the Americans in the agora, where it had become re-buried
2.   Hobhouse I 286
3.   According to William R. Hamilton, it was in fact the discovery by Elgin's agents of vases in the same style in Attic tombs which proved decisively their Greek origin. But Clarke (above, Chapter 7) must surely have suspected it, even if he had not read Sir William Hamilton's *Engravings* of 1791 in which he argued conclusively for their Greek provenance. Hamilton was so eager to defend Elgin that he attributed to him more than he truly achieved
4.   See D. Watkin, *Thomas Hope and the Neo-Classical Idea*, 1968
5.   Dodwell, I. 322
6.   F. S. N. Douglas, *Essay on certain Points of Resemblance between the Ancient and Modern Greeks* (1813), 86–9
7.   Hobhouse, I 318
8.   Cit. St Clair 170 f
9.   St Clair 190
10. He means Herostratus (see p 228)
11. M. E. Chamberlain, *Lord Aberdeen*, 1983. But perhaps these two were Henry Gally Knight and J. H. Fazakerly, who later offered to buy out the Germans' share in the Aigina marbles
12. H. Tregaskis, *Beyond the Grand Tour*, 1979
13. Welcker (Chapter 10) I, 402, citing Gropius
14. Cited in Watkin, *C. R. Cockerell*, 1974, 17. Vitruvius (III.3.12f) had stated the existence of entasis, so Cockerell was really only verifying his hitherto unnoticed statement
15. E. A. Gardner, *Journ. Hellenic Stud.* 6, 1885, 143–52
16. Stackelberg, *Der Apollotempel*, 1826 23; Rodenwaldt n.d., 22
17. *Life of Byron*, 83
18. H. H. von Hallerstein 1983, 198
19. This account of Gropius is in sharp contrast to the favourable opinion formed of him by later visitors, notably Lamartine in 1832. He deserves to be quoted at length: 'Austrian consul in Greece, and a man of learning and

genius, M. Gropius joins to the most scrupulous and profound erudition, that *naïve* simplicity and good-nature which are the type of the truly worthy sons of Germany. Unjustly accused by Lord Byron, in his sarcastic notes on Athens, M. Gropius has not returned evil for evil to the memory of the great poet. He, indeed, lamented that his name had been dragged by him from edition to edition, and delivered up to the rancour of ignorant antiquarian fanatics; but he never once attempted even to justify himself; and when one is on the spot, to witness the constant efforts made by this distinguished individual to restore a word in an inscription, a displaced fragment of a statue, or a date on a monument, we feel certain that M. Gropius has never prophaned what he adores, nor made a vile traffic of the most noble and the most disinterested of studies – the study of antiquity.' (*Travels* 99)

Gropius and Wagner were clearly a mismatched pair, doomed by the difficulties of their positions to fall out. Cf R. Wünsche, in *Glyptothek*, 1981, 60–62

20.   Ludwig's biographer suggests that Britain was willing to let them slip in gratitude for Ludwig's hostile attitude to Napoleon: surely an overestimation of Bavaria's importance on the international scene. (E. Corti, *Ludwig I von Bayern* 1937/1979, 102)
21.   Quoted in St Clair 213 f
22.   Quoted in J. Aicard, *La Venus de Milo*, 1874
23.   See Stoneman 1984, 249–52
24.   *La Venus de Milo*

Chapter nine

1.   Cited in J. M. Crook, *The British Museum* 1972, 48
2.   Beaufort, *Karamania*, 1817
3.   F. V. J. Arundell, *Discoveries in Asia Minor*, 1834
4.   K. Jeppesen *The Maussolleion at Halikarnassos* I, Copenhagen 1981; M. Ashley (1980), 204 ff; *JHS*, Archaeological Reports 1985, 87 f
5.   Harry Edgel *A Letter written . . . on board HMS Siren at Malta, February 27th 1846*, 1850, 1–31
6.   Eg, author of the obituary in *Athenaeum* 1894, II 797. 'His manner to those whom he did not care to conciliate was not engaging, and provoked opposition which militated against his success'
7.   A closer parallel to the Mausoleum is a tomb at Mylasa which may actually be a copy of the Mausoleum: a plinth, a colonnade of square pillars, and a pyramid; whatever stood on top is lost, but there will have been no room for a quadriga
8.   Eg, at Petworth; cf A. Bammer 1984, plate 38
9.   J. Evans, *Time and Chance* 1956, 288–9
10.   Wood, *Ephesus*, Supplement I
11.   *Ibid* III

Chapter ten

1.   O. Hederer 1964, 105–111. A less favourable view in H. C. S. Ferguson, 'The Acropolis at Athens', in *Greek Gazette* November 1985

2.   *Travels* I 270
3.   S. Dow, *Amer. Jnl. Arch.* 72, 1968, 154–5
4.   O. Hederer 1964, 101
5.   Exhibition catalogue, M. C. Hellmann and P. Fraisse, *Paris Rome Athens*, Houston 1982. The first extended discussion was J. J. Hittorf, *De l'Architecture Polychrome chez les Grecs*, 1830
6.   A. Laing, *Country Life* May 17 1984, 1383
7.   E. Lovinesco, *Les Voyageurs français en Grèce au XIXe siècle* (1909)
8.   Leake, *Morea* I 42–44
9.   In 1768 he was hoping for funds from Cardinal Stoppani: letter to C. G. Heyne, 13 Jan 1868; see Boetticher 18, 53
10. His attendant artist was the architect Thomas Allason
11. Ross, *Wanderungen*, 1851
12. The treaty is translated in full in C. W. Ceram 1966, 36 ff

Chapter eleven

1.   A. Bammer 1984, p. 16
2.   H. Döhl 1981, 44; D. F. Easton, *Antiquity* 58 1984, 197–204
3.   Exhibition catalogue, *Het Goud der Thraciers en Schliemanns Troje* Museum Boymans – van Beuningen, Rotterdam 1984
4.   C. T. Newton, 'The British Museum,' in *Essays*, 1830
5.   J. Evans, *Time and Chance*, 1943; S. Horwitz, *The Find of a Lifetime* (1981); A. Brown, *Arthur Evans and and the Palace of Minos*, Oxford 1983
6.   See Michael Wood, *In Search of the Trojan War*; L. Foxhall and J. K. Davies, *The Trojan War*, 1985
7.   Cited in Seling 1967
8.   *Das Akademische Kunstmuseum zu Bonn*, 1827
9.   Cf Pevsner, *Burlinton Mag.* October 1968, 584
10. *Gesammelte Schriften* III 215
11. F. M. Turner, *The Greek Heritage in Victorian Britain*, 1981, especially p. 56. As the canon of great works became established, the need of museums worldwide for copies became ever more urgent. From Amsterdam to Athens, from Oxford to Cambridge, from Austin, Texas to Ithaca, NY, the Olympia pediments and the Parthenon frieze gazed benignly down on studious youth and improved their characters with visions of the highest
12. *Memoir of Pliny Fisk*: A. Bond, Boston 1828
13. Cockerell 1903, 138
14. Y. Karkar, *Railway Development in the Ottoman Empire 1856–1914*, New York 1972; see also Bammer 1984, 26–30 and works cited in his n. 40, for the importance of railway construction to archaeological progress
15. Cited from C. W. Ceram 1966, 312

Chapter twelve

1.   English Notebooks for 29 September 1855
2.   Bickford-Smith 1893, 223
3.   David Lowenthal, *The Past is a Foreign Country* (1985) 66, 68 f)

Index

Canning, Stratford 218, 221, 255

Canova (sculptor) 195, 199, 206

Cape Malea, ship sinks off carrying
treasures to Rome 6

Capitol, Washington – Grecian
style of 127

Capodistria 241, 245

Capuchin Missions in Greece 59; as
influence on Transfeldt 72–3

Carcavy, Pierre de 62, 85, 86, 89

Carlo II, Venetian ruler of
Cephalonia and Zaleynthos 28

Carlyle, Rev. J. D. 97, 171

Caroline, Princess 154, 155, 298

Cast Gallery established 250

Castiglione, Fra Sabba 40

Castle Howard 169

Castor, Tomb of 100

Castri 28; location of site of Delphi
70

Catholic Church in conflict with
Orthodox church 59

Catholic missionary travellers in
Greece 59

Cave of the Seven Sleepers,
Ephesus 68

Caylus, Comte de 103, 107, 109,
136, 229

Calymnos, Newton digs at 219

Cecrops, legendary king of Athens
48

Celebi, Evliya See Evliya

Cephalas, Constantine 18

Cephalonia 63

Cephisodotus (sculptor) 9, 160

Ceres, destruction of temple of
169

Cerigo (Cythera) 63

Cerigotto, discovery of wreck
containing treasures 7

Chambers, Sir William 128, 130,
135

Chandler, Richard 132–5, 165, 169,
208, 231, 237, 259; expedition
to Asia Minor 130

Charlemont, Earl of 97, 118, 135,
137

Charles I, King of England 42, 45,
65, 85

Charles II, King of England 81

Chateaubriand, François René 89,
101, 109, 139, 177

Chersiphron (architect) 227, 230

Child levy under Turkish rule of
Greece 60

Childe Harold, by Lord Byron 178

Chimaera Tomb, transportation to
British Museum 214

Chios 13; Fourmont in 97; Galland
visits 88; Lady Montagu visits
118

Chishull, Edmund 117, 118, 131,
135, 266

Choiseul-Gouffier,
Marie-Gabriel-Florent-
August, Comte de 136, 137,
138–9, 165–6, 259, 268

Choniates, Nicetas See Nicetas

Chryse 146

Chrysida, River 63

Chrysoloras, Manuel 26; catalogues
statues in Constantinople 20

Cicero 5, 7

Cimonian Wall 78

Çiplak, suggested as site of Troy
268

Clarke, Edward Daniell 80, 147,
148, 151–5, 158, 159, 160, 167,
168, 171, 174, 248, 268

Claude (Lorrain) 140, 142

Clazomenae, Dilettanti Society
expedition members visit 132

Clement IX, Pope 82

Cnidus 39, 113, 114, 132, 207, 223;
Dalton's publications on 137;
Gell and Dodwell visit 149

Cnossus 24

Cockerell, Charles Robert 126,
142–3, 175, 182, 184, 185, 186,
187, 188, 189, 190, 191, 192,
194, 248, 253, 286, 301; objects
to restoration of Aigina
Marbles 195; visits Myra 210

'Codinus' 16